A volume in the

DOUGLASS SERIES IN EDUCATION,
edited by HARL R. DOUGLASS, Ph.D.,
DIRECTOR OF THE COLLEGE OF EDUCATION,
UNIVERSITY OF COLORADO

Teaching in Elementary School

MARIE A. MEHL

ASSISTANT PROFESSOR OF EDUCATION
UNIVERSITY OF COLORADO

HUBERT H. MILLS

PROFESSOR OF EDUCATION
UNIVERSITY OF COLORADO

HARL R. DOUGLASS

DIRECTOR OF COLLEGE OF EDUCATION
UNIVERSITY OF COLORADO

SECOND EDITION

THE RONALD PRESS COMPANY , NEW YORK

Library of Congress Catalog Card Number: 58–5641
PRINTED IN THE UNITED STATES OF AMERICA

PREFACE

This book is a comprehensive treatment of the fundamental theory and practice of teaching in American elementary schools. It is intended for use by students in courses in elementary education emphasizing methods and by teachers in service who wish to acquaint themselves with modern concepts of the child's physical, emotional, and social, as well as intellectual development and related educational procedures.

Elementary education, as considered in this book, encompasses the all-round growth of children at the ages of six through thirteen years. Its objective is the acquisition of mental, social, and physical skills, attitudes, ideals, interests, concepts, understanding, and information that will help children to improve their living in the home, at work, at play, and in the community. The present and future attainment of this objective depends upon the development of the child into a well-integrated and balanced personality. This calls for a maximum opportunity for directed self-expression and a minimum of frustration and detailed direction, a great amount of successful experience and feeling of belonging rather than of failure, social isolation, and insecurity. Among the modern practices designed to achieve these ends, the two emphasized in this book are the avoidance of teaching methods which have been found to arouse unnecessary or excessive worry on the part of the child and the use of cooperative learning activities.

Most of the chapters deal with everyday activities of the modern classroom teacher. These require a knowledge of concepts and techniques such as child growth and development, course-of-study planning, use of problems and projects, learning outcomes, creative learning, cooperative selection and organization of learning materials and activities, discussion procedure, functional units, use of audio-visual aids, review and practice, and community resources and relations, all of which are described and explained. The responsibilities of the classroom teacher also discussed include directing pupil extraclass activities, counseling, measuring and evaluating pupil growth, assisting in planning the curriculum, and using research materials. The volume concludes with suggestions for the continued personal and professional growth of teachers.

The authors have synthesized the widely accepted modern views of the elementary school teacher's functions and procedures in the role of stimulating and guiding desirable growth and learning. They have no "new" philosophy or procedure to present. They do not subscribe to the idea that the elementary school exists in a vacuum, with problems unrelated to those of secondary schools or of society in general. In using this book as a text, therefore, instructors will find it adaptable to their own courses and methods of teaching. The basic principles of education presented are those commonly accepted by modern educational thinkers, and there is no special emphasis on any one of the various modern philosophies of education or "plans" of procedure. Instructors can employ the textbook for basic discussion purposes and supplement it with special assignments as they wish.

The authors have a combined experience in the elementary school field that includes teaching in a one-room rural school and in city schools, serving as supervisor and as superintendent of schools in a city system, supervising student teachers in elementary schools, teaching courses in pre-service and in-service education of elementary school teachers and principals, and visiting, advising, and lecturing to elementary school teachers in cities in the United States.

Marie A. Mehl
Hubert H. Mills
Harl R. Douglass

January, 1958

CONTENTS

v

Teaching in
Elementary School

1

OPPORTUNITIES AND RESPONSIBILITIES
OF THE TEACHER

In the middle half of the nineteenth century, the graded elementary school replaced the separate and relatively ungraded reading and writing schools and primary schools. Throughout the development of the elementary school system the basic pattern of a free education for all children has held its ground. The fundamental skills or three R's which are imperative to the progress of learning by an individual and to the intelligent participation of citizens in our democracy, have maintained their place in the curriculum throughout the history of American education. Since children from all levels of society meet daily to work and play together, the elementary school always has been and will continue to be one institution in the American way of life that will be a powerful influence in preserving our democracy.

CHANGES FROM THE OLD TO THE NEW

The first decades of the twentieth century saw the beginning of widespread criticism of traditional teaching. Influenced by John Dewey's formulation of the philosophy of education and by the development of testing, educators began to level their fire on many aspects of contemporary schools. Among other things, they charged the schools with:

1. Wastefulness through using the lesson-hearing recitation method.
2. Indefiniteness in conventional assignments and inadequate instruction in methods of effective study.

3. Tendency to focus attention on words rather than on ideas and meanings.
4. Overemphasis on a multitude of petty facts, too numerous to learn and too easily forgotten.
5. Failure to use visual, auditory, and other concrete learning aids.
6. Failure to correlate instruction around centers of application and interests, such as lifelike problems and projects.
7. Relative lack of group cooperative activities.
8. Bad effects of tyrannical and fear-inspiring class methods upon mental balance and personal development of the individual child.
9. Failure to use effectively the out-of-class learning activities of the child.
10. Inability to measure accurately and objectively a pupil's progress.

In the past half-century much progress has been made in correcting these and similar weaknesses. Indeed, the process of transition is still under way in spite of vigorous opponents who for various reasons champion a return to narrow, authoritarian, and unpsychological teaching.

New teaching principles

During the first few decades of the twentieth century, revolutionary changes took place in the American elementary school. Most of these changes are still in process. Perhaps the major force at work has been the spread of John Dewey's ideas about education. Dewey's philosophy stressed the interest approach to learning, clarified the concept of learning as an individual and continuous process, and emphasized the schools' responsibility for making it possible for children to get valuable social education by participating as useful members of a social group. Out of these teachings have grown basic principles of today's teaching:

1. Education means improving the quality of living.
2. The child can best be educated as a whole, as a unit organism.
3. Children learn by doing.
4. Learning comes largely through sense impressions.
5. Learning depends upon the individual child's ability.
6. Learning should be gradual and continuous, not discrete.
7. Natural social settings should constitute learning situations.
8. Motivation should be intrinsic and natural, not artificial.
9. Instruction should be adapted to individual needs.
10. Teacher-pupil and interpupil relationships should be cooperative.

Even a brief comparison of the instructional materials and methods of the conventional school with those of its modern counterpart reveals that far-reaching changes have taken place. These changes have resulted from developments in educational philosophy, in educational psychology, and in the scientific movement in general. Where yesterday's education was thought of as preparation for adult life, today's teaching is designed to help children live also more fully day by day. The scientific movement has made educators conscious not only of aims but also factual results. It has made teachers critical of the effects of method, content, and materials of instruction upon the individual child.

Emphasis upon the learner

The simple curriculum of reading, writing, and arithmetic followed in the time of our grandfathers has been replaced by a much more complex body of studies. The three R's retain a prominent place, but instead of being almost the whole of instruction, they are now regarded as fundamental tools for learning many other things. In addition to the three R's, today's elementary curriculum includes music, social studies, science, health, directed and free play. Emphasis is being placed upon such creative work as art, through which the child expresses his attitudes, impulses, and appreciations. If a child has a chance to enjoy a variety of experiences, it is now believed, he is more likely to develop those attitudes, appreciations, and understandings that are basic to emotional stability.

The conventional school, on the other hand, placed its main emphasis on intellectual development. Through memorizing the content of reading and arithmetic assignments, it was unwarrantedly believed, the child would also develop industry, stick-to-itiveness, and patience. Skills and work habits thus acquired would somehow be transferred to natural life situations as well as to all phases and types of learning situations. Little or no definite plans and no provision were made for development of social skills. Little or no thought was given to development of concomitant learnings, such as attitudes toward classmates or school work, self-direction, or appreciation of the contributions of others.

Today, in almost every school, emphasis is placed not only on the child's intellectual growth but also on his physical, social, and emotional development. Subject matter still plays an important role in education, but the child has access to many different books, bulletins, periodicals, and audio-visual materials. Teachers are concerned with the prevention of emotional blocks and frustrations through adjustment of learning situations to the individual child's interests, background, relative maturity, and readiness, through reducing competition and rivalry in working toward goals, and through avoidance of humiliation and fear. Physical health is also a concern, as emphasis on proper classroom equipment, hot lunches, and physical examinations indicate. Schools help the child to learn to take his place in his social group, sometimes as leader and sometimes as follower, through play programs, units of instruction, and situations which involve creative effort.

Respect for the individual

All the new trends in teaching are premised on the theory that each child is an individual, that he learns as an individual, and should be respected as such. Hence the emphasis on individual initiative and responsibility, on the importance of experiencing success, and on the development of a healthy personality. Modern teaching respects the self-confidence and integrity of the individual child.

Today's teaching is also much more realistic. The principles of learning by doing, understanding before memorizing, and learning through sense impression had been voiced as theory by forerunners of the twentieth-century revolution. Now they are put into practice.

Through all the new developments, the trend toward more friendliness, cooperation, and sympathy between teachers and pupils is easily discernible. Although millions of children have come into the public schools from lower socio-economic levels, lower levels of culture in the home, and with lower levels of intellectual ability, discipline has become less and less of a problem. This fact offers convincing testimony to the soundness of the new relationship between instructor and instructed.

Development of personality

In recent years much attention has been given to the fact that a large number of individuals have unstable personalities or at least do not enjoy good mental health. Some of these difficulties are believed to result from, or at least to be materially aggravated by, feelings of inadequacy or inferiority acquired during school life. Such feelings can be acquired by a child who is forced to meet standards of achievement beyond his potentialities. A child who is compelled to participate in activities in which he has no interest, or is deprived of opportunities for success in activities in which he has real possibilities of succeeding, can easily feel both inferior and frustrated.

Modern schools seek to avoid damaging the personality of young learners. On the positive side, the better schools adjust educational methods and materials so as to assist the development of healthy personalities. Every child should have opportunities to measure his capacities or powers by experiencing success in many activities as well as a limited amount of failures and fear of failures in others. It is the teacher's responsibility to arrange situations in which the child will participate without external compulsion and will have a reasonable chance of success.

New methods and techniques

Children in earlier American schools learned by memorizing and proved they had "mastered" assignments by reciting them back to the teacher. The teacher of today believes that the child learns most fully and economically only when he is participating in a purposeful and meaningful manner in the school's activities. The teacher guides and directs learning by working with the child and by providing a rich, meaningful environment which will arouse his interest, train him to apply what he learns, and challenge him to higher levels of learning.

In the early schools, a child's progress and status were measured in terms of the reading textbook he was studying ("first reader," "second reader," etc.). Often he was retained in a grade until the material was "mastered." Today's teachers believe in advancement according to each child's pattern of growth. In modern schools, children remain with their social group and work with materials on their individual levels of achievement. At the end of the school year they move on to the next grade, where they are again grouped according to their needs and where materials and problems are paced to their present abilities.

New concepts of discipline

Discipline was harsh in the traditional school. The teacher's word was law. Fear, physical pain, and humiliation were used to motivate study. The disobedient child was often punished severely by whipping, standing in the corner, or sitting for hours with a dunce cap on his head.

The modern teacher understands that children are organisms in the process of development. Children learn responsibility for conduct by being treated as honest, sincere individuals who will cooperate if given increased opportunities for exercising decision and self-control. The lazy child, the bully, and the clown are no longer regarded as wicked individuals who must be disciplined by corporal punishment. Instead they are guided in developing interests in the objectives which their group hopes to achieve. The timid child and the quiet child are no longer thought of as being the best behaved but rather as children who need guidance in learning to participate actively in their own social group.

Developments in measurement and evaluation

Since 1910 great strides have been made in methods of measuring growth and the results of learning. Teachers today generally employ more objective and more reliable means of measurement. Furthermore, in recent years much attention has been given to measuring advancement in fields other than general information and subject matter. The superior teacher today understands how to measure growth in attitudes, ideals, interests, and understandings.

The development of mental tests and formulation of the concepts of mental age and I.Q. have given tremendous impetus to the provision of better means of dealing with individual differences. Recent research of factor-analysis is revising concepts relative to intelligence. Instead of having a single score for mental age, at least nine primary abilities may be measured; thus relative weaknesses and strengths of mental abilities can be pictured on a graph. The results of achievement tests take on greater meaning if they are interpreted on the basis of the child's capacities for learning and become an effective means in guiding children in their schoolwork and various school activities.

Closely related to the improvement of testing is the increased use of controlled experimentation as a means of evaluating techniques. This scientific approach to the problem of judging the merits of proposed procedures has not been as fruitful of definite conclusions as was hoped. Yet it has thrown much light upon the relative efficacy of various plans in contributing to such educational outcomes as can be measured—chiefly information and subject-matter skills. It constitutes a most promising improvement over the prevailing armchair and forensic approach to new techniques and has already brought into serious question the somewhat extravagant claims made for various new teaching plans or techniques.

Advances in measurement have also included: [1]

1. Development of new types of tests, such as nonverbal and performance tests.
2. Improvement of teacher-made tests.
3. Development of a relative marking system.
4. Methods of discovering individual needs, interests, and readiness for learning in many fields.
5. Evaluation of educational aims, materials, and methods.

[1] See chap. 3 for additional discussion of learning about individual children.

6. Development of measurement of other than intellectual capacity, attainments, and growth, e.g., interests, attitudes, and various aspects of personality.

At the same time there has been increasing concern about problems of developing and evaluating children's social behavior. Skills and abilities involved in this area do not lend themselves to evaluation by tests. Hence there have been developed new instruments of measurement and evaluation, such as interviews with children, clinical or case-study work, sociometric instruments, discussions, analyzing group behavior, various mechanical aids for recording such behavior, and observation of individuals or groups. These are explained and discussed in Chapter 3.

Use of audio-visual aids

Effective teachers in the past have supplemented reading and study with such aids as pictures, natural objects, maps, and observation. But the use of visual and auditory aids and other tangible objects has now developed beyond the dreams of the nineteenth century. Much greater use is being made of the simpler aids mentioned above, and manufactured models and objects are found in many schools. Technology has given the teacher of today the radio, phonograph, lantern slide, sound moving picture, television, and trips outside the school. Hence it is becoming possible for the majority of teachers to address themselves seriously to the task of instruction rather than lesson hearing.

THE MODERN TEACHER'S RESPONSIBILITIES

The great advances which have taken place in elementary education have served not only to increase opportunities for children to learn and develop, but they have also increased the responsibilities of teachers who must guide today's children in adjusting themselves to the everchanging world in which they are living and will live.

Directing learning activities

By far the teacher's most important responsibilities are to plan and direct activities which will result in desirable growth. In the modern school the teacher is considered the director of learning. This means that she must conceive, provide, and arrange for motivation, materials, activities, and measures of growth which will ensure that the children under her guidance acquire skills in reading and writing, gain an understanding of numbers, acquire abilities to read with comprehension and to communicate intelligently, and develop habits of work and proper attitudes. A teacher must carry on innumerable activities in directing the learning of children. She must:

1. Learn to know each child.
2. Plan, arrange, and evaluate learning materials.
3. Choose methods of teaching in the light of goals to be achieved, needs and abilities of children, and materials on hand.
4. Maintain effective person-to-person relationships.
5. Maintain physical environment conducive to learning.
6. Guide in the solution of problems.
7. Evaluate growth.
8. Record progress.
9. Keep parents informed.
10. Study research so as to clarify educational problems.

Building curriculum

Teachers realize that an effective school program attains its success through carefully planned curriculum organization. Since the teacher is the key person in knowing what should be in the curriculum, she has the responsibility to take part in building it. In curriculum construction, the modern teacher is called upon to:

1. Develop criteria which can be used in the selection of curriculum materials.
2. Provide for continuity in various areas of learning.
3. Discover and review interests, needs, and capacities of children.
4. Find out how the home and community can cooperate with the school in the on-goings of learning.
5. Study the relationships of content and materials from grade to grade.

Developing character

Greater emphasis is being placed upon the development of character and consequently the development of appropriate ideals and habits. Character is the result of one's own thoughts, words, and actions. Since habits may result only from doing, it is imperative that real-life situations be provided so that children may experience individually those patterns of conduct which are acceptable in a democratic society. Children must be motivated toward those objectives that have intrinsic values.

The modern teacher is increasingly concerned with providing experiences in which children have opportunities to render service to others, to be courteous, courageous, cooperative, honest, and kind, and to make decisions which are concerned with moral values. The group situation in the classroom offers endless opportunities for providing such experiences.

A teacher's behavior during a class may have a more lasting effect than the subject matter being discussed. By respecting the child as a person, giving him a helping hand when he is discouraged, being fair with him, being his friend in time of need, and being patient, the teacher will instill in the child those feelings of appreciation and security which he will cherish; thus he will learn how others feel when he in turn is kind and thoughtful to them.

Children select certain adults as models and draw from them inspiration which helps them raise their own level of achievement in building proper habits of conduct. Since teachers are with children several hours five days a week, they may be admired and imitated. The teacher's attitude and behavior toward children often have a lasting effect on the lives of most of them.

Guiding children

Many teachers know that the strains and stresses in today's living often cause social ills, such as delinquency, crimes, and mental illness. As living becomes more complex, the need to make constant adjustments adds to the strain of coping with changing conditions. Since many children and adults do not have the stamina to withstand these stresses, they must be helped. It is believed that guidance service that will help people face reality, have worthy goals, and yet know how to relax and enjoy creative recreation can do much to conserve human resources. The modern teacher feels that the program of building strength into people must begin in the elementary grades.

Good classroom teachers work hard at developing good interpersonal feelings in children. They help children learn how to play and work together. Many attitudes are clarified for the children through their experiences and observations of what the teacher does and says. If children are expected to respect the rights of others, teachers must respect the personality of each child.

To render effective guidance the teacher must understand child society so that patterns of conduct will be evaluated on the level of the child and not on the level of adults. The teacher realizes that through the development of effective habits, attitudes, and appreciations the child will need less and less of her guidance. Thus he will grow into an independent member of society who will understand that, for privileges received, he must also assume responsibilities.

Diagnosing difficulties and evaluating growth

The teacher is responsible for adjusting all learning situations as closely as possible to the interests, backgrounds, and maturity of children. She is also responsible for evaluation of the achievement and progress of children, for diagnosis of their needs, and for organizing remedial procedures. Intelligent use of tests and observation of children at work are very desirable in pacing the work of children so that they do not face learning situations that are beyond their potentialities. By this precautionary device, the careful teacher may avert the precipitation of personality problems.

Diagnostic tests and critical observation are also very helpful in locating children's specific deficiencies and in determining the bench mark at which they are working. A superior teacher must be proficient in constructing tests in line with the immediate and specific objectives, in preparing remedial materials such as work sheets, and in understanding the value as well as the methods of commercial materials.

Conducting and utilizing research

A teacher's success in helping children learn rests in part on her willingness to improve her work constantly by utilizing the techniques of research. While research conducted by teachers may be of a relatively simple nature, it has the advantage of being conducted in actual teaching situations. Teachers very definitely have the professional responsibility, as do physicians, dentists, engineers, and other professional people, of utilizing the findings of careful research work conducted by trained investigators. The superior teacher of today is not only diligent in keeping abreast of research pertaining to her field of work, but she has learned how to evaluate and interpret research critically.

Understanding the community

The modern teacher realizes that she cannot work effectively in any given community if she has only general or incomplete knowledge of it. In order to understand the culture of its people and learn about their needs and interests, it is essential that the teacher live in a full sense in the community, including week ends.

The child's growth is also influenced by other forces in the community. Attitudes and opinions of children are influenced by their religious background, their economic status, the tensions in the neighborhood, and the organizations which provide out-of-school experiences. In order to understand the aspirations of the children and the customs of the various groups, the teacher must be always oriented with respect to those sources which have a great influence upon the lives of the people, young and old. Important points of contact are churches, clubs, recreational activities, welfare organizations, and homes.

The most effective curriculum is based upon the needs and interests of the children. These are determined to a large degree by the community in which the children live. It is essential therefore that the teacher understand the social pattern and life of the community. One section of a city may be a district in which the parents are on relief and the children undernourished. In another section, the children may hear little or no English spoken in the home. Teachers in the first section will be concerned with health problems, and teachers in the other section may find it necessary to build an understanding of the English language before they introduce reading to the children.

The teacher of today also should quickly assume the full responsibility of a citizen. She should understand the form of government of the community. She should know who the city officials are, and she should participate in civic groups. By sharing in community activities, the teacher may assist in explaining the work of her school to the community, take her school into the community, and let the public know what is needed in the school in order to have the best institution possible for their children. Through an understanding of community problems the teacher will be able to present community needs to the children in a realistic way and thus vitalize the curriculum.

Developing an understanding of democracy

The goal of education in a democracy is to produce democratic individuals. A democratic individual respects the rights of others, is worthy of being respected, realizes that in a cooperative society we must give as well as receive, and understand that the value of an individual is determined by his contributions to the group. He also appreciates the fact that in a democracy he has the right to make his own decisions and both the right and the responsibility to participate in group decisions. Therefore, if an elementary school is to be an effective institution in a democracy, it is essential that the teachers understand the nature and problems of a democratic society, thus they can recognize and assume the responsibility of guiding the children in the development of those skills which will enable them to meet life with confidence and discover and develop full potentialities even in the least promising pupils.

Teaching for world peace

In recent years development of the means of human destruction has been so accelerated that there appear to be only two alternatives—world suicide or mutual understanding among peoples of the world. This means that children must be trained in the ways of peace. Teachers must begin in the primary grades to develop pupils' understanding and appreciation of different peoples, their cultures, and their interdependence. Interracial and intercultural relations in our own communities can be made significant by talking, playing, and working with persons representative of these groups and coming to know and appreciate some of the music, art, and scientific contributions of other peoples. A social consciousness can be developed by helping children realize that they must live peacefully in groups, that they must learn to take their turns, and that their needs are no more important than the needs of other children. By the time children leave elementary grades they should understand that the people in a wider community, or the world, are almost as interdependent economically and politically as the people in smaller communities and that in order to survive, cooperation of all peoples is needed. At this age, children also should understand the shrinking of world distances and have some comprehension of its international, economic, and political implications.

It is necessary that teachers in the classroom lay the basis of mutual understanding and tolerance between peoples without which international treaties are but scraps of paper and armaments are inadequate security antidotes.

PROFESSIONAL OPPORTUNITIES

Teaching is a calling of great importance. It offers an opportunity and challenge to service far greater than other callings do. The effective teacher does not follow a prescribed formula but creates ways and means that will bring out the best in each child. The teacher can, if she will, be one of the most highly respected individuals in her community. She can live a life of great service to her pupils as well as to her nation and the world.

Types of positions

The individual who is willing to work hard and bring out the best that is in her will find that the teaching profession offers a wide range of choices. Whatever a teacher likes to do best, she usually will find an opportunity to do. She can teach in nursery school, kindergarten, primary or intermediate grades. Opportunities are available in elementary schools to teach in special areas, such as music, art, physical education, and speech.

The opportunities for many and varied experiences are great. During the summer and holidays the teacher may travel and/or work on a hobby, such as painting or writing. She may extend her information by attending summer school, through self-directed reading and study, by serving as a salaried camp assistant for children, or by serving in social work or summer projects organized by the city for children.

Opportunities to teach overseas

Some teachers expand their experiences by exchanging jobs with teachers overseas for a year. By teaching children in other countries, the teacher gains a deeper knowledge and understanding of the history, educational system, and culture of peoples in other lands. By exchanging visits in a neighborly way, teachers have an opportunity to develop a deeper understanding of all children. Teacher exchange is a wonderful opportunity to learn and understand the values of other nations, to present abroad a true picture of life in the United States, and to develop a rational relationship among peoples of the world. Information relative to teaching in schools overseas may be obtained from Teacher Exchange Section, Educational Exchange and Training Branch, Office of Education, Department of Health, Education, and Welfare, Washington 25, D.C.

Opportunities for advancement

Teaching is a profession which offers opportunities for various kinds of advancement. The teacher interested in new challenges from year to year may ask for new assignments such as teaching a different grade or assuming important responsibilities on committees. After some experience and successful teaching in a system, and frequently by preparing for a position ahead, she may advance to a position as principal, supervisor, coordinator, or head-teacher. Almost all school administrators started their careers as classroom teachers.

Advancement in salary is assured in many school systems. Some give annual increments up to a maximum amount. Others recognize by salary increases attendance at summer school, superior classroom work, participation in regional and national meetings, or travel in other countries.

QUESTIONS, PROBLEMS, AND EXERCISES

1. Be prepared to give a five-minute talk on "The most important purposes of elementary schools."

2. Visit a local elementary school and note characteristics of the environment and the educational program.

3. List the traditional practices that persist in your local school, the modern practices.

4. Write a critical appraisal of a newspaper or magazine article written by a layman relative to educational problems.

5. Study the comic books read by a child whom you know.

6. List some children's books that have the same qualities as comic books liked by children.

7. View a television program for children several times and evaluate the program on the following points:

    a) Does it meet the needs of children for entertainment purposes?

    b) Does it provide wholesome humor, adventure, etc.?

    c) Does it provide constructive information?

    d) Does it present acceptable standards of behavior?

    e) Is the acting good?

8. Characterize three cultural groups in your local community.

9. What are the major problems of children today? How do these problems differ from those of a generation or more ago?

10. Be prepared to discuss characteristics of a good elementary teacher in terms of a "world at peace."

11. What are the major differences between educators and schoolmarms or schoolmasters?

SELECTED SUPPLEMENTARY READINGS

ADAMS, FAY. *Educating America's Children,* 2d ed. New York: The Ronald Press Co., 1954.

Part I. "Understanding and Protecting Our Elementary Schools" is an excellent treatment of the present status of elementary education. The author clarifies the responsibilities of teachers in providing a better education for children.

ASSOCIATION FOR SUPERVISION AND CURRICULUM DEVELOPMENT. *Growing Up in an Anxious Age, 1952 Yearbook.* Washington, D.C.: National Education Association, 1952.

Problems of this age that are related to children are clarified by specialists—educators, sociologists, psychologists, economists, guidance personnel, social workers, and others. The emphasis is upon helping boys and girls solve problems they face today. Major areas covered are: sec. i. "Living in a Confused World"; sec. ii. "Cultural Experiences for Children"; sec. iii. "Continuity and Change in a Technological World"; sec. iv. "How Relationships Develop."

ASSOCIATION FOR SUPERVISION AND CURRICULUM DEVELOPMENT. *Forces Affecting American Education, 1953 Yearbook.* Washington, D.C.: National Education Association, 1953.

An excellent discussion of the pressures that affect education.

BUTTS, FREEMAN R., and LAWRENCE A. CREMIN. *A History of Education in American Culture.* New York: Henry Holt & Co., Inc., 1953.

The purpose of this book is to present changes in American schools as related to the cultural background in the various stages of America's growth.

HERRICK, VIRGIL E., JOHN I. GOODLAD, FRANK J. ESTVAN, and PAUL W. EBERMAN. *The Elementary School.* Englewood Cliffs, N.J.: Prentice-Hall, Inc., 1956.

Part I. "Our American Heritage and the Elementary School," discusses very effectively the forces that brought about the organization and educational program of today's elementary schools.

MILLARD, C. V., and ALBERT J. HUGGETT. *An Introduction to Elementary Education.* New York: McGraw-Hill Book Co., Inc., 1953.

The following chapters are pertinent here: chap. 6, "The Child in Our American Culture"; chap. 7, "The School in Our American Culture"; chap. 8, "The Teacher in Our American Culture"; chap. 13, "Opportunities in Elementary School Teaching."

OTTO, HENRY J., HAZEL FLOYD, and MARGARET ROUSE. *Principles of Elementary Education.* New York: Rinehart & Co., Inc., 1955.

Chap. iii presents description of the major factors in the child's total educational environment as a person. The educative experiences presented include activities and interactions that children meet in living day by day in and out of school. The discussions are restricted to children in the elementary and upper grades.

THOMAS, R. MURRAY. *Ways of Teaching in Elementary Schools.* New York: Longmans, Green & Co., Inc., 1955.

Chap. v, "Society and the Schools," is an excellent summary of the origins of American education and changes that have taken place in education up to 1900. The author also selects and discusses problems of the present century that are affecting our schools. These are the changing family, citizenship and internationalism, intergroup relations, and contemporary stratification.

2

GROWTH AND DEVELOPMENT
OF CHILDREN

The basic ideas of child development date back to the days of Rousseau, Pestalozzi, and Froebel. From simple observations and intuition, these pioneers concluded that the educational program should be planned in accordance with the development of the individual or in harmony with nature. With the advent of measurement in the early twentieth century, child development became a field of study. In 1953, The Society for Research in Child Development was organized to coordinate and disseminate research findings. It publishes *Child Development Abstracts, Monographs of the Society for Research in Child Development,* and a periodical, *Child Development.*

Child development is a comprehensive field of study. It selects from other fields those ideas that aid in understanding the development of an individual. It adopts and integrates ideas from physiology, psychology, sociology, psychiatry, nutrition, pediatrics, anthropology, religious education, and other fields. Even though child development is a new field of study, it already has developed generalizations that appear to be true of all humans.

An understanding of the characteristics of children at various developmental levels will strengthen the teacher's sensitivity to needs of children and her insight into ways of pacing the presentation of goals, materials, and techniques in all areas of learning. Since the teacher in the elementary and upper grades works with children ranging from ages five to fourteen, the following discussion of developmental patterns will be restricted to this age range.

BASIC CONCEPTS, TERMINOLOGY, AND PRINCIPLES

Every professional field has a technical vocabulary of terms, the meanings of which are specific to that field. Terms which are used to designate basic concepts in the field of child development are *growth, maturity, maturation, development* and *normal development*. To avoid confusion and misunderstanding, an effort will be made here to set forth the meaning of these basic concepts.

Growth

Growth is a quantitative increase of existing substance or structure and generally is characterized by biological changes in an individual as he progresses toward maturity. Growth may be described in terms of increase designated as "rate of growth." Physical growth is very obvious. The various parts of the body grow at different rates. By the age of six the brain and spinal cord are nine-tenths of full size. Six- and seven-year-olds grow two or three inches in height in a single year and gain from three to six pounds. The pre-adolescent experiences a spurt in physical growth and seems to "shoot up" suddenly. Next follows a period of growth in weight, girls frequently gaining about eighteen pounds in a year. At the same time the preadolescent's arms grow longer and his hands bigger. Apparent imbalance in the various rates of growth are only temporary and tend to stabilize each other in the total growth pattern of the body.

Considerable research has been done in language growth. When the number of words used by children from upper and lower socio-economic levels have been compared, it has been found that those from the upper level have a larger vocabulary than lower level children. An only child usually has a larger vocabulary than children who have brothers and sisters.

All growth or change in an organism is attributed to two sources —heredity and environment. These interact in many ways. Heredity, for example, seems to preselect or delimit those environmental influences that will affect the growth process. In turn, environment brings forth the innate potentialities of each person and determines as well the degree of realization of the capacities of each individual.

Environment has little or no influence upon the human as to the number of eyes, ears, legs, or arms. These and many other physical characteristics are strictly a matter of heredity—species heredity, racial heredity, family heredity, or a combination of these. The color of one's eyes, the shape of one's nose, fingers, and ears are only very slightly matters of environmental control, as is the normal color of one's skin.

Growth, while the result of both heredity and environment, is more a matter of heredity. In other respects, environment is the more important factor. Even in physical growth, environment may wield an important influence within the limits set by heredity. Height and weight can be influenced to a limited extent in most individuals through nutritional processes. Height can be so influenced only in childhood but weight at any age. Speech and other skills in expression are acquired, not inherited. So are ideals, most (if not all) attitudes and interests, social behavior, and physical and mental skills.

In all directions, however, limits to growth are set by heredity— by the species of the animal and the heredity of the individual. These hereditary limits are apparently laid down in the character of the tissues of the cortex and nervous system especially but also in all his physical structure. The capacity of a bird, for example, to acquire a language is indeed very limited as compared to the capacity of a normal human being.

Maturity and maturation

Maturity is the state or condition that must be reached in the developmental process of an individual before he can perform successfully at the various levels of growth—mentally, physically, socially, and emotionally. The term mental maturity means that the individual has reached the maximum point of his pattern of mental growth.

Maturation is the normal progression of growth toward maturity. The maturation process is due to internal natural growth factors of the various capacities and structures (physical, sensory, motor) of an individual. We think of muscular maturation as the growth of the muscles until they function effectively for specific purposes or can do the job. For example, when eye-hand muscles coordinate effectively and when the smaller muscles in the hands, wrists, and fingers have matured so that the child can handle tools for cursive writing, we say that the child has reached the physical maturity level needed for cursive writing.

In the process of maturation, elementary and upper-grade children are modifying or abandoning behavior patterns as they advance from early childhood to adolescence. Emotional behavior patterns characteristic of the normal child in early childhood are indications that the child has arrived at the maturity level of early childhood in the maturation process. If, in the process of growth, the child does not abandon or modify responses and use more effective behavior patterns in situations, we say that he is emotionally immature. A four-year-old is mature if his behavior patterns are normal for a four-year-old but immature compared to responses of a normal six-year-old.

It must be remembered that if those factors inherent in the performance of any activity have not reached in the maturation process those levels of skills needed for the performance of the activities, meaningful learning cannot take place. Essential for all learnings are an organism that has reached those physical, social, intellectual, and emotional maturity levels needed for each learning and an environment favorable for effective learning. For example, speech sounds are produced by the speech organs which are controlled by the nervous system; if the essential organs have not matured sufficiently and if the environment is not conducive to learning, the child cannot learn to speak effectively.

Development

Development refers to perfecting qualities and abilities in a person. It may involve a change in structure, capacity, function, and/or efficiency. Developments intellectually, socially, emotionally, and spiritually are interrelated. Hence teachers are concerned with the "whole child." When the child's nervous system, muscles, social adaptations, and emotional factors needed in learning to read have matured sufficiently so that he can cope with beginning formal reading, then the abilities and capacities involved in the process of learning to read will continue to develop. During the process of learning to read, the development of the eyes will be great. The child will develop the abilities of having the eyes follow a line of print from left to right and make the return sweep correctly. The eyes will note the general configuration of the words, similarities and differences in the beginning and ending of words. In oral reading the eye will be ahead of the voice, since the content is read silently before the words are uttered aloud; as the idea is being expressed orally, the eyes do not stop but read ahead to get the next idea. Concurrently, real experiences are being associated with the pictures; spoken words and printed symbols are being associated.

As the child is learning to read, he also is developing socially and emotionally. Socially, he is learning to be an effective participant in a group that is working on a specific problem—learning to read. He will learn to share ideas, consider contributions of other children, control himself by refraining from talking when he is supposed to be listening.

Whatever the goal that the child is hoping to achieve, it is accompanied by feelings or emotions. If his responses are acceptable, if no activities or responses have been blocked, he has pleasant feelings or pleasant emotions. If day by day he faces the reality that learning to read involves work, and he succeeds in the task, then day by day he will develop self-confidence in attacking jobs, as objectives take on wider and greater meanings.

Development is ordinarily a slow process. Teachers must not push children beyond the point of being able to cope with the situation. The first appearance of an ability or the first attempt at a new skill does not indicate that the child is ready to pursue the learning at that particular time, any more than the appearance of the first tooth means that the child is ready to eat all solid foods.

Teachers must keep their eyes on the children and not on the calendar. They should be aware that children are always ready to learn something. Five-year-olds and some six-year-olds may not have developed enough to be able to learn to read but they have good eyes and can see things themselves; they have tongues and are incessant talkers; there is nothing wrong with them. They are ready to learn about those things that they can see, touch, taste, smell, feel. Since the time clock of some children is running fast, it is imperative that we do not cut down on their diet but challenge them with problems which they are ready to attack.

Normal development

The term *normal development* has two different meanings. It is very important for teachers to understand both concepts for they will be using both ideas in working with children and much harm can be done if the concepts are not interpreted and used properly. One meaning of normal development refers to the developmental pattern of each child as an individual. Each child has his own pattern of growth that is normal to him. One six-year-old may be forty inches in height and weigh forty pounds; another six-year-old may be forty-seven inches tall and weigh forty-nine pounds—for each child the measurements are said to be normal. Academically some children consistently do superior work in all areas of learning; others do average work in reading and have difficulties in arithmetic and spelling. We know that the intelligence of the first group is greater than that of the second and, therefore, say that the accomplishment of each child is normal for him as an individual. Individual growth patterns of children are obtained by longitudinal studies which reveal that no two children are alike and that individual differences are great and varied.

The second concept of normal development is a statistical concept. In this sense it applies to children of the same chronological age. The ages at which the stage of development referred to is reached are used as a base, and the average is calculated. This average is said to be the normal age for whatever fact was being considered. Children who reach the stage referred to at or near this average age are said to be experiencing normal development with respect to that particular trait.

Teachers must be cautious in interpreting norms of standardized achievement tests. These norms are a statistical description of the average or median achievements of many children taken from many different schools. They are not intended to be used as standards of accomplishment for all children in a grade. Since schools vary in content of curriculum and in skills developed in each grade, it is evident that each school must decide what to expect of its pupils. Two of the purposes for using the norms on standardized tests should be: (1) to determine how much growth a child has made during the year; and (2) to determine the growth that he makes from year to year.

Every heterogeneous group of children in any grade will include some children whose performance is below and other children whose performance is above the grade-norm on any test. Some children will vary within themselves and will be below the grade-norm in some areas of learning and at the same time will be above in other areas.

Teachers should not be satisfied if they find a superior child doing average work. If a child who is a slow learner has made acceptable progress, even though working below the norm for the grade in which he happens to be, we should accept it as satisfactory work for him. To expect more of a child than he has the ability to accomplish is harmful but no more harmful than to fail to challenge him to work up to capacity.

Basic principles

Among the more important general principles of child growth and development are the following:

1. Learning is experiencing.
2. Learning implies a change in behavior patterns and attitudes— acquisition of ideals, interests, new information, and skills and re-organization of old skills and old information.
3. Readiness for any learning task is determined by the growth of the child as a whole.
4. The individual acts as a whole.

5. The various component traits—mental, physical, social, and emotional—develop at different rates, and each learner possesses his own unique pattern of growth.
6. The learner varies not only within himself in the development of these various traits but differs to a greater or lesser degree from established norms.
7. Each child has his own unique pattern of development.
8. A child will absorb from his environment and his experiences those learnings for which he is ready.
9. Instruction beyond the child's level of maturity will not result in permanent learnings.
10. The process of growth and development follows a sequential pattern.
11. Growth within the individual is continuous.
12. Growth is the result of interaction of nature and nurture.
13. Many forms of behavior patterns are normal for different age levels.
14. Emotional reactions often are influenced by motor development.
15. Mental and physical reactions may be influenced by emotions.
16. There are sex differences in growth and development.
17. Children are alike in many ways.

NORMAL STAGES OF DEVELOPMENT

The growth characteristics at designated age levels in any outline relative to developmental growth patterns of children must be considered as norms, for no child will fit perfectly into any one age level. There is great overlapping of all characteristics at each level with the same characteristics on the level immediately above or below. However, an understanding of the normal stages of development aids the teacher in being alert to behavior patterns that deviate from the general. It also will be a guide in determining the readiness of children for various learnings so that learnings and materials can be effectively paced or adjusted.

The facts presented in the following outline were taken from *A Chart of Normal Development* by Jenkins, Shacter, and Bauer.[1]

CHILD DEVELOPMENT CHARACTERISTICS AND NEEDS

I. Infancy—Preschool Years
  A. Physical Development
    1. Most rapid growth rate of any period.
    2. Mastery of walking, running, climbing, jumping, skipping, using tricycle.

[1] From *These Are Your Children* by Jenkins, Shacter, and Bauer. Copyright, 1949, by Scott, Foresman & Co., and used with their permission.

   3. Learning by touching, tasting, feeling.
   4. Desirable habits of eating, sleeping, elimination, usually well established.
   5. Motor coordination gradually developing, permitting cutting, pasting, coloring.
   6. Four-year-olds beginning to wash and dress themselves, lace shoes, brush teeth.
B. Characteristic Reactions
   1. At one—sociable, beginning to explore environment; enjoys nursery rhymes, pat-a-cake, and simple rhythmic play.
   2. At two—often negativistic, ritualistic, more responsive to humor or distraction than to discipline; increasing understanding of and beginning use of language; solitary or parallel play; possessive.
   3. At three—more conforming, anxious to please, better motor control, interested in other people, cooperative, less rigid or ritualistic, highly imaginative, beginning to share, responsive to verbal guidance.
   4. At four—lively, highly social, talkative, much out-of-bounds behavior, expressive, high motor drive, imaginative, dramatic, versatile, constantly asks "Why?"
C. Special Needs
   1. Sureness of parental support and love.
   2. Consistency and patience from adults.
   3. Regular daily schedule which fits needs of individual child; plenty of sleep.
   4. Chances for self-help but without pressure.
   5. Companionship of other children.
   6. Play equipment to develop large muscles and challenge creative imagination.
   7. Opportunity for plenty of activity.

II. At Five
A. Physical Development
   1. Has entered period of slow growth.
   2. Girls are usually about one year ahead of boys in physical development.
   3. Good general motor control, though small muscles not so fully developed as large ones.
   4. Sensory-motor equipment not ready for reading; child apt to be farsighted.
   5. Speech has very little infantile articulation.
   6. Handedness established by five.
B. Characteristic Reactions
   1. Stable—good balance between self-sufficiency and sociality; home-centered.
   2. Beginning to be capable of self-criticism, eager and able to carry some responsibility.
   3. Noisy, vigorous, but his activity has definite direction.
   4. Shows purposiveness and constructiveness; knows what he's going to draw before he draws it.
   5. Uses language well; loves dramatic play.

     6. Can wash, dress, feed, and toilet himself, but may still need occasional help.

     7. Individuality and lasting traits beginning to be apparent.

     8. Interested in group activity.

C. Special Needs

     1. Assurance that he is loved and valued at home and at school.

     2. Opportunity for plenty of activity; equipment for exercise of large muscles.

     3. Opportunity to do things for himself; freedom to use and develop his own powers.

     4. Background training in group effort, sharing, give and take, and good work habits that he will need next year in first grade; kindergarten experience if possible.

III. At Six

A. Physical Development

     1. Growth proceeding more slowly; a lengthening out.

     2. Large muscles better developed than small ones.

     3. Eyes not mature, tendency toward farsightedness.

     4. Permanent teeth begin to appear.

     5. Heart is in period of rapid growth.

B. Characteristic Reactions

     1. Eager to learn, exuberant, restless, overactive, and easily fatigued.

     2. Self-assertive, aggressive; wants to be first; less cooperative than at five; keen competition and most boasting.

     3. Whole body is involved in whatever he does.

     4. Learns best through active participation.

     5. Inconsistent in level of maturity evidenced, regresses when tired; often less mature at home than with outsiders.

     6. Inept at activities using small muscles.

     7. Relatively short periods of interest.

     8. Has difficulty making decisions.

     9. Group activities popular; boys' and girls' interests beginning to differ.

    10. Much spontaneous dramatization.

C. Special Needs

     1. Encouragement, ample praise, warmth, and great patience from adults.

     2. Ample opportunity for activity of many kinds, especially for use of large muscles.

     3. Wise supervision with a minimum of interference.

     4. Concrete learning situations and active, direct participation.

     5. Some responsibilities, though without pressure, and without being required to make decisions and choices or achieve rigidly set standards.

IV. At Seven

A. Physical Characteristics

     1. Growth slow and steady.

     2. Losing teeth; most sevens have their six-year molars.

3. Better eye-hand coordination.
4. Better use of small muscles.
5. Eyes not yet ready for much near work.

B. Characteristic Reactions
1. Sensitive to feelings and attitudes of both peers and adults; especially dependent on approval of adults.
2. Interests of boys and girls diverging; less play together.
3. Full of energy but easily tired; restless and fidgety; often dreamy and absorbed.
4. Very little abstract thinking yet; seven learns best in concrete terms and where he can be active while learning.
5. Cautious and self-critical; anxious to do things well; likes to use hands.
6. Talkative, exaggerates; may fight with words instead of blows; highly competitive.
7. Enjoys songs, rhythms, fairy tales, myths, nature stories, comics, radio, movies.
8. Able to assume some responsibility; concerned about right and wrong, though often prone to take small things.
9. Rudimentary understanding of time and money values.

C. Special Needs
1. The right combination of independence and encouraging support.
2. Chances for active participation in learning situations with concrete objects.
3. Must make adjustment to rougher ways of playground; needs adult help to do this without becoming too crude and rough.
4. Warm, encouraging, friendly relationship with adults.

V. At Eight

A. Physical Development
1. Growth still slow and steady; arms lengthening, hands growing larger.
2. Eyes ready for both near and far vision; nearsightedness may develop this year.
3. Permanent teeth continuing to appear.
4. Large muscles still developing, small muscles better developed, too.
5. Poor posture may develop during this year.

B. Characteristic Reactions
1. Often careless, noisy, argumentative, but alert, friendly, interested in people.
2. More dependent on mother again, less so on teacher; sensitive to criticism.
3. New awareness of individual differences.
4. Eager, more enthusiasm than wisdom, higher accident rate.
5. Gangs beginning; best friends of same sex.
6. Allegiance to peer group instead of to the adult in case of conflict.
7. Greater capacity for self-evaluation.

       8. Much spontaneous dramatization; also ready for simple class-room dramatics.
       9. Understanding of time and use of money.
     10. Responsive to group activities, both spontaneous and adult-supervised.
     11. Fond of team games, comics, radio, adventure stories, collections of all kinds.

  C. Special Needs
      1. Much praise and encouragement from adults.
      2. Must still be reminded of his responsibilities.
      3. Wise guidance and channeling of his interests and enthusiasm, rather than domination or overcritical standards.
      4. A best friend.
      5. Experience of "belonging" to peer group; opportunity to identify with others of same age and sex.
      6. Adult-supervised groups also; planned afterschool activities.
      7. Exercise of both large and small muscles.

VI. At Nine
  A. Physical Development
      1. Slow, steady growth continues; girls forge further ahead, some children reach the plateau preceding growth spurt of pre-adolescence.
      2. Lung and digestive and circulatory systems almost mature; heart especially subject to strain.
      3. Teeth may need straightening; first and second bicuspids appearing.
      4. Eye-hand coordination good; hands ready for crafts and shop work.
      5. Eyes almost adult size; ready for near work with less strain.

  B. Characteristic Reactions
      1. Decisive, responsible, dependable, reasonable, strong sense of right and wrong.
      2. Individual differences distinct and clear; abilities apparent.
      3. Capable of prolonged interest; often makes plans and goes ahead on his own.
      4. Gangs strong and of one sex only, of short duration and changing membership.
      5. Perfectionistic; wants to do well, but loses interest if discouraged or pressured.
      6. Interested less in fairy tales and fantasy, more in his community and country and in other countries and peoples.
      7. Loyalty to his country and pride in it.
      8. Much time spent in talk and discussion; often outspoken and critical of adults.
      9. Much arguing over fairness in games.
     10. Wide discrepancies in reading ability.

  C. Special Needs
      1. Active rough and tumble play.
      2. Friends and membership in a group.
      3. Training in skills, but without pressure.

4. Reasonable explanations; no talking down to him; definite responsibility.
5. Frank answers to questions about the coming physiological changes.

VII. In Preadolescence
  A. Physical Development
    1. A "resting period," followed by a period of rapid growth in height and then growth in weight; this usually starts somewhere between nine and thirteen; boys may mature as much as two years later than girls.
    2. Secondary sex characteristics beginning to develop.
    3. Rapid muscular growth.
    4. Uneven growth of different parts of the body.
    5. Enormous but often capricious appetite.
  B. Characteristic Reactions
    1. Wide range of individual differences in maturity level among this age group.
    2. Gangs continue, though loyalty to the gang stronger in boys than in girls.
    3. Interest in team games, pets, radio, comics; marked interest differences between boy and girl groups.
    4. Much teasing and antagonism between boy and girl groups.
    5. Awkwardness, restlessness, and laziness common as result of rapid and uneven growth.
    6. Child approaching adolescence often becomes overcritical, changeable, rebellious, uncooperative.
    7. Interested in activities to earn money.
  C. Special Needs
    1. Knowledge and understanding of the physical and emotional changes about to come.
    2. Skillfully planned program to meet needs of those who are approaching puberty as well as those who are not.
    3. Warm affection and sense of humor in adults; no nagging or condemnation or talking down to him.
    4. Sense of belonging and acceptance by peer group; increasing opportunities for independence.

VIII. In Adolescence
  A. Physical Development
    1. Rapid weight gain at beginning of adolescence; enormous appetite.
    2. Sexual maturity, with accompanying physical and emotional changes; girls are usually about two years ahead of boys.
    3. Sometimes a period of glandular imbalance.
    4. Bone growth completed; adult height reached; improved muscular coordination.
    5. Heart growing rapidly.
  B. Characteristic Reactions
    1. Going to extremes; emotional instability with "know-it-all" attitude.

      2. Return of habits of younger child—nail biting, tricks, impudence, daydreaming.
      3. High interest in philosophical, ethical, and religious problems; search for ideals.
      4. Preoccupation with acceptance by the social group; fear of ridicule and being unpopular; oversensitiveness; self-pity.
      5. Strong identification with an admired adult.
      6. Assertion of independence from family as a step toward adulthood.
      7. High interest in physical attractiveness.
      8. Girls usually more interested in boys than boys in girls, resulting from earlier maturity of girls.

C. Special Needs
      1. Conformity with and acceptance by the peer group.
      2. Adequate knowledge and understanding of sexual relationships and attitudes.
      3. Adult guidance which is kindly, unobtrusive, and does not threaten the young person's feeling of freedom.
      4. The assurance of security; adolescents seek both dependence and independence.
      5. Opportunities to make decisions and to earn and save money.
      6. Provision for constructive recreation and if possible a "worthy cause."

DEVELOPMENTAL TASKS OF CHILDREN

Growth is the result of both heredity and environment. With respect to basic physical growth, for example stature, color of hair and eyes, general shape of various parts of the body, etc., heredity is a much more potent factor. With respect to behavior, environment is a much more important factor, and behavior, therefore, is much more susceptible to influence, direction, and determination by environment.

Growth, as far as development of behavior and behavior patterns are concerned, is influenced to a very great extent by experiences that learners have. This is why we have schools. The school is an institution established for the purpose of causing learners to have experiences which are believed to contribute more to desired growth than those they would have outside of school. In order to cause youngsters to have experiences believed to make the greatest contribution to the desired patterns of growth, textbooks and other learning materials are employed, learning activities are planned, students are motivated, discussions are held, papers and other projects are planned and worked upon by learners, and examinations and evaluation are planned. All of these have come in recent years to be referred to as developmental tasks, although the word "tasks" is somewhat of a misnomer since it implies imposition from without and, perhaps, distastefulness. Developmental activities would have been a better term.

Examples of appropriate developmental tasks for middle childhood or elementary school children have been furnished by a leading student of child growth and development as follows: [2]

A. Developmental Tasks of Middle Childhood (ages 6–12)
1. Learning physical skills necessary for ordinary games.
2. Building wholesome attitudes toward oneself as a growing organism.
3. Learninng to get along with age-mates.
4. Learning an appropriate masculine or feminine social role.
5. Developing fundamental skills in reading, writing, and calculations.
6. Developing concepts necessary for everyday living.
7. Developing conscience, morality, and a scale of values.
8. Achieving personal independence.
9. Developing attitudes toward social groups and institutions.
B. Developmental Tasks of Adolescence (ages 12–18)
1. Achieving new and more mature relations with age-mates of both sexes.
2. Achieving a masculine or feminine social role.
3. Accepting one's physique and using the body effectively.
4. Achieving emotional independence of parents and other adults.
5. Achieving assurance of economic independence.
6. Selecting and preparing for an occupation.
7. Preparing for marriage and family life.
8. Developing intellectual skills and concepts necessary for civic competence.
9. Desiring and achieving socially responsible behavior.
10. Acquiring a set of values and an ethical system as a guide to behavior.

QUESTIONS, PROBLEMS, AND EXERCISES

1. Describe the physical appearance of a seven-year-old child whom you know.

2. Measure the height and weight of seven eight-year-old children. Compare your findings with some good standard height-weight table and explain any observed discrepancies. What do you find as you compare your measurements of the children?

3. In a panel discussion, summarize the basic principles of child development.

4. Write a summary paragraph on: "How an understanding of child development aids the teacher in her teaching."

5. Clarify the fact that individual differences in an intermediate grade are greater than individual differences in a primary grade.

6. From the point of view of the teacher, what are the implications relative to differences in maturation rates of girls and boys?

7. Why is it good training to have children on an allowance?

[2] Robert J. Havighurst, *Developmental Tasks and Education* (2d ed.; New York: Longmans, Green & Co., Inc., 1954), pp. 2, 6–12, 33–62.

8. Give an illustration of the following generalization: Asking children to perform tasks for which they are not ready may cause them to become frustrated.

9. Why do children respond differently to the same subject matter in instruction?

10. Be prepared to give a five-minute talk on the significance of the relatively long period of childhood in the human species?

11. Visit an elementary classroom and note the developmental tasks in which the children are participating.

12. How may the teacher of a class of average size recognize exceptional children in her class?

SELECTED SUPPLEMENTARY READINGS

BEAUCHAMP, GEORGE A. *Planning the Elementary School Curriculum.* Englewood Cliffs, N.J.: Allyn & Bacon, 1956.

Chap. 6, "The Nature and Demands of Children," is very readable. It stresses the general concepts of child growth and presents ways for measuring growth patterns. A concise presentation of characteristics of five growth periods—infancy, early childhood, middle childhood, later childhood, and adolescence.

GESELL, ARNOLD, FRANCES L. ILG, and LOUISE B. AMES. *Youth: The Years from Ten to Sixteen.* New York: Harper & Bros., 1956.

Major concentration is on the behavior patterns of the development of normal adolescents in the home, community, and school.

HAVIGHURST, ROBERT J. *Developmental Tasks and Education,* 2d ed. New York: Longmans, Green & Co., Inc., 1954.

Excellent clarification of what is meant by the term, "developmental task." Developmental tasks of middle childhood and of adolescence from twelve to eighteen are presented.

HERRICK, VIRGIL E., JOHN I. GOODLAD, FRANK J. ESTVAN, and PAUL W. EBERMAN. *The Elementary School.* Englewood Cliffs, N.J.: Prentice-Hall, Inc., 1956.

Chap. 5, "Children: Their Learning and Developmental Processes," presents clearly and concisely the developmental characteristics of children in elementary grades.

ILG, FRANCES L., and LOUISE BATES AMES. *Child Behavior.* New York: Harper & Bros., 1955.

Major emphasis is upon ways that growth changes affect behavior of children. The book contains specific suggestions on how to help children up to eleven years of age who have behavior problems.

JENKINS, GLADYS GARDNER, HELEN SHACTER, and WILLIAM A. BAUER. *These Are Your Children,* Expanded ed. Chicago: Scott, Foresman & Co., 1953.

An excellent guide on child growth and development for parents and teachers. Many examples and pictures of child behavior clarify special needs of children at various age levels. The book also presents a survey of physical, mental, social, and emotional growth arranged in seven age levels by means of summaries, charts, diagrams, graphs, and tables.

JERSILD, ARTHUR. *Child Psychology.* Englewood Cliffs, N.J.: Prentice-Hall., Inc., 1954.

A thorough treatment of problems related to human growth and child development in all aspects about which teachers are concerned. A clear presentation of how "selfhood" affects and is affected by growth. Information is based on scientific evidence and treated in a way that is remarkably clear and readable.

OLSON, WILLARD C. *Child Development.* Boston: D. C. Heath & Co., 1951.

Olson is an outstanding educator of today who is known for his contributions to child development. Research by Olson and others is interpreted so that the results can be understood. Every teacher should study the book.

OTTO, HENRY J., HAZEL FLOYD, and MARGARET ROUSE. *Principles of Elementary Education.* New York: Rinehart & Co., Inc., 1955.

Chap. xi is an excellent treatment of children growing up and learning. Terms related to growth and development are clarified in such a way that teachers should have a clear understanding of the concepts in various contextual settings. There are excellent generalizations relative to the educative process.

STRANG, RUTH. *An Introduction to Child Study.* New York: The Macmillan Co., 1951.

An excellent summary of facts pertaining to development and the learning process. Many practical methods as aids for studying and understanding children are presented.

3

KNOWING THE PUPIL

The extent to which the teacher knows her pupils determines in no small measure her effectiveness in assisting their growth and development. A sympathetic understanding of pupils is essential to making intelligent decisions concerning selection of appropriate learning materials, utilization of suitable teaching procedures, diagnosis of learning difficulties, assistance to individual pupils with problems of personal and social adjustment, discipline, provisions for individual differences, guidance of pupils, evaluation of pupil achievement and progress, and pupil accounting, including report cards and conferences with parents.

INFORMATION AVAILABLE TO THE TEACHER

A teacher can obtain information from many sources to supplement her knowledge of her pupils obtained by observation and other first-hand methods. Some of these sources are discussed in the following paragraphs.

Cumulative school records

When the child enrolls in the first grade, the school should begin to assemble information about him. Information about his home and family background is especially significant. For purposes of identification, the school must record parents' (or guardians') names, addresses, and telephone numbers. Their race, nationality, marital status, citizenship, educational background, and occupations may help to understand the child's temperament and feeling of well-being. Information about the number, ages, educational or occupational status of brothers and sisters provides insights into the pupil's social adjustment.

The family's economic status and the attitudes of its members toward the school provide cues for understanding the child's attitudes. A knowledge of neighborhood conditions also helps identify factors which influence the child's behavior. This information can be obtained by interviews with parents at school but should be supplemented by visits to the home. It is also important to have physical health data including records of childhood diseases, condition of sense organs such as eyes and ears, nutritional status, and any abnormalities. In brief, the cumulative record that usually accompanies a pupil from one grade to another should contain information concerning:

1. Community conditions.
2. Home background.
3. Education achievement test scores.
4. Intelligence test scores.
5. Physical health examination records.
6. School attendance record.
7. Conversations and informal interviews with pupil.
8. Records of conferences with parents and home visits.
9. Dated samples of pupil's work—compositions, drawings, test papers, etc.
10. Results of sociometric devices.
11. Notes or records of pupil's play and other extracurricular activities.
12. Special interests—reading, hobbies, pets.
13. Anecdotal records and logs of the pupil's significant behavior observed by his teachers in the lower grades. Entries in these records should be dated.
14. Periodic summaries of pupil's progress.

Periodic summaries may reveal trends in the pupil's emotional, social, physical, and intellectual development.

The value of a cumulative record is dependent upon its accuracy, completeness, availability to teachers, and use. The teacher can contribute to the value of the record especially in regard to accuracy and completeness. Frequent entries of measures of achievement and objective observations greatly enhance the value of the cumulative record as a source of information about the pupil.

Community backgrounds

The culture of the community in which the child lives greatly affects his attitudes. The cultural backgrounds of children living in the various regions of the United States differ so markedly that they produce great differences in individuals' attitudes toward race, religion, politics, and manners. The out-of-school experiences of pupils living in a rural community vary greatly from those of children living in an urban community. Other matters in communities which influence children's outlooks are recreational, health, and educational facilities. Provisions for these facilities vary considerably from one community to another. Unless the teacher can see the pupil against his background of community life, it is doubtful that she can truly understand the pupil's motivations, interests, and attitudes toward many aspects of living. Constructive community influences such as supervised playgrounds, libraries, museums, youth organizations, and church groups tend to counteract slum housing, overcrowding, minority group prejudices, unwholesome commercial enterprises which cater to youth, and other poor community conditions.

Home background

The home situation is one of the major influences on the elementary school pupil. Indeed, the transition from the sheltered life of the family to the larger school group requires some of the most important emotional and social adjustments the individual is called upon to make. Feelings of insecurity and frustration often result when the young child finds himself suddenly removed from his protected position in the home and placed among strangers in the school. This severing of home ties is especially confusing until the child finds acceptance by the teacher and other pupils.

An indication of the school's awareness of the pupil's strong interest in his home during his first two or three years in school is revealed by the inclusion of topics pertaining to the home in the course of study for the primary grades. The child's attitude in school also is influenced by the interpersonal relationships in his home. The child who feels rejected by members of his family often feels rejected in school. In the school as in the home, unsatisfied emotional needs for acceptance, approval, and security may produce such symptoms of maladjustment as temper tantrums, thumb-sucking, acts of hostility toward other children, and other tension-reducing forms of behavior.

The teacher needs to know various other features of the home situation which influence the child's attitude and performance in school. Parental occupation, irrespective of income, may affect the child's educational goals. Standards of conduct and methods of disciplining children vary considerably among families of different economic and social levels. The teacher who comes from a middle-class home often finds it difficult to understand the attitudes and values held by children of upper-class and lower-class families. The attitudes of parents of minority cultures may be reflected in the child's attitude toward the school and other social agencies.

In planning activities for children in the present-day school, the teacher should know that in all but the poorest modern homes children's work experience is very largely limited to manipulation of household gadgets in which physical effort is reduced to a minimum.

In the interpretation of information about the pupil's home situation, no one of the factors in the situation should be overemphasized. Many children from unsatisfactory home situations make a good adjustment to school and life. The teacher should recognize that many children's maladjustments result from the school environment rather than from the home.

General intelligence test scores

Children at any given grade level differ markedly in their ability to learn and to remember what they have learned. Psychologists have constructed intelligence tests as measurements of a person's ability to learn. Although teachers occasionally may attach too much weight to intelligence test scores, they represent one important source of information concerning a learner.

The I.Q. is an index number of intelligence computed by dividing the mental age (M.A.) by the chronological age (C.A.). An I.Q. of 100 indicates average intelligence. If a child of 5 years gets as high a score as the average child of 7 years, he has an I.Q. of 140. If he does only as well as a child of 4 years, he has an I.Q. of 80. The M.A. is ascertained by the total score on an intelligence test containing items which reveal understanding of words, ability to work with numbers, ability to solve logical problems, memory, and ability to plan ahead.

By using tests such as the Thurstone Primary Mental Tests, it is possible to obtain a score on each of several different abilities. These separate scores reveal the child's weak and strong points which an over-all score cannot indicate. In recent years many psychologists have expressed the opinion that a sound concept of general intelligence embraces volitional and emotional aspects of behavior as well as strictly intellectual abilities.

In line with the organismic concept of human behavior, Wechsler [1] has suggested that a person's general intelligence is in-

[1] David Wechsler, "Cognitive, Conative, and Nonintellective Intelligence," *American Psychologist*, V, March, 1950, pp. 78–83.

fluenced by anxiety, drive, perseverance, persistence, and security. Evidence from recent studies of general intelligence indicates that environmental factors may greatly influence the constancy of the I.Q. There is some evidence that most intelligence tests are geared to our middle-class culture.

Significant differences are frequently observed in the scores made on intelligence tests by children from families representing various occupational groups. The teacher should be aware that there may be considerable overlapping of the scores made by individual pupils of low and high occupational and social status. The variations in the scores of children of different language groups are usually considerably less on nonverbal tests.

The intelligence test is useful in predicting when used along with the previous marks on prognostic tests for predicting and measuring potentiality for success. It should be borne in mind that, while scores on intelligence tests do correlate positively with marks received in courses, the correlation is not high enough to permit accurate prediction in individual cases. Great caution should be exercised against overemphasizing the significance of an I.Q. determined by a single group intelligence test. The scores of two or more tests administered at different times may give a more accurate measurement of a pupil's intelligence. In the event a pupil makes an extremely high or low score on a group intelligence test, it is feasible to give him an individual intelligence test.

Educational achievement

In many schools, batteries of standardized tests are given. These tests are designed to measure children's mastery of the basic skills in reading, arithmetic, spelling, and writing and their knowledge of content subjects such as geography, literature, and history. The teacher can compare the scores of the pupils in her class on these tests with the scores of pupils in other schools. Comparisons also can be made between the achievement test scores of pupils in a class with their intelligence test scores to ascertain whether or not the pupils' achievement is up to the standards of their mental abilities.

The results of various types of teacher-made tests (see Chapter 19) also provide information concerning pupil's achievement and progress. If the test items are sufficiently detailed and specific, an analysis of the scores may be useful in the diagnosis of specific learning difficulties.

Records of a pupil's previous achievement in school represent another important source of information about him. These records usually include marks given by former teachers. The achievement record also may include samples of the pupil's written work, test papers, and written comments of his former teachers.

In the interpretation of the pupil's previous school achievement, the teacher should be aware that the correlation is not perfect between marks received by children in the various grades of the elementary school. A positive correlation between the marks received by children at different grade levels indicates that previous school marks have some value in predicting a pupil's future school achievement. There are many reasons, however, for considerable variation in a pupil's achievement at different grade levels. Changes in his motivation, maturity, and social adjustment which may occur from time to time may cause great differences in his behavior or achievement in school. The elimination of a defect in vision which may have handicapped a pupil at one time may represent the difference between unsatisfactory and satisfactory progress in school. It is essential that the teacher explore the reasons or combination of reasons for a pupil's previous school achievement. This record should be used to understand him, not as evidence against him.

Work-study skills. Emphasis is being placed upon the development of work-study skills which include ability to read maps, graphs, charts, use of table of contents and the index in locating information, and intelligent use of the library. Tests at the elementary school level follow:

Iowa Tests of Basic Skills. Boston: Houghton Mifflin Company.
New York Rating Scale for School Habits. Yonkers, N.Y.: World Book Company.

Critical thinking ability. Increasing emphasis is being placed upon critical thinking whenever the child faces a problem in reading, arithmetic, social studies, or the like. A test on critical thinking in the social studies may be obtained from the Bureau of Publications, Teachers College, Columbia University, New York. This test checks work-study skills and abilities to draw conclusions and apply generalizations. Most teachers should spend more time observing the quality of the skills and habits of clear thinking of individuals in their classes.

Physical health examinations

Medical examinations of pupils are administered periodically in many schools. These examinations are given either by a school physician or a private physician who supplies the school with a report of the child's physical condition. These general medical examinations are usually supplemented by dental examinations and check-ups by the school nurses when pupils return to school after illness.

Records of these examinations are available to teachers. In addition to the data in the health records, the alert teacher can detect defects in pupil's vision and hearing as well as other types of physical disabilities. Low physical vitality caused by poor nutrition and the effects of various children's diseases which handicap pupils in their schoolwork can be identified by the teacher. Pupils with these disabilities should be referred to the proper authorities for treatment. The teacher can also modify her classroom procedures and seating arrangements to alleviate some of the difficulties.

The child's physical development represents a crucial aspect of his total growth during the elementary school years. The child's physical well-being is intimately connected with his educational achievement and social adjustment. Feelings of inferiority, frustration, and inadequacy are quite common among children who have physical defects.

Eighty-seven per cent of absences in the elementary school are caused by illness. The amount of absence from school caused by illness is much higher among children ages six to nine than in the general school population. Illness not only contributes to absenteeism but also contributes to retardation, and partly explains unsatisfactory school achievement and other forms of maladjustment of individual pupils.

A general knowledge of various aspects of a child's physical development is useful to teachers. In assigning tasks involving manual dexterity, such as penmanship, the teacher should be aware that in the muscular development of children ages 6 to 8 the large muscles of the arms and legs develop much earlier than the smaller muscles of the hands and fingers. Physical growth of children ages 6 to 12 is slower than in infancy or during adolescence. Just prior to puberty, which usually comes earlier for girls than boys, there is a lag in physical growth. During their period of relatively slow growth, children manifest boundless energy. In finding the health status of the child information is needed on:

1. Family background
2. Height, weight, age
3. Condition of teeth, eyes, ears, nose, throat, heart, chest
4. History of illness and accidents
5. Immunizations, etc.
6. Physical defects
7. Rest habits and eating habits

Anecdotal records

The anecdotal record is a written record of one or more teachers' observations of a pupil's behavior and reactions in various situations. Entries in the anecdotal record made once or twice a week during a year may give a valuable sequential picture of the development of the child during that period. The record should include items of information obtained from informal conversations between the teacher and the child, samples of the pupil's school work, reports of how he spends his free time, comments about his parents, other teachers, and classmates, samples of his free creative work, and his playground activities.

An illustration [2] of a part of the anecdotal record of a fourth-grade pupil follows:

Jane is ten years of age. She is fifty-five inches tall and weighs seventy-three pounds. Her physical status is good.... She is in the fourth grade. She spent two years in the first grade. She is a blond with blue eyes. Her eyes are crossed and she wears very thick lenses in her glasses. Her eyes test normal with her glasses on. She is next to the youngest of six children. She has two brothers in the army who are eighteen and nineteen, twin sisters who are sixteen and married, and a brother who is eighteen months old. Her father is fifty-two years of age and her mother is thirty-nine.

On the friendship test she was given rejections by three of her classmates. They gave these reasons: (1) Sally—I do not like Jane because she cheats in almost all of the games. (2) Lela—I like Jane and have tried to be her friend but she is so fussy and is always going to tell on someone. (3) Beth—I do not like Jane very much because she does not like to do anything the rest of us like to do and she always finds something to fuss about.

Jane came in from recess complaining that Olive had hurt her. She said that Olive had put her whole weight on her shoulder.

She told me that Beth stole her pencil sharpener. She said this before the whole room. Beth got out the sharpener and returned it, saying that she had borrowed it. Jane went home at noon because she said that I didn't believe that Beth had stolen the sharpener. She told the children that she was going and why.

At recess today she ran after some of the girls and when they would not let her be the mother she would not play, and went over to watch a hopscotch game.

She brought me a note written by two of the girls saying, "You think you are smart." She was indignant and said, "What are you going to do about it?"

She told me at noon that Jeff took the volleyball off the school ground at noon. She said, "I would be afraid to do that."

Jeff said that Jane would not let him play with the volleyball today. She said that he was too rough, but the other children said that he was not.

She came running in from recess saying the other side cheated and that somebody pulled her coat.

2 Anna Belle Donalson, "A Sociometric Study of Fourth-Grade Children" (Master of Arts thesis, University of Colorado, 1945), pp. 57–58.

The children complained that she didn't play fair at recess. They said that when she was caught she always quit and then started playing again in a little while.

She was leader of one team of chase. She said that none of the girls wanted to be on her side. The girls said that she was so bossy with those on her side and that they did not like for her to be leader for that reason. They said she wanted to tell everyone just what to do.

INFORMATION GATHERED BY THE TEACHER

The teacher in the elementary school who has one group of children in her class most of the school day has an excellent opportunity to know her pupils. As a child progresses through school, he can be observed in his role of individual learner and as a member of a group of his age-peers. The classroom offers opportunities for acquiring information in regard to these matters that is unavailable in any other situation.

Observation of the child as he reacts to the numerous aspects of his school environment provides the basis for understanding his personal and social adjustment. An accurate gauge of his general and special abilities can be obtained on the basis of actual achievement and performance in various formal and informal school situations.

Over a period of time, by means of conversations with him, observations, and various instruments of measurement, including interest inventories, the teacher can obtain information in regard to:

1. Special interests
2. Special abilities—artistic, athletic, dramatic, musical, and scientific
3. Voluntary free reading
4. Degree of socialization
5. Participation in extraclass activities
6. Out-of-school activities
7. Use of leisure time
8. School citizenship record
9. Supplementary information in regard to general abilities and special aptitudes as revealed by test scores.

The teacher is in a good position to make an honest appraisal of the pupil's strengths and shortcomings. She can discover what the pupil can do well, whether it be mathematics, typewriting, sports, or organizing parties. She can ascertain his weaknesses in reading, spelling, composition, and making things. She can identify evidences of physical weakness or disease.

Since satisfactory social adjustment is so important in the development of the pupils, the teacher should be especially sensitive to any symptoms of social maladjustment. Ordinary observational and sociometric techniques are helpful in this respect.

While much of this information can be obtained in the year in which the pupil is a member of the teacher's class, many schools are organizing their programs to enable each teacher to stay with the same group of children longer than one year. The reorganization of the elementary school into two divisions to take the place of the present organization of six grades makes it possible for one teacher to keep in close touch with each pupil for a three-year period.

The teacher can supplement in various ways her knowledge of pupils gained by a careful analysis of cumulative school records. Some of the techniques of studying pupils are described briefly in the following paragraphs.

Conversations and informal interviews

Many teachers create opportunities to chat informally with individuals or small groups of students before the school day begins, during intermissions, or during the day. These informal friendly conversations may be directed by an interested, skillful teacher to topics which give clues to the pupil's interests, reactions to his school, as well as out-of-school experiences, motivations, and aspirations.

Information obtained in these situations is a valuable supplement to that obtained in more formal group situations in which many pupils may be reluctant to express their feelings. The teacher also may conduct a series of informal interviews with each member of a class in which the child is encouraged to discuss his favorite activities, hobbies, etc. If these conversations are to help the teacher know the pupil, she must establish good rapport with him so that he will express his ideas freely.

Informal observations

The elementary school teacher has many opportunities each day to observe the pupils she teaches. Observations of the pupil's classroom activities provide clues to his abilities and attitudes toward school activities, and his participation and interpersonal relationships in various work and study groups. Observations of the pupil's play activities reveal important physical and social skills. Since child behavior is subject to frequent change, conclusions relative to a pupil's behavior based upon a single observation may be very misleading. A series of observations represent a much sounder basis for an accurate evaluation of the pupil.

The value of the observations made by the teacher is highly dependent upon her sympathetic interest in the pupil. This interest is necessary to provide the "drive" which is essential for making careful observations. Even though the teacher has a strong personal interest in the pupil, she must make an objective, impersonal evaluation of her observations. Despite her professional involvement in the pupil's welfare, the teacher at all times must be cognizant that the value of her observations in understanding the pupil is determined to a very great extent by the objectivity of her evaluations.

In the interpretation of the observation of a pupil's behavior, consideration should be given to the various factors in the situation which may have affected his behavior. If records of the teacher's observations are to be used by other teachers or guidance workers, accurate and complete descriptions of the pupil's behavior and the situation are necessary.

Knowledge of interpersonal relationships

The social development of the learner represents an important aspect of his total pattern of growth. A pupil's interpersonal interactions, acceptance, and affiliations within his class largely determine his feelings of satisfaction and security in the school. These feelings influence not only his overt behavior but also his motivations in learning activities. Many items of information concerning a pupil's behavior and progress in school can be interpreted only upon the basis of a knowledge of his position as a member of a group of his age-peers.

The techniques which may be employed by the teacher to obtain information about the interpersonal relationships among her pupils, include not only observations of individual pupils in group situations and informal conferences but also sociometric devices. When the results of a sociometric test are recorded as a sociogram, the teacher can substantiate some of the information obtained by the more subjective means of individual conferences and observations. A sociogram indicates the relationships among the members of a group; it does not reveal *why* the relationships exist. Thus the construction of a sociogram of a class must be followed by a careful study of the causes of each individual pupil's acceptance or rejection by the members of his peer group. If the pupil is encountering difficulty in making a satisfactory social adjustment, information concerning the reasons for his difficulty is necessary in planning a program to help him find and fill his place as a member of his peer group.

Figure 1 is a sociogram of the girls in a fourth-grade class in Corpus Christi, Texas.[3] The sociogram was made upon the basis of three choosing situations as follows:

1. Write the name of your best friend.
2. Write the name of your next best friend.
3. Write the name of your third best friend.

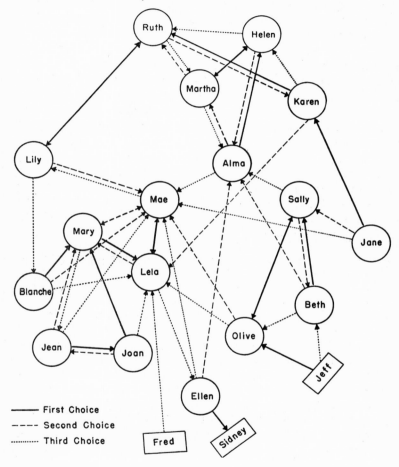

Figure 1. Sociogram of Seventeen Fourth-Grade Girls

It will be observed that a clique existed within the class, that certain pupils were isolates, and that certain children outside the clique chose members of the clique but were not chosen by mem-

[3] Used by permission of Anna Belle Donalson, Fourth-Grade Teacher, Furman School, Corpus Christi, Texas.

bers of the clique (usually referred to as *fringers*). The sociogram also reveals that at the fourth-grade level girls choose girls and seldom choose boys.

An analysis of the sociogram reveals that Jane was an *isolate* since she was not chosen by any of the other pupils. Mae, who was chosen by the greatest number of pupils, could be designated as the *star* of the class. There were few mutual first choices among the pupils, indicating the absence of cliques in the class, with their attendant *fringers*.

Identifying emotional needs

Especially significant among the basic emotional needs common to all children are the need for acceptance, affection, and security. Failure to satisfy these needs often results in frustration and other forms of mental disturbances. As no two individuals react alike in meeting their problems, no set procedure can be followed by the teacher in identifying the symptoms of maladjustment of different pupils. There are, however, some symptoms of frustration which are useful to the teacher in understanding pupil behavior. Some indication that a child is encountering difficulty in satisfying his basic emotional needs may be revealed by one or more of the following types of behavior:

1. *Shyness and other forms of withdrawing behavior.* Child may refuse to play with other children, prefers classroom activities that isolate him from others. He may be overstudious, or, on the other hand, indulge in excessive daydreaming.
2. *Extremely aggressive behavior.* A certain amount of aggressive behavior from time to time is normal for most elementary school pupils. Frequent displays of strong aggressive behavior of a pupil, however, may be symptomatic of emotional disturbances. Pupils may reveal their aggression in name-calling, bragging, loud yelling, hitting, pushing, and bullying other children, or destroying school property.
3. *Submissive behavior.* The behavior of the oversubmissive pupil is characterized by docility, great efforts to "please," dependence upon others, and self-depreciation. The oversubmissive pupil is likely to be exploited by other pupils.
4. *Somatic symptoms of illness.* Physical symptoms frequently associated with emotional disturbances are headaches, skin diseases, speech defects, tics, and recurrent attacks of bronchitis and heart palpitation.

In interpreting the symptoms of pupil maladjustment, too much importance should not be attached to isolated acts of behavior.

Frequent recurring symptoms of pupil frustration are danger signals which call for a study of the causative factors in the pupil's behavior. The difficulties of a pupil may have their origins in the home situation or in unfavorable factors in the school situation.

The teacher should not direct all her attention to the negative aspects of pupil behavior. Desirable positive personality traits in pupils can be fostered by judicious praise and recognition. Favorable group relationships contribute to the individual pupil's development.

Emotions are intrinsic factors in every experience. The understanding of the nature of each child is essential in guiding him to take his place in a social world. Information about the child's emotional behavior patterns can be obtained by:

1. Studying children's creative work, such as paintings, drawings, stories, and poems.
2. Recording projection techniques, such as how the child treats his pet, toys, etc.
3. Noting on anecdotal records wishes, desires, worries, tantrum patterns, etc.
4. Using devices such as the Haggerty-Olson-Wickman Behavior Rating Schedules, World Book Company, Yonkers, N.Y.

Daily informal observations should reveal a great deal about the emotional development and the emotional stability or instability of individuals. In notable cases of emotional instability some record should be made to indicate the situation and the particular pattern of behavior indicating emotional instability.

Ascertaining personality traits

The practice of giving and recording a personality inventory is spreading. These inventories furnish rough measures of such qualities as relative seriousness, frankness, steadiness, extroversion, introversion, dominance-submission, sociability, neuroticism, persistence, and relative adjustment and maladjustment to home, school, and companions. Typical of instruments for this purpose are the following:

California Test of Personality. E. W. Tiegs, W. W. Clark, and L. P. Thorpe. California Test Bureau. Kindergarten through adult. Factors tested: self-reliance, sense of personal worth and personal freedom, belonging, freedom from withdrawal tendencies, freedom from nervous symptoms, social standing, social skills, freedom from antisocial tendencies, family relations, vocational relations, and community relations.

Vineland Social Maturity Scale. Training School at Vineland, New Jersey. Ages 0-1 to 21 years.

The Symonds Adjustment Inventory. Teachers College, Columbia University, New York City. For use in upper grades.

A personality evaluation form that focuses the attention of teachers upon clinically pertinent observations and questions has been constructed by C. Buhler and G. Howard, Western Psychological Service, West Los Angeles, California. It includes instruction on the selection and organization of knowledge about the child according to the clinical aspects of the child's needs and values and reactions to the realities of live situations. Using the personality evaluation form, teachers select and record data so that patterns of the child's personality structure become easily identifiable. These include such patterns as psychological needs, demands made upon the child by his family and society, and the values and goals cherished by himself and family.

Similarly useful is a projective technique published by the same authors, *World Tests*. One of these tests employs real objects, and the other employs pictures. Both forms may be administered in a comparatively short time and scored and interpreted according to very definite instructions. Use of this test is most likely to furnish useful information relative to certain specific areas of personality, including the individual's unconscious goal-striving.

Ratings by former teachers are also employed as are other records of pupil behavior which throw light on the honesty, temperament, disposition, and other important character and personality traits of the pupil. Testimony of parents frequently reveals information in this area.

Learning pupils' interests

A knowledge of pupils' interests is essential to the teacher in selecting instructional materials and planning learning experiences. The learner's interests can be used to guide him into new areas of knowledge and experience. Appropriate provision for motivation of the individual learner can be made only in terms of his interests.

Listening to the pupil's informal conversations, analyzing his written work, and observing his free play activities contribute to the teacher's knowledge of the pupil's interests. *What I Like to Do*, a standardized measure of interests for pupils in grades four to seven, has been constructed by Louis Thorpe, Charles Meyers, and S. Marcella Ryser, Science Research Associates. The measuring instrument is designed to ascertain what the pupil would like to do in the areas of art, music, social studies, active play, quiet play, creative and mechanical activities, "around the house" activities, and curiosity about and interest in nature. Typical of the 294 questions on the test are:

Would you like to . . .	No	?	Yes
Paint pictures of people	☐	☐	☐
Collect snapshots	☐	☐	☐

Other techniques which are used by teachers in ascertaining the interests of children are:

1. Evaluating withdrawals of books from public library and school libraries.
2. Using questionnaire in order to detect various areas of interests, such as hobbies, favorite games, health interests.
3. Recording activities which children choose during free periods.

From pupil autobiographies and compositions teachers also may be able to discover status and changes in interests which reveal pupils' growth or deterioration in several very important areas. Among these areas are family relationships, hobbies, attitudes toward the other sex, religious attitudes, educational and vocational intentions, excessive or inadequate self-confidence in general or specific areas, unfortunate experiences which may explain some types of behavior, and unsatisfied inner yearnings which may also throw some light on otherwise inexplicable behavior.

Studying creative products

The child reveals many of his feelings about his school, home, and peer group in his creative products. When encouraged by the teacher to express his ideas freely, the pupil tells much about his reactions to various school and outside activities. Analyses of auto-biographies, original compositions, drawings, spontaneous conversations, informal storytelling, free play and make-believe activities provide a valuable basis for understanding some of the concerns, hopes, and worries of the learner. The following short essay [4] written by a boy of thirteen years on "What I Would Like to Be" reveals his longings for adventure and as an avenger of wrong-doing:

The Person I Would Like To Be Like—If I had my wish, I would like to be about 14 years old and my character would be kind and law-abiding. My appearance would be sort of slender, have a black mask across my eyes, trunks, a short-sleeved shirt, and a black cape across my back.

[4] Association For Supervision and Curriculum Development, *Fostering Mental Health in Our Schools, 1950 Yearbook* (Washington, D.C.: National Education Association), pp. 252–53.

My occupation would be catching bandits, crooks, robbers, and murderers. I would have a swell recreation. The recreation would be collecting the rewards.

The child's creative activities also give a good indication of his abilities and skills in drawing, writing, and oral expression. A diagnosis of the learner's specific strengths and weaknesses provides a basis for planning remedial and developmental programs for the learner. In the process of expressing his feelings the individual acquires greater understanding of himself. For example, the child who is confused and emotionally disturbed may be assisted in clarifying his feelings and reducing his tensions by the opportunity to express his attitudes in a permissive classroom situation in which the teacher and other pupils accept and help him clarify his feelings without censure.

Listening to informal discussions

In Chapter 16, the *Show and Tell* technique is described. In these informal discussion periods, each pupil is free to report his experiences and observations of the preceding day. If these discussions are conducted in a friendly, permissive manner, the teacher can gain valuable information about each pupil.

The topic the pupil chooses to discuss provides not only a clue to his daily experiences but also some indication of his interests. The type and variety of activities in which the pupil engages in school and outside may suggest to the teacher the direction which some of the classroom learning activities should take. By listening to the reports of the pupil, the teacher can gain insights into how he reacts to various experiences and his ability to cope with and adjust to different situations.

A knowledge of how the child feels about his experiences in the school and home may reveal the extent to which his basic emotional needs are being met. The pupil's feelings of self-confidence and security are frequently indicated by his discussions of various topics.

Careful evaluations of the oral reports and discussions in the Show-and-Tell period can indicate the pupil's strengths and weaknesses in expressing his ideas to others. This evidence can be used as the basis for planning various developmental and remedial learning activities for individual pupils and for the group.

Conducting parent-teacher conferences

Reference is made in Chapter 20 to the use of the parent-teacher conference as an opportunity for the teacher to report and interpret to parents the child's progress in school. These conferences also can be useful to the teacher in learning about the child's home situation, including his relationships with other members of the family. Buhler and others [5] have compiled a list of suggestions teachers have found useful in conducting conferences with parents. The suggestions are as follows:

Don'ts	*Do's*
Compare or discuss other children in the classroom. This distracts attention from the problem at hand, encourages competitiveness, and often harms school and neighborhood relationship.	Begin with a positive statement of the child's abilities, assets, or interests. This helps parents to be less defensive because it conveys interest and liking of the child.
Criticize or blame past school experience, or teacher, because this destroys confidence in all education. Attention should be centered upon present needs and plans, not past mistakes.	Accept parents' goals or wishes for their children, even though they differ from the school's. Try to extend narrow goals of "learning to read" or "doing numbers" to broader ones of social adjustment and personal development.
Describe personal experiences to interpret behavior, because human beings and situations are different and the same solutions often do not apply.	Encourage the parents to formulate their own statement of the child's need and to search for causes rather than depending upon others' opinions.
Use blanket words such as immaturity, insecurity, etc., without specific descriptions of the child's behavior.	Share observations about children, comparing responses at school and at home before making an interpretation or judgment.
Imply that the parent or the home is to blame for the child's behavior or overlook all the other influences upon the child's life.	Remember that criticism or evaluation of children is taken emotionally as criticism or evaluation of the parents themselves.
Become immediately defensive when questions about school practices are raised.	Listen to parents' complaints or criticisms of the school, accepting them as evidences of interest or suggestions to be considered.
Give advice unless asked and never as the single successful solution.	Be ready to offer several suggestions which are within the parents' ability to carry out when problems are discussed.

Making case studies

In a case study, various items of information about an individual obtained from many sources are assembled into a single pattern.

[5] Charlotte Buhler, Faith Smitter, Sybil Richardson, and Franklyn Bradshaw, *Childhood Problems and the Teacher* (New York: Henry Holt & Co., Inc., 1952), p. 251.

The chief value of the case study in understanding the pupil is that it provides a total picture rather than a number of isolated bits of information concerning the pupil. The different items of information can be studied in their proper relationship to each other. If the data are assembled over a period of time, it is possible to observe the developmental patterns of the pupil.

While it would be extremely valuable for a teacher to make a thorough case study of each of the pupils in her class, usually it is necessary for her to select a limited number of pupils for very intensive study. Many teachers make case studies of a few of the most seriously maladjusted pupils and a few who are exceptionally well adjusted.

Procedures. The various techniques for obtaining information about a pupil which are described in this chapter can be utilized in making a case study. One teacher used the following procedure in making a case study of one of her maladjusted pupils:

1. Made a careful study of the pupil's cumulative school record.
2. Observed his classroom and playground activities.
3. Talked with other teachers who knew the pupil.
4. Observed the reactions of his classmates to him and his reactions to them.
5. Conducted a series of individual conferences with the pupil.
6. Made an analysis of the pupil's written work and scores on tests of general intelligence, achievement, special abilities, and interests.
7. Visited the pupil's home and conducted conferences with his parents.
8. Summarized the information about the pupil.
9. Interpreted the data.
10. Planned a program to assist the pupil.

Recording the information. The information obtained in the study of a pupil can be classified under general headings as follows:

A. General Information
   1. Name and address
   2. Parents' names
   3. Chronological age
   4. Schools attended
   5. Grade
B. Community situation—especially the factors which directly influence children
C. Home Background
   1. Formal education of parents
   2. Occupations of parents

3. Brothers and sisters—formal education and occupations of older brothers and sisters
4. Status in the family—acceptance or rejection, favorite child
5. General economic and social status of family
6. Mobility of the family

D. School Record
1. General school achievement and attendance
2. Record as a school citizen
3. Achievement in different subjects
4. Significant changes in progress in school
5. School activities
6. Social relations with other pupils

E. Mental Abilities
1. General abilities—M.A., I.Q.
2. Special abilities and aptitudes

F. Physical Condition
1. General physical vitality
2. Stature
3. Overweight or underweight
4. Vision and hearing
5. Health habits—eating, sleep
6. Physical skills

G. Out-of-school Experiences
1. Leisure-time activities—kind and amount of time devoted to each
2. Playmates—age (one symptom of social maladjustment is the child's preference for playmates much older or younger than himself)
3. Chores around the home

Interpreting the information. The mere acquisition of information concerning pupils does not ensure that the teacher will gain a clear understanding of them. The data require careful interpretation. Some of the information concerning deep-seated emotional problems can best be interpreted by a person especially trained in that area of child adjustment. The same is true of certain data concerning the child's physical and social development. There is, however, a considerable body of nontechnical data which the alert teacher can interpret and use in her endeavor to understand pupils in her classes. As a result of scientific studies of child growth and development by Dr. Arnold Gesell and others, there is available to teachers considerable information about the biological and psychological traits of children at different maturity levels. These studies have made it possible to formulate certain generalizations which offer the teacher insight into "what children are like" at different ages.

In the study of the individual child, however, environmental and hereditary factors which contribute to great differences in children's physical, social and emotional development must be taken into account.

QUESTIONS, PROBLEMS, AND EXERCISES

1. What are the chief difficulties encountered by teachers in learning to know their pupils?

2. Suggest some of the errors teachers make in their relationships with pupils because of their failure to understand them.

3. What preparation should the teacher make for a conference with the parents of a pupil whose school achievement is unsatisfactory?

4. Suggest how the teacher may involve the shy, withdrawing type of pupil in group activities in the classroom and on the playground.

5. How may the teacher assist a pupil who is rejected by members of his class gain social acceptance by his peer group?

6. Suggest a list of guiding principles which should be followed in making anecdotal records of pupils.

7. The effectiveness of pupil-teacher conference as a means of knowing the pupil is dependent upon the teacher's ability to establish good rapport with the pupil. Indicate how this rapport may be achieved.

8. Suggest other items which should be included under each of the general headings of the case study outlined in this chapter.

SELECTED SUPPLEMENTARY READINGS

ASSOCIATION FOR SUPERVISION AND CURRICULUM DEVELOPMENT. *Fostering Mental Health In Our Schools.* Washington, D.C.: The Association, 1950.

Part 3, "Knowing and Helping the Child," contains chapters on use of anecdotal records, sociometric grouping, informal talks with children and parents, and children's creative products as sources of information.

BUHLER, CHARLOTTE, FAITH SMITTER, SYBIL RICHARDSON, and FRANKLYN BRADSHAW. *Childhood Problems and the Teacher.* New York: Henry Holt & Company, Inc., 1952.

Chap. viii, "The Teacher's Study of Individual Children," describes techniques a teacher can use to increase her understanding of her pupils.

CROW, LESTER D., and ALICE CROW. *Understanding Our Behavior.* New York: Alfred A. Knopf, Inc., 1956.

Chap. iii, "Personality Evaluation," describes the use of various instruments and techniques for personality evaluation.

CUNNINGHAM, RUTH, and others. *Understanding Group Behavior of Boys and Girls.* New York: Teachers College, Bureau of Publications, Columbia University, 1951.

Chap. xi presents techniques and instruments for studying individual and group behavior.

FOREST, ILSE. *Child Development.* New York: McGraw-Hill Book Co., Inc., 1954.

Chap. i, "Toward Understanding Children," contains section devoted to evaluating social development.

HASKEW, LAURENCE D. *This Is Teaching.* Chicago: Scott, Foresman & Co., 1956.
Chap. iii, "These Are the Learners," contains section dealing with the various techniques of studying students.

OTTO, HENRY J., HAZEL FLOYD, and MARGARET ROUSE. *Principles of Elementary Education,* rev. ed. New York: Rinehart & Co., Inc., 1955.
Chap. x, "The Children," discusses what a teacher should know about a child with an excellent description of how a teacher studied her class.

WINGO, G. MAX and RALEIGH SCHORLING. *Elementary-School Student Teaching,* 2d ed. New York: McGraw-Hill Book Co., Inc., 1955.
Chap. ii, "Learning to Understand Pupils," illustrates a technique for learning about an individual pupil.

4

CHILD GROWTH
THE GOAL OF INSTRUCTION

Much superficial thinking about the curriculum and instruction is the result of failure to understand their relationship to the growth of human beings toward the objectives of education. Many teachers and administrators have never thought through the function of instruction and learning activities in education and thus have accepted the status quo, as represented by the subjects authorized by the board of education and the textbooks adopted for teaching them.

Changes in curriculum usually grow out of immediate practical considerations, such as the desire to have children succeed in spelling certain words or reciting the multiplication tables, or the need to please parents or other adults in the community. Some changes are the result of a teacher's attempt to follow a "trend," often without knowing just what the trend really is and involves, or why it has occurred.

Whatever is taught is likely to be justified by fallacious interpretation of some psychological principle (such as transfer of training) or by reference to some consideration which is really of secondary importance. Basic to any effective selection of curricular materials is recognition of the principle that the curriculum and related learning activities are designed to provide an environment for a given group of learners, so selected, arranged, and presented as to influence the growth and future behavior of these children.

RELATION OF INSTRUCTION TO GROWTH

Modern education is based on the principle that human beings, like other living organisms, are in a constant state of change. The organism that flourishes is likely to be that one in which change or growth is a continuing adaptation to environment.

Education is the process of influencing growth to facilitate the best possible adaptation of a human being to his environment, of bringing about changes in him that will enable him to function adequately in the world in which he lives. *Teaching* is the directing of this process. It is the management and control, so far as possible, of the changes that take place in the immature individual. In the following paragraphs, this theory of education will be examined.

Importance of early years

Living organisms grow most rapidly during the first part of their normal life span. During this early period, growth is more positive and integrated than during the concluding period of life, which is characterized by a tendency toward degeneration. For example, the cat, with a normal life span of 15 to 18 years, and the dog, with a span of 10 to 12 years, do most of their physical and mental growing during the first year of life. In succeeding years, growth takes place at a greatly decreased rate.

Since growth is so rapid in the first period of normal life span, those organisms for whom this period is relatively long appear to have a greater chance to make positive and more complicated adaptations to their environment. The human organism, therefore, is indeed favored by nature, for the period of infancy is many times that of other forms of life and the period of plasticity of the cortex and neural systems is correspondingly greater.

Importance of school environment

Growth is determined by both heredity and environment. But hereditary factors are fixed from the beginning of embryonic life, and nothing can be done to change them. If growth is to be influenced at all, it must be through environment. Experience is indeed the best teacher, for it is the *only* teacher. If growth is affected in any way except through experience (environment), the result is not learning but inheritance.

If the aim of education is to produce desirable growth, the school must provide an environment that will stimulate such growth more effectively than experiences which the individual would have otherwise. *The curriculum and methods of teaching are means of assur-*

ing for the child desired educative experiences. Anything may be included that will cause the learner to act, feel, and think now in such a manner as will cause him to act, feel, and think in desired ways in the future.

Hence the curriculum and classroom procedures are not merely means of getting youngsters to learn certain sets of materials or even their cultural heritage. No element of the heritage is a thing of intrinsic value to be "passed on" to the young. It is a means to an end. That end is the kind of individual a teacher sets out to produce—the kind of individual who lives happily and with benefit of society.

Acceptance of this general goal for education facilitates assessment of the value of guidance and other extracurricular activities, as well as the course of study and instructional methods. Failure to use this basic concept is probably the reason why certain curriculum materials have a privileged place in the school, regardless of their functional contributions to the growth of the learner.

By one basic criterion—Does it contribute to desirable growth?—the validity of all curriculum materials and methods of teaching may be judged. Not only the traditional reading material, recitation, writing, and instruction but also the use of pictures, discussions, assembly programs, excursions, and community participation may be so judged.

Any materials or pupil activities, in school or out, in books or not, within subjects or outside them, that will cause pupils to have educative experiences—that is, experiences that result in desirable growth—may legitimately be considered for educational programs. Hence it is clear that (1) the educational environment of the school includes guidance, clubs, and other extracurricular provisions for learning experiences and (2) all such activities and services should be planned, carried on, and evaluated according to the same broad principles as the rest of the curriculum.

OBJECTIVES OF LEARNING AND TEACHING

The objectives of learning and teaching must be stated in terms of desired growth in individual children. Teaching is the process of bringing a youngster into contact with his environment under conditions that will influence his growth in the desired direction. The whole process is based on knowing what actions, feelings, and thoughts are desired. To influence growth, a teacher must first answer the fundamental questions: Growth toward what? What kind of an individual should be produced?

Hundreds of notable statements of the objectives of education have been drawn up. Some are in terms of *abilities* desirable in an individual, such as clear thinking, forceful thinking, getting along with other people. In recent decades, the more notable statements have been formulated in terms of types of growth that are apt to result in better *functioning* in areas of life activity common to almost everyone.

Some of these statements emphasize the fullest possible development of the powers of the *individual*. There is differing emphasis, however, upon whose benefit should govern: the individual's personal benefit, that of society, or both.

Complete development of an individual's powers is an objective that is not acceptable, for there are "powers" that had better be left undeveloped. Powers to be developed must be selected in terms of some *set of ultimate values*, such as communication of need or social cooperation. Otherwise, the objectives of education might include development of powers that are actually destructive or are at best of little value to anyone.

Many statements of the objectives of education have been made by important individuals, committees, and commissions. Some of these have been in terms of subject matter to be mastered, some in terms of areas of life for which children ought to be prepared, and some in terms of types of growth. In recent years there has been a tendency to place more emphasis upon stating objectives in terms of types of growth, fitting one for specified areas of life and with mastery of subject matter as means rather than objectives.

Probably the most widely circulated and most commonly accepted statement of objectives of education in the last twenty years has been that made by the Educational Policies Commission of the National Education Association, as given in the following paragraphs. Note that some of these objectives are in terms of types of growth, the acquisition of certain types of information, skills, ideals, attitudes, and habits. For example, an educated person, under the objectives of self-realization, has found the inquiring mind. The educated person has an appetite for learning. This means that one of the objectives of education is to develop interests in acquiring information, in acquiring skills and, indeed, in acquiring various types of learning. To take another example, in self-realization the educated person works to improve the health of the community. This means that one of the objectives of education is to develop in each child the interest, attitudes, ideals, knowledge, and understandings that will enable him to work to improve the health of all of those living in his community, including himself.

OBJECTIVES OF EDUCATION

I. The Objectives of Self-realization

The Inquiring Mind. The educated person has an appetite for learning.

Speech. The educated person can speak the mother tongue clearly.

Reading. The educated person reads the mother tongue efficiently.

Writing. The educated person writes the mother tongue effectively.

Number. The educated person solves his problems of counting and calculating.

Sight and Hearing. The educated person is skilled in listening and observing.

Health Knowledge. The educated person understands the basic facts concerning health and disease.

Health Habits. The educated person protects his own health and that of his dependents.

Public Health. The educated person works to improve the health of the community.

Recreation. The educated person is participant and spectator in many sports and other pastimes.

Intellectual Interests. The educated person has mental resources for the use of leisure.

Esthetic Interests. The educated person appreciates beauty.

Character. The educated person gives responsible direction to his own life.

II. The Objectives of Human Relationship

Respect for Humanity. The educated person puts human relationships first.

Friendships. The educated person enjoys a rich, sincere, and varied social life.

Cooperation. The educated person can work and play with others.

Courtesy. The educated person observes the amenities of social behavior.

Appreciation of the Home. The educated person appreciates the family as a social institution.

Conservation of the Home. The educated person conserves family ideals.

Homemaking. The educated person is skilled in homemaking.

Democracy in the Home. The educated person maintains democratic family relationships.

III. The Objectives of Economic Efficiency

Work. The educated producer knows the satisfaction of good workmanship.

Occupational Information. The educated producer understands the requirements and opportunities for various jobs.

Occupational Choice. The educated producer has selected his occupation.

Occupational Efficiency. The educated producer succeeds in his chosen vocation.

Occupational Adjustment. The educated producer maintains and improves his efficiency.

Occupational Appreciation. The educated producer appreciates the social value of his work.

Personal Economics. The educated consumer plans the economics of his own life.

Consumer Judgment. The educated consumer develops standards for guiding his expenditures.

Efficiency in Buying. The educated consumer is an informed and skillful buyer.

Consumer Protection. The educated consumer takes appropriate measures to safeguard his interests.

IV. The Objectives of Civic Responsibility

Social Justice. The educated citizen is sensitive to the disparities of human circumstance.

Social Activity. The educated citizen acts to correct unsatisfactory conditions.

Social Understanding. The educated citizen seeks to understand social structures and social processes.

Critical Judgment. The educated citizen has defenses against propaganda.

Tolerance. The educated citizen respects honest differences of opinion.

Conservation. The educated citizen has a regard for the nation's resources.

Social Applications of Science. The educated citizen measures scientific advance by its contribution to the general welfare.

World Citizenship. The educated citizen is a cooperating member of the world community.

Law Observance. The educated citizen respects the law.

Economic Literacy. The educated citizen is economically literate.

Political Citizenship. The educated citizen accepts his civic duties.

Devotion to Democracy. The educated citizen acts upon an unswerving loyalty to democratic ideals.[1]

These statements are not fundamentally different from that of Herbert Spencer. He defined education as preparation for "complete living," with activities in five principal categories in the following order of importance: (1) self-preservation, (2) rearing and discipline of offspring, (3) economic life, (4) social and political relations, (5) leisure.

By way of summary, it may be said that it is the purpose of education so to stimulate and guide the growth of the individual

---

[1] *The Purposes of Education in American Democracy* (Washington, D.C.: The Educational Policies Commission of the National Education Association, 1938), pp. 50, 72, 90, and 108.

that he will function effectively in areas and activities of life which most careful students of education believe to be important—vocation, home, citizenship, and enjoyment of leisure—and will also possess in high degree mental and physical health and vigor and the skills and interests appropriate to most effective learning in the future. The curriculum must be the best possible selection and arrangement of stimuli to experience resulting in maximum growth toward effective functioning in the areas indicated by a sound statement of the objectives of education.

At all times in the organization and revision of the curriculum, the general objectives of education must be kept in mind and a balance maintained so that growth will be stimulated toward all objectives. Education for citizenship and for health education should, for example, never be neglected in favor of education for leisure, or vice versa. Each general objective of education must be analyzed and broken down into limited objectives or types of human growth which are essential to, or contribute greatly to, the attainment of the objective. Such an analysis will not only contribute to the selection of curriculum materials and to planning for instruction and learning activities; it is essential to any effective educational planning.

TYPES OF EDUCATIONAL OUTCOMES

It is convenient and practical to think of the outcomes of learning experiences of different types classified according to their nature. Types of educational outcomes together with examples follow:

1. Detailed, factual information
   America was discovered by Columbus in 1492
   A foot is equal to twelve inches
   Six and eight are fourteen
   London is the capital of England

2. General principles
   A sentence is a group of words expressing a complete thought
   To divide by a fraction, invert the fraction and multiply
   Distance = rate × time

3. Understandings, meanings, definitions, general concepts, orientations
   The meaning of democracy
   The concept of evolution
   Orientation in a new community, school, or field of thought
   The meaning of cooperation

4. Skills emphasizing mental activity
   Ability to add, subtract, multiply
   Ability to think logically

Ability to outline or summarize printed materials
Ability to express self in written form
Ability to read rapidly
Ability to conduct group conferences

5. Skills emphasizing motor activity
   Riding a bicycle
   Handwriting
   Dancing
   Swimming
   Painting
   Clear enunciation

6. Habits
   Various habits of courtesy, e.g., saying "Thank you" when favored
   Various habits of neatness, e.g., putting away tools after use
   Various habits of healthful and sanitary living, e.g., brushing of teeth before retiring
   Various habits related to personal appearance, e.g., combing hair every morning
   Capitalizing, crossing all "t's", and dotting all "i's"
   Checking all arithmetical computations

7. Ideals
   Ideal of being courteous
   Ideal of being honest
   Desire to become a good citizen
   Desire to be like a certain person
   Desire to be respected as a good worker
   Desire to be helpful to playmates and friends

8. Interests
   In national public affairs
   In flowers
   In airplanes
   In skillful speech
   In improving one's own social graces
   In new scientific discoveries

9. Tastes
   Liking for good literature
   Dislike for rowdiness
   Liking for exercise
   Liking for company of intelligent persons
   Dislike of cheap literature and low-grade movies

10. Attitudes and beliefs
    Open-mindedness in matters of religion
    Appreciation of the good qualities of persons of other races
    Acceptance of persons of low economic status
    Belief in democracy
    Opposition to unfair practices
    Various attitudes towards issues, people, practices

Each of the major objectives of education is achieved only by the development of contributory psychological outcomes of several, if not all, of the ten types in the foregoing. The curriculum has the purpose of providing experience that will guide and stimulate the growth and development of the appropriate psychological outcomes. Therefore it must be so chosen, arranged, and brought into contact with the learner as to produce those outcomes which are indicated from an analysis of the objectives of education.

Outcomes in curriculum planning

To decide what should be included in the curriculum, teachers might follow these steps:

1. Determine the objectives of education in terms of the kind of ultimate end product desired, for example, the good citizen, vocational competence.
2. Determine for each of the characteristics of the kind of person desired the necessary or more important contributory information, attitudes, interests, skills, habits, tastes, concepts, principles, and understandings.
3. Select and arrange according to pupils' interests, abilities, and previous growth such curricular materials and learning activities as will result in the development of the necessary information, understandings, skills, habits, ideals, attitudes, tastes, and appreciations.

On first thought, these steps seem logical and practical. If these determinations and selections could be made objectively and accurately, teachers would be well on their way toward a science of education. Needless to say, however, the matter is not as simple as that. There are too many factors involved, and too much information that is needed is not available, particularly in step 3. Curricular materials result in different experiences in different individuals, and experiences apparently alike result in different influences upon growth, to say nothing of the fact the school is only one, though an important one, of the sources of environmental influences upon growth.

Outcomes and behavior for good citizenship

Nevertheless it is a useful procedure, almost indispensable to clear thinking about the curriculum, to break down each of these principal areas or objectives of education into smaller units. There is no one thing called good citizenship. It is made up of a great variety of components, and each of these is a phase of growth which requires guidance and stimulation. To enumerate even the majority of the smaller units would involve more space and time than are available here. They tend to fall into categories, however, and the good curriculum does not fail to provide stimuli for all categories.

Categories as they apply to good citizenship are reviewed below. Being a good citizen involves each of the following:

1. *Knowing what is right and effective in the society in which the person is a citizen.* This knowledge consists of some which must have been learned previously, particularly fundamental principles, some which the citizen will most probably obtain incidentally to his life in the society, and some which he will have to acquire as the specific needs arise.

2. *Being willing to behave in a way which is right and effective.* This may be in part a matter of heredity, but it is probably in larger part a matter of learning. To insure right and effective behavior, the individual must be invested with appropriate ideals and attitudes, and he must be kept from the development of unfavorable ideals and attitudes, such as excessive personal power or gain, racial, national or regional supremacy, attitudes of ill will or contempt toward other groups or classes of society, and attitudes of indifference to matters of honesty, sexual regularity, the welfare of others, etc.

3. Being willing and able to behave in an appropriate and effective manner also involves the *possession of interests which will lead one to read and investigate and to become informed about matters upon which intelligent decisions must be made* by the citizenry of the society in which one lives and to discharge the duties of any office to which one might be elected—e.g., labor problems, international relationships, various types of private and public social security.

4. *Developing appropriate skills*—skills in getting on with others, in self-expression, in thinking clearly, in reading and listening critically, and in evaluating what he may read or hear on questions confronting or likely to confront citizens of his time.

5. *Acquiring a wealth of appropriate habits,* so that right and effective behavior is only to a small extent a matter of conscious decision.

6. *Acquiring a working collection of useful concepts and basic general ideas* which enables the citizen to understand and evaluate human experience and proposed lines of social action. He knows, for example, what constitutes democracy, communism, fascism, and socialism. He is not satisfied with cheap substitutes for democracy and is not stampeded by fine-sounding but fallacious doctrines or deceived by the application of terms like *communism* or *fascism* to practices which are really democratic in nature.

The foregoing brief analysis might well be expanded into a sizeable volume. No teacher would be capable of carrying in mind all the possible skills and attitudes, or *behavior components,* even should she be capable of listing all of them. Indeed she must become so oriented in such matters that she recalls them in service as an artist, not as a scientist.

The teacher and any one else participating effectively in course-of-study construction must think through what information, concepts, habits, skills, interests, ideals, attitudes, tastes, and appreciations are required for good citizenship, health, recreation and leisure, vocational efficiency, and home leadership and efficiency. This is an important intermediate step which can be eliminated or skimped only at the peril of poor course-of-study construction. Only after such a determination can one safely proceed to plan experiences for learners which will result in anything like the maximum contribution of school subjects to the aims and objectives of elementary education.

Concomitant behavior outcomes

The process of curriculum construction is further complicated by the fact that the attempt to develop desired behavior components always gives by-products—sometimes quite important, sometimes quite undesirable. This sort of outcome of instruction or learning may appropriately be called *concomitant outcomes.* Perhaps they are more the result of the methods of instruction than of the content, but it is hard to draw the line, and it is clear that some grow directly out of content.

A child's attitudes toward school, authority, learning in general, himself, his parents, and his classmates are usually influenced by the degree to which he finds the curriculum or parts of it interesting and apparently useful and himself capable of mastering it. His interests in various fields of learning or vocations are undoubtedly affected by his experiences with school subjects as they are taught.

Those who are familiar with child guidance, mental hygiene, and problem boys and girls are well aware of this phenomenon and can cite impressive instances in which teachers have caused the development of most powerful growths in personality—some of them malignant and systemic, some of them fortunately wholesome as well as pervading. Very often the concomitant or by-product outcome is much more important than the growth actually intended as a direct result of the learning activities.

This is particularly important in the use of incentives in instruction. Learning activities which appeal to children as pleasure-giving or otherwise worth doing result in favorable attitudes toward everything associated with their learning activities, including the subject, the school, and the teacher. To a much smaller degree learning and instructional activities will result in these favorable attitudes if they appeal to the learner as worth doing for the sake of the resulting learning, even though not pleasurable in themselves.

Less effective in developing favorable attitudes are instruction and learning activities which are both unpleasant and seemingly unlikely to result in worthwhile learning. It is important to bear in mind that the learner must not only be convinced that the learning likely to result is worth while to him, but also that it will bring him returns not too far in the future.

Also very important with respect to concomitant learning is the degree to which the learner succeeds in mastering the tasks involved in the learning activities. If he fails consistently or frequently, he is most likely to develop unfavorable attitudes toward the materials, the subject, the schools, and the teacher and is quite likely to develop a lack of confidence in himself, at least with respect to the particular field of learning.

OTHER FACTORS INFLUENCING GROWTH

The teacher, as well as other curriculum-makers, should bear in mind at all times that the effect produced upon the child is the result of a considerable number of factors, of which the curriculum is only one. The direct effect is the resultant of a number of component forces, one of which is the curricular materials.

Among the other environmental components may be mentioned the following:

1. The previously acquired background of the learner including:
   a) Vocabulary
   b) Interests
   c) General information
   d) Background in the particular field
   e) Out-of-school experience
   f) Attitudes
2. The home background of the learner including:
   a) Interests and attitudes of the parents
   b) Opportunities for study—physical aspects, books and periodicals, assistance of parents
   c) Experiences and activities which are a part of home living
3. Other contemporary influences, such as:
   a) Radio

    b) Movies
    c) Newspapers and periodicals
    d) Library
    e) Companions
    f) Work experience
    g) Contacts with adults

Instruction cannot disregard the environmental forces which influence the individual's growth, any more than it can afford to ignore the hereditary factors in growth. The school is indeed a supplementary institution. This fact has important implications for the teacher and for her functional activities which should be mentioned at this point.

Supplementary nature of school instruction

By reason of its supplementary character, the school must keep in at least fair adjustment to the rest of the learner's environment.

1. The specifications for the desired product of the schools must be drawn in the light of the conditions and demands of society as the learner will find it, including those conditions in contemporary society which call for compensatory or corrective education.
2. When some other social institution or area of the learner's environment no longer influences growth toward the objective of education as it did formerly, the school must follow one of three alternatives. It must (a) re-educate the particular social institution or some other agency to take over and serve as a replacement, (b) allow the particular educational service to go unperformed, or (c) adapt the school program so as to assume the particular function no longer operative.
3. When the educative influences of out-of-school experiences duplicate those of the school, the school should (a) determine the degree to which certain instructional activities are no longer necessary and (b) adapt instruction so as to eliminate superfluous activities.

Curriculum and changing American life

It is unfortunate that careful research and the ingenuity of the best minds cannot develop a perfect or even near-perfect curriculum. The bases upon which instructional programs and activities must be built are in a constant state of change. In the first place, the pattern of responsibility of the school changes from time to time. With changes in the home, in modes of amusement, in national and international problems, in vocational life, and in numerous other areas, the responsibility of the school for education, for vocation, for intelligent citizenship, for home membership, for recreation, and for other things increases or decreases. Changes are likewise required in the nature of school education itself.

In another place in this volume will be found a discussion of important changes in American life to which the school must adjust itself. No more will be said on the subject here other than to point out two very important facts:

1. The course-of-study maker and the teacher must possess a workable orientation to American life, its conditions, its problems, its currents and changes, and they must be able to evaluate American life in terms of the changing demands which it makes upon education.
2. The course-of-study maker and the teacher must visualize accurately the other components of human growth—the influences of home, church, the press, commercial entertainment, the radio, industry, and social companions upon the development of information, skills, habits, concepts, ideals, and attitudes.

It follows naturally that, if school instruction is to remain in anything like adequate adjustment to the needs and conditions of American society as the learner will find it and to the learner's needs and responsibilities in that society, teachers, textbook writers, and other curriculum-makers must be in touch with American society—its institutions, its problems, its trends, and the implications of all these for the curriculum. It is also a logical corollary that the curriculum should be regarded as a growing, living thing which in all probability is at least a few steps behind in its adjustment to the needs of learners and of society. As a matter of fact, the lag of the curriculum behind conditions and requirements of the times is in many respects a matter of decades rather than of years.

Curriculum and changes in pupils

Not sufficiently recognized is the fact that the interests of children of any given age also change with the passage of time. Their customs, what they read, what they like to do, how they like to play, their attitudes toward parents and teachers—all these and many other characteristics of children important in the adjustment of curriculum to the individual are matters that do not remain the same from one generation to another. Textbook writers and publishers and the more discerning teachers and principals have learned this fact.

Education is an individual matter. The growth of a group of individuals may be stimulated or guided by a common stimulus—a book, a lecture, or a picture—but it is not the group that grows; it is the separate individuals who compose the group. There are as many separate and different growth results as there are individuals within the group. From any poem or short story one individual may increase his interest in reading and a confidence in school and the teacher, while another pupil may develop a prejudice against poems and stories, an increased dislike for school, and an increased lack of confidence in the teacher. Still another may develop an appreciation of good reading, a respect for the teacher, and a lack of confidence in himself.

One is reminded of an experiment in chemistry employing a rack of test tubes containing different liquids and a beaker with still another liquid. Upon being mixed with some of the fluid in the beaker, the liquid in one test tube will turn brown, in another green, in another black or maroon. What transpires in a child's mind, and indeed in his nervous system, is a matter both of the outside stimulus and the inside apperceptive mass of knowledge, tastes, interests, and attitudes. Therefore it is necessary not only to offer different subjects but also to lead the children in one class learning one subject to do, read, say, think, and feel different things. The curriculum must be flexible enough to provide for this.

There is also a pronounced tendency to adapt all aspects of learning situations to the individual. Whether sections for instruction are formed on the basis of general mental ability, of probable need, or of any other criterion, there will always remain a wide variety among the abilities, capacities, interests, present needs, future needs, and experiential background of the individuals who compose the sections.

Because of these ever-present significant changes and variations, courses of study must always be regarded as flexible, tentative outlines. It is well to have courses of study, as it is often well to have textbooks, but in practice they must be adapted to the individuals in the class. This of course is largely the responsibility of the teacher.

It is the teacher's responsibility to bring the pupil into contact with problems and challenges which will facilitate the exploration of his interests. It is a responsibility of the teacher to bring the pupil into contact with things to do, read, say, make, hear, feel, see, and challenge, and thereby insure future behavior that will be desirable in terms of the objectives of education and of the potentialities of the individual. To live up to such responsibility the teacher must have a fund of knowledge about the individual pupils. She should have convenient access to pertinent data on the pupil's special interest, vocational, recreational, and social; on the expanse of his vocabularies, especially his listening and reading vocabularies; on his general intellectual ability; on his special aptitudes, mechanical, musical, and the like; on his out-of-school experience; on his physical development; on his stock of schoolbook information, the areas of his maladjustment, if any; and his most pronounced attitudes, ideals, and prejudices.

It is upon all these types of background of the individual learner, and more, that experience is projected for interpretation. The degree and nature of effects of experience upon the growth and future conduct of the learner are conditioned by his background. With respect to many of these items, the majority of learners of a given school grade or section may be relatively homogeneous, but there are always significant deviations. Because of these deviations, principals, supervisors, and teachers are, to a far greater extent than formerly, systematically gathering and recording data concerning pupils. Whereas formerly the data were not made available to teachers (at least not conveniently available), in many schools today such data are gathered for the teacher's use. Naturally, an alert teacher who has trained herself will soon come to note and carry in mind many impressions and facts concerning each learner. She should record these data for future use by herself and other teachers.

Curriculum and methods

While it is serviceable for the purposes of discussion to differentiate between curriculum and methods, they are inseparably interrelated and are associated parts of the educational environment of learners in school. While methods may be thought of as the procedure to bringing the learner into contact with the stimuli to experiences that will result in influencing his growth, teachers must not lose sight of the fact that methods are in themselves also educational stimuli or important parts of educational experiences.

Pupil growth is determined both in nature and amount by the method of causing learners to have the experiences thought to be effective in developing the desired types of growth. What happens to the learner educationally is determined in part, and often in large part, by such aspects of methods as:

1. The degree and adequacy of adaptation of learning materials and activities to the maturity, interests, and background of the learner, to the objectives of the unit, and to the subject of instruction
2. The nature of questions and questioning evaluated in the light of their adaptation to the interests, abilities, and backgrounds of the

learner, the objectives and sequence of the unit, and subject of instruction

3. The opportunity provided for initiative, planning, and responsibility on the learner's part
4. The definite efforts of the instructor to emphasize ideals, attitudes, tests, judgments, and understanding as contrasted with factual knowledge and subject skills
5. The evaluation techniques of the teacher and the consequent relative emphasis upon such things as those mentioned in Number 4
6. The opportunities provided for such experiences as applying principles to life, projects and other "doing" activities, group cooperation, discussion, and community participation
7. The manner of speech and other aspects of the teacher's personality

While the opportunities for writing method into textbooks and courses of study are limited, the final determiner of the curriculum is the teacher. She should not fail to recognize her responsibility for providing the most effective school environment for growth toward the objectives of education.

QUESTIONS, PROBLEMS, AND EXERCISES

1. To what extent do teachers in all their planning think of education as assisting young people to be happy, useful, healthful citizens and parents? Give examples for your answer.

2. Be able to give a five-minute talk on the significance of the relatively long period of infancy in the human species.

3. Make a list of ten areas of growth which are controlled largely by heredity, and ten which are controlled largely by environment.

4. Make a list of ways in which one learns or grows that are determined largely by out-of-school or preschool experience.

5. Be prepared to give a five-minute talk on "The teacher as a determiner of growth."

6. Write in your own words your idea of the objectives of elementary education.

7. List three specific examples of each of the ten types of educational outcomes.

8. For one of the objectives of education list at least one of each of the ten types of educational outcomes.

9. What are concomitant outcomes? Give several examples. What is their relative importance in later life?

10. What, if anything, do you think the school can and should do relative to out-of-school environmental influences upon the child?

11. Prepare a five-minute talk on "The curriculum and changing American life," considering the inferences to be drawn from the material of this chapter.

12. Why do individuals respond differently to the same subject matter in instruction? What can, or should, the teacher do in regard to these differences?

SELECTED SUPPLEMENTARY READINGS

ADAMS, FAY. *Educating America's Children,* 2d ed. New York: The Ronald Press Co., 1954.

Chap. 2, "The Basic Task: Helping Children Become Good Citizens." Most important objective and basic principle.

CASWELL, HOLLIS L., and A. WELLESLEY FOSHAY. *Education in the Elementary School,* 2d ed. New York: American Book Co., 1950.

Chap. 4, "Aims of Education in the Elementary School." Good statement of objectives and their relationships to learning activities.

HERRICK, VIRGIL E., JOHN I. GOODLAD, FRANK J. ESTVAN, and PAUL W. EBERMAN. *The Elementary Schools.* Englewood Cliffs, N.J.: Prentice-Hall, Inc., 1956.

Chap. 4, "The Objectives of the Elementary School," pp. 69–94. Over-all statements of objectives; types of statements; developmental tasks as objectives; functions of objectives.

HILDRETH, GERTRUDE. *Child Growth Through Education.* New York: The Ronald Press Co., 1948.

Chap. 1, "Education and Life Today," presents a discussion on the "old" and "new" methods and defines modern problem solving.

KEARNEY, NOLAN C. *Elementary School Objectives.* New York: Russell Sage Foundation, 1953.

In this report prepared for the Mid-Century Committee on Outcomes in Elementary Education, recommended goals for the elementary school are presented in part ii.

OTTO, HENRY J., HAZEL FLOYD, and MARGARET ROUSE. *Principles of Elementary Education.* New York: Rinehart & Co., Inc., 1955.

Chap. 4, "The Purposes of Elementary Schools." Especially good section on translating objectives into school activities. Chap. 5, "Educating for Self-Realization." A good, short survey of subject-matter areas and how related to self-realization. Chap. 6, "Educating for Satisfying Human Relations." Describes how practical school situations may be used in teaching desirable human relations. Chap. 7, "Educating for Economic Efficiency." Clarifies the position of the elementary school regarding vocational preparation. Chap. 8, "Educating for Civic Responsibility; Developing appropriate ideals, attitudes and knowledge." Describes democracy and how it functions in elementary classrooms through child activity. Chap. 9, "Organizing the School Program." Emphasizes a program which meets the needs, interests, and abilities of the children in all school activities.

SMITH, B. OTHANIEL, WILLIAM O. STANLEY, and J. HARLAN SHORES. *Fundamentals of Curriculum Development.* Yonkers, N.Y.: World Book Co., 1950.

Chap. 11 sets up criteria for judging the validity of educational objectives.

WOLMAN, BENJAMIN. "Scientific Study of Educational Aims," *Teachers College Record,* 50:471–81, (April, 1949).

An analysis of statements of educational aims formulated by great philosophers.

5

BASIC CURRICULUM PROBLEMS

The character of the curriculum is largely determined by the teacher. The manner in which the teacher exercises control varies considerably from school to school. In some situations, the whole curriculum is constructed by teachers working in cooperation. If she is an official member of the curriculum committee, the teacher assists in determining the scope of the curriculum for the entire school, or she may participate in preparation of source units and other suggestive instructional materials with a given area of the curriculum. In other schools, the curriculum is largely predetermined by state legislative enactments, state department of education requirements, or local school administrative and supervisory regulations. Governmental agencies usually indicate the broad outlines of the curriculum in terms of subjects, grade placement, and time allotment. They also attempt to implement these requirements by means of written courses of study.

A course of study is the teacher's guide to the curriculum. It usually contains suggested objectives, content, teaching procedures, and methods of evaluating pupil achievement within a particular area of the curriculum. Whether the course of study is teacher-inspired or dictated by outside agencies, the classroom teacher is its final arbiter. In the last analysis, it depends on the emphasis placed by the teacher on various items of content and on her manner of presentation. Even when the course of study was regarded as the "directions and specifications" having the force of law in respect to required subjects, grade placement, sequence of topics, and time allotment, the qualitative aspects of the curriculum were in the hands of the teacher.

74

The modern concept of the course of study as the function of suggestion rather than presumption places a much greater premium upon the teacher's initiative and resourcefulness. Regardless of its origin or degree of completeness, the official course of study can merely indicate general guiding principles. Source units can do little more. They are blueprints, subject to modification by individual teachers. Valuable as the official guides may be, adaptions and refinements must be made in terms of the students involved; hence, use with different classes requires modification and change. These changes are so far-reaching in scope and significance that the resulting product is sometimes referred to not as a course of study but as a course of instruction. More recently, courses of study are being referred to as course-of-study guides or curriculum guides. They do not, in themselves, constitute courses of study.

BASIC CONSIDERATIONS

The curriculum is as broad and varied as the child's school environment. Broadly conceived, the curriculum embraces not only subject matter but also various aspects of the physical and social environment. The school brings the child with his impelling flow of experiences into an environment consisting of school facilities, subject matter, other children, and teachers. From the interaction of the child with these elements learning results. Not only is the learner an ever-changing personality resulting from a continuous series of new experiences, but the constituent elements of his environment are constantly evolving and unfolding. The interactions between the two factors which comprise the learning situation, therefore, are manifold and varied. The inherent character of the learner and the environment give learning its dynamic quality.

The one static element in the situation has been the subject matter. It also has been the one foreign element in the learning situation. Until recently subject matter was suggested, if not actually imposed, by individuals or agencies outside the school. The individuals were in most cases subject-matter specialists, who assumed that the chief function of the school is to transmit from one generation to another the culture of the race in the form of subject matter. They also believed that the organizing principle for school activities lies within the body of subject matter itself. Many of them accepted the theory of formal discipline and justified the retention of much obsolete material on the ground that these materials were difficult for children to learn and therefore of value in training their minds. The chief difficulty, however, was that these specialists were unfamiliar with the interests and needs of contemporary elementary school children.

This procedure has been generally abandoned in schools today. Now children participate at least to various degrees in the planning of learning activities. These activities are planned in terms of the interest and need of these same children. Subject matter is an accessory means and not an end in itself or a framework in which planning must be done.

Philosophy of education

Basic to planning a curriculum and to teaching is a clear philosophy of education, or statement of ideals toward which the school strives. Philosophy of education is a group of objectives and principles that help in deciding which experiences may be truly educative and which miseducative.

Several factors which influence educational philosophy have been mentioned, including its basis in the needs of the child, both as an individual and as a member of society. Such needs in turn are largely determined by the ideals of the society in which the child and his elders live. Another important influence on educational philosophy is that a society depends for its existence on effective intercommunication between individuals and between groups.

In the formulation of an adequate basic philosophy of elementary education, consideration should be given to:

1. Concepts of the function and nature of elementary education as formulated by recognized leaders in education, philosophy, and sociology
2. The educational philosophy formulated by teachers in other schools
3. The nature of the learning process
4. The ideals of the culture out of which the school grows
5. The role of elementary education in that culture
6. Characteristics of the local community which the school serves
7. The unique characteristics of the children to be educated

Curriculum and social change

The schools which are training modern children must adjust their curriculums to a rapidly changing world. During the past ten or fifteen years, more important changes have taken place in American life than previous generations experienced in a whole lifetime. Scientific claims for the future are fantastic which makes us aware of the fact that life is everchanging. Interests of children are being enlarged. Many children are now thinking in terms of an air age far removed from the land-and-water age in which their teachers grew up. Today's citizens must adjust their thinking to the atomic bomb and the jet airplane. In addition to technological changes, political and economic changes require that children develop capacity for being good citizens of the world as well as their own country, state, and community.

Illustrations of some important social changes and problems which challenge the curriculum determiner follow:

Inculcation of democratic values. Since the votes of citizens largely determine the basic policies of a democracy, it is essential for schools to develop children who will be effective citizens. But democracy is more than a form of political organization. It is a way of life. Hence it is of the highest importance that schools provide experiences which will inculcate in children the ideals, behavior patterns, and processes that go to make up democratic living. Such experiences are characterized by cooperation, with every person working for the good of the group and the good of every group member, sharing in planning and leadership, understanding that for privileges received, responsibilities must be accepted, and being open-minded and having faith in other persons. Every teacher at every instructional level has the responsibility to provide experiences which will produce in a child a socially moral character and social intelligence.

Importance of world-mindedness. Today the world is divided between free peoples and those who live under totalitarian rule. The free peoples wish to live at peace, with justice and equity for all. World War II and subsequent strife have shown them the need to develop understanding of other peoples' problems so as to bring about a peaceful world in which the welfare of every human being is cherished and protected. Moreover, they have learned about the economic interdependence of all nations.

All school programs, beginning at the elementary level, must therefore emphasize world-mindedness, economic interdependence, and the need for international cooperation. Schools, parents, and other community members must develop in young children a feeling of security, of being needed, and of being loved. We must make it possible for all children to make worthwhile contributions in child and adult society, thus gaining respect for themselves and for others, and also to cooperate with others in achieving common goals.

Children who have lived in a community where people work and play together peacefully and respect the right of all, regardless of race, color, creed, economic status, and intelligence, are not likely to be antagonistic toward others at home or abroad. To them a united, peaceful world will be possible and sensible.

Increase in delinquency. Another problem affecting the curriculum is the increase in juvenile delinquency and crime, which is due, in part, to inadequate education. Criminologists have discovered that a close relationship exists between delinquency and school failure. Children are discouraged and drop out of school when the school curriculum is too difficult for them and is not paced to meet their everyday needs and experiences. Hence, in order to prevent crime and delinquency, the curriculum must provide experiences that will fit the needs of all children, so that they can experience success in various activities and cooperate effectively in group enterprises and recreational activities. Such experiences should be available not only during the school year but also during vacation periods.

Mass media of communication. Radio, movies, television, and comic magazines are an important part in the environment of everyone. They are means whereby our culture, thinking, and ideas are transmitted to others. Many are resisting the use of mass media of communication in the classroom and insist that children get their information mainly by reading books. Instead of berating the new communicative media, it would be more practical to assist in removing the abuses, overcome the weaknesses, and develop the new challenging resources as educative tools.

The interests, concepts, and vicarious experiences of children are influenced greatly by television broadcasts. In social studies and science the sequence of units is from the immediate environment (the home) to more remote regions in distance and time in the intermediate grades. Will television extend the near-at-hand environment to include cultures and peoples remote in time and place? Is the time near at hand to re-evaluate children's interests, concepts, and informational background? Are those responsible for planning curricular patterns, preparing instructional materials, and implementing the educational program aware that a new era with respect to children's interests, understandings, and experiences is at hand? It is hoped that mass media of communication will be used to enrich the curriculum, thus serving more effectively the needs and interests of children.

Depletion of natural resources. The need for conservation of natural resources also affects the curriculum. Water and wind have destroyed millions of acres of productive soil. Forests, minerals, and wild life in many areas are threatened with destruction. Basic to conservation are our attitudes toward the preservation of natural resources upon which we depend for survival. Since very young children can understand many of the elementary concepts of conservation, it is the schools' responsibility to develop an awareness, understanding, and appreciation of this problem.

CURRICULUM PATTERNS

An understanding of the characteristics of types of curriculum organization is a prerequisite for designing or redesigning the curriculum. Attention will be given here to types which are, and have been, in wide use.

Isolated subjects

The use of separate, unrelated periods for spelling, handwriting, language, reading, etc. characterized early American education and to some extent the schools of today. During the early part of this century, children usually studied twelve or more subjects during one school term. The various subjects neither related to each other nor to the needs and interests of children. Each subject was taught in isolation, and each had its own time period. Often a basic textbook was selected on its own merits without considering the child who would be using it and a page-by-page assignment made daily.

Correlated subjects

The movement toward curriculum correlation was an attempt to escape the highly artificial segmentation of the curriculum. An attempt was made to present similar topics in two or more subjects concurrently so that children would better understand what they were studying. For example, United States history and geography would be taught in the same grade. History and geography each retained its own assigned period, but the content was related to the same area or interest center. In this organization the number and fields of subjects taught remained the same as in the isolated subject program.

Broad fields

Both the broad fields curriculum and the subject curriculum are dependent for their content upon the various school subjects. They differ partly in the method used to divide the school day into class periods. The broad fields curriculum achieves fewer and longer class periods by including several subjects in a broad field. For example, the broad field in language arts would include reading, oral and written communication, spelling, and handwriting. Social studies would include history, geography, and civics. In each broad field one subject may be selected as the core area. The other subjects in the field may be correlated with the core subject.

Child-centered program

The child-centered program of the 1920's and 1930's rejected the traditional subject curriculum, which did not consider the real experiences of children outside of school. The new approach to the curriculum emphasized activities, interests, and needs of children rather than the three R's. Teachers planned the program in advance and included activities representing the play life of children, such as excursions, stories, etc. It was said that the knowledge and skills inherent in subject matter would be achieved by enriching the children's various activities.

Some teachers who favor child-centered programs do not believe that the interests, needs, and activities of children can be anticipated satisfactorily and a curriculum pattern set up in advance. They believe they must start with the group of children they are teaching. Therefore, they select and plan the program in cooperation with the children. The resulting curriculum is referred to as the experience program.

The core program

In the core or large block unit type of program class, isolated subjects are abandoned; skills, facts, information may be taken from any subject or reliable source in solving related problems. A typical core or large block class is made up principally of language arts and social studies, which are not taught as separate subjects. Very frequently closely related learning activities in art, music, and occasionally arithmetic or science may be included in the various units taught in the core or large block, but these subjects are also taught as separate subjects. Units of work in the core are based upon social studies materials. The language arts skills are usually integrated in learning activities involved in the solution of the problems identified with the unit. Usually the experiences are suggested in outline form in advance. From these suggestions pupils and teachers cooperatively select, plan, and develop units of work that fit abilities, interests, and needs of children. The principal characteristics of the core or large block program are cited below.

1. Class periods are equivalent to about two regular class periods per day.
2. Time schedule is flexible.

3. One teacher is responsible for teaching the core class; frequently, in upper grades, she remains with the same group of children in the core class for two years.
4. Teacher and pupils cooperate in selecting problems and materials pertinent to the unit of work.
5. Learning activities are related to abilities, interests, and needs of children, and whenever feasible applied to out-of-school activities.
6. Subject matter serves as a means to an end in solving problems.
7. A wide variety of materials are used, such as literature, reading, arithmetic, audio-visual aids, community resources, art, music.
8. Problem-solving techniques are utilized cooperatively by pupils and teacher in planning, solving problems, group discussions, evaluation of pupil's progress toward achievement of goals.
9. Pupils engage in different types of activities as they solve problems such as reading, making graphs and charts, group discussions, making observations, making models and murals.
10. A variety of evaluation instruments and techniques are used as observation by the teacher of pupils' behavior, attitudes and skills; pupil self-evaluation based upon standards set up by pupils and teacher cooperatively; tests of factual information.

Success of the core program or unit type teaching depends upon many factors, the major factor being the teacher. Upon her rests the responsibility of analyzing the behavior of children and suggesting treatment for problem children; keeping records of pupils' growth in identifying problems, applying study skills, and making social adjustments; providing leadership in activities in which children engage; serving in the capacity of counsellor or guide; selecting, organizing, and unifying learning materials and activities; cooperating with school personnel, parents, and lay people in the community. The teacher also helps children understand the interrelationships of skills, facts, attitudes, and appreciations in solving problems and in working and living democratically with each other.

Eclectic program

The eclectic program strikes a balance between the two extremes: subject-matter and child-centered organization. An attempt is made to select the best from all curricular types and integrate these various elements into a program fitted to the interests and needs of children according to the maturity of the learners. A scope-sequence pattern is worked out in advance, and the details are worked out daily by teachers and children. Part of the day is devoted to direct teaching of skills or tools of learning and the other part to unified activities or units of work in content areas, such as social studies. This curriculum also includes opportunities for creative work in areas such as fine arts and writing stories. Throughout the day children are developing an appreciation and understanding of democratic principles. The time devoted to each of the various activities is distributed according to goals to be accomplished. The daily schedule is quite flexible and may be adjusted by the teacher and children to fit all phases of the work.

CURRICULUM SCOPE AND SEQUENCE

In discussing and constructing courses of study the terms scope and sequence are used frequently. *Scope* refers to what is included in the curriculum; it may be used to indicate specific experiences or major elements of the program within which learnings will take place. *Sequence* may be defined as an orderly succession of learning experiences planned grade by grade, year by year, or level by level so that the learnings of children will be continuous throughout the elementary grades. Level by level sequence is now the preferred form.

The idea of scope and sequence is not new, but the content as worked out in certain curriculum studies is quite different. In the traditional school the scope and sequence were represented by the areas covered by the text within particular fields. The statements of scope and sequence today reflect clearly the desire on the part of curriculum workers to focus attention upon selecting problems with reference to basic human needs and to the essential conditions of social living. It is designated to help the school to pay attention to some orderly development of the major aims of education, conceived in a transitional society still wishing to develop both a unity for group action and competence for personal uniqueness.[1]

Most curriculum makers determine the scope of the program by selecting certain areas of human experience. The areas may be classified as:

1. Social relationships—social studies, geography, history
2. Elementary concepts in general science, biological and physical science—nature study, animals, plants, and rocks, soil, and other geological formations in local community
3. Physical and mental health—physical education, health instruction
4. Language arts—reading, oral and written communication, handwriting, and spelling
5. Computational experiences

[1] John Dewey Society, Third Yearbook, *Democracy and the Curriculum* (New York: Appleton-Century-Crofts, Inc., 1939), p. 490.

Planning scope and sequence

Arithmetic. A good illustration of planning scope and sequence is a chart for teaching the computational phase of arithmetic. Here study is paced according to the mental level at which normal children can master the skills with appropriate experiences and developmental patterns. The chart is arranged in four columns. This helps the teacher see the skills that are comparable in difficulty. In using it, the teacher must know the approximate mental age of the child as well as his arithmetical development.

RECOMMENDED GRADATION OF ARITHMETIC PROCESSES [2]

Mental Age	Whole Numbers	Fractions	Decimals	Per Cent
6-7	1. Counting	1. Contacts in activity units and in simple measurements	1. Tens as basis of number system	
	2. Identifying numbers to 200			
	3. Writing numbers to 100			
	4. Serial idea			
	5. Using numbers in activities of all kinds			
7-8	1. Reading and writing numbers to 1000	1. Recognizing fractional parts	1. Place value	
	2. Concept development		2. Zero as a place holder	
	3. Addition and subtraction facts to 6			
8-9	1. Addition and subtraction facts and simple processes	1. Extending uses of fractions in measurement	1. Reading money values	
	2. Multiplication and division facts through threes	2. Finding part of a number	2. Addition and subtraction of dollars and cents	

[2] Leo J. Breuckner and Foster E. Grossnickle, *Making Arithmetic Meaningful* (Chicago: John C. Winston Co., 1953), pp. 96-97.

Mental Age	Whole Numbers	Fractions	Decimals	Per Cent
	3. Multiplication by one-place numbers		3. Multiplication and division of cents only	
	4. Related even division by one-place numbers			
9-10	1. Completion of all multiplication and division facts	1. Extending use and meaning of fractions	1. Computing with dollars and cents in all processes	
	2. Uneven division facts	2. Easy steps in addition and subtraction of like fractions by concrete and visual means		
	3. All steps with one-place multipliers and divisors	3. Finding a part of a number		
10-11	1. Two-place multipliers	1. Addition and subtraction of like fractions; also the halves, fourths, eighths family	1. Addition and subtraction through hundredths	
	2. Two-place divisors— apparent quotient need not be corrected			
	3. Zeros in quotients			
11-12	1. Three and four place multipliers	1. Addition and subtraction of related fractions; as ⅓ and ⅙, also of easy unrelated types, ½ and ⅓	1. Addition and subtraction extended to thousandths	

	2. Two-place divisors— apparent quotient must be corrected	2. Multiplication	2. Multiplication and division of decimals by whole numbers	
		3. Division of whole numbers and mixed numbers by fractions		
12-13	1. Three-place divisors	1. Addition and subtraction of types: $\frac{3}{4} + \frac{5}{8}$ $4\frac{5}{8} - 3\frac{5}{6}$	1. Multiplication and division of whole numbers and decimals by decimals 2. Changing fractions to decimals, and vice versa	1. Cases I and II in percentage using whole per cents
13-14	1. Extending uses of whole numbers	1. Extending uses of fractions	1. Extending uses of decimals	1. Case of III of percentage 2. Fractional per cents

Social studies. In social studies, the scope of the program is influenced by the interests and abilities of children as well as the facilities of the community and school. Usually the content and experiences are organized as units of work of which the sequence or grade placement is determined on the basis of interest, understanding, and needs of children at the various levels of maturity. The general philosophy is to begin in the primary grades with the immediate environment of the child and widen the scope as he matures. At the primary level there is little variation from school to school in the basic units used, but at the intermediate and upper-grade levels the variation in areas or scope studied is great. In social studies, for example, the Denver, Colorado, curriculum provides the units listed on the following page in elementary and upper grades.[3]

[3] Social Studies Program Committee, *The Social Studies Program of the Denver Public Schools* (Denver, Colorado: The Department of Instruction, 1954), Table of Contents, vii-viii.

Grade	I.	The Family; Pets; Toys
Grade	II.	The World Through Our Senses; Our Community; Communication in Everyday Living; Water
Grade	III.	Money; Animals Near and Far; Living in Denver; Learning about Plants
Grade	IV.	Ways of Living Then and Now; Physical Forces That Work for Man; The Earth; Transportation; Ancient Plants and Animals
Grade	V.	How Our Country Began; How Chemical Changes Affect Our Everyday Living; United States Today
Grade	VI.	World Geography; People of the Western Hemisphere; Astronomy; Communication
Grade	VII.	How Did Early Man Develop? What Were Some of the Contributions of Past Civilization? What Contributions Were Made by People Who Lived in Europe During the Middle Ages? How Do People of the Eastern Hemisphere Live Today?
Grade	VIII.	How Did Europeans Discover and Explore a New World? Why Did People from Different Lands Come to America? How Did the Colonies Achieve Independence from Britain? How Did the New Nation Form a Union? How Did Democracy and Patriotism Develop in the 1800's? How Did the United States Acquire and Settle the Great West? How Did Internal Conflict Help to Confirm the Union? How Did Industrial Expansion Effect Changes in Living in United States? What is the Role of the United States in Today's Interdependent World?

The State of Oklahoma notes in its *Curriculum Guide* the following sequence of major areas for units of work in social studies: [4]

Grade	I.	Living in Home and School
Grade	II.	The Immediate Community
Grade	III.	The Expanded Community
Grade	IV.	Oklahoma and Community Life in Other Lands
Grade	V.	Life in the Western World
Grade	VI.	The Old World and Its Culture
Grade	VII.	Our American Heritage
Grade	VIII.	Democracy in Action

Basic nonsubject areas. The nonsubject areas cannot be planned definitely as to scope and sequence, but the teacher and anyone else who participates effectively in curriculum construction must

[4] State Department of Education, *Curriculum Guide for Elementary Schools,* Bulletin No. 11. (State of Oklahoma: Department of Public Instruction, 1950), Table of Contents.

know what information, concepts, habits, skills, interests, ideals, attitudes, tastes, and appreciations are required for these areas of which one is *good citizenship*. Good citizenship is made up of a great variety of components in behavior; each of these is a phase of growth requiring guidance and stimulation. To enumerate even the majority of these would involve more space and time than are available here. They tend to fall into categories, however, and the good curriculum must provide stimuli for all categories.

Being a good citizen involves:

1. Knowing what is right and effective in the citizen's society. This knowledge consists of some fundamental principles learned previously, some which the citizen will probably possess incidentally to his life in the society, and some which he will have to acquire as the specific needs arise.

2. Being willing to behave in a way which is right and effective. This may be in part a matter of heredity, but it is probably more a matter of learning. To insure right and effective behavior, the individual must be invested with appropriate ideals and attitudes, and he must be kept from the development of unfavorable ones, e.g., ideals of excessive personal power or gain, ideals of racial, national, or regional supremacy over others, attitudes of ill will or contempt toward other groups or classes of society, and attitudes of indifference to matters of honesty, etc.

3. Being willing and able to behave in an appropriate and effective manner also involves being interested in reading, and investigating, and becoming informed on matters regarding which intelligent decisions must be made by the citizenry of the society in which one lives and being willing to discharge the duties of any office to which one might be elected.

4. Developing appropriate skills in getting on with others, in self-expression, in thinking clearly, and in evaluating what he may read or hear on questions confronting or likely to confront citizens of his time.

5. Acquiring appropriate habits so that right and effective behavior is largely automatic. It becomes more and more automatic due to habits of industrious, honest, and thoughtful behavior.

6. Acquiring useful concepts and basic general ideas which enable the citizen to understand and evaluate human experience and proposed lines of social action. He knows, for example, what constitutes democracy, communism, fascism, and socialism. He is not stampeded by fine-sounding but fallacious doctrines or deceived by the application of terms such as communism or fascism to practices really democratic in nature.

CURRICULUM PLANNING PROCEDURES

As teachers gain new insight into the educational objectives and the needs of children, they will realize the need for continuous evaluation and improvement of the curriculum. The following principles may serve as a guide for teachers who are interested and engaged in evaluating and reorganizing their curriculum.

1. Curriculum improvement depends on teacher growth.
2. Changes in curriculum should be based on research, planning, and organization.
3. When an evaluation of the curriculum reveals that certain changes should be made, a carefully planned program of curriculum revision should be put into effect.
4. The school should be the planning center.
5. Persons who understand and know children must be leaders in curriculum planning.
6. Administrators, teachers, parents, lay people, and children should participate in curriculum planning.
7. The trend in elementary and upper grades is toward a more unified curricular organization.
8. The curriculum must consider all experiences needed to accomplish the objectives of a democratic society.
9. The evolving curriculum must include experiences to aid children in making adjustments to their present life, thus preparing for the more complex problems of tomorrow.
10. The curriculum must provide experiences to assist children in developing intellectually, physically, socially, emotionally, and spiritually.
11. The curriculum must be concerned with high moral qualities as characterized by the democratic way of life.
12. The curriculum must provide for interrelations in the content subjects.
13. There must be definite planning for achieving balance in the content subjects.
14. There must be definite planning for social interactions among children within all areas of learning.
15. There must be definite planning for creative abilities of children.
16. Curriculum organization must provide direct instruction in the development and mastery of basic tools of learning and in the acquisition of effective work and study habits.
17. The content of the curriculum must provide continuity in children's learning experiences as related to principles of child development.
18. The curriculum must provide for the many differences found in children's needs, interests, abilities, and rates of learning.

19. Curriculum must provide experiences in which learnings will move gradually from the concrete to the abstract.

Since the curriculum includes so many learning experiences, it is advisable not to attempt to revise all areas of learning in one year. Teachers and administrators should recognize curriculum work as a part of their load and, therefore, should be capable of identifying those areas in need of immediate revision. The agenda for the year may be prepared at a preschool conference or some time during the first month of school by a planning committee of administrators and teachers.

Readiness for planning

In any program that needs change, the attitude of people who take part in the revision and of those who will be affected by the change is very important. Important elements in readiness for curriculum planning are understanding that in a changing society the curriculum must change also, discontent with present curriculum, interest in curriculum study, and effective leadership. In developing a readiness for curriculum improvement, some administrators start with those teachers who are interested and gradually add others who become concerned about the problem and ready to participate. In many places, there are workshops led by carefully selected college instructors or other very competent persons. Frequently, college credit is earned by participation in these workshops.

Organizational patterns

Some schools have employed curriculum experts from outside the school system or small committees within the system to revise their programs. Even though the results were technically superior, little change was noted in the classroom activities. Since teachers did not participate in organizing the new curriculum, they did not understand the reasons for including much of the content, the value of suggested materials, and the usefulness of procedures for developing ideas and skills. Whenever teachers do not participate in curriculum organization, the implementation of the new program is negligible.

Other schools have a system-wide curriculum council responsible for a program from kindergarten through high school. This council is made up of individuals working in the central office and staff members from various schools in the city. Each school has committees working on various curricular problems directly related to their school but also related to the over-all pattern. They cooperate with the curriculum council and receive help from it in attacking their own problems. Often the system-wide curriculum council is a policymaking group. It may develop bulletins needed by teachers. Teachers may be relieved from classroom duties for curriculum work, such as screening and editing materials.

Frequently the improvement of the curriculum is left to each individual school usually with help from leaders in the department of curriculum and instruction. In this situation, a teacher or principal will lead in organizing the program and obtain the help of other teachers, parents, lay people, children, school board members, or the county superintendent in evaluating and revising specific phases of the curriculum.

Personnel

A significant development in curriculum planning is the classroom teacher's acceptance of leadership in this area. Today many teachers do not wait to be told what to do but endeavor to develop the best curriculum possible for the children in their community. This is as it should be. Who is better qualified to evaluate children's needs than the person directing their learning activities? If teachers take part in curriculum planning, there will be more continuity in purposes from grade to grade, and teachers will do a better job of teaching.

Various plans are being used to make it possible for the classroom teacher to work on curriculum problems or committees. Frequently they are released from classroom duties for a specific period of time. Some school systems pay their teachers for ten months' teaching, nine of which go into teaching, the other to duties including curriculum work. Many school boards pay the expenses of teachers attending evening curriculum classes or curriculum workshops at higher institutions of learning during summer sessions.

Today's concept of curriculum planning is cooperative and includes school personnel, people from other professions, parents, lay people in the community, and children. Each individual works on the committee where he can make worthwhile contributions when the services of the committee or individual will fit most effectively into the program. Parents and laymen can give suggestions and make recommendations relative to educational problems in the community and society at large and evaluate school experiences related to various professions, business enterprises, jobs, etc. Children may be of service when the curriculum is being tried out in classrooms. Under the guidance of the teacher and with her approval children help in setting up immediate goals, determining ways of solving problems, selecting materials, and evaluating the activities in which they are participating.

Committee responsibilities

The working centers in a curriculum improvement program are the various committees. The desirable number and type of committees depends upon the size of the school system and the goals to be achieved. Committees should be relatively small, but there should be good representation from different schools. Members should understand their specific problem and its relation to the whole program. Each committee reads widely and studies research that is related to its problem; they also may consult specialists and authorities in the field. Ideas are shared, and various points of view are crystallized. Findings are organized and submitted to a group or a committee designated to act as coordinator, serve as a screening and/or evaluating center, or prepare materials for printing. Frequently, after the proposals have been examined and evaluated, the materials are returned to the original committee for revision, condensation, and organization so that anyone interested in the curriculum will be able to understand the content and remember it.

Introduction of the new curriculum

The new curriculum should be reviewed by every teacher. For teachers employed after completion of the course-of-study revision, an orientation program relative to the new curriculum may be necessary. Where this is not done, each new teacher should study the courses of study carefully at the beginning and during her first year of teaching in the system.

The curriculum will serve the needs of children and society only if it is constantly evaluated and if those who are implementing it realize that as long as society changes there will be a need for constant revision.

QUESTIONS, PROBLEMS, AND EXERCISES

1. List the communication values to be shared by people living in America. Be sure that the terminology used will have meaning for anyone who should read your list.

2. Write your own definition for the terms curriculum and course-of-study.

3. Organize a panel discussion on important changes in our society in the past decade.

4. In your judgment, which of the curricular patterns would enable you to guide the learning of children most effectively? Why?

5. Examine several recently published readers to determine which help children to develop objectives for civic responsibility.

6. Identify current patterns of curriculum organizations in four different school systems.

7. Observe a class for half a day and list all situations in which oral communication was used.

8. List special activities in a social study unit for bright children.

9. What are the effects of a program in which children must make too many choices? Of a program in which they seldom make a choice?

SELECTED SUPPLEMENTARY READINGS

ASSOCIATION FOR SUPERVISION AND CURRICULUM DEVELOPMENT. *Action for Curriculum Improvement, 1951 Yearbook.* Washington, D.C.: National Education Association, 1952.

An excellent treatment on problems related to curriculum improvement. The book tells how pupils, teachers, supervisors, administrators, parents and others interested in the school can cooperate in bringing about changes in a curriculum.

BEAUCHAMP, GEORGE A. *Planning the Elementary School Curriculum.* Englewood Cliffs, N.J.: Allyn & Bacon, 1956.

Part III, "Planning Activities and Procedures," is a thorough and systematic study of all the more important aspects of curriculum selection and organization.

BECK, ROBERT H., WALTER W. COOK, and NOLAN C. KEARNEY. *Curriculum in the Modern Elementary School.* Englewood Cliffs, N.J.: Prentice-Hall, Inc., 1953.

Chap. 12, "Curriculum Structure," clarifies four types of curriculum which are: separate-subjects, correlated, broad-fields, and developmental-activity. Criteria for the selection of curricular content are presented in clear-cut terms and are: frequency of use, quality, cruciality, universality in time, place, and use, decreasing returns, difficulty, and educational shortages.

FEATHERSTONE, WILLIAM B. *A Functional Curriculum for Youth.* New York: American Book Co., 1950.

Various approaches to designing the curriculum are presented. Special emphasis is on subject and broad-field approaches.

HERRICK, VIRGIL E., JOHN I. GOODLAD, FRANK J. ESTVAN, and PAUL W. EBERMAN. *The Elementary School.* Englewood Cliffs, N.J.: Prentice-Hall, Inc., 1956.

Chap. 6, "Planning and Organizing the Curriculum," is a timely analysis of advantages and disadvantages of various curricular organizations. Specific suggestions for improvement of elementary school curriculum.

LEE, J. M., and D. M. LEE. *The Child and His Curriculum,* 2d. ed. New York: Appleton-Century-Crofts, Inc., 1950.

A thorough presentation of the development and building of elementary school curriculum. Special emphasis is placed upon the work of the teacher in curriculum building.

RAGAN, WILLIAM B. and CELIA BURNS STENDLER. *Modern Elementary Curriculum.* New York: The Dryden Press, Inc., 1953.

An excellent book for teachers and administrators who are concerned about curriculum building. The major areas presented are: (1) Curriculum Foundations; (2) Curriculum Organization; (3) Curriculum Areas; (4) Curriculum Evaluation. The problems and projects at the end of each chapter are excellent in arousing the reader to do some thinking for himself.

SAYLOR, J. GALEN and WILLIAM M. ALEXANDER. *Curriculum Planning for Better Teaching and Learning.* New York: Rinehart & Co., Inc., 1954.

A comprehensive treatment of problems related to curriculum development in public school systems. The book is easy to read. Drawings, tables, charts, etc. are aids in clarifying concepts. The book is organized in five parts:

Part 1. Why is Better Curriculum Planning Needed?
Part 2. What Major Factors Must be Considered in Curriculum Planning?
Part 3. How Shall the Curriculum Framework be Organized?
Part 4. How Shall We Plan the Curriculum for Better Teaching?
Part 5. How Shall Curriculum Planning be Organized and Evaluated?

6

BASIC PRINCIPLES OF LEARNING
AND MOTIVATION

For half a century, various students of learning have attempted to discover and state the "laws of learning." Nothing like common agreement has been obtained though in most instances it is obvious that the so-called "laws" do express the operation of real and effective principles which condition learning.

That no statement acceptable to the great majority of advanced students of education has yet been made may be attributed to a number of causes. First, instead of *learning*, there exist *learnings*. These learnings, e.g., the learning of facts, the learning of skills, and the learning of ideals, are not alike with respect to nature and phenomena. They do not take place in exactly the same manner; consequently there is no underlying set of laws applicable to all learnings. Secondly, it is quite difficult to differentiate completely the various operative principles of learning. They seem to overlap.

FACTORS CONDITIONING LEARNING

On the following pages, no attempt will be made to set forth or defend a consistent, complete system of laws of learning. Instead, the most important principles and factors which condition learning and which a successful teacher must consider will be described briefly. The teacher who understands the nature, importance, and more important implications of these laws and factors will not only understand and better evaluate suggestions for teaching procedures, but, if possessed of at least average capacity for creativeness and imagination, will be able to plan the details of teaching procedures for herself.

Activity, use, or repetition

One learns only by some activity in the neural system: seeing, hearing, smelling, feeling, thinking, physical or motor activity, or some other kind of activity. The learner must actively engage in the "learning," whether it be of information, a skill, an understanding, a habit, an ideal, an attitude, an interest, or the nature of a task. Sometimes being "active" only once modifies the individual to such an extent as to result in a desired degree of learning of more or less permanency. An individual may never forget a certain happening or some aspect of it. Ordinarily, however, the activity must be repeated if the desired learning is to be achieved.

Other factors being equal or inoperative, learning is in proportion to the frequency of the repetition of the activity. Other factors— interest, vividness, attention, effect of the activity, interval between repetitions, readiness for the activity, and background of the learner —are, however, rarely equal or inoperative. Mere repetition, if conducted under unfavorable conditions, may not result in learning what is desired. It may in fact result in learning other things not desired; there may be concomitant undesirable outcomes or misunderstandings. For some reason repetition under favorable conditions tends to result in more permanent learning in the fields of skills and habits than in the fields of information and memory in general.

The learning effects of repetition are conditioned by the spacing of the repeated operations, though no general rule can be stated. In learning to spell a long word, operate a complicated machine, or type, one repetition a day is usually not effective. At that rate one forgets between repetitions all, or practically all, he has learned previously. On the other hand, continued successive repetitions may reach the stage where further repetition yields no learning dividends because of fatigue, loss of interest or attention, or other reasons, some of which are not easily identifiable.

Disuse and relearning

What one forgets, how quickly, and how completely depends upon so many factors that it is not possible to predict exactly the effects of forgetting. It is obvious, however, that what one has learned but not used or recalled for some time is for the time less well learned. If a fact is well learned, one may not be able to recall it at all after a period of disuse, depending upon the period of disuse, the degree of overlearning, and the interest of the learner in it. Skills and habits, particularly motor skills and habits, do not fade nearly so quickly or completely as facts. To a lesser degree, the learning of attitudes and interests likewise persists longer than the learning of facts. It is surprising how a telephone number or a street address, one's own for example, which was once well learned, may escape recall after a year or two, while the skills involved in riding a bicycle, playing a piano, or rowing a boat will persist in considerable degree until the general physical deterioration of old age sets in. The necessity of use in order to prevent forgetting suggests to the teacher the following: cumulative reviews and programs of maintenance of important facts, principles, interests, skills, and habits.

Ordinarily, however, relearning requires less time and effort than original learning. Quite frequently when it is necessary to relearn, e.g., to restore a skill or knowledge in a certain field to a former level, the saving is often at least three-fourths in terms of time. This is especially true with skills. Usually it is much less than a third or a half when the learning has to do with verbal memory. The greater the learner's understanding and meaning for him of the subject matter, the greater the saving in relearning.

Effect, satisfaction, or annoyance

The immediate effect of any activity upon the future activity of an organism is conditioned by the richness of the experience. One remembers best those experiences which were particularly painful or pleasurable. One avoids repeating an activity which is likely to cause a repetition of unpleasant experience. "The burnt child dreads the fire," and he remembers well the pain of the burn. Likewise an individual remembers a humiliating experience, though he may forget what he was trying to learn when the humiliating experience occurred.

The results of many experiments performed to discover how far the effects of learning activities influence learning seem to indicate clearly that rewards and punishments are effective and that pleasant and unpleasant effects condition learning. However, the principle of effect operates unevenly and is influenced in its operation by other principles. It is clear too that the by-products or concomitant effects of the use of artificial rewards and punishments are often very undesirable and more than offset the value of the learning. If learning experiences are unpleasant—for example, if they are compelled and unaccompanied by success and the accompanying pleasant feelings—the subject being studied and even the teacher in the school are associated in the child's mind and emotions with unpleasantness.

One of the most desirable and powerful pleasurable effects is the knowledge of progress, achievement, or praise discreetly bestowed.

The immediate effect of a learning activity, pleasurable or otherwise, is dependent to a considerable extent upon whether there is mind set, purposiveness, or consciousness of meaningful relationships. If to participate in a certain learning activity forces one to cease effort in an area or in a direction in which one is interested before one is ready to desist, it is most likely to produce irritation or resentfulness, at least at first. If the learning activity fits in with activities in which one is interestingly engaged or seems to contribute to a purpose which is in the mind of the learner, the effect is pleasurable and therefore favorable to learning.

Knowledge of success and failure toward known goals

Hundreds of experiments have been conducted to discover the effects of knowledge of progress or lack of progress upon learning progress. It has usually been found that knowledge of success improves learning more than lack of information concerning progress. The results of these experiments are not entirely consistent and are difficult to interpret. It seems clear, however, that in the first stages of learning the majority of learners, especially young learners, are more effectively influenced by commendation than by condemnation. Continued scolding usually has a negative effect. Commendation is most beneficial when the learner needs encouragement to revive his flagging spirits.

Teachers must remember that individuals respond differently to adverse criticism and to praise. Censure is relatively more effective with capable learners and with confident extrovert learners than too much praise. Criticism, except of the most friendly sort, is likely to do more harm than good with less capable learners and sensitive learners of the introvert type. In general, teachers who frequently give mild encouragement mixed occasionally with mild, friendly, and frank criticism are more effective than teachers who are adversely critical or lavishly commendatory or who vacillate from severe criticism to extreme praise. Knowledge of failure seems to have different results upon different individuals according to circumstances. Knowledge of failure, especially chronic or complete failure, is harmful to many and beneficial only (1) to those who have not made very sincere efforts to learn or (2) when the knowledge of failure is diagnostic and not too discouraging. Knowledge of failure may be helpful in bringing into focus just where the failure is and what has caused it, without giving the individual the impression that greater achievement is impossible for him.

In most instances motivation is improved if definite, achievable, and not too remote goals are set up in the mind of the learner. Remote general goals and objectives should whenever possible be broken down into smaller and more immediate goals. Practical goals and objectives of learning activities are abilities to do, abilities to recite, the solution of problems, the answering of questions, the completion of projects, the attainment of skills or elements of skills, the formation of habits, and the like. Abilities "to do" include such things as to be able to tell a funny story, carry on a conversation, and follow directions. Assignments should be formulated in terms of such goals—specific, attainable, and seemingly desirable—not in terms of amounts of materials to be read or number of repetitions or of general remote goals such as "to be able to speak more effectively," "to understand the history of the American people," or "to appreciate music." These general objectives should not be ignored. The learner should be usually conscious of them and desirous of attaining them, but they must be broken down into more immediate subgoals.

Phenomenon of association

Since the time of Aristotle at least, the principle of association in learning has been recognized as important. In the eighteenth and nineteenth centuries, the English Associationists, who constituted an important school of thought in psychology, centered their attention upon theories or philosophies of learning based upon the phenomenon of association. They believed that ideas which are associated in the mind with other ideas tend to be recalled more readily than unassociated ideas. When one of a pair or group of ideas is recalled, the other or others tend to be recalled also. The more associations a particular idea forms in the mind of the learner, the more readily it is recalled.

Several types of association should be recognized, including association in time, contiguity in space, and contiguity of meaning. If two or more experiences occur at the same time or are in consciousness at the same time, the subsequent presence of one in mind tends to bring into consciousness the other or others. When one idea, feeling, or act has occurred in the experience of an individual immediately preceding another idea, feeling, or act, the recurrence of the former tends to cause the recurrence of the other. Likewise ideas which have been in the mind of the learner, associated as to their place in space, develop the property of association so that the recall of one tends to bring the other into consciousness. Ideas which are associated in meaning in the mind of the learner tend to be tied to each other in future consciousness. A special type of this principle is the principle of *sequence*. The applications of this principle in learning are varied and widespread, being operative especially in learning which involves sequence in the formation of habits, the development of skills, and memorizing.

The implications of this principle for learning and teaching are many and of great importance. Experiences which we would like to have occur together, or in sequence, in future thought, action, or feeling, should be experienced together or in sequence in learning. By so arranging the learner's experiences, one may go far in conditioning future experience. The applications are not confined to the area of skills, habits, or ideas but are found also in the area of emotional reactions. It is unavoidable that a feeling of sadness, anger, humor, reverence, joy, or duty shall be so conditioned that it will recur when an experience recurs which has been previously associated with the same feeling. A person may be conditioned to feel sad in a certain house, to feel reverent in the presence of a cathedral, to feel inferior in the presence of a certain person or situation, to feel belligerent when a certain idea, for example, fascism, is mentioned, to feel admiration when strength is exhibited, to feel friendly toward a given word, idea, or type of person, and to feel afraid in the presence of a snake, a large body of water, or of a certain type of responsibility in connection with which one has previously felt unsuccessful or unhappy.

For teaching, one of the more important implications of the principle of association is that what one wishes the pupil to retain, subject to ready recall, should be associated with a variety of other things, particularly with needs and applications of what is being learned. This phase of learning is important in transfer of training, discussed later in this chapter. The degree and certainty of "transfer" is proportional to the number and strength of associations between the situation first experienced and the situation to which transfer is to take place.

An important factor in retention is understanding. The better a passage, a skill, a definition, or the basis for appreciation of an experience is understood, the more quickly learning will reach the state of mastery and the more recallable and lasting it will be. The relative inefficiency of learning and teaching in schools of previous generations was a natural consequence of the attempt to "learn" without understanding. The expenditure of time in teaching for understanding is usually, particularly where permanence is desired, economical of time and effort in the long run. "The longest way round is the shortest way home" in many instances.

Phases and applications of the principle of association may be seen in such schools of thought in educational psychology as the "organismic," with its "field property," and the "integration" or "unity" idea and movement. Learning things in relation to each other and in relation to some fundamental unifying principle is not the same as learning things separately. Ideas, facts, or actions experienced in association are not the same as the identical ideas, facts, and actions experienced individually. There are meanings, new ideas, new facts, new actions, which are not in any one or in the sum of the individual ideas, facts, and actions, but grow out of and upon the relationship of the components. There are events and movements in history, attitudes and actions of peoples, scientific phenomena, and other things worth learning which are the outgrowth of combinations of facts, ideas, chemicals, and so forth and which cannot be explained or understood from experience of any one component of the combination. The components must be associated, often in a particular way, to produce the resultant which is worthy of learning. Conversely, when a complex learning situation is analyzed and experienced one step at a time, great care must be taken that relationships and properties of the complex whole are not lost sight of. Otherwise, highly important things may not be learned.

Mind and emotional set, apperceptive mass

The learning effects of any given instruction upon any given individual vary with the individual's mental background at the time, regardless of his previous mental content. By *mind set* is meant the degree of absorption of the mind at any particular moment and the content of consciousness at that time—the ideas, thoughts and purposes of the moment.

Everyone has had experiences which demonstrate this principle in a humorous way. For example, when a person expects a telephone call, he may answer the telephone when the doorbell rings. A friend's remarks may be ridiculously misunderstood because someone expected something different from what the friend actually said. To some extent, a person experiences what he expects to experience—sees what he is looking for even if it is not really there to see.

The current emotional set or mood also determines, to some extent in most instances and to a great extent in some, how a learner will react to teaching and to learning activities and materials. If the learner is at the time optimistic, critical, weary, enthusiastic about something else, worried, happy, or depressed, what he learns will be associated with his mood when he learned it. It is difficult to make any adequate adjustment to the varying moods and mind sets of each of a number of individuals in a class. Nevertheless, a teacher should realize that these factors condition learning.

The number is legion of schoolboy howlers or boners which result from the natural tendency to interpret one experience in the light of previous experience, as indicated in the following examples.

> Reciting the Lord's Prayer one little boy was heard to say, "Harold be Thy name." Another begged, "Give us this day our jelly bread." A New York child petitioned, "Lead us not into Penn Station."
>
> When certain pupils were told classes would be dismissed because of teachers' institute, Lonnie Leonard, eight, startled his parents with: "No school tomorrow. The teachers are going to an innocent toot."
>
> A first-grader volunteered to recite a nursery rhyme. "Little Miss Muffet sat on a tuffet," he intoned, "eating her curves away."
>
> The children were singing "Oh, Susanna." Suddenly three-year-old Billy had a version all his own. He sang lustily, "I come from Alabama with a band-aid on my knee."

Many suggestions for making teaching effective grow out of this principle, which possesses great validity and underspread application. Explanations must be made in the light of the background vocabulary and previous experience of the learner. Care must often be taken (a) to fill in gaps with necessary background for understanding new materials, sometimes in the form of a review; (b) to put learners in an appropriate frame of mind for many new ideas or learning activities—perhaps sometimes by developing interest or a desire to learn, sometimes by explaining the purpose of the learning activity.

Often the failure to utilize this principle occurs not because the teacher does not realize its importance but because she does not know the background, previous experience, interests, and present frame of mind of the pupil. The teacher is usually prone to over-rate the pupil in this respect and to presuppose a background which exists only to a very limited extent if at all. To be most effective, teachers should acquire as much knowledge as possible about pupils in their classes by means of interest and experience inventories, vocabulary tests, and other exploratory devices, employed at the beginning of a year or at the beginning of a unit of instruction.

It is fortunate when a teacher is aware of the goals and interests of the individual pupils in her class and is able to arrange the learning activities and experiences so that they seem to contribute to those goals rather than divert the child or frustrate him.

The principle of "mind set" also conditions the nature of the effect of any learning activity or the suggestion to a learner that he engage in a given activity. When there is present in the mind of a prospective learner a purpose upon the accomplishment of which he is intent, an interruption is very likely to be resented. When Harry is intent upon reading a newspaper, playing a game, or even perhaps working a problem in arithmetic, an interruption in the form of a suggestion to quit and read a magazine, or go to assembly, or study spelling is likely to be unwelcome. Unless the suggested activity is one which keenly interests or immediately excites him, the effect upon him is much more likely to be one of annoyance than of pleasure. The more absorbing and pleasurable the activity in which he is engaged, on which he has a particular mind set, the more he dislikes interruption.

Many teachers think that to the growing child the *complex* is not only synonymous with the *psychological,* but also with the *concrete.* They are convinced that when complex behavior situations are broken up into small units of behavior they become atomistic, artificial, and unnatural. They also are definitely of the opinion (in particular, those believing in the gestalt school of thought in psychology) that the child has very great capacities for learning behavior of a very complex type, and give many illustrations of a youngster's acquiring a behavior of a complex type with apparently not too great difficulty. It is also claimed that, when the complex is broken up artificially into simple units, the youngster is less interested in learning because of the apparent lack of applicability in real life. Furthermore, the child finds it difficult to reconstruct these units into forms of complex behavior which are really the objectives of the instruction.

At least three important general principles of teaching seem to grow obviously out of this principle of learning: (1) the approach to new learning activities should be made in such a manner as to utilize current mind sets; (2) quite frequently time and care must be devoted to setting the stage by reviews, discussions, observation trips, and so forth to prepare the learner for coming learning experiences; and (3) the probable effect of any learning stimulus, materials, methods, or activities upon the learner must be considered in the light of what he already knows or does not know, his interests, abilities, concepts, and tastes.

Certainly specific teaching procedures have their source of validity, at least in part, in this principle of learning. Among them may be mentioned the following procedures.

1. From the simple to the complex
2. From the concrete to the abstract
3. From the near to the remote
4. From the fundamental to the accessory
5. From the psychological to the logical

Readiness

Naturally one of the more important considerations in directing learning is that of the learner's readiness. Algebra can be taught with some degree of success to an average child in the fifth grade but with great difficulty and uneconomical expenditure of time. The same is true of attempts to teach reading to learners 3 or 4 years of age. Whatever may be postponed until later will be learned more easily provided the learner in the meantime is growing through learning. Naturally, not everything can be postponed; even if it could, valuable opportunities for learning would not be fully utilized. Something must be taught each year. It is a matter of relative readiness. Years ago, there was a tendency to force learning materials earlier and earlier in the life of the child. Long division, for example, which had once been taught in high school, was introduced in many schools as low as the fourth grade. The result was not only uneconomical efforts at learning but the development of undesirable attitudes in the relatively unsuccessful child and misconceptions of his own capacity for learning mathematics.

With a growing understanding of child psychology and a growing realization of the folly of crowding nature too much, there has been a greatly increased attention to the matter of readiness and an increased recognition of the value of a greater experiential background upon which instruction may be based. As a result, there has been a tendency to relocate many items of instruction in later grades, particularly in the subjects of reading, mathematics, grammar, and literature. There have been many attempts to discover at what grade, in accordance with the principle of readiness, the various topics or phases of topics of courses of study should be taught. Many investigators have entertained the hypothesis that, just as in the maturation of a chick there comes a time when it learns most naturally and economically to peck for food, so in the life of a child there is probably the time of golden opportunity, if a person could locate it, when each of the important things to be learned could be best taught. Up to the present, no means have been discovered whereby teachers may identify the "golden age." They have, nevertheless, learned that some ages are better than others for some things, and this approach to the improvement of instruction is still under way. For example, reading may be best begun on a systematic basis at about the mental age of 6½ or 7 years, whatever the chronological age of the child may be.

Teachers are beginning to discover that in order to make rapid and successful progress in learning to read the individual child must acquire an appropriate experiential background. If he does not have this at the time reading is begun in school, he must be put with others of a like deficiency and given the necessary experiential background before he attacks systematically the acquisition of reading skills. In the cases of a considerable number of learners, progress in the learning of reading will not go on satisfactorily until the child has acquired a desire to be able to read.

More intensive study of this principle seems to reveal, among other things, that (1) it is not practical to attempt to force nature too fast in developing understandings, tastes, interests, attitudes, ideals, habits or skills; (2) the optimum time for teaching various items is conditioned not only by the maturation and growing background of the learner, but by his developing and changing interests and his growing needs for the outcomes in question; (3) the decision must be made on the basis of a consideration of various factors, including (a) the necessity for learning much before leaving school and (b) the necessity for learning something early as a basis and background for understanding and learning other things. With few exceptions, there is no very special time at which the human is "ready" for any particular subject matter; it is a matter of adapting the instruction to the learner's degree of readiness both in terms of basis for understanding and in terms of his interests and needs.

Interest and effort

The contribution of repetition to learning is a matter not only of frequency but also of other factors, including the attitude of the learner and his ability to attach meaning to the materials. Perfunctory drill or repetition is relatively ineffective, as in reading passages with a low level of attention and interest. Experimenters have discovered that repeating materials for the subjects of the experiment to learn does not always result in any appreciable degree of learning. Learning is dependent largely, in addition to accurate repetition, upon a type of experience in which there is a high level of attention and in which there is upon the learner's part an interest in the learning activity and an interest in achievement of learning. Learning is achieved most quickly and completely when the learner is an *active* and a *willing* participant in learning activity.

Many experiences are retained indefinitely even though not repeated. In this category are experiences of unusual intensity or meaning to the individual. A person rarely forgets the sight of a dying person, a violent storm, a very humiliating incident, a most eagerly sought reward or victory. He also remembers longer his more vivid learning experiences of a less spectacular nature—the visualized, concreted, colorful, more or less dramatic and lifelike ones.

Because of the prime importance of this principle and because of the difficulty in obtaining a high level of interest, attention, and active participation among learners for what teachers try to teach in school, a later section of this chapter will be devoted to discussion of the approaches to motivation, interest, and attention.

Physiological factors

Several physiological factors condition learning to an appreciable extent. Learning declines with fatigue, particularly learning of very difficult or abstract materials or procedures, but physical fatigue must be of a very marked degree before it in itself interferes seriously with learning. Ordinarily, fatigue affects learning principally by interfering with or dividing attention or is of the nature of mental fatigue, ennui, or boredom. It tends to interfere more with the acquisition of understanding than with rote memory, more with acquisition of complex and fine skills than with habits.

Pain tends to interfere with learning much in the same manner as does fatigue, serving to distract attention rather than to prevent learning if attention can be maintained. Drugs have various effects upon learning, most of them inimical or negligible.

Learning is materially conditioned by the general physiological condition of the individual. Persons with nutritional defects, chronic fevers or systemic infections of any sort, very low blood pressure, or glandular malperformance are almost certain to be handicapped in learning. Such effects are noticeable not only in individuals, but in whole groups who live in regions where these physiological maladjustments are common.

Intelligence

What an individual can learn and how rapidly he learns are dependent upon his capacity for learning—apparently upon the composition and modifiability of the cortex and the nervous system. Learning capacity is not greatly dependent upon race or sex. A teacher should learn the limits set by heredity for each of the individuals in each of her classes (I.Q.) and the stage of mental maturity or ability (M.A.) and adapt teaching materials and methods accordingly.

For the slow or dull learner there must be concrete, sensory, life-like, simple, practical materials and activities; for the bright pupil there must be challenges in the form of complex abstract materials and materials and methods calling for ingenuity, generalization, and creativeness.

Transfer of training and formal discipline

Learning outcomes achieved in a specialized situation or restricted field may function under certain conditions in other specialized situations or restricted fields, or in all fields. Ideals of honesty and honest behavior developed in the classroom tend to carry over to life outside the classroom. However, neatness developed in arithmetic may not necessarily be expected to carry over to neatness in person or in room because neatness in person and neatness in arithmetic, though both referred to as *neatness,* are two different things. The degree of carryover or transfer depends upon certain principles which may be stated as follows:

1. The degree to which there is identity or similarity between the training situation (stimulus-response) and the field or situation to which transfer is made as to (a) content: ideas, facts, principles, concepts, vocabulary; and (b) procedure: of study, of action.
2. The degree of general intelligence and imagination of the learner which will enable and cause him to recognize that the effects of training in a previous situation or situations apply to various new situations; to think in a given new situation of the possibilities that might be employed.
3. The degree and extent to which in the original training a general ideal was held before the learner (e.g., the ideal of neatness) and the extent of the possible areas to which transfer could be made was emphasized (e.g., the transfer of the study of general rules of English grammar to oral and written expression).
4. The degree to which the gap between the learning situation in the school and the situation or situations or application is bridged by discussions and learning activities. In other words, all subjects should be taught in terms of their application to everyday life.

Teachers must be constantly alert to the possibilities and point out the more useful applications or "transfers" of what is learned to areas or situations in which specific training could not be given for reasons of lack of time or equipment.

INTEREST AND INCENTIVES

The teacher must see to it that her pupils engage in appropriate learning activities eagerly and attentively to assure substantial learning progress. If the learning activities are selected and arranged appropriately and the approach and the personality of the teacher are attractive, most younger children will be eager to learn. That the child loses interest as he becomes older is in part attributable to the failure of teachers to adapt materials and methods to his acquired and potential interests. Many well educated and scholarly teachers often have very limited success in teaching, because they cannot get learners to engage in the activities emphasized for learning.

The most successful teacher has the knack, know-how, or personality (usually a combination of these) to get children willingly to do those things which they must do if they are to learn, with a spirit which they must have if they are to learn well. She must be able to put pupils in a receptive frame of mind and to plan learning activities that are interesting, meet specific felt needs of the learners, and are entered upon and continued with vigor because of genuine values rather than artificial incentives such as rivalry, marks, and love of approval.

Evaluation of incentives

The relative value of motives or incentives to learning activities may be judged by the following criteria:

1. *Power of appeal:* the degree to which the incentive stimulates the learner to continued learning activity
2. *Universality of appeal:* the proportion of the learners involved who will be motivated by the incentive or motive
3. *Concomitant educational outcomes:* the nature of the educational effects of the use of the incentive (a) upon the learner's attitude toward and interest in the subject, (b) upon the learner's attitude toward the teacher and the school in general, (c) upon the learner's attitude toward himself and his capacities, and (d) upon the development of social and ethical characteristics

Unfortunately, some teachers, especially beyond the lower grades, use incentives primarily upon the basis of the first two criteria above and ignore the third. This is shortsighted, fallacious, and unjustifiable. Many teachers sacrifice long-term educational gains by destroying or failing to develop permanent interests in order to meet immediate difficulties.

No matter how effective the use of a given incentive may be (appeal to rivalry, use of honor rolls, threats of failure, for example) as a means of goading children to do problems and exercises in arithmetic or study spelling lessons, it is unwise to employ it, if by so doing the teacher fails to develop an interest in the subject or activities involved. Indeed it is actually reprehensible to resort to that kind of incentive if it causes the pupil to dislike the subject and to develop attitudes likely to cause him to avoid further participation in these activities.

Horace Mann, the great evangelist for public education in New England, wrote the following: "If a teacher desires that his pupil should be a great man rather than a good one, or that he acquire wealth rather than esteem; or that he should master Latin rather than ride his own spirit, or attain high official preferment rather than love the Lord his God with all his heart and his neighbor as himself—then he will goad him on by the deep driven spur of emulation or any other motive until he will outstrip his fellow, at whatever peril to his moral nature."

It is not difficult to appreciate the observation of a parent who protested, "Even if my son did make a B in that teacher's course, I would have preferred that he not have studied under her at all. He will soon forget the scientific information he learned and certainly it is poor return in comparison with the unfavorable attitudes developed."

Using artificial devices to stimulate learning activities has other objectionable qualities. They encourage children to study for artificial rewards rather than for interest or education itself. They fail to lead children toward intellectual interests, and children often cease to study when the artificial pressures are removed.

Many of these artificial incentives breed undesirable character traits such as conceit on the part of the brightest and despair on the part of the least able, overdeveloped appetite for competition and for winning, destruction of the tendency to work with and for others as opposed to working against others, and a willingness to cheat, to use various devices to mislead teachers, and to "learn" only what will be checked up on.

Some incentives commonly employed have much power but apply to only a few learners. Honors and distinctions do not apply to all the superior pupils and have little appeal to the pupil who realizes that his chance of attaining them is negligible. The possibility of failure is of little motivating value to children who with little effort can be certain of passing.

Some incentives appeal to all or nearly all pupils but not in a manner likely to result in vigorous learning activity. In this category may be placed the desire to be a good citizen or to be of service to humanity, to be a learned rather than an ignorant person, to be a success in life, and many others which are too general or remote to stimulate immediate learning.

Types of interest, attention, and needs

John Dewey in his *Interest and Effect in Education* pointed out clearly that attention is essential for economical learning and is directly dependent upon, and grows out of, interest. Where interest is lacking, learning activity is handicapped by divided attention. Dewey said, "External mechanical attention to a task as a task is inevitably accompanied by random mind-wandering along the lines of the pleasurable. The spontaneous power of the child, his demand for realization of his own impulses, cannot be suppressed." [1] Wherever there is effort to attend, there is an inherent weakness, and while "effort" or the "will" to attend must be resorted to occasionally, it should not be overworked, as it so commonly is in classrooms.

Interests are of two kinds, direct (intrinsic) and indirect (mediate). Attention may be spontaneous, growing out of interest, habit, or sensory insistence, or it may be forced by the will or by unwelcome distraction.

Needs are classified as generic or specific. For example, working for a grade is a generic need since many things can be done in many subjects in working for a grade; there is no specific answer to the need for a good grade. In contrast, a specific need means a need for a specific thing—a specific bit of knowledge, a specific skill, or a specific habit. Needs also may be classified as immediate or deferred and as intrinsic or mediate. From a mediate need, a need not for the thing itself but as a means to an end, indirect interest and forced attention usually follow.

Direct and indirect interest

It is not always easy to distinguish sharply between direct and indirect interest. There are some things that persons are interested in doing merely because to do them affords pleasure. Individuals are interested in these activities because they satisfy predispositions, yearnings, and tastes which may be either inherited or acquired. Examples of direct interests are those commonly exhibited by chil-

[1] John Dewey, *Interest and Effort in Education* (New York: Houghton Mifflin Co., 1913), p. 9.

dren in hearing funny stories, in "reading" picture stories (comics), in playing some forms of games, and the interest some children have in drawing or making a stamp collection.

An indirect interest is one such as that in studying because of the need to know something, (to know a certain fact in order to plan a purchase, a party, or a trip) or the desire to make a good mark or not to appear stupid in class. An indirect interest may and often does become a direct interest. Often pupils study because of an indirect interest. With good curricula and a good teacher, these pupils, or many of them at least, should eventually become interested in learning activities. One of the most important functions of teaching is to develop a variety of keen, desirable interests. Unfortunately most teachers sacrifice interests to the much less valuable outcome of temporary mastery of subject information or skills.

Most individuals have certain identifiable predispositions. Some things they just like to do. Most children like to be active physically, though this desire decreases as they approach maturity. Most children are curious, particularly about things that are strange. Most boys and girls like contests, particularly group contests. Many other interests common to children may be identified by the observing teacher.

What is interesting depends upon current value to the learner and to those of his age group at the time. Children usually like to do what other persons of their age are doing and think worth doing. To some extent, varying with different individuals, what is interesting depends also upon what others in general seem to like to do and believe worth doing.

Interests are also individual. What interests one child may not interest another. One enjoys making things with tools. Another prefers to talk about airplanes. One likes to play in sand, another to be with a group, another to read stories, and another to work with clay. Many teachers began their work not because of their interest in teaching but as a means of livelihood and later developed an interest in teaching for itself.

Spontaneous and forced attention

An individual usually gives spontaneous attention to that which is of direct interest to him. No effort of will is required. To those activities which are performed not because of any direct interest but for some ulterior purpose one is compelled to force his attention. It is, to be sure, a matter of degree. Some activities are of sufficient direct interest or have become so nearly a matter of habit and routine that little effort is required to pay attention to them. Spontaneous attention is given also to loud noises, moving objects, and strange sights, which may or may not be pleasurable or even interesting in themselves.

Wherever there is forced attention, the learning situation is not at its best; attention is divided. At least some consideration must be given to the matter of forcing attention, and always there is competition for attention. There is rarely the degree of attention often thought of as absorption. Physical discomfort and distracting noises and sights, which result in the necessity for more forcing of attention, should be kept at a minimum.

While there are those who believe that children should engage only in activities which are intrinsically interesting, they find it difficult to convince many of the wisdom of their position. There is much of value to be learned which, at least at first, must be learned by means of *motivated* activity. The learner must be caused to engage in the activity necessary for learning not because of direct interest but because by so doing he may gain something he wishes or avoid something he does not like. He operates with forced attention from indirect interest and is stimulated by a motive.

Specific and generic need

Motivation is a very effective approach to interest. To be motivated one must feel a *need*. He must wish something and must feel that to engage in a given activity will enable him to satisfy that desire. Quite often, in fact almost daily, teachers themselves must develop motivation, either specific or generic. Often a person needs a particular knowledge or skill for a specific purpose. He may, for example, need to know the location of certain cities to understand the significance of certain current news, to be able to type in order to get the position he desires, to know certain facts in order to operate or to repair a radio or an automobile, to be able to use a certain tool or machine in order to make something he wishes to construct, or to develop skill in speaking or acting in order to make a debate squad or to take part in a play. All these are *specific* needs. For the purpose of motivating and developing interest in the performance of learning activities the specific need is of relatively great effectiveness, depending upon the keenness with which that need is felt.

There is another specific need which plays an important part in the techniques of the best teachers. It is the *felt* need created by bringing pupils to see what are the specific deficiencies in their learning achievements. For this purpose diagnostic tests constructed by the teacher (if not otherwise available in textbooks) should be used frequently and teachers should observe for deficiencies young learners at work.

Generic needs do not ordinarily constitute as powerful a motivating force. The appeal to generic need does not develop a permanent interest in the activities or field of study. In addition it is likely to result in harmful concomitant outcomes—dislike for the subject, the teacher, the school, or all of these. Yet appeal to generic need must be made frequently because commonly learners will not feel a specific need for the outcomes of the learning activities contemplated or for the activities themselves. Appeal to generic need should, therefore, be made only when there seems to be no intrinsic interest or practical felt need. Generic need is a need for some outcome of learning activity which is not a need for the particular instructional or learning materials, an outcome to which other materials or outcomes will also minister. Of this broad type is the need for good marks, for approval, for education or knowledge in general, and for preparation for higher grades. Also included are the needs felt to satisfy the desire for achievement, to help a team, to satisfy a sense of duty, or to avoid criticism. Almost any subject may be motivated by appeal to generic needs.

The appeal to some specific need or needs is to be preferred wherever such a need exists, not only because it is likely to be of greater motivating power and less likely to result in undesirable outcomes, but because it associates the learning materials, activities, and outcomes with their practical applications and thereby provides training in application as well as understanding of the practical significance of the outcomes acquired.

Immediate and deferred needs

One of the most important characteristics of a need is the proximity of the time when the need will become *immediate*. The degree of motivating power is in proportion to the nearness of the time when what is to be learned will be useful. What is needed today is of much importance. What will be needed next week is less impelling. What is needed next year seems not at all pressing. What will be needed when the child is five, ten, or twenty years older may appear to be of great value theoretically, but it is not likely that many young learners will be keenly motivated to study such matters at the present time. They are not likely to be vigorously motivated by learning activities which serve remote needs, in preference to alternative activities which are intrinsically interesting and therefore pleasurable or activities which minister to current or immediate needs.

Positive and negative motivation

Generic and specific needs seem to fall readily into one or the other of two categories, *positive* and *negative*. Human beings do many things in order to achieve something desired and many other things to avoid something undesirable. A child may practice on his violin because he wishes to be able to perform well on it, or he may practice because his parent or teacher will censure him if he does not practice. A learner may study a selection in literature because he enjoys it or because he fears being unable to perform satisfactorily when called upon in class.

It must be recognized that often the positive and the negative are different aspects of a single motive. A student may engage in learning activities both because he wishes to excel, or at least to achieve a fair mark, and also because he wishes to avoid appearing inferior or making a low mark. Specific needs, as well as generic needs, may be either positive or negative or both. For example, a student may learn what is involved in making a good table on which to study, or what information is needed to understand certain current news not only to achieve a desired object but also to avoid failure in a specific undertaking.

While the degree to which the need appeals to a learner is most important, it is also true that positive incentives or needs are usually more effective than negative incentives or needs. While a slightly attractive reward is less motivating than the prospect of a serious punishment, rewards usually are more effective than punishments. They are, on the average, not only more effective as motivation, but they are definitely much less likely to possess undesirable concomitant outcomes such as distaste for the subject matter or learning activity, dislike for the school and the teacher, and untoward effects upon personality that result from fear and compulsion through fear. The fact that teachers employ negative incentives does not establish a presumption in their favor but stands as a testimonial to the lack of ingenuity, time, or industry, on the teachers' part. Sarcasm, humiliation before classmates, and other punishments are disappearing from practice among the more successful teachers.

Natural and artificial incentives

Whenever it is necessary to resort to motivation which is of the nature of a reward or a punishment other than the natural outcome of learning, an *artificial incentive* is employed. This is always the case in the appeal to generic need. Artificial incentives are broad in their scope of application in that they appeal to the large majority of learners. They also quite frequently possess considerable motivating power. However, from the point of view of developing permanent interests, effects upon personality and upon pupil-teacher relationship, and other concomitant outcomes, they are most likely to be definitely harmful and should be employed only in the absence of natural incentives, specific needs, or intrinsic interest which will motivate learning activity sufficiently to result in a high degree of attention.

QUESTIONS, PROBLEMS, AND EXERCISES

1. Different authorities use different terms in speaking of repeated experience as the basis of learning, e.g., *activity, use, frequency, exercise,* and *repetition.* What differences do you see between the meanings of these terms as employed in formulating a fundamental principle of learning?

2. Think of two examples of "learning" more or less permanently a fact or an attitude from one repetition only, and two examples of relative failure to learn after many repetitions. Explain why there was learning or not in each case. What laws or principles were involved in the cases where there was learning?

3. Think of two examples of forgetting from lack of recent repetition—one of a fact or facts and one of a skill. Which tends to be more completely forgotten from disuse?

4. Mention some ways of employing "associations" to insure retention of facts or habits.

5. Give a five-minute discussion of "readiness"—its meaning and application to learning.

6. What are the principal unique or different elements, and what is the common element, in the meanings of *interest, effort, attention, vividness, intensity?* What is the relation between interest and effort, interest and vividness or intensity, attention and vividness?

7. What are some of the implications for classroom work of the effect of fatigue upon learning? The effect of malnutrition upon learning?

8. Select one school subject and think of some learning outcomes of that subject which transfer to broad areas in life—outcomes that ordinarily transfer in large amounts. Do any other subjects result in the same transferable outcomes?

9. Mention three methods of getting learners to apply themselves which you think are good and three which you think are bad. Evaluate each on the basis of (1) power of appeal, (2) universality of appeal, and (3) concomitant outcomes.

10. Give two examples each of:
   a)   direct and indirect interest
   b)   spontaneous and forced attention
   c)   generic and specific need

d) immediate and deferred need
e) positive and negative motivation
f) natural and artificial incentives

11. Discuss the role of goals in learning—the effectiveness of specific goals upon effectiveness of learning activities and the possible effects of knowledge of relative success or failure upon learning.

12. Take one side of the following question and be able to defend it in class. "Forcing children to perform unpleasant learning activities is desirable educational experience."

SELECTED SUPPLEMENTARY READINGS

ADAMS, FAY. *Educating America's Children,* 2d ed. New York: The Ronald Press Co., 1954.

Chap. 7, "The Basis of Individual Effectiveness: Mental and Physical Health." Some good suggestions are offered for the classroom teacher to prevent children from acquiring certain mental and physical impairments.

BEAUCHAMP, GEORGE A. *Planning the Elementary School Curriculum.* Englewood Cliffs, N.J.: Allyn and Bacon, 1956.

Chap. 7, "The Nature of the Learning Process," pp. 113–33. Nature of different kinds of learning and relationship to the curriculum.

BECK, ROBERT H., WALTER W. COOK, and NOLAN C. KEARNEY. *Curriculum in the Modern Elementary School.* Englewood Cliffs, N.J.: Prentice-Hall, Inc., 1953.

Chap. iii, "Motivating Educational Behavior." Physiological and psychological needs in relation to motivation. Chap. ix, "Principles of Learning Basic to Curriculum Development." Goal directed activity, emotional learning, learning as a creative process, learning as a developmental process.

BURTON, WILLIAM H. *The Guidance of Learning Activities,* rev. ed. New York: Appleton-Century-Crofts, Inc., 1952.

Chap. ii, "Certain Misconceptions Concerning Learning." Contrast of how learning took place in the past with how it is viewed today. Chap. iv, "The Characteristics of Educative Experience." The learner is the central focal point of educative experience today. Chap. v, "The Nature of the Learner." Different learning theories are described along with the one gaining popularity today.

HERRICK, VIRGIL E., JOHN I. GOODLAD, FRANK J. ESTVAN, and PAUL W. EBERMAN. *The Elementary School.* Englewood Cliffs, N.J.: Prentice-Hall, Inc., 1956.

Chap. 5, "Children: Their Learning and Development Processes," pp. 95–124. Developmental characteristics of children; types, natures and concepts of learning; mastery motivation; transfer; frustration; role of child and role of teacher.

JERSILD, ARTHUR T. *Child Development and the Curriculum.* New York: Bureau of Publications, Teachers College, Columbia University, 1946.

Chap. ii, "Principles of Child Development as Applied to the Curriculum." Reports some basic assumptions and principles which are evidenced in research. These assumptions and especially the principles should prove helpful to the teacher.

KLAUSMEIER, HERBERT J., KATHARINE DRESDEN, HELEN C. DAVIS, and WALTER ARNO WITTICH. *Teaching in the Elementary School.* New York: Harper & Bros., 1956.

Chap. 3, "The Learning Process."

MacLean, Malcolm S., and Edwin A. Lee. *Change and Process in Education.* New York: The Dryden Press, Inc., 1956.

Chap. 11, "The Emotional Basis of Teaching and Learning," pp. 343–79. Many types of emotional development are described and its relation to democratic classroom procedure is discussed.

Saylor, J. Galen, and William M. Alexander. *Curriculum Planning for Better Teaching and Learning.* New York: Rinehart & Co., Inc., 1954.

"The Learning Process and Curriculum Planning," pp. 186–212. An excellent discussion of the learning process and its ramifications in the classroom.

Thomas, R. Murray. *Ways of Teaching in Elementary Schools.* New York: Longmans, Green & Co., Inc., 1955.

Chap. iv. Theories of child behavior from Rousseau to present with emphasis on the need for understanding.

Wingo, G. Max, and Raleigh Schorling. *Elementary-School Student Teaching.* New York: McGraw-Hill Book Co., Inc., 1955.

Chap. iii, "Child Growth and Development." Contains a section on characteristics and needs of various ages of children in the elementary school with some helpful suggestions for teachers.

7

TEACHING FOR TYPES
OF LEARNING OUTCOMES

A person may grow educationally in a variety of ways—by acquiring *information* (specific or general) and by acquiring knowledge of the location of cities, mountains, and rivers, or of the rules of grammar, mathematics, or science, or knowledge in the form of understandings, that is "knowing" in the sense of knowing the significance and characteristics of a person, species, object, process, institution, or idea.

A person may grow educationally by acquiring intellectual skills, social skills, and motor skills and by acquiring habits of thought, habits of feeling, and habits of action.

He may grow educationally by acquiring *ideals*—desired goals in the form of traits one wishes to acquire or standards one wishes to attain and support—and by developing *attitudes*—relatively fixed tendencies of emotional reaction to individuals, groups of people, ideas, institutions, social practices, and philosophies.

Finally, he may grow by acquiring *interests* in various types of intellectual, physical, and social activities and in individual persons, animals, or objects, and by acquiring *tastes*—preferences for certain kinds of experiences in reading, hearing, seeing, or doing. For example, he may acquire interests in historic places, inventions, sports, drama, dress and appearance, and tastes for certain types of literature, art, music, games, social intercourse, or theatrical presentations.

In this chapter there will be presented general basic concepts of (1) the relationship of learning and teaching to each of these types

117

of educational growth and (2) the procedure in promoting learning of each of these types. In subsequent chapters, more detailed discussions of techniques of teaching for various types of growth will be presented.

ACQUISITION OF KNOWLEDGE

An individual may grow educationally by acquiring knowledge (a) in the form of *verbatim statements* as, for example, being able to state that "a sentence is a group of words expressing a complete thought" or to recite a selection from literature or a passage from a book; (b) in the form of the *gist* or *general idea* of a paragraph or other passage, or of an event, a person, a movement, a process, or some other part of experience which one can state in one's own words; (c) in the form of a *general principle, concept,* or *rule* which one can state in one's own words or can apply to a given situation, case, or problem. These three types of knowledge vary characteristically with respect to the degree of understanding necessarily involved. Within each of the three categories learnings also differ in the amount and nature of understanding. Reciting verbatim from memory may be achieved with little or no understanding of meaning although it is frequently accepted as implying understanding and in lieu of more valid evidence of understanding.

Fortunately the tendency in teaching has been to put much less emphasis upon memorizing. Not only is it difficult and time-consuming, quickly forgotten, and of little value unless accompanied by a high degree of understanding of the meaning of the words memorized, but there are relatively few statements or passages which there is any real need to memorize. Nothing can be gained by reciting a set of words verbatim unless there is understanding of the meaning of the words.

Throughout the nineteenth century, much of the activity of the schoolroom had verbatim or memoriter learning as its main objective. Verbatim recitation was impressive and was commonly accepted as evidence of learning of meaning. This was particularly true among persons who were in awe of formal statements, long and unusual words, and bookish materials. Ability in verbatim recitations tended to put its possessor in a favorable light. In recent decades there has been a growing tendency to be more concerned with abilities to apply knowledge than with the mere possession of knowledge or what passed for it.

It may be desirable sometimes to memorize beautiful passages of literature and statements or rules of procedure, the ability to use which depends materially upon recalling exact words and making fine distinctions. Nevertheless, verbatim recitation without rich understanding not only possesses little utility, but to most learners it is a very difficult and distasteful task. Even the ability to use rules and precepts which are employed completely and continually is aided very little by verbatim memorization.

In studying procedures of teaching for acquisition of knowledge, a person must continually be on guard to distinguish learning verbatim or near-verbatim from learning the "gist" or general content and import of information. Many of the conclusions from experimental work in the psychology of learning are based upon experiments involving only verbatim learning, and inferences from these conclusions are subject to so many limitations as to decrease the value of the so-called basic scientific principles of acquiring knowledge.

Authoritative vs. development methods

Procedures of teaching for the purpose of acquiring information and understanding tend to fall into two general categories: (1) the method of learning accepted facts or conclusions on the basis of assumed competent authority and (2) the method of developing the student's stock of information and understanding by processes of observation and reasoning.

The learning of materials from the printed page or from the spoken words of the teacher, the radio speaker, or other persons constitutes the first type. The second type is represented by procedures in which the learners' efforts are centered upon developing through problem solving or the inductive procedure the information or general principles being learned. These two types of learning and teaching may be designated as the *authoritative* and the *developmental* types of procedure.

Not all techniques of teaching fall precisely into one or the other of these two general types. Nevertheless, most techniques tend to be predominantly one or the other. Among those which are largely authoritative are:

1. Learning from textbooks or other references
2. Learning from lectures
3. Learning from visual or other sensory presentation by the teacher
4. Learning from class recitations made by oneself and others

Among those which are predominantly developmental are (1) the *inductive procedure* by which the learner arrives at a general conclusion—for example, the concept of cause and effect, a rule for capitalization, the "a" formula in arithmetic (i.e., $a = wl$), certain laws of science—by examining a number of individual cases; (2) the *deductive procedure* by which the learner arrives at an inferred conclusion or solution by reasoning from previously known or given facts or principles—for example, a learner or a class may be attempting to derive a general principle or to deduce a specific conclusion and yet receive so much help from the teacher as to make the result at least partly dependent upon "authority." It frequently happens also that as a teacher is explaining she so stimulates the learners or at least some of them to think through the matter for themselves as to make the procedure at least partly developmental.

Distinct advantages are claimed for both the authoritative and the developmental methods of teaching. The values claimed for each method may be summarized as follows:

Advantages of authoritative methods:

1. Economy of time
2. Presentation of subject matter in a logical manner
3. Requirement for ability and ingenuity of teacher lessened
4. Definite, formal presentation preferred by many students
5. Body of tangible subject matter given to pupil
6. Mastery of material presented by authoritative methods ascertainable by accepted instruments of measurement
7. Nature and difficulty of the material may justify the direct, authoritative method instead of more time-consuming methods
8. Retention facilitated by reference to textbooks

Advantages of developmental methods:

1. Concomitant learnings may be highly important outcomes such as (a) initiative, (b) independent habits of study, (c) techniques of problem solving useful in meeting problems outside school.
2. Self-activity required of learner satisfies conditions of effective learning.
3. Retention can be reinforced by the learner's repeating the developmental process.
4. More complete response of the learner in the initial learning makes it more permanent, thereby reducing need for excessive drill and repetition.
5. Reality and vividness of the pupil's experience in reaching a conclusion or solving a problem for himself contribute to greater understanding.
6. Activities involved in developmental methods make a greater appeal to active energetic children than do the methods which foster passivity.

7. Method presents greater opportunity for the teacher to observe and diagnose the individual pupil's methods of study, personal qualities, and needs.

It is evident that, except for the saving of time, in general the advantages of developmental methods greatly outweigh those of authoritative methods.

Developmental methods require more skill and background than authoritative methods. For this reason, beginning or mediocre teachers are inclined to use the latter. After having experimented with and attained some mastery in developmental technique and having become conscious of its limitations, the teacher who is desirous of improving the quality and effectiveness of her teaching will make increasing use of developmental practices. Developmental methods may be employed with marked advantage if good judgment is exercised in determining whether the necessary outlay of time is disproportionate to the educational outcomes which will probably result.

Direct and indirect methods

Fortunately an individual can learn from the experience of others as well as from his own experiences. Otherwise, for a given individual the scope of learning would be limited and time-consuming. An individual can learn, for example, about the appearance of an object without seeing the object, about a process without seeing the procedure, about sounds without actually hearing them, about pains without feeling them, about a person, a business, a war, a legislative body, or a treaty without having any direct experiences with them. Learning can result, and a great deal of it does, from *vicarious* experience—the experience of others at second hand. Practically all that a person receives from newspapers and the radio, in fact from all printed or written material, all spoken words, and all forms of graphic art (pictures, graphs, models, and the like), is vicarious experience.

The relative advantages of direct and indirect methods are similar to the relative advantages of developmental and authoritative methods, as will be recognized from a comparison of the two types of methods. In learning from one's own personal experience one is likely to learn more accurately, to retain what is learned longer, to understand more completely, to be more interested in the process of learning, to see better the value of the things learned, to enjoy more greatly the learning activities, and to learn more quickly and more completely.

Nevertheless, many of the things which are desirable to learn must be learned from vicarious experience. It is not possible, for example, to experience those things which have already happened and which cannot be caused to happen again for the purpose of teaching history. A similar situation exists with respect to most of the content of science, geography, and the social studies, and of some of the content of all other subjects.

The teacher should at all times recognize the limitations of the use of vicarious experience in learning, and she should so plan the learning experience that it will suffer as little as possible from those limitations. Pictures, models, field trips, dramatization, and other representations should be employed frequently in order that vividness, accuracy of details, interest, and understanding may be achieved. The learning situation should possess as much of reality as is possible, subject to limitations on the expenditure of time and money. Because of the great superiority for the purposes of learning and teaching of various approaches and substitutes for reality and personal experience, Chapter 12 is devoted to the discussion of the values, uses, types, and techniques of both visual and auditory aids.

Teaching for retention

Quite often information once acquired remains with one; more often it does not. Information is retained in the sense that one's neural tissue is so modified that the mental content may be experienced again in the absence of the original sensory stimulus. Whether every experience permanently modifies the tissue involved so that there is always the possibility of recall, or only a portion of experience so modifies the tissue that retention is permanent, is not definitely known. Everyone knows, though, that much of what he experiences cannot be recalled. Whether in a given instance this results from failure of retention or failure of recall cannot be reliably determined.

The pupil does not retain all the information he acquires, or if he does he is not able to recall it. Much of what he has read, or what has been told, soon slips away beyond recall. What he has experienced directly, visually or otherwise, and what he has developed for himself inductively or deductively, he is usually able to recall even after the passage of a considerable time.

Several factors operate to determine what elements in a learning experience will be retained. One of the chief factors is the *intensity* or *vividness* of the experience. The degree of intensity of an experience is conditioned by these factors.

1. Degree of interest in the experience, its stimuli, and its outcome
2. Elements novel to the situation
3. Understanding of the significance of the experience
4. Impressions made by emotionally charged experiences
5. Variety and intensity of the sensory reactions involved in the experience
6. Absence of irrelevant distracting factors such as hunger and worry
7. Degree of attention to and concentration upon the experience
8. Physical fitness

Because of the difficulty of arranging classroom learning situations in which favorable conditions with respect to all these factors are present, it is necessary to strengthen initial learnings by drill and review. Properly used, developmental methods are effective in promoting satisfactory retention. While appropriate recitation procedures such as skill in questioning and giving assignments are important, they are poor substitutes for really challenging, lifelike problems in the classroom.

The principles of drill applicable to retention of knowledge are analogous to those for the development of skills and habits. These principles are discussed in Chapter 14.

Teaching for understanding

The distinction between acquiring information without understanding it well and acquiring information which is relatively well understood is of great importance in teaching. To acquire information with relatively little understanding (1) is difficult and requires more time than it is worth in most instances; (2) taxes student interest and tends to build unfavorable student attitudes toward the subject, the teacher, and the school; (3) yields the learner little satisfaction in its acquisition; (4) means that the student will be able to make little use of it and is likely to misapply it; and (5) fails to furnish the learner with basic understanding which would enable him to learn and understand other things better.

Many schoolboy boners are the natural results of learning without understanding, for example,

The circulatory system consists of veins, arteries, and artilleries.
Socrates died from an overdose of wedlock.
Wifehood indicates a woman's martial status.

A large proportion of misunderstandings and hence limited, ineffective, or wrong learning results from the learner's lack of knowledge of the precise meaning of words. No matter how much he may recite acquired information, it is of little or no value to him if he does not know the meaning of the words or the significance of the information with respect to its uses and implications. For this reason alone, if for no other, teachers should take especial care to see that learners know the meaning of all important words in the more important materials being studied.

Understandings involve a knowledge of the implications, meanings, and significance of units of information, e.g., the importance of a knowledge of the relative merits of different brand names of canned foods in a unit on consumer buying. Understanding also involves the answers to questions as to how something behaves under various conditions, its uses, and its properties—e.g., what happens to a copper wire when too much resistance is developed to an electrical current.

Understandings are also concerned with the significance of each of the steps in a process and of the sequence of steps. In problem solving, for example, one gets the problem in mind, searches for pertinent data, arrives at a tentative hypothesis, and checks the tentative hypothesis for verification.

Understandings likewise deal with cause and effect and other relationships such as concomitant variation (e.g., height with weight, salary and experience, intelligence and scores on art aptitude tests). In the development of understandings, the following procedures, discussed more fully elsewhere in this volume, are useful:

1. Explanations—verbal and with illustration
2. Problems of application
3. Problems of evaluation
4. Discussions among learners
5. Visual and auditory aids
6. Methods; developmental methods as opposed to authoritative methods

Another important type of knowledge is the general concept, e.g., the nature of social responsibility, of a typhoon, of the poverty of India. Concepts include definitions. The increase and enrichment of concepts is one of the most valuable educational services a teacher can render a pupil, and yet the "schoolmarm," the novice, and the lesson-hearing type of teacher are ineffective at producing this precious type of educational growth.

ACQUISITION OF HABITS AND SKILLS

The psychology of habit formation and the psychology of the development of skills are very much the same. A *habit* is an acquired propensity for the organism to behave in the same pattern every time a certain condition or set of conditions is present in the environment or behavior of the organism or in both. A *skill* is the developed efficiency in some procedure. Both habits and skills may be physical in nature, or social, or intellectual. Handling a knife and fork or tying a bow tie are physical skills, getting along with people or managing a meeting are social skills, and reading and thinking are intellectual skills. Our procedure of dressing in the morning is very largely physical habit, our greetings to individuals when we meet them through the day is social habit, and our insisting upon having adequate data before arriving at conclusions is intellectual habit.

The fundamental principles underlying the acquisition of habits and those underlying the acquisition of skills are very much the same. Fundamental is the factor of *repetition*. A habit results from going through the same behavior pattern a number of times under the same environmental situation or conditions. A skill results from repeating a certain behavior pattern and improving it with respect to speed and accuracy, accuracy meaning effectiveness with respect to a given objective.

In acquiring both habits and skills, it is most important to repeat the behavior pattern without exceptions. Failure to perform in the given pattern under the given situation in forming a habit and failure to behave in exactly the same way and in the same sequences (except as limitations of the present ability of the individual may prevent) in developing a skill should be avoided in the establishment of satisfactory behavior patterns.

In both types of learning, opportunities for repetition should not be spaced far apart, especially in the first stage of learning. For economical and effective learning there must be interest and understanding of need, use, skill, or desire to be able to achieve the skill. This is especially true of the development of a skill. To insure the certainty of performance in the case of habit and improvement in the case of a skill, the performance must be associated in the mind of the learner with pleasurable consequences, especially in the case of skill development, e.g., satisfaction resulting from the knowledge or the expectation of improvement which more than compensates for whatever fatigue or boredom accompanies practice. Unpleasant experiences associated with habits or skills tend to cause the habit or skill to disappear or to slow down its development.

Skills and habits, both physical and mental, when once developed to a reasonably high degree of certainty and efficiency are relatively permanent acquisitions, far more so than detailed information. For that reason, as well as by reason of the essential nature of a great many skills and habits as integral parts of important education, the teacher must be alert to realize when the opportunity is at hand to contribute to the formation of a desirable habit or the development of a useful skill.

ACQUISITION OF IDEALS AND ATTITUDES

Teachers are ordinarily not so effective in developing the ideals and attitudes which are desired outcomes of school experiences as they are in developing skills, habits, information, and generalized ideas and concepts. This is unfortunate, for ideals and attitudes are very powerful determinants of human behavior. They constitute the sine qua non in education for good citizenship, the most important objective of education.

The teacher's relative ineffectiveness in developing ideals and attitudes results from three factors: (1) the degree of possession of an ideal or an attitude is relatively difficult to measure; (2) the contribution made by teaching for a week, a month, a semester, or a year is rarely measurable in the case of most ideals and many attitudes; and (3) the development of almost all desired ideals and most attitudes is the result of school experiences in many school subjects and in all grades, and out-of-school experiences at home, at play, in leisure reading, at church, and elsewhere.

Procedures in development

The methodology effective in developing ideals and attitudes is not as well developed as is the methodology of stimulating the acquisition of information, or that of developing habits and skills. Ideals and attitudes cannot always be approached directly and in a simple fashion. The learning of a number fact, a date, a rule, or other sort of fact or the acquisition of a skill is something which may be assigned as a lesson for a day or a week or a month, and teacher and learner may proceed consciously and directly to facilitate the learning process. On the other hand the development of an ideal of being helpful to others or an attitude of openmindedness with respect to people of other nationalities is the outgrowth of many experiences distributed over a number of years.

The development of ideals and attitudes does not lend itself to a simple, direct procedure. A given ideal or a given attitude can rarely be assigned for study. In fact, contributions to the development of ideals and attitudes almost invariably accompany the acquisition of more specific skills, habits, and information. Naturally, teachers tend to focus upon developing the outcomes which are the immediate objectives of the particular day or unit, toward which progress can be measured easily.

It is clear however that ideals, attitudes, and interests are powerful influences on and determinants of human and social progress and happiness, and that, once acquired, they continue to function long after the great bulk of information has sunk below the level of ready recall.

Ideals. Educationally and psychologically speaking, an ideal is a standard of perfection accepted as such by a particular individual or group of individuals. The meaning of *ideal* therefore involves the element of subjectivity. It is most commonly used to connote a standard of excellence or a person or object possessing excellence toward which or whom the individual or individuals who experience the idealizing have an emotionalized systematic reaction. This emotionalized reaction is one of admiration, or of wishing to be or to be like.

Among ideals which are important educational objectives may be mentioned the following examples, which are classified as to types:

1. Honesty, reliability, fairness, thrift, capacity for service to others, characteristic repayment for services and favors
2. Certain dimensions and patterns of bodily figure, physical beauty, physical strength, physical skills
3. Facility of speech, ability to think clearly
4. Social popularity, social graces, leadership, good fellowship

All the ideals listed above meet social approval. Many persons accept less desirable ideals, e.g., sharpness in business deals, power over other persons, sexual sophistication, social toughness, lack of conscience, ostentatious display of bravery or of material possessions, and ability to deceive others.

Obviously it is of great importance that the ideals of the greatest value to society are inculcated. Wherever high ideals are not present, lower ones are certain to exist. The behavior of any individual is determined to a great extent by the character and strength of his ideals, for it is in great part an attempt to realize those ideals.

The basic psychology and methodology of the development of ideals cannot easily be expressed in terms of specific procedures or techniques. It involves many procedures and techniques used in working toward other types of outcomes. The most important principle probably is that the learner shall have contact with the desired ideals in the form of reading, discussion, or observation of individuals possessing the ideal qualities under such conditions as will present the ideal in a favorable light.

Opportunities occur daily in almost every class for children to establish some desired ideal or to strengthen those they already possess. Either directly or by implication one or more of the desired standards can be brought into the consciousness of learners in such a way as to promote acceptance. The most effective type of approach is through personification. Children, especially, are likely to accept or develop ideals which are characteristic of some individual whom they admire. Perhaps members of their own group possess the same ideals, or perhaps the individual represents an ideal already held by the youngster. For example, if a much publicized war hero, athlete, or movie star or some well-liked older relative or neighbor possesses a good characteristic, manner, or standard of thought or action, there is considerable likelihood that a child will idealize that characteristic, particularly if the characteristic is logically associated in some way or another with the success of the one admired. To be sure, there is no certainty that the admirer will idealize all or any of the good characteristics of the hero, but the chances are favorable that the hero will become one source of ideals.

The opportunities to bring to the attention of young learners desirable ideals as portrayed by fictional characters and historic personalities are very great in teaching literature, history, and current events. There are also numerous opportunities in teaching science, art, music, and other subjects to point out leaders in these fields deserving of emulation and likely to inspire. It is effective to bring to the attention of learners contemporary, conspicuous individuals who possess one or more of the desirable characteristics. Opportunities to present ideals in the abstract—e.g., accuracy of calculation, neatness of written work, intellectual honesty, and service to humanity—occur in teaching every subject. Perhaps one major caution should be stated here as a fundamental principle: *teachers must be adroit in the development of ideals.* Methods too obvious, too energetic, or seemingly lacking in sincerity are not only likely to prove ineffective but may actually tend to arouse antagonism or to promote indifference.

Attitudes. Educationally and psychologically speaking, an *attitude* is an individual's predisposition toward other persons, ideas, institutions, practices, or questions. Following are some illustrations of attitudes to the development of which teachers should make important contributions:

> *Favorable attitudes toward:* our social institutions, practices, and principles, e.g., democracy, right of free speech, cooperation, education, freedom of religious worship, thrift, peace, and logical thinking
>
> *Attitudes of tolerance toward:* individuals of races, nationalities, and religions other than one's own; beliefs, practices, and opinions of others which are contrary to one's own but which are not clearly contrary to the welfare of the nation and society
>
> *Unfavorable attitudes toward:* immoral, unethical, and antisocial principles and practices, e.g., waste, class distinction, physical violence, superficiality, cruelty, hypocrisy, and dishonesty

It is not easy or necessary to make sharp distinctions between ideals and attitudes or to attempt to plan a different method of teaching for each. They are quite similar in nature, overlapping in characteristics, complementary and mutually supporting each other, and the methods of developing the two types of outcomes are almost identical. It is important for teachers to realize the educational importance of ideals and attitudes, to watch alertly for opportunities to contribute to the development of desirable ideals and attitudes, to avoid attempts to force them unwisely by lecturing, "preaching," or compelling conformity, and to seek their development in concrete and specific situations rather than in verbal and abstract forms.

Noncurricular contributions

The ideals and attitudes of children tend to grow out of and be influenced by the ideals and the standards of their playmates and of their teachers as they come to know them in the daily school work. They grow out of reflection and daydreaming stimulated by biography, literature, and other factual and fictional materials. The fairness, patience, forcefulness, aggressiveness, pleasantness, democracy, sympathy, neatness of appearance, masterliness, frankness, poise, and good judgment of a classroom teacher do much to help shape ideals and attitudes of pupils. They also may have their origin in all sorts of group activities and associations, such as a playground, games, scouting, and camp fire activities. They are continually being strengthened or reshaped by experience within and outside the class. They are rarely developed well by continued "preaching."

ACQUISITION OF TASTES AND INTERESTS

Whether or not one is educated is as much a matter of what tastes and interests he has acquired as what he knows, if not indeed more so. The truly successful teacher is one who not only can assist learners to acquire a considerable degree of mastery of the subjects taught, but also leaves her students with a desire to learn more and with abiding interests which will cause them to continue to learn and to engage in activities based upon what has already been learned. John Ruskin, the great nineteenth-century English philosopher and writer, said, "Education is not so much coming to know what one ought to know as it is coming to behave as one ought to behave."

Opportunities for development

The master teacher is always conscious of the importance of guiding learners in the acquisition of desirable tastes and interests and always watching for opportunities to contribute to their development. The superior teacher of elementary school science, for example, utilizes the available opportunities to develop interests in various fields of her subject, in procedures, discoveries, unsolved problems, scientific movements, and the pioneers and great men of science.

The superior teacher of social studies leaves her class with interests in new developments in government; in group approaches to the solution of problems of living; the people of other countries and our relationships with them; and current local, state, national, and international problems.

The superior teacher of English strives to develop not only a taste for and interest in good reading in general, but also an urge to understand the relationships between literature and life, in human nature, social and psychological behavior, and human emotions and customs.

Teachers of art and music have always had as a most important objective the development of interests in and tastes for reasonably good art and music, though teachers may properly attribute their ineptness in attaining such objectives to their emphasis upon information and skills, a weakness shared by many teachers of literature.

Procedures in development

Individual tastes and interests have their origin in meaningful experience. Initial experiences do not always breed tastes and interests; indeed, often there is at first a slight distaste and lack of interest sometimes amounting to boredom. This constitutes a challenge to skilful teaching. Continued contact with ideals under favorable circumstances will, except in a minority of cases, beget interest.

The most effective teachers are neither discouraged nor irritated by evidence of initial dislike or lack of interest and are not too much encouraged by immediate interest or what apparently is the quick development of taste. Continuing development of worthy interests is dependent to a large degree upon the teaching.

The master teacher also recognizes and makes appropriate provision for the fact that tastes and interests are individual matters. Not all children can be expected to be, nor is it desirable for all to be, interested in the same thing and possessed of the same tastes. The important consideration is that each child increases the keenness of his interests and tastes for better things.

Much teaching is of the type sometimes referred to as "appreciation teaching." It involves not only the development of tastes and interests and frequently of ideals and attitudes, but also the information, understandings, and skills involved in analysis and evaluation. Since it involves the development of all these outcomes, the successful appreciation "lesson" is in practice a combination of several of the principles and techniques for developing all those various types of outcomes.

Following are suggestions which may prove useful to teachers in teaching for development of tastes. Most of them apply with appropriate modification of wording to the development of ideals, interests, and attitudes.

1. Employ subject matter appropriate to the age and maturity of the pupils. Developing taste is a slow process, and the level of subject matter cannot with success be elevated abruptly. Subject matter beneath the level of development of the child is likewise ineffective.

2. The teacher should show some enthusiasm for the material. She should not be effusive or gushing, but sincerely appreciative.

3. Care should be taken to avoid overanalysis. The mechanical dissection of a beautiful piece of literature is not likely to arouse the desired appreciation.

4. Do not force the student to express his reaction. While opportunity should be provided for spontaneous expression, and while such expression should be mildly and judiciously commended, no pressure should be brought to bear. A premature expression, especially if forced, is likely to be unfavorable or hypocritical. It must be remembered that the better tastes develop slowly.

5. Do not attempt to standardize results in developing appreciations. Tastes differ, and they develop unevenly. Wide individual differences must be expected, and these will require patience and careful procedure.

6. Students should not be talked into "appreciation." Appreciation should grow out of direct experience. A pupil should be led to discover points of beauty or enjoyment and should not have these thrust upon him.

7. The pupil's possession of productive technique may enhance appreciation, and usually does, but compulsory training in productive technique may develop attitudes which will hinder the development of the desired attitudes or interests.

8. Ideals are best acquired in the concrete. Performance, even if fictitious or imaginary, is superior to abstract concepts.

9. Care must be taken to prevent digression or distraction which will arouse conflicting or incongruous feeling-states.

10. Care should be taken to keep in the background the teacher's intention to develop appreciation.

11. Appreciation of thought should not be sacrificed to appreciation of form; the former is intellectual, the latter sensuous.

12. Newly found interests and tastes should be cautiously directed into satisfying activities. Care must be taken, however, not to force these. Haste never made waste more certainly.

13. If after a fair "exposure" the material used does not bid fair to arouse favorable attitudes, persistence may not avail anything. A change of diet may serve much better.

14. As far as possible, the student should find esthetic or moral values himself. Ideals are naturally discovered; they are rarely taught. Moralizing is ordinarily unwise and to be avoided.

CONCOMITANT OUTCOMES

Every teacher knows that when she is teaching for certain objectives, to produce certain outcomes of teaching, the effects upon the pupil and his educational growth are never confined to effects relative to the objectives and outcomes sought. The incidental or by-product effects or outcomes are commonly rather important; indeed, they are frequently more important than the outcomes intended.

This is a matter of prime importance in connection with the incidental effects of types of motivation of learners. As was pointed out more fully in Chapter 6, teachers who induce their students to engage in learning activities in such a manner as to develop unfavorable attitudes "kill the goose that lays the golden eggs." Such a procedure is clearly one that obtains an immediate and often ephemeral educational growth at the expense of forever stunting or preventing a greater growth through the years to come.

A multitude of ideals, attitudes, interests, tastes, general ideas, and information are in the process of growth, or ready to be stimulated, at all times. The teacher is often unconscious of the effects of teaching and learning activities in regard to these outcomes. Care must be taken to keep to a minimum such concomitant outcomes as:

1. Development of misunderstandings, misconceptions, and false impressions
2. Development of unfavorable attitudes toward subjects, persons, ideas, or practices, attitudes which are either unfair, uncalled for, or not to the interest of the learner or of society, e.g., an attitude of hostility toward all Russians, an attitude of superiority toward Chinese, or an attitude of resentment toward constituted authority
3. Destruction of potential or existing interests in any field of thought and study or any worthwhile activity
4. Development of unworthy tastes, e.g., for cheap literature, movies, or recreational activities
5. Development of indifference toward thrift, the feelings of others, responsibility for the general welfare, good speech, or good manners
6. Development of rivalry, selfishness, self-centeredness, superiority, inferiority, dislike of teacher and school, etc.

Merely because it is difficult to measure adequately pupil growth in ideals and interests, the teacher should not permit herself to underestimate the importance of these types of educational outcomes. The fact that they are not objectives peculiar to the particular field or subject taught by a given teacher should not cause her to shelve responsibility for contributing her share to the development of important outcomes.

QUESTIONS, PROBLEMS, AND EXERCISES

1. What is the difference between "knowing" a specific fact and knowing its meaning—between learning a specific fact and learning its meaning?
2. Which is more important: our knowledge or our interests and attitudes? knowledge or conduct? habits or skills?
3. What is a concept? Mention three. Give some suggestions for leading young persons to acquire a given concept.
4. Select some school subject (e.g., science). Mention several developmental methods commonly employed in it; several authoritative methods.
5. Be able to discuss in class "teaching for understanding," mentioning its importance and its methods as applied to some one school subject or field with which you are familiar.

6. Select a school subject and mention four to six skills to the development of which that subject should contribute.

7. What are the most important principles to observe in developing a skill? a habit?

8. Select a school subject and mention four to six ideals or attitudes to the development of which that subject should contribute.

9. What are the most important precepts for teachers for developing desirable ideals and attitudes?

10. Select a school subject and be able to tell what tastes or interests the subject should contribute.

11. Mention several very important general or concomitant outcomes to the development of which every teacher and every subject should contribute.

12. Which types of outcomes are usually overemphasized and which ones underemphasized and why?

SELECTED SUPPLEMENTARY READINGS

BALDWIN, ALFRED L. *Behavior and Development in Childhood.* New York: The Dryden Press, Inc., 1955.

Chap. xvii, "The Acquisition of Habits." Discusses the importance of habit formation as a learning process and conditions which favor the reinforcement of this type of learning.

GATES, I. ARTHUR. *Educational Psychology,* 3d ed. New York: The Macmillan Co., 1948.

Chap. xiii, "The Development of Meanings." Offers suggestions for assisting students in acquiring concepts and meanings.

McCLOSKY, GORDON, ZENO B. KATTERLE, and DELMAR T. OVIATT. *Introduction to Teaching in American Schools.* New York: Harcourt, Brace & Co., Inc., 1954.

Chap. viii, "What is Learning?" Presents the modern concept of the process of learning, with especial attention to basic intellectual and motor skills.

MURSELL, JAMES L. *Developmental Teaching.* New York: McGraw-Hill Book Co., Inc., 1949.

Chap. x, "The Development of Aesthetic Responsiveness." Presents the nature of aesthetic responsiveness and the basic psychology of its development.

QUILLEN, I. JAMES. "What Are the Basic Concepts to Be Developed in Children," *Readings in Educational Psychology,* JEROME M. SEIDMAN (ed.). Boston: Houghton Mifflin Co., 1955. Chap. x.

Suggests that the social concepts to be developed in children should be selected on the basis of their social significance and persistence.

SAYLOR, J. GALEN, and WILLIAM M. ALEXANDER. "Outcomes Desired from School Experiences," *Curriculum Planning for Better Teaching and Learning.* New York: Rinehart & Co., Inc., 1954, pp. 213-41.

A short history of the selection of educational objectives by various groups based on ever changing concepts.

8

CLASSROOM SOCIAL BEHAVIOR

One of the most important outcomes of a program of elementary education is the personal and social adjustment of pupils. Misbehavior is a symptom of the disorganization of organic and environmental factors which are basic to satisfactory personality development. Since many causes of maladjustment often occur in the early years of a child's life the symptoms should be identified and a program of correction should be initiated in the elementary school. If the causes are not removed until the child becomes an adolescent or adult, the problems of maladjustment become increasingly difficult of solution. A constructive program is especially needed in the lower elementary grades to prevent the child from becoming confused and frustrated as he transfers many of his activities from the home to the school situation.

The principal function of discipline in the elementary school is to assist each pupil to develop the abilities, attitudes, and habits essential to intelligent self-direction. The teacher has the responsibility of arranging opportunities for the pupil to acquire sound personal values and social adequacy through participation in his play and work group. The factors which prevent effective learning also hinder personal and social adjustment. Thus the establishment and maintenance of a school environment which stimulates and promotes effective learning also contributes to the pupil's personality development. A child's success or failure in one aspect of his total personality growth affects his development in all other aspects. The difficulties encountered by a child in his relationships with other pupils and his teachers may appear to grow out of his general dissatisfaction with school.

Most teachers who are genuinely interested in helping children become happy, well-adjusted individuals can acquire the necessary understandings and skills by diligent study. To assist pupils in making satisfactory personal and social adjustments, it is essential that the teacher—

1. Possess clear insights into the psychological and sociological concepts of rational human behavior.
2. Be aware of the implications of school discipline for individual character development and democratic living as well as success in teaching.
3. Perceive the interaction of environmental and organic factors in personality development.
4. Recognize the necessity of studying children as individuals and as members of groups to discover clues to each child's concerns, needs, interests, and behavior patterns.
5. Possess effective techniques of studying children.
6. Acquire the skill and artistry to assist children in finding their own solutions to problems in the area of personality development.
7. Understand social peer adjustments.

INFLUENCES UPON CHILD BEHAVIOR

Social and economic status

In order to understand and direct a child's behavior in an intelligent manner, the teacher should recognize that individual behavior is in part the resultant of many forces in the local community operating singly and in combination. Some of these forces are economic; others are rooted in the mores of the community, including the prevailing standards of conduct of adolescents and adults.

Children's normal idealistic outlook and sense of fairness tend to cause them to ignore superficial differences and judge persons on the basis of their intrinsic worth. However, if contrary attitudes are deep-seated in the community, and especially if parents emphasize differences in wealth in their conversations with their children, these ideas may be reflected in the behavior of elementary school children.

Gangs may be formed on the basis of financial or social standing of families. It is not uncommon for the "dead-end boys" or ostracized minority groups to clash in acts of violence with the sons of the elite. Students of juvenile delinquency among boys are convinced that the inability of many boys to have the things their associates possess is the source of many crimes against property.

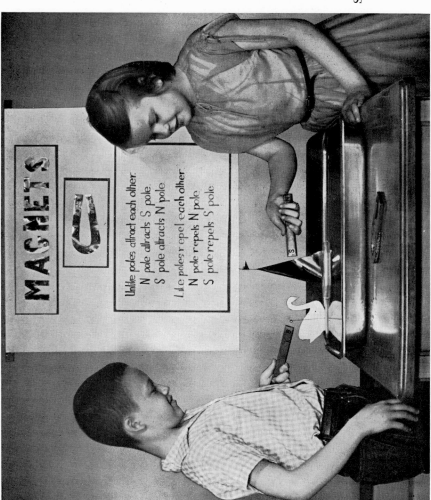

Science—Language Arts. Application of language skills.

Learnings and materials paced to children's abilities and interests practically eliminates disciplinary problems. (Weymouth Public Schools, Weymouth, Massachusetts)

The responsibility of the teacher is to assist pupils in the development of a sound set of values. There is need also for the schools to exercise leadership in the education of adult members of the community regarding what should constitute the basis of respect for human personality.

Home and family

A child's behavior is particularly influenced by his home environment. The standards of conduct of his parents are very commonly reflected in the child's acceptance or rejection of their behavior patterns. The parents' desire to dominate the child's thinking or their willingness to emancipate him in this respect is an important factor in the pupil's ability to assume responsibility for his own behavior in school. Discord in the family resulting from differing opinions of the mother and father in regard to the severity or the methods of discipline often results in confused and inconsistent child behavior. Discord and bickering in the home, growing out of financial strains or marital incompatibility, are conducive to emotional disturbances of the child.

The presence of a more talented brother or sister, or a "favorite" child in the home, may cause deep resentment on the part of the less favored child. This may take the form of an attitude of indifference ("don't care") or one of shame and humiliation. The child who is a member of a foreign family or minority race which has been subjected to acts of discrimination in the community may encounter difficulty in making satisfactory adjustments to the school group. He may become unduly sensitive to the normal reactions of other children to him and react in turn by withdrawal or overcompensation.

Emotional tensions growing out of home conditions can frequently be alleviated by assisting the child in interpreting the situation in relation to the long-term factors in his development. Interviews with parents and discussions of the problems of child behavior in parent-teacher association meetings may be fruitful. Adult education courses for parents also present opportunities for discussion of the rearing of children.

Physical health and development

Studies of school children reveal that at least one-third are handicapped by serious defect or illness and that another third have minor defects. Intellectual, social, emotional, and physical traits are so intimately interrelated in their development that diagnosis and treatment of physical defects are essential in an education program. Many problems of learning and behavior can be traced directly to the child's physical handicaps. Feelings of physical inadequacy frequently result in social maladjustment and acts of overcompensation. This is especially true if the handicap is serious enough to prevent the child from participating in games and sports.

Many problems of discipline grow out of the restlessness of children resulting from the overactivity of certain endocrine glands. Malnutrition, poor vision, skin disorders, and defective hearing may contribute to unsatisfactory achievement and irritation with the school situation.

While the teacher cannot be expected to become an expert diagnostician of physical disease, she should be able to recognize the signs of malnutrition and of mental and physical fatigue as bases of irritability and other forms of maladjustment. Proper seating arrangements, adequate lighting, hot lunch programs, and health instruction represent a few of the most important things a school can provide in assuming its responsibility for the physical welfare of children.

Basic needs

About 60 per cent of discipline problems involve both individual case history and psychological structure of the group. Basic to an understanding of child behavior is a recognition of their basic needs. Every child needs to have feelings of security and belonging and a growing sense of adequacy or success. Failure of the teacher to take these emotionally charged factors into consideration inhibits the development of satisfactory personality traits and effective learning on the part of children.

Feelings of security are developed in young children through expressions of affection, confidence, interest, and understanding by parents and teachers. The child who is continually thwarted acquires feelings of resentment against adults. He feels that he is helpless against what he believes is unfair treatment by teachers and parents. Typical of this attitude is the expression, "Wait till I grow up; I'll show them." This feeling of injustice may cause the child to react to the teacher by surly withdrawal or open defiance. These attitudes can be changed in time by patience, kindness, and good will. On the other hand, if these feelings of injustice are allowed to remain, attitudes of ill will, envy, and bitterness toward other persons may characterize a person throughout his life.

Feelings of adequacy are a result of the child's finding success in his school work. In planning pupil activities, the teacher should consider means by which each child can achieve a proper balance between success and failure. The teacher's understanding of each child's abilities, concerns, and needs is essential to planning such a program.

The blocking of voluntary action is recognized by psychiatrists as one of the conditions that result in emotional upsets. Failure in school blocks the learning process. Occasional failure is disturbing. Frequent failure is tragic. Repeated failure does irreparable damage to the child's personality. One of the most stupid acts of teachers is to require or expect the child to perform tasks he cannot do. School tasks which are too easy for the child are likewise detrimental. Resentment on the one hand and boredom on the other are natural responses of the child.

In her efforts to assist the child in adjusting to a situation in which he has not been successful, the teacher should avoid calling the child's attention to his difficulty by urging him to greater efforts, by pleading with him to "try hard," or by telling him that his parents want him to succeed. The emotionally charged problem can best be solved by assisting the child to analyze the difficulty and by providing some other stimulus to action in which he may have the satisfaction of success. The teacher should avoid making the failing child feel conspicuous before his classmates. The emotional disturbance is usually only one aspect of a total complex.

Emotional blocks may also develop in school situations in which the child is subjected to very rigid requirements of conduct or achievement. The examination and marking systems in use in many schools are detrimental to the development of feelings of self-confidence and security, both of which are essential to good mental health. The feelings of inadequacy developed by the domination of parents and perpetuated by the enforcement of arbitrary school standards often become the basis of useless fears which prevent the individual from achieving social and vocational efficiency.

A sense of belonging results when the child is accepted by his teacher and group and has an opportunity to share in making plans and participating in the activities of his own age group. A skillful teacher can direct the activities of a group of children to bring all of them into both small group and general group activity. The information obtained by a study of the sociograms (See Chapter 20) of the class provides a basis for the teacher's understanding of the social structure of the group, including the social distances of the isolates from the socially accepted members of the group.

Mental ability

The type, frequency, and seriousness of disciplinary difficulties are often determined by the mental maturity of the individual. The child of low intelligence is susceptible to the suggestions of other persons without discriminating as to their efficacy. He may also encounter difficulty in seeing the implications of his behavior. The lower his level of intelligence, the less able he is to learn from his own experience or that of others.

Many of the problems of discipline, however, arise among children of high intelligence. If the school situation fails to present a challenge for the bright child to exercise his mental abilities, boredom and restlessness may cause him to seek outlets for his powers in undesirable overt behavior. The maintenance of high standards of conduct is dependent, therefore, upon learning experiences of considerable variety and different degrees of difficulty which are appropriate to various levels and types of intelligence.

CLASSROOM BEHAVIOR PROBLEMS

The roots of misbehavior of children in elementary and upper grades lie in early experiences which determine basic adjustments of factors in the home, schoolroom, and themselves. The same disturbing factor will affect children differently. Some become negative, others overaggressive. Even though understanding on the part of the teacher and a friendly school climate will help children overcome problems, some will need special help. Following are some common behavior problems which occur in the classroom, with possible causes and ways of dealing with them.

Having temper tantrums. Causes of temper tantrums are varied. The child may be tired or frustrated by new and difficult experiences. He may be imitating behavior patterns seen in the home, or, if he is insecure at home, he may seek through misbehavior to receive attention from members of the family.

When a child has a temper tantrum, he may be helped by isolating him so that he can gain self-control. An effort should be made to detect the experiences before outbursts and confer with parents or nurse. It is not advisable to aggravate these emotions by punishment. When he is calm and not disturbed he should be rewarded with personal favorable attention. He should be guided and helped in facing new experiences that may be somewhat frustrating.

Being irritable, quarrelsome, and restless. A child may be irritable, quarrelsome, and restless because he is not being stimulated by his school work or because he feels that what he has done is not acceptable. He may be tired or unwell. He may feel insecure or find it difficult to work and play with children.

This situation may be relieved by giving the child work at his own level of accomplishment and by varying his activities so as to maintain his interest. If a lower grade child is obviously fatigued and tired, he should be permitted to lie down and rest.

Being a constant disturber. The child who is constantly disturbing others may be trying to distract attention from his unpreparedness; he may want the approval or attention of the other children; or he may feel inferior and thus be bidding for acceptance. If he has always been the center of attention during his preschool days, he may now be craving the teacher's whole attention.

If a child is not disturbing the class or other children too much, much of this behavior may be safely ignored. If the class is really disturbed, then limits must be set for the disturber. If these limits do not aid him in controlling himself, he must be isolated from the group. By giving the disturber responsibilities so that he can receive legitimate recognition, it is possible that he may give up disturbing others.

Being overdependent. A child may be overdependent on others because his mother has done everything for him and he has not learned to help himself. He also may have demanded his mother's help so as to keep her attention; his early training may have been too severe; or he may not have been able to accomplish whatever he has attempted to do and as a result has given up.

The child who depends on others must be taught how to help himself and how to learn to assume small responsibilities. He needs to be praised for successful efforts. His work and materials must be paced according to his needs and abilities so that it will be possible for him to succeed.

Being passive or indifferent. A passive child may have experienced many failures and so find new situations overwhelming. During his early childhood his training may have been very severe. On the other hand he may have been waited on constantly and as a result is afraid to try new things for himself. He also may be fatigued or hungry. In some cases the work is too easy, so that the child does not need to be an active learner.

There are various ways of inducing active participation from passive children. The teacher may read stories of children who are interested in doing new things. She should find out what the passive child can do and what interests him. She should try letting him work first by himself and then with one or two children.

Assignments in the various areas of learning must be made challenging and significant to passive learners.

Being timid or fearful. Factors related to timidness may be limited experience with other children, feelings of inferiority, doubts about being accepted, or harsh treatment in the home. Many children and adults are fearful of situations or activities that are unfamiliar or strange. As children mature, these fears often increase.

Younger children who are timid may be helped by doing things that they enjoy with the teacher, then with one or two other children, and gradually with a larger group. They respond well to quiet praise for successful efforts. Older children must be helped to find a place in, and acceptance by, their peer group; often they must be helped in facing their difficulties with courage.

Being overaggressive. Overaggressiveness or bullying may be forms of compensation for feelings of insecurity with adults, a sense of inferiority as related to sisters or brothers, a feeling of not being liked by other children, failure to be chosen "it" in games, inability to do the schoolwork or to make contributions in various classroom activities.

To help the overaggressive child, look for evidence of insecurity and try to win his confidence. Let the child know that you like him. Help him to understand that there are certain things that he must do and that, if he will not conform to the accepted behavior of the group, he must be isolated until he can cooperate. Some outbursts of anger frequently are an accumulation of irritations; children should be kept from brooding by taking part in activities that take their minds away from the "hurts." After the storm of anger has subsided, the teacher should talk with the child and discuss his problems with him.

Being a daydreamer. The daydreamer would rather not face reality and prefers to get what he wants through fantasy. He also gains self-satisfaction and security in this manner.

The teacher should note when the child daydreams and find out whether this behavior is related to a certain work period. Observe the things that he can do successfully and provide opportunities for him to do those things. The teacher should consult parents and school social workers.

Being an isolate. An isolate may be a child who is selfish, timid, demanding, either immature or too intelligent in relation to his peer group. He may be shy of being with other children and prefers being with adults, or he may simply not have learned how to participate with other children.

The teacher should provide many opportunities and experiences in which isolates will meet with success, such as making contributions in a group project that will be enjoyed and appreciated by other children. Stories can help them realize that they have social responsibilities, and activities can assist them to get the feeling of being socially accepted. Parents could invite other children to the home and also have the child go to a camp or join a club. The skillful teacher can enlist children who are leaders to assume some of the responsibility in helping rejected children feel comfortable in their groups.

Playing with younger children. Children who constantly prefer to play with younger children usually do so because they are not being accepted by their own age group to the extent that satisfies them. They may wish to dominate the situation at all times. Among this group are children who have poor motor skills, or who are retarded mentally and socially.

To help these children, find out about their mental capacities and motor skills. If the child is mature enough to participate in the games with his peer group, help him develop the necessary skills so that he can take part and thus not interfere with the progress of the activity. Discover his interests and make provisions so that he can work and play with a limited number of children near his own age.

Cheating. Often the classroom situation is responsible for cheating. Exaggeration of the value of grades and rewards, as well as assignments which the child does not understand and cannot do, may lead him to copy the work of classmates and submit it as his own effort. If fear of failure is intense, children will cheat so as to escape this torture.

Usually cheating can be prevented if the teacher evaluates her objectives, attitudes, procedures and adjusts the instructional program so that it will be paced properly. The teacher should be concerned with the kind of effect that the instructional program has on the child. The child should be praised privately for honest efforts, and he should also be given credit for what he does on his own.

Stealing. Young children do not understand the concept of ownership and therefore cannot be said to be stealing when they use or take things that belong to other children. Some children steal because it is the accepted pattern in the home and/or neighborhood. Theft may be the result of poor home training. Again, it may be compensation for rejection or an effort to secure recognition from peers.

Parents should make it possible for children to earn money to buy small things. This helps children to get the feel of proper ownership and thus learn to respect other person's rights to their possessions. The teacher must accept the child's social and economic status and at the same time help him understand that society does not condone theft. The child must learn to accept the consequences of his behavior. The teacher also should ask aid from the principal or visiting teacher in studying the case and in deciding upon treatment.

Violating school regulations. Rules are laws of conduct which have been agreed upon as being necessary to maintain order in a society. These rules or laws have been set up to benefit and protect the majority of individuals.

Freedom in a democracy does not mean that each one does as he pleases, in whatever manner he chooses to achieve his end. Freedom does not mean that children are released from all adult control and from following standards or rules of conduct that have been set up in order to protect all from hazard or harm. Each child must learn that it is necessary to obey rules so as to protect himself and others in a group. Children must understand the reason for rules; they must develop habits of self-control in obeying the rules; they must acquire respectful attitudes for rules and appreciate the efforts of those who are abiding by the rules. Children must be given opportunities to understand and to learn the basic principles of right and wrong and their application to all areas of human relationships. Faulty concepts must be clarified as children develop.

If children cooperate with the teacher in developing rules of conduct for various situations, they will develop an understanding of the value of rules and will acquire the proper kind of attitudes related to the observance of law. As children mature, concepts related to law-abiding citizens will take on wider meaning.

PREVENTIVE MEASURES

There are a few basic considerations which teachers may find helpful in preventing individual violations of good behavior. If at all possible, it is better to prevent undesirable behavior than to try to cope with a classroom situation that has become unruly. Following are some general suggestions:

1. At the beginning of the year, learn the names of the children quickly.
2. With the help of the children, arrange the classroom favorably for work, giving particular attention to—

    a) Grouping chairs and tables as activity demands or, if desks are fastened to floors, using same materials in same area of room.

    b) Arranging the classroom for good group living.

3. Manifest a courteous, friendly attitude toward all children.

4. Guide each child into active participation in a committee, small group, or general class at least once during each phase of the work.

5. Establish friendly relationships with children by—
    a) Talking freely with children.
    b) Listening to the spontaneous comments children make and the ideas and opinions they express as they talk of in-school and out-of-school experiences.
    c) Interpreting the stories they write and the pictures they draw in order to gain clues to their interests and needs.

6. Avoid extreme forms of—
    a) Competition among students.
    b) Pupil dependence upon teacher.
    c) Group pride.

7. Use praise judiciously. When deserved, do not hesitate to make comments on written work and in presence of supervisor or principal.

8. Set standards of achievement in terms of the child's ability.

9. Accept suggestions of children made in group discussions for changes in the classroom situation.

10. Adapt learning activities to the abilities and needs of the children in the group.

11. Utilize children's interests as point of departure in planning, managing, and appraising their activities.

12. Encourage pupil participation in planning pupil activities.

13. Avoid harshness, sarcasm, or nagging.

14. A deterrent to child misbehavior lies in the effective handling of classroom routine—checking attendance, collecting and distributing papers, and arranging instructional materials for prompt and expedient use.

15. Alertness on the part of the teacher to what is happening in the classroom at all times is essential. Eyes that see and ears that hear what is transpiring prevent incipient misbehavior from becoming serious disaffection.

16. The possibility of pupil inattention in the group discussions is greatly minimized if the discussion is truly a clearinghouse for ideas. A repetition of ideas with which children are already familiar is not conducive to genuine interest. When children cannot hear the child who is reciting because of the poor seating arrangement of the class or because of his failure to speak in audible tones, they have a tendency to lapse into habits of inattention and indifference.

17. Children who are given a part in planning and evaluating their classroom activities have less inclination and time for misconduct.
18. Announcing in advance what will happen in the event of misbehavior precludes the possibility of treatment in terms of the needs of the offender.

Every good teacher knows that helping children to use their freedom intelligently and at the same time to be self-directive is not an easy task. She understands that in order to guide children effectively in acquiring those attitudes, habits, and skills needed in adult life, she must continue to improve her understanding of problems related to self-directed control by studying research, by observing other teachers, and by critical self-evaluation. Out of careful analysis of all methods or techniques used in guiding children can come effective ways to help each child build a good foundation for a life that is well adjusted and self-adjusted.

TREATMENT OF MISBEHAVIOR

Pending the arrival of more ideal conditions in home, school, and society, it is not realistic to expect that all forms of pupil maladjustment can be prevented. If an individual's overt behavior is detrimental to his own best interests and those of the school group, it is necessary that his behavior be adjusted directly and immediately. While the child's misconduct may have its origins in the general situation, the form of his behavior is usually specific and individualistic. It is, therefore, impossible to formulate a list of suggestions which a teacher may follow as a general prescription.

Not all children should be reprimanded in the same manner. The shy child must be treated kindly while the deliberately mischievous child may require more vigorous methods of control. There is need at times for placing restraints upon the activities of individuals and groups of children. The way in which the restraints are imposed is especially significant. Under wise teacher leadership, groups can usually be depended upon to set up restraints upon the behavior of the young child. The teacher should remember that the child is usually required by most adults to accept immediately and without question the taboos of human behavior that have required centuries for civilized man to develop.

Punishment approach

Punishment may be necessary at times, but it should be used only when the child does not respond to more positive appeals. Before using a punishment the teacher should evaluate it in terms of the following criteria: (1) Will it modify the child's behavior? (2) Is it adapted to the child's temperament and disposition? (3) Will it help the child in making an adjustment to his environment? (4) Is it related to the offense? (5) Is it reasonably severe? (6) Will it leave little or no resentment, antagonism, or excessive embarrassment?

Punishment is a very difficult technique to use effectively. One child can take it and profit thereby, whereas another child will be injured by it. Punishment in many schools takes the form of isolation or removal of privileges. Teachers frequently isolate children who are disrupting the group. This technique is effective in some cases but does not work well in others. Advantages of isolation are (1) the other children may continue with their work without being interrupted; (2) the offender learns that isolation is the result of not cooperating with the group; (3) it gives him time to become calm in order to be able to work with the group; (4) the disturber learns that in order to be accepted by others, he must meet the standards of behavior established by the group. Disadvantages of the use of isolation as punishment are (1) a child who is emotionally insecure may feel that he is not wanted and therefore become more disturbed; (2) the offender has no opportunity of learning self-control in a group.

Removal of privileges is a good technique to use in many cases if the teacher uses it discreetly. Whenever a child abuses a privilege, an effective punishment is to take away the privilege. Whatever is taken away must be connected with the misbehavior. For example, if a child cannot work without annoying others at the various centers of interest, such as reading table or art center, he is deprived of the privilege of leaving his seat until he can take care of himself. Depriving a child of a privilege that is not related to the offense is very likely to cause him to become resentful. Depriving a whole class of privileges as a punishment for the offense of one or two children is a very ineffective method for all children may become resentful at what is obviously unfair.

Group positive approach

Group control is used very effectively as a positive approach to discipline. Children take part in setting up standards of conduct and therefore know and understand what is expected of them. By using these standards as criteria, each child evaluates his own behavior patterns, and the whole group evaluates the effectiveness of the group working as a unit.

The group should not be used to reward or punish an offender. Children should not be placed in a situation in which they must pass judgment on their friends or playmates. If children are asked to pass an opinion on the misconduct of a special friend the response may be to give him another chance. If they are asked to evaluate the misconduct of an unpopular child, even though his behavior was not as disturbing as that of the friend, the group can be more cruel in giving a verdict than any adult would be. Situations that require children to report the misconduct of their classmates to the teacher often will cause them to lose a friend or to be rejected by the class as a whole or by their peer group. The classroom should be a place where children are kind to each other and not a place where they are encouraged to be cruel.

Natural consequences approach

The method of allowing natural consequences to take their course is very closely related to depriving children of privileges. Every child should have experiences resulting in a natural way from unwise behavior which will help him understand what is meant by a reasoned response. Teachers use this technique frequently when children understand that work must be completed during a certain period and that it is possible for them to complete the task in the allotted time. If instead of doing the work they waste time and do not complete the work, they must use the free time that normally follows the work period. If it should happen to be the recess period, then the play period must of course be forfeited.

A specific case of the use of natural consequences is illustrative: A child deliberately broke an outdoor thermometer that another grade was using in recording temperature over an extended period of time. The teacher, mother, and child decided that the proper thing to do was to replace the instrument and since he deliberately had broken it, he must pay for it out of savings which he had planned to use for a bicycle. Before this incident, this child had caused much grief by destroying things that belonged to other children, but this experience thoroughly put an end to his destructive behavior in school.

Teachers must think through this technique very carefully, for it also does not fit the needs of all children. In some instances, children deliberately may not complete their work; indeed, they would rather suffer the consequences in order that they might avoid certain activities or perhaps to gain prestige in their peer group.

Praise and approval approach

Most children grow and are nourished by praise and approval. If their ideas and suggestions that are practical are recognized, they will be more responsive and cooperative. One of the best ways to motivate learning is the recognition for a job well done. The teacher must be on the alert to give praise at the opportune time. The child who is doing careless work may be spurred on to put forth more effort by a deserved comment as, "Your work is much neater today than it was yesterday. I am wondering if you can do as well or better tomorrow."

Approval can be overdone and lose its effectiveness. Excessive approval may make a child feel insecure if he is not complimented every time that he does a job well. It may also breed jealousy and feelings of injustice on the part of others. Distributing praise carelessly has no merit, since children can quickly detect shallowness and usually will resent it and also may react in unfavorable ways.

CONSTRUCTIVE SCHOOL PROCEDURE

The immediate objective of school discipline is to maintain effective work conditions. One who takes a realistic view of the school must recognize the necessity of a school environment which is conducive to constructive pupil endeavor. Stated in negative terms, it is difficult to establish effective habits of study in a situation characterized by disorderly, antisocial conduct. Children appreciate and profit by mature, intelligent teacher leadership in the maintenance of conditions which prevent confusion and a needless waste of time in their work.

The ability to maintain good order in the classroom has long been considered one of the chief measures of teaching competence. Parents and the general public evaluate the teacher's success largely on the basis of her skill in establishing and maintaining pupil morale. Superintendents and principals attribute more failures of teachers to failure in this area than to any other cause.

The emphasis placed upon this aspect of the teacher's work has caused many teachers to consider maintaining order as an end in itself and thus to isolate and treat it as a separate problem. The evidence is conclusive, however, that effective teaching procedures constitute the surest guarantee of success in discipline. Good order and morale are natural results of the teaching which provides pupils with significant, challenging problems along with facilities and freedom to attack these problems. In considering the relation of ability in discipline to teaching success, the teacher should avoid the error of placing disciplinary practice on the low level of force and arbitrary authority rather than on the plane of social and self-direction.

Planning the constructive program

In planning a constructive program the teacher may need the cooperation of the principal, other teachers, parents, visiting teachers, or community agencies. Often school counsellors can work out effective procedures. All corrective measures must be directed toward the goal of helping each child develop a self-control that will lead to mature self-control. It should be remembered that readjustments often take a long time.

Ascertaining causes of misbehavior

Whenever behavior problems do not improve under normal working conditions but are repeated and become increasingly disturbing, the teacher realizes that something is wrong. She knows that the chronic disturber is as much in need of special help as the child who is deficient in reading or arithmetic. She knows that the cause or causes must be determined and that corrective techniques must be planned accordingly.

In ascertaining causes of misbehavior in the classroom, every teacher should critically evaluate her relationship with the children. Lack of rapport naturally leads to an undesirable classroom situation. If the child finds that the teacher is stable, friendly, pleasantly firm, and understanding of his needs, he usually tends to adjust himself to the conditions and cooperates in maintaining an orderly classroom. He also tends to assume his responsibility as an individual and as a member of a group in solving problems.

Inattention on the part of children, arguing with the teacher, listlessness, and boredom are largely the results of poor teaching. The teacher who does not understand how children learn, who is not familiar with the content that she is teaching, and who does not know how to analyze the various difficulties in the areas that she is teaching will not feel secure. As a result the children are frustrated. A teacher who tries to bluff her way through the day's work usually deceives only herself; even a kindergarten child is usually aware of unpreparedness and lack of planning.

Giving children social responsibility

The social forces present within each school group can be utilized to give children actual experience in making decisions on a cooperative basis. Participation in the democratic process of accepting and sharing responsibility for the general welfare is basic to living in a democratic society. Each individual should fully recognize that his actions are not only significant to himself but also affect the welfare of other members of a group.

In many areas of school life children may properly be given opportunities to make individual choices and assist in making group decisions. In many schools children make decisions under teacher guidance for carrying school tasks through to completion. They make decisions with regard to sources of information, study procedures, and methods of presentation and evaluation of their own activities. The main value of pupil participation in school affairs is that it provides opportunity for the pupils to make value judgments. The number of decisions is of less significance than the manner in which they are made. The important thing is that intelligent, democratic processes are utilized and growth in accepting and discharging responsibility takes place.

Pupil cooperation and participation in management are based upon a concept of pupil-teacher relationship that is far removed from the authoritative teacher role. However, the difference is one of degree and may not be as great as it appears. Pupil responsibility is a sham and pretense unless the teacher is thoroughly convinced that children are capable of developing a system of inner controls of behavior which is superior to any system of external controls that can be devised by teachers or parents.

Basic, therefore, to the effective operation of any plan of pupil participation is belief on the teacher's part in the ability of pupils to participate in planning their own activities in an intelligent manner. The assumption on the part of pupils of such responsibility should be a gradual process, preceded and accompanied by careful guidance in procedure and evaluation of actual problems. Children resent the hypocrisy of make-believe problems.

QUESTIONS, PROBLEMS, EXERCISES

1. Discuss the meaning of discipline and purposes of discipline.
2. How can you distinguish between serious emotional problems and those problems that are a part of normal child development?
3. Write a paragraph on "how setting limits to a child's behavior will help him gain self-control."
4. Explain and defend or refute this statement: "The fundamental reason why children do not act right is because they do not have the conditions for right action"—Francis W. Parker.
5. Organize and present to the class a panel discussion on ways in which effective work situations may be produced.

6. Visit a classroom in which the teacher has good rapport with children. Make a record of what the teacher says and does and note the children's reactions; determine the factors responsible for the teacher's success.

7. Outline a plan of obtaining information in regard to a child whose behavior makes him a problem (that is, plan a case study).

8. Visit a child guidance clinic. Learn about the problems of preadolescent children and the methods used in diagnosing the difficulties and treatment recommended in several cases.

SELECTED SUPPLEMENTARY READINGS

BARUCH, DOROTHY. *New Ways in Discipline.* New York: McGraw-Hill Book Co., Inc., 1949.

This is a book that every teacher and parent should read. Common everyday problems that we face in working with children are discussed in a practical and helpful way. The author cites many concrete examples of children.

McDANIEL, HENRY B. *Guidance in the Modern School.* New York: The Dryden Press, Inc., 1956.

Chap. 3, "Guidance in the Elementary School," thoroughly discusses eight basic principles related to guidance and child development. The elementary classroom teacher's responsibility in school guidance is clarified very effectively.

OHLSEN, MERLE M. *Guidance, An Introduction.* New York: Harcourt, Brace & Co., Inc., 1955.

Chap. 4, "Guidance and School Discipline," presents suggestions that will aid teachers in identifying causes of children's unacceptable behavior patterns. A section is devoted to staff responsibilities for discipline.

OTTO, HENRY J., HAZEL FLOYD, and MARGARET ROUSE. *Principles of Elementary Education.* New York: Rinehart & Co., Inc., 1955.

Chap. xii, "Living With Children." An excellent treatment of teacher's philosophy as related to effective discipline. Definite descriptions of effective discipline are presented in following areas: teacher-pupil planning; first day of school; managing classroom routines; controlling classroom environment; meeting all school problems; meeting individual needs; independent work periods.

THOMAS, R. MURRAY. *Ways of Teaching in Elementary School.* New York: Longmans, Green & Co., Inc., 1955.

Chap. vi, "Modern Techniques in Discipline." Typical causes including teacher-causes of discipline problems are analyzed and positive approaches for the prevention of unacceptable behavior are presented. The problem of applying punishment is discussed.

WINGO, G. MAX, and RALEIGH SCHORLING. *Elementary-School Student Teaching.* 2d ed. New York: McGraw-Hill Book Co., Inc., 1955.

A clear-cut presentation of today's meaning of discipline. Concrete suggestions relative to effective discipline techniques and preventive measures are presented in chap. xii.

9

PLANNING FOR TEACHING

Teaching is one of the most complex and significant of human endeavors. It is complex because of the many intangible values and numerous human factors involved. Its significance lies in its power to shape human destiny for good or ill. No teacher who is mindful of the trust placed in her can be content with anything less than excellence in her work. Although perfection in teaching is achieved by few teachers, it is an ideal worth seeking. It is doubtful that any teacher ever failed to become a better teacher by planning her teaching in advance. It is likewise doubtful that impromptu thought and action ever resulted in peak teaching performance.

In brief, planning—
1. Gives the teacher a clearer comprehension of the objectives of elementary education and the relationship of her teaching to those objectives.
2. Helps the teacher clarify her thinking about the distinctive contribution her teaching subject makes to the objectives of education.
3. Tends to insure that the relative values of various instructional materials and procedures are given proper consideration.
4. Serves to make the teacher more resourceful in recognizing pupils' needs, utilizing pupils' interests, and providing more satisfactory means of motivation.
5. Reduces the amount of trial and error in teaching through a better organization of curricular materials, use of more appropriate methods, and greater economy of time.
6. Wins respect of pupils. They appreciate the teacher who is a learner with them and makes preparation for her work as she expects them to do.

7. Presents one of the teacher's best opportunities for continuous personal and professional growth.
8. Contributes to the teacher's feeling of self-confidence and self-assurance.
9. Aids the teacher in recapturing waning enthusiasms, thereby insuring a fresh, up-to-date presentation of instructional materials.

The majority of teachers in elementary schools have accepted instructional planning as a prerequisite to effective teaching. But it is amazing to discover that not all school teachers recognize the need for planning. The confusion and doubt in regard to planning which seem to exist among many teachers and outright rejection of planning by others can be traced to the following causes:

1. The requirement that lesson plans be made according to certain specifications in order to serve the purposes of supervisors in checking up on the work of the teacher.
2. The heavy teaching schedule of many teachers, which leaves little or no time for any but superficial planning.
3. The apparent success of planless teaching. Many teachers have achieved a fair degree of success, as teaching is measured, without planning.
4. The willingness of many teachers to follow the line of least resistance and thus accept mediocrity.

The scope of adequate planning is as broad as the work of the teacher. Every aspect of her work requires thoughtful consideration in advance. Broadly conceived, planning involves the curriculum, guidance, extracurricular activities, pupil appraisal, and methods of procedure. The discussion in this chapter will be limited to classroom procedures.

PRELIMINARY PLANNING

Teachers and students must make many adjustments in the first days of a school year. The elements in the new situation are novel, and they exist in different combinations from those which the teacher and the students have experienced in any other situation. As new groups are formed for work and play, the teacher faces the problem of helping pupils to establish satisfying personal relations with one another and with her.

The teacher can help reduce any feelings of frustration and insecurity which may arise in the early phases of a course or activity by careful planning of the initial stages of the work. Equally important is the creation of a favorable first impression among the students of the subsequent work in the course. The need for preliminary planning is especially urgent in the case of the beginning teacher or the teacher in a new school.

As a basis for intelligent preliminary planning, the teacher should obtain information concerning the nature of her duties, the school, the students, and the local community prior to the beginning of the school term. While the responsibility for becoming informed in respect to her duties in a new teaching position rests primarily with the teacher, administrative and supervisory officials in many schools utilize various materials and procedures to familiarize new teachers with their duties, such as:

1. Administrative guide or personnel policy handbook
2. Teacher's manual
3. General curriculum guides and courses of study
4. General instructional guides
5. Special bulletins containing suggestions for teaching various subjects
6. Superintendent's bulletin
7. Special bulletins to teachers, such as information for home-room and school club sponsors
8. Reports of special studies of students made by the school
9. Student handbooks
10. Descriptive materials of the local community
11. School records of pupils

In addition to these materials, the new teacher may avail herself of information obtained from other teachers, supervisory and administrative personnel, and local citizens.

Planning for the school year

Prior to the beginning of the school term, the teacher should do some general long-range planning for the school year. A reference to the school's curriculum guides and courses of study will supply facts about the knowledge and skills students should acquire at different grade levels. The broad outlines of the course can then be planned, including a tentative selection of the major units or topics of the course.

The first step in planning a course is to decide on the objectives of the course. This should be followed by a consideration of the scope of the course in terms of the objectives. The third step consists of organizing the content around significant problems or into units of interest. The approximate time allotment for each of the units should be made in terms of its relative value in attaining the objectives of the course. Finally, general plans should be made in regard to the methods of teaching each of the units. Basic to all these decisions is a consideration of the needs, interests, and abilities of the pupils who are to be taught. Less important perhaps, but deserving of consideration in formulating the long-term plan, are the inventories of available equipment, supplementary reading materials, and opportunities for guided field trips to obtain firsthand information on each of the units.

It is usually feasible to make subdivisions of the course for the purpose of establishing a series of more immediate and definite goals than the complete course affords. The work of the semester or year may be divided in one of several ways: (1) It may be organized around a *series of problems or projects*. (2) It may be divided into several coordinate subdivisions of subject matter or *subject-matter units*. (3) It may be organized around some central theme of child interest by setting up *experience units*. (4) It may be divided in terms of intervals of time, that is, by the week or the month. Regardless of the basis upon which the division is made, planning is essential.

If the work is organized into projects, the teacher should become familiar with the various methods of selecting and teaching projects. It is well to remember that pupil purposing is the essence of the project.

While decisions concerning the general scope of the work in a subject can be made in advance, detailed planning of the course should be postponed until the teacher becomes well acquainted with the students as a result of her day-to-day contacts with them.

Planning for the first day

Despite the teacher's limited knowledge of her students, it is necessary for her to make definite plans for the first meeting of the class. Some of the students may attempt to "try out" the new teacher. Other students may come to class with a strong dislike for the subject because of previous unhappy experiences with other teachers of the subject. All the students are returning from a summer vacation during which their interests have been far removed from classroom work.

In planning the first day's work, the teacher should decide definitely how she will handle routine matters and what procedures and instructional materials she will use. Consideration should be given to student seating arrangements, roll call, and distribution of papers.

In formulating plans for the first class meeting, the teacher should decide what approach she should make—whether she should lead the students in a discussion of the course, perform a demonstration, or call on the students to relate some incident which occurred during summer vacation. Some teachers have found the latter procedure effective in breaking down the formality that often characterizes the first meeting of a class.

The teacher should decide in advance what information about the objectives and scope of the course she will give the class and how she will present it. The teacher's plan should provide also for giving the students definite information about the textbooks and other learning materials they will use.

If student participation in planning the learning activities is expected, the teacher should decide what statement to make concerning the possibilities and nature of that participation. The plan should provide for a definite task or assignment for the next meeting of the class.

In planning how the first class period is to be spent, the teacher should consider how the students can be kept busily engaged for the entire period and how the class can be conducted in a friendly yet businesslike manner.

CONTINUOUS PLANNING

Preliminary planning represents an important phase in the endeavor of the teacher to fulfill her teaching responsibilities. Preteaching plans, however, can be formulated only on a tentative basis as broad, general guides to teaching. Continuous adaptation and projection of the initial plans, with due consideration of the students involved, are essential. Appropriate plans for the organization of learning experiences and the methods designed for motivating and directing learning activities can be made only in terms of a particular learner or class. The understanding of students acquired by an alert teacher in her daily contacts with them affords a sound psychological basis for planning classroom teaching.

In contrast to rigid teaching plans made in advance, the development of flexible plans which can be modified as the work of the class proceeds tends to insure the utilization of significant interests of students as points of departure for learning experiences. The evolving development of teaching plans to meet the emerging needs of the students gives the curriculum its truly dynamic character. This is not to imply that the teacher has no responsibility for pre-planning learning activities in situations in which students are involved in the planning. The contrary is true. Careful planning by the teacher, in which she integrates the interests of students into the framework of the essentials of a field of knowledge, is a basic requirement for the successful operation of cooperative learning activities. Thus in planning for teaching, consideration must be given to both the learning materials and the learners.

Cooperative planning

One of the most significant trends in teaching in the elementary school is *cooperative planning* of activities by the teachers. In many schools the need has been recognized for preparing "resource units" as advance guides. The pooled judgments of a great many teachers, principals, supervisors, and curriculum workers are used to build a "frame of reference" for the individual teacher's use in teaching a unit. The resource unit, which should be distinguished from the teaching unit of the individual teacher, is merely suggestive in content and arrangement. It constitutes an outline of the broad scope of the unit prepared on the basis of the combined judgment of a group of teachers, supervisors, and the director of instruction in the schools. The chief features of a resource unit are described in Chapter 11.

Cooperative planning by teachers not only serves the purpose of providing blueprints of a general character for the use of the individual teacher but affords also a valuable experience in mutual professional endeavor. Under the supervision of a competent director of instruction, group planning can serve as an effective means of in-service education of teachers.

Pupil-teacher planning

Another noteworthy development in modern elementary education has been the inclusion of the interests and preferences of children in the teacher's plans for teaching. The acceptance of the idea that the learner should be taken into account has been difficult for many teachers. The theory that the child is immature and therefore not capable of participating in the making of important decisions, even though the decisions affect him directly, appears unsound in the light of our present knowledge of child psychology. Likewise untenable is the narrow concept of democracy upon which many school practices have been based. Democracy implies the opportunity for making choices and assuming responsibility for the results of these choices. It is essential that the teacher have a functional respect for the personality of the child as well as a strong faith in the power of education to make desirable changes in the thoughts and actions of the individual.

The most convincing evidence, however, of the advisability of pupil participation in planning various school activities comes from schools in which the practice has been put into effect. Pupils have demonstrated their ability and willingness to assume intelligent responsibility for their own acts. Pupil morale has been enhanced. Problems of pupil control have greatly decreased, and conditions for satisfactory learning have been established. The teacher who encountered difficulty in leading pupils to accept her purposes as worthy has discovered that shared pupil-teacher purposing is an open sesame to success.

The cooperation of pupils in planning activities may be used in practically every aspect of the life of the school. In matters pertaining to school citizenship, the curriculum, social activities, and classroom procedure, the pupils' active participation has been utilized. In instructional procedures involving the project method, pupils have participated in setting up objectives of the unit, selecting topics for study, choosing curricular materials, making decisions in regard to the methods of study, selecting the manner of presentation of the findings of their study, and evaluating the success of their various activities in connection with the unit.

The leadership of the teacher is essential in guiding these activities into desirable channels but not dictating to the pupils. Many teachers have exercised this guidance function by suggesting lists of activities or readings from which pupils make choices. Other teachers have encouraged pupils to suggest their own lists of activities. A combination of these two procedures by cooperative pupil-teacher planning as the work proceeds is perhaps the best plan.

Teacher-pupil planning does not imply that preplanning by the teacher is nonessential. Effective teacher-pupil planning is a result of reflective preparation on the part of the teacher. The teacher should anticipate and study the needs and the interests of the children in the light of opportunities for cooperative learning, thus making it possible for her to guide children to higher levels of accomplishment. She has thought through the activities that will aid in the development of objectives which are important for various levels of accomplishment in her group. She should evaluate available sources of information. Her plans should be flexible so that they can be adjusted to fit the plans which the children may set up for themselves.

With young children, much of the planning depends upon the teacher's ability to guide their participation in planning. As children become more mature, they should be able to assume more of the responsibilities of establishing the goals to be achieved for the good of all. At any level of the pupils' development, it is the responsibility of the teacher to be able to evaluate the goals set up by children and to give guidance when needed (See Chapter 10 for illustration of pupil-teacher planning of a unit).

LONG-TERM PLANNING

In the section on preliminary planning, it was suggested that the teacher become familiar with the general requirements of the course she is assigned to teach by a careful examination of the courses of study or curriculum guides, textbooks, and other instructional materials available. In many schools, the teacher has considerable freedom in adapting the suggestions in the official course of study to her particular students. In other schools, the teacher is expected to follow rather closely the requirements outlined in the course of study. At the beginning of the school term, the teacher should ascertain the policy of the school in regard to the use of the course of study and, regardless of the school's policy regulating its use, she should acquaint herself with its contents as a basis for planning to teach the course.

As the work in the course proceeds and the abilities and interests of the class become increasingly evident, the teacher should reexamine the course of study with a view to modifying it to the extent permitted by school regulations and to the extent necessary to serve the students' needs. These modifications should and usually can be made within the broad framework of the course of study which can be planned on a long-term basis by the teacher.

Long-term planning of a course involves the following:

1. Formulating the objectives of the course in terms of its distinctive contribution to the total educational experiences of the students
2. Selecting content and learning activities in terms of the objectives of the course
3. Organizing the content into significant units of learning
4. Arranging, at least tentatively, the sequence of units of learning on the basis of their relationship to the objectives of the course and the maturation of the students
5. Making a tentative selection of the teaching procedures to be used
6. Considering the methods of evaluation to be used

Planning units of instruction

In preparing to teach an instructional unit, the teacher should study the suggestions contained in resource units or other source material which may be available to her.

The following suggestions for planning a unit were formulated by a group of teachers and supervisors in the Denver Public Schools:[1]

A. *The teacher does some preplanning.*

The teacher and children will make plans together for carrying on and evaluating the unit which has been selected; but, before approaching these planning situations with the children, the teacher will consult many sources of help and explore possibilities for developing the unit. Having thought through the problems, objectives, and activities involved, she will feel free to let the children express their ideas. Through this background she will be able to supplement their suggestions, broaden their vistas, and help them to set up problems and goals in terms which have meaning to them. The teacher will understand that this preparation on her part is not for the purpose of determining plans for the class but rather is to serve as a background and reservoir of ideas which will assist the class to identify in the unit every problem which may be of concern to the children.

1. She anticipates problems.

During discussions while the children have been agreeing upon their unit of work, they have made comments, expressed ideas, and raised questions. The teacher has noted these and jotted down significant ones. She now examines them to determine special problems which will be of immediate concern to her children. From her own background of knowledge and experience she identifies additional problems which she will suggest for consideration. As an illustration, toys and games which the children bring in to show and to play with just after Christmas may stimulate a general interest in how toys work. The teacher has watched and listened to the children as they examined and played with the toys and equipment. They have discussed the possibility of basing a unit of work on this interest, and have agreed upon it. The teacher will now in her preplanning think through their spontaneous questions and comments and find that they group themselves around such specific problems as ways in which mechanical toys work; ways in which other toys operate through balance, friction, rolling, and so forth; why some toys are self-propelling and others have to be pushed, pulled, and manipulated in various ways; the part that toys play in the everyday life of a child; how all persons, children and grownups, are helped by playing; how toys help us to learn; and why we share toys with others. The teacher will think through such problems in terms of the questions which the children may ask and those which she will suggest for consideration. The teacher should keep in mind the maturity level of the group and should not try to cover all possibilities for learning in this one experience.

2. She identifies objectives and considers ways in which she may evaluate behavior change.

The teacher understands that behavior is fostered and developed most effectively when children are solving problems that are meaningful to them. She understands as well that growth takes place in relation to experience.

---

[1] *Planning and Developing A Life-Experience Unit.* Prepared under the direction of Maurice R. Ahrens, Director of Department of Instruction, Denver Public Schools, 1948, pp. 13–31.

There is continuous development in the over-all pattern of physical, mental, social, and emotional growth. Every experience which the child has contributes in some way to growth in one or more of these areas. Next, there is development in relation to general objectives which apply to all units of work. Every unit should contribute to such broad objectives in social living as ability to work well with others; growing skills in leadership and cooperation; habits of independence in thought and action; attitudes of responsibility, open-mindedness, and consideration of others; and growing skill in critical thinking and making choices, with an attitude of willingness to accept the consequences. As the teacher preplans she will identify experiences which should promote growth toward these objectives. Lastly, there is development in relation to specific objectives which apply to a particular unit. For instance, children may cooperate, make choices, and appreciate the contributions of others equally well whether their problem is "How shall I spend my money?" or "What is there in music for me?" The specific attitudes and appreciations, habits and skills, interests, and ways of thinking which grow from these two problems, however, will be very different.

Specific objectives for the first problem might be "To remember first to buy things I must have" and "To learn to choose things that mean most to me." The second problem might include such objectives as "To make an instrument that I can play in the rhythm band" and "To build up my own list of favorite composers and selections." The teacher will analyze the chosen unit to find opportunities it offers for fostering attitudes and appreciations and for developing specific habits and skills.

In her preplanning the teacher will state the objectives in simple and direct terms so that they may be evaluated in relation to what the child thinks and says and does. She will plan to use objective means whenever possible in measuring growth: observation and recording of behavior, discussion, conference, records of various kinds, tests, and other devices. Then, knowing what the problems are, what behaviors may grow out of them, what techniques may be used to measure growth, the teacher next asks herself, "How?" and considers experiences which must be provided to meet the objectives.

3. She explores possibilities for learning experiences.

The teacher must understand that it is through experiences that the children will grow toward the goals set up. She will anticipate many types of experience and activity necessary to solve the problems. She will consider new types of activity, having discovered, for example, that the children have had many experiences in giving reports and making booklets and movies and need wider experiences in doing, experimenting, going places, and making community contacts.

She thinks of the various ways in which children record information they use in solving their problems: keeping scrapbooks, writing and illustrating stories and articles for group or individual books, organizing information in simple outline form on charts, making diagrams and simple graphs, and keeping a daily "log." If it is a science unit, the teacher considers the possibility of setting up a "laboratory corner" where, with simple equipment gathered by teacher and children, they may carry on experiments which will make their learnings real. The teacher will explore possibilities for field trips and will try to find persons in the community with special interest or experience who may be invited in to talk to the group. The teacher will realize that children learn as they express their feelings and ideas through art and construction activities, through song and rhythm, through poems and stories and dramatizations. Through such experiences the child will have many opportunities to listen, to participate, and to create. The teacher will plan to use available films, film strips, slides, phonograph records, radio recordings, and current radio programs when possible. The teacher realizes that the best learning takes place when as many avenues as possible are opened up, that children learn through their five senses and through emotional and physical responses as well as through mental processes.

The children, when their turn comes to plan, will usually suggest activities in terms of past experience, so the teacher needs a wider list to supplement their ideas.

4. She explores sources of material.

The teacher finds out what materials are available from as many sources as possible. She explores her own room for materials, she scouts about the building for suggestions, and she refers to catalogs from the Department of Special Services. She plans to get pictures, pamphlets, and books from the professional and public libraries. She lists commercial agencies, such as dairy and food councils, railroads, airlines, travel agencies, and industrial companies which furnish film strips, movies, pictures, pamphlets, and other educational materials. She finds that many free and inexpensive materials are available through educational publishing houses and governmental agencies. The children will later locate many other resources and will be responsible for writing to various agencies (only one child's letter to each, however) and for gathering many of the materials. The children will draw upon home and community for all sorts of material: rocks, birds' nests, leaves, fruits, vegetables, boxes, boards, scrap material, recipes, utensils—almost anything that is needed. Persons in the community are also sources for obtaining information.

5. She increases her own background of knowledge.

In her preplanning the teacher studies all available materials which she has collected. She gets some firsthand information from persons in the school or community. She visits places of interest to increase her own knowledge and to find out what the children should look for on their visit. She reads selected books and articles, which she will later put in the hands of the children. She realizes that sometimes she will need to say, "I'm not sure about that. We will look it up together."

6. She considers techniques and ways of organizing the class for work.

In her preplanning the teacher has tentative ideas for ways in which the group should be organized for work. Later as she and the children plan together, she will help them to see the need for these various ways of working.

a. Participating as an entire group in some experiences. The teacher will anticipate class activities, such as taking field trips, seeing movies, listening to speakers, radio programs, and recordings, making general plans, discussing problems and matters of importance to the whole class, and summarizing completed work.

b. Working in small groups to solve definite problems. A child's interest, attention, and participation are more easily stimulated when he is a member of a small group of five, six, or twelve children rather than when he is one of thirty or forty. He feels greater responsibility to the small group and, also, greater security in making his contributions. Small groups can make more effective use of materials, for the children will be referring to varied materials adapted to specific problems and interests. Usually no one text or pamphlet is provided in sufficient quantity to be used by an entire class at the same time. Many varied materials are used because no one book could provide answers to questions which each group of children will ask in relation to their specific problems and interests. The teacher will understand, then, that working in small groups will provide for more effective learning and more adequate use of materials.

The teacher will consider ways in which children may be organized in small groups. One way would be in relation to individual interest in specific problems set up. This plan may be used when a problem, or group of related problems, is to be worked on by only one group of children who would bring their information to the rest of the class. In this case, after a discussion of various problems, materials, and experiences related to each one, every member of the class would identify the problem or group of problems of greatest interest to him and indicate his first, second, and third choices. A committee, with the help of the teacher, would then make up groups based on these choices. Each group would accept responsibility for exploring a particular problem or group of problems and sharing their learnings with the rest of the class. The children would understand that shared experiences must be varied and graphic in order to challenge the attention and further the learnings of all members of the class.

In the elementary school, and especially among the younger children, it often seems best, when all problems are of general interest and concern, for every group to work in turn on each of the problems set up. Each group at a specific time might be working on a different problem and might approach it in a different way, but in the end they would all have done some simple research on every problem, recording information and expressing and sharing ideas. Sometimes groups may be organized by having children choose those with whom they wish to work. This may be done informally or by the use of a sociogram based on each child's choices in response to the question, "With what three children in this class would you like to work in solving the problems we have set up?" Each child, then, in a group so organized feels that he is working with someone whom he has chosen and with those who have chosen him.

As a rule, when working together on common problems and interests, children are not grouped as to mental maturity level. The teacher will realize that this is a situation in which the child who is slower mentally will profit by the discussion, help, and leadership of other children. The teacher will provide, if possible, a few easy reading materials for each problem being worked on and may sometimes have to rewrite material. She will remember that children of any level of ability, but especially the slow-learning child, will gain much information through out-of-school experiences, pictures, discussions, ability to get some information from a page which he cannot read word-for-word, group discussions, and special help from other members of the group. These and many other learning experiences will help the slow-learning child to feel that he is making his contributions to group work along with some of the brighter children of the class. Frequently a special aptitude may help to give the slow learner status—like Ben, who could not read but had a remarkable memory, or Lynn, who was usually chosen to letter charts which the other children organized.

c. Working in flexible, changing groups on art, construction, and other creative activities. The groups organized to work together in gathering, recording, and sharing information on specific problems usually remain the same throughout the unit of work. The grouping, however, during the period when art, construction, and other creative activities are being carried on will be more spontaneous and fluid, the children coming together in twos and threes, or fives and sixes, to work on a common interest. When the picture is painted, the boat completed, the poem written, or the play planned, the little group may dissolve, or it may stay as it is already set up and go on into a new activity. If the entire class is planning a culminating program, such as a play, a puppet show, a movie, or an exhibit, definite groups may be organized to take care of such specific problems as scenery, costumes, script, stage settings, and display centers.

The teacher will do little preplanning for grouping in this freer type of work. She will know only that she must keep ahead of the children with her materials, ideas, and ability to organize the situation from day to day so that worth-while work may be accomplished.

d. Providing for individual contributions to the work of the entire class. The teacher will plan to have each child, as far as possible, make his individual contributions. She will think through the ways in which children, often with the help of their parents, may be provided additional materials and experiences which they will share with the group.

Outlining the unit

In the actual preparation of the unit, the material may be tentatively arranged according to the following outline:

Title of Unit

Subject _____   Grade Level _____
Date _____   Teacher _____

   I. Statement of the major problem (based on student needs)

  II. Teacher objectives—desired student behavior changes including appreciations, attitudes, knowledges, skills, and interests, cooperative work skills

 III. Student objectives—basic understandings, concepts, generalizations, habits, skills, abilities to work with others

 IV. Preliminary teacher planning
    A. Anticipated outcomes
    B. Necessary materials
    C. Preliminary discussion with students concerning unit

  V. Launching the unit
    A. Challenging statement or question by the teacher
    B. Picture displays

C. Striking demonstration before the class

D. Film pertaining to unit

VI. Teacher-student planning

A. Questions and suggestions from students concerning unit

B. Questions growing out of introductory remarks of teacher

VII. Suggested activities

A. Field trips, interviews, group work, reports, panels, committee work, class discussions, etc.

B. Reading and discussing specific assignments in textbooks or other source materials

VIII. Suggested materials

A. Basic and diversified reading references

B. Audio-visual: moving pictures, television, radio, recordings

C. Resource persons

IX. Culminating activities

A. Summarizing findings by individuals and committees

B. Displaying models, pictures

C. Determining what has grown out of the study

X. Evaluation in terms of anticipated outcomes—by teacher and class

XI. Bibliography

A. Teaching materials

B. Student texts and references

C. Audio-visual materials

A unit plan

The following is an example of a plan for teaching a unit which was prepared by a student teacher.

Title of Unit: Birds

Subject: Nature Study   Grade: III
Date: May 1956   Teacher: Margaret Bell

I. Primary Objectives:

1. To stimulate and arouse an interest in the study of birds

2. To help children understand and appreciate the value of birds

3. To develop skills and habits needed in solving problems and in obtaining information about birds such as listening, observing, and reading

4. To provide experiences that will aid each child in developing those habits and skills needed in sharing information, such as discussing and reporting

II. Outline of Teacher's Informational Background on the Robin, Sparrow, Bluebird, and Wren:

A. The bird; its place in nature and relation to man
    1. The bird's place in nature
    2. The bird's relation to man
       a. Scientific relation
       b. Economic relation
       c. Aesthetic relation

B. The bird; its form and function
    1. The wings, form and use
    2. The tail, form and use
    3. The feet and legs, their form and use
    4. The bill, form and use
    5. Sketch of a bird

C. The migration of birds
    1. Origin of migration
    2. The route of migration
    3. The height and speed of migration flight
    4. Orientation and route finding
    5. Distances travelled by birds

D. The domestic life of birds
    1. The nesting season
    2. The nest
    3. The eggs

E. How to study birds
    1. When to look for birds
    2. Where to look for birds
    3. How to study birds

F. Teaching bird study
    1. Show how birds are beneficial
    2. Projects for class work

G. Birds of local neighborhood
    1. Division into life-zones
    2. Nesting birds of local neighborhood
    3. Common birds to study

H. Specific information on the robin, sparrow, bluebird and wren
    1. Descriptions of birds
    2. Their nests, eggs, brood, size of eggs, and color
    3. Their food and habitats

I. Specific information on constructing bird houses

III. Initiating the Unit:

A. Arrange a stimulating and challenging environment by displays
    1. Attractive pictures of birds and a colorful chart showing their nests, eggs, and broods on the bulletin board
    2. Books and magazines obtained from the Audubon Society in the library corner
    3. An exhibit such as bird nests or houses on the science table

B. Tell and/or read stories about different birds

C. Let the children listen to some records of bird songs

D. Show authentic slides of birds in the region

IV. Exploration: (Select the activity that is best suited to the group of children.)

Discovering what children know about birds in a—
A. Class discussion in which—
1. The teacher asks questions and keeps notes on concepts that are inaccurate.
2. Children present their own ideas about a slide that they have seen without any preparation for the experience.
B. Show and tell period: Children volunteer their information about birds. They should not prepare the content beforehand.

V. Purposing and Planning:

In a teacher-pupil discussion period—
A. Find out what the children wish to learn about birds
B. Determine some specific problems to be solved
C. Plan ways of solving the problems
D. Occasionally, but not always, decide upon the culminating activities

VI. Solving the Problems: (Note: One problem out of a total of six is presented.)

Problem I. In what ways are birds important to man?
A. Content
1. Birds make the world happier and more pleasant and beautiful.
2. Birds help man by destroying harmful bugs and insects, eat weed seeds and help to reseed forest areas.
3. Birds help man by destroying rodents such as rats and mice.
4. Birds furnish food for man (game and domestic birds).
5. Birds furnish feathers for pillows, penpoints, and decorative hat bands.
6. Birds have had the greatest interest and fascination for artists, sculptors, and poets.
B. Experiences suggested for this problem
1. Plan ways of solving the problem
2. Read for information
3. Listen to stories and poems about birds
4. Listen to records on songs of birds
5. See colored pictures of birds
6. Discuss ways in which birds help us
7. Give oral reports on observations of birds doing something for us
8. Write original stories on "one way in which (name of bird) helps me."
9. Learn to recognize bird calls
10. Draw and label their own posters and/or pictures relative to the problem
11. Make a frieze of ways in which birds help us
C. Suggested materials
1. RCA Victor Record: The Bird Call Game, WY 4002
2. Victor Record 17735, Songs and Calls of Our Native Birds, Gorst. No. 1, 2, 3, 4

3. For dramatic play use Victory Rhythm Album No. 1, Flying Birds—soaring, dipping, circling

VII. Culminating Activities:

A. Major (one of the following activities may be used)
 1. A program for parents or another grade in school including original stories and poems; giving bird calls; showing and telling about pictures, posters, frieze; singing songs
 2. An exhibit in classroom displaying pictures, posters, frieze, class scrapbook on birds, individual books, bird houses made by the children, bird books, original stories and poems
 3. Enroll in Junior Audubon Society

B. Minor (using the materials not used in the major culmination)
 1. Sending the class or individual scrapbooks on birds to a children's hospital
 2. Placing the frieze about birds in one of school building's halls

VIII. Evaluation:

 1. Anecdotal records on leadership, assuming responsibility in solving problems, cooperation as revealed by adjustments and responses
 2. Teacher observes children as they solve the problem
 3. Children and teacher use the standards planned cooperatively during class work

IX. Leads into Other Units:

A. Unit on other forms of nature
B. The idea of flight may lead into a unit on airplanes
C. Unit on preservation of wild life
D. Unit in geography on outstanding landmarks and also inhabitants of cold and hot climates (related to the problem on the migration of birds)
E. Unit in science on weather
F. Unit on how other animals are beneficial to man

X. Bibliography:

A. For Teacher
 1. Barruel, Paul. *Birds of the World; Their Life and Habits.* New York: Oxford University Press, 1954.
 2. "Birds," *The World Book Encyclopedia.* 1956 Edition. Field Enterprises, Inc., Educational Division, Chicago, Ill. Vol. 2, pp. 788-815.

B. For Children
 1. Craig, Gerald. *Science Everywhere.* Boston: Ginn and Co., 1956.
 2. Parker, Bertha. *Birds.* Evanston, Ill.: Row, Peterson & Co., 1947.
 3. ———. *Birds in Your Backyard.* Evanston, Ill.: Row, Peterson & Co., 1949.
 4. Williamson, Margaret. *The First Book of Birds.* New York: Franklin Watts, Inc., 1951.

XI. Integration and/or Correlation with:
  A. Reading
  B. Oral and written language
  C. Geography
  D. Art
  E. Numbers

DAILY AND WEEKLY PLANNING

In many schools each teacher is supplied with a commercially published lesson plan book. Spaces are provided for the teacher to record a brief statement of her plans for teaching each day for a period of a week in advance. In reality, the plan book does not require weekly plans but rather a series of brief outlines for five daily plans prepared a week in advance. In many of the plan books, spaces are provided for the teacher to write a statement of the aims, assignment, teaching materials, and approaches for each subject for each day of the week. While this planning in advance has considerable merit, it is more a brief memorandum than a plan. A series of brief daily plans made a week in advance should be considered as merely tentative, subject to modification as the class work proceeds. The teacher should recognize that this type of planning does not obviate the necessity of making more detailed lesson plans. In fact this type of "lesson plan" can hardly be thought of as a plan.

Planning the daily work

A well-established principle of psychology is that, everything else being equal, the more immediate the goal the more impelling is its influence. The remote goals of the large learning units should be supplemented by several immediate objectives. The daily recitation, in spite of its limitations, has the distinct advantage of providing a series of immediate goals for the learner. The work of the daily class period should be related to the larger objectives of the unit and the course. There is nothing inherent in the daily recitation to make it an isolated activity. The best assurance that the work of the daily class period will be related to the other important aspects of the course is in careful planning of each day's work.

If the daily class period includes recitation and directed study, the plan should provide for both activities. The teacher's work is not ended when the recitation is concluded. Teacher leadership wisely exercised during the directed study period may be more essential to pupil learning than are the activities of the recitation period.

Planning for the directed study of pupils involves a consideration of the following:

1. Physical environment favorable for pupil study
2. Accessibility of study materials
3. Means of motivating pupils in their study
4. Diagnosis of learning difficulties of individual pupils
5. Procedures in directing the study of individual pupils, particularly slow-learning and superior pupils
6. Methods of eliminating difficulties common to the group
7. Means of checking on the efficiency of the pupils' study habits

The daily lesson plan

In formulating a daily lesson plan, it is necessary to give consideration to the following:

1. Worthy attainable aims (both general and specific) clearly formulated
2. Good selection and arrangement of instructional materials for use in attaining the objectives
3. Carefully chosen procedures, in considerable variety and detail, for effective use of the materials
4. Indication of the tentative amount of time to be devoted to each part of the lesson
5. Applications of materials to school and out-of-school situations noted
6. Bibliography of reading materials for pupils and teacher and other supplementary materials
7. Provisions for evaluating pupil progress
8. Suggestions for revision of the plan, added after actual use

An erroneous belief has been prevalent that, while planning is important, the form of the plan has little significance. The usefulness of the plan is dependent to a considerable extent upon its form. No one form may have optimum value for all types of recitations or teachers. Some teachers may find that a detailed written plan is the most desirable. Other teachers may prefer brief notes on content, procedures, and assignment. It is extremely doubtful that a teacher can obtain the maximum benefit without reducing the plan to written form. Since memory is ephemeral, the written plan is the most satisfactory record for future use. A plan revised after actual use provides an excellent basis for future planning.

A complete plan contains proper captions, indicating topic, date, grade or grade section, class period, and room number. This information makes the plan more valuable to the teacher for future reference. In large schools in which the plans of many teachers are submitted to one central administrative or supervisory office, the inclusion of this information is necessary for systematic and effective use of the plans.

The following represents a form which many teachers have found useful.

EXAMPLE OF DAILY PLAN

Reading Activities

Grade: Third   *Room:* 202
Hour: 10:00   *Teacher:* _____

Topic: Story entitled "Ups and Downs" in *Streets and Roads,* Curriculum Foundation Series, by William S. Gray and Mary Hill Arbuthnot.

I. General Suggestions:

    1. Motivation of pupils for story.
        Get children interested in reading the story by—
        a. Showing pictures
        b. Discussing any experiences or ideas children have about the subject—relate to children's experiences
        c. Telling part of story
        d. Using pictures, concrete objects, music, etc., related to story

    2. Give the main thought question dealing with the entire story—can be given orally or written.

    3. Present difficult words and phrases pupils will encounter in story.
        a. Guessing games
        b. Map study
        c. Pronunciation—vital to story
        d. Study of words—prefix, suffix, base words, ending, plurals
        e. Use dictionary

    4. Start questions in a variety of ways, e.g., What, why, show, tell how, etc.

    5. Be sure all understand assignment, where it is, where books and materials are, time allotted, etc.

    6. Provide for individual differences.
        Present material orally, written, charted, etc.
        Supplementary lesson—books, magazines, texts, clippings, reference books
        Individual research
           Preparing bibliography
           Extra report for reading lesson
           Correlated report—science, social studies, etc.
           Reading Center—recreation, book reports, reading record; some pupils continue or complete other work
           Group work (help others, dramatize)

II. Aims:

    1. General—To develop understanding and appreciation of elevators in modern buildings (as part of a unit on means of transportation)

2. Specific—(a) To increase children's powers of reading and comprehension
      (b) To extend vocabulary of children

III. Preparation for Reading:
  1. What kinds of buildings besides department stores have elevators to take people from floor to floor? (Office buildings and tall apartments)
  2. Discuss the buttons marked "Up" and "Down" that are used to signal the elevator to stop for passengers. (Be sure the class is familiar with the self-service type of elevator.)

Presentation of Phrases and Words

1. stamped her foot	1. Scamp p. 38
2. sly little monkey	2. monkey p. 38
3. pushed the button	3. buttons p. 40
4. rushing up and down	4. also p. 40
	5. fifth p. 39
	6. anybody p. 39
	7. purple p. 41
	8. I'd (Stands for?)

Questions to Guide Study

  1. How were Mrs. Brown and Jack alike?
     (Both trying to catch Scamp running down the hall. Neither could catch him.)
  2. *How* did Scamp escape Nancy?
     (He jumped into elevator.)
  3. *Give* two reasons why Nancy's idea was wrong.
     (Door wouldn't open and elevator started down.)
  4. *Tell* three things about the fun Scamp had.
     (He pushed one button after another.)
     (He kept going up and down many times—nobody could stop him.)
  5. *When* did those on the fifth floor laugh?
     (When Jack told the woman who wanted a ride he couldn't take anyone because a monkey was in the elevator.)
  6. What idea did Jack have?
  7. How did Nancy feel?
  8. When Jack's idea came true how did he fool Scamp?
  9. What made Nancy feel better?
  10. Read aloud just what Nancy said to Scamp.
  11. What shows Jack took over his job right away?

Word Drill

monkey	buttons	also	purple
money	mittens	already	burst
Monday	better	almost	further
month	rattle	almost	burden
	rotten	always	curtain

IV. Children Read Story Silently.

V. Questions After Reading Story: (to be written or discussed orally)

    1. Why couldn't Mrs. Brown and Jack catch Scamp?

    2. How did Nancy try to catch him?

    3. Show that Scamp fooled her.

    4. Describe the lady in the purple dress.

    5. What words show that the lady in the purple dress was irritated?

    6. Be ready to read aloud the sentence that tells that Scamp was a funny elevator boy.

    7. Why is Scamp a good name for Mrs. Brown's pet? (Main thought question)

VI. Suggestions for revision of plan for future use.

The use of the plan

There should be tangible evidence of planning in the teacher's activities in the classroom. As a result of the judicious use of the plan, the value of planning is revealed in the higher quality of classroom instruction. If the details of the plan are designed with facility of use in view, the skillful teacher can easily acquire the ability to use the plan to serve her purposes to the best advantage in the classroom. While there is little objection to fairly close adherence to a well-formulated plan, to rely too much upon its details is unwise. However, the chief values of intelligent planning can be dissipated by a disregard of the plan in teaching.

Deviations from the planned activities can be justified only when it is clearly evident that the best interests of the class can be served by content and procedures which were not incorporated in the original plan. Immediately after a plan has been used and while the class activities are still vivid in the memory of the teacher, any necessary modifications of the plan should be made. After this preliminary revision the plan should be filed for future use. Further adaptations will, of course, be necessary in terms of the interests, capacities, and needs of other groups of pupils.

QUESTIONS, PROBLEMS, AND EXERCISES

1. What part should pupils have in planning the activities of the daily class period? the units? the entire course?

2. In cooperation with other members of a class committee, plan a resource unit as a guide for planning by the individual teacher of a given elementary school grade.

3. Write a detailed daily lesson plan in the subject you are interested in teaching.

4. How can the teacher anticipate pupils' reactions to a particular item of content or procedure?

5. What factors should be taken into consideration in decisions regarding the form of a daily lesson plan?

6. Write a statement of two or three paragraphs on: "The Use of the Lesson Plan in the Daily Class Period."

7. Discuss the statement: "If the objectives of a course are to be accomplished, it must be planned in advance and in considerable detail."

8. Make a critical analysis of the suggestions in this chapter for preplanning a unit and indicate how the procedure might be improved.

SELECTED SUPPLEMENTARY READINGS

Association for Supervision and Curriculum Development. *Creating a Good Environment for Learning, 1954 Yearbook* Washington, D.C.: National Education Association, 1954.

Chap. ii, "A Day in a Primary Grade." An account of a teacher and her pupils planning and working together.

Baxter, Bernice, Gertrude M. Lewis, and Gertrude M. Cross. *The Role of Elementary Education.* Boston: D. C. Heath & Co., 1952.

Chapter x, "Planning Educative Experiences for Children." Excellent suggestions for planning the learning environment of pupils in the various areas of study.

Haskew, Laurence D. *This Is Teaching.* Chicago: Scott, Foresman & Co., 1956.

Chap. vi, "What Teachers Do in School." Contains section on teacher planning teaching procedures in terms of learning outcomes.

Herrick, Virgil E., John I. Goodlad, Frank J. Estvan, and Paul W. Eberman. *The Elementary School.* Englewood Cliffs, N.J.: Prentice-Hall, Inc., 1956.

Chap. xiv, "The Learning-Teaching Day." Section devoted to planning an initial schedule and continuous planning in the classroom.

Lane, Howard, and Mary Beauchamp. *Human Relations in Teaching.* Englewood Cliffs, N.J.: Prentice-Hall, Inc., 1955.

Chap. iv, "The Functioning of Group Intelligence." Presents some of the characteristics of group planning.

Miel, Alice, and Associates. *Cooperative Procedures in Learning.* New York: Bureau of Publications, Teachers College, Columbia University, 1952.

Chap. v, "Planning Studies." Presents suggestions for planning within the limits of subjects and courses of study. Contains a description of planning for cooperative learning outside a course of study.

Saylor, J. Galen, and William M. Alexander. *Curriculum Planning: For Better Teaching and Learning.* Chap. 5. "The Pupil as a Factor in Curriculum Planning." New York: Rinehart & Co., Inc., 1954.

Chap. xiii, "Planning and Developing Learning Experiences with Learners." Presents many excellent illustrations of pupil-teacher planning.

Wingo, G. Max, and Raleigh Schorling. *Elementary-School Student Teaching.* 2d ed. New York: McGraw-Hill Book Co., Inc., 1955.

Chap. vii, "Teacher and Pupils Plan Together." Discussion of the importance of planning and suggestions for involving pupils in planning.

10

INSTRUCTIONAL UNITS OF LEARNING

Recognizing the inadequacies of prevailing classroom practices, various leaders of educational thought have formulated plans for the organizing and teaching of learning units which are more comprehensive in scope than those utilized in the daily recitation. Some of the early unit plans of teaching attracted considerable attention, and a few won fairly wide acceptance. They failed to become the predominant classroom practice because of the prevailing stimulus-response concept of learning, with its emphasis upon the mastery of isolated bits of knowledge rather than upon total patterns of learning.

As a consequence of acceptance of the Gestalt concept of the nature of learning, the unit idea grew in favor as a guide in the organization of curricular materials, even though methods of teaching were not greatly different from those used in textbook teaching.

The concepts of Gestalt psychology which served to bring about refinements in the unit method of teaching were (1) that the nature of the total learning situation is determined not merely by the sum of the elements which comprise it, but rather by the relationships which exist among the different parts; (2) that the parts of a learning situation have meaning only in terms of their relations to each other and to the whole; and (3) that the unifying factor in organizing the elements of a learning situation is the purpose of the learner.

Another factor which contributed to acceptance of the unit method of teaching was growing recognition of the need for more adequate provisions for individual differences. The failure of various administrative plans, such as ability grouping, to provide satisfactory means of individualizing instruction caused many leaders of educational thought to consider the classroom teacher as the proper person to meet the needs of individual pupils. As a result, supervised study, differentiated assignments, enriched curricula, and the unit method became the vogue. One of the main arguments advanced for use of the unit method of teaching was its value in providing for individual differences. The possibilities of the unit in this respect have too seldom been realized. The opportunity for different pupils to work on different aspects of a unit presents an excellent method of providing for their individual abilities, interests, and needs. More significant, however, is the demonstrated value of individual projects in making adequate provision for individual differences.

The instructional unit emphasizes total patterns of learning rather than isolated bits of knowledge presented in a series of daily assign-study-recite topics. In addition to being comprehensive in scope, the learning materials and activities of a unit must be organized in such a manner as to possess *unity* or *wholeness*. This essential unity may be achieved by a logical arrangement of subject matter either around a significant topic, theme, or generalization or around the learner's interest, a recognized need, or a significant social problem.

TYPES OF LEARNING UNITS

A superficial analysis of the various unit plans of teaching may lead to the conclusion that they are essentially alike except for terminology. The unit plans do possess a certain similarity in that all of them recognize larger units of learning than that of the daily recitation and are therefore characterized by the long-term assignment. The different plans, however, are identified with different educational philosophies and psychologies of learning. For example, one school of thought regards the unifying element as residing within the body of the subject matter, whereas another group recognizes the purpose of the learner as the integrating factor in the organization of learning materials. Thus, units are frequently classified as *subject-matter units,* in which the materials are organized according to the logic of the subject matter involved, or as *experience-type units,* in which the learning experiences are bound together by some central theme of child interest or significant social problem. This distinction is misleading in that in both types of units subject matter is employed, although it is used differently. In the experience-type unit, the learner's interest is the point of departure in the learning activities; thus it has a psychological organization, in contrast to the logical organization of the subject-matter unit.

Subject-matter and experience units

The word subjects in the curriculum represents knowledge that has been organized logically and systematically, such as geography, arithmetic, and natural science. In a subject-matter unit all information is centered around a division of a certain subject-matter field. The learning experiences are formal. Textbooks are the main source of information. The time devoted to the unit is relatively short. The teacher plans the unit and directs the work of the children accordingly. For example, in a unit on *Safety* all information is based on safety and is obtained by reading a basic textbook on safety in the hope that, through transfer of learning, children will apply the understanding and the habits of safety to real life situations. In a topical unit on *Birds,* children learn facts presented in their readers or science books but perhaps disregard the common birds of their own community that do not happen to be mentioned in the particular book used.

Experience units are based upon life experiences in which the children are interested. First graders are interested in the care of their pets. Fathers of three fourth-grade children worked in coal mines and, as a result of their immediate interest, the class wished to learn about the mines. A group of sixth graders decided that they wanted to landscape the school grounds. In experience units children and teacher cooperate in planning the experiences. The plans are flexible so that changes may be made from day to day. Information is obtained by cutting across subject-matter lines. The amount of time devoted to the unit will vary with groups and the type of experience which is being pursued.

Since the core of the curriculum is based upon interests of children, the development of the tools of learning is incidental and depends upon the utilization of those skills in the learnings which come out of the units. However, the teacher is concerned about the realization of the objectives of education and guides the children in the selection of their units so that the activities in which they will engage will provide for the utilization of those skills and habits essential in acquiring information and in communicating with others.

Comparison of units

Some of the differences of the units presented may be clarified by presenting major characteristics of each.

Characteristics:	Subject-Matter Unit	Experience Unit
Selected by:	Teacher	Teacher and child
Purposes are:	Based upon textbook or course of study	Teacher's and child's
Plans are developed:	According to textbook	By teacher preplanning and children and teacher filling in details as unit grows
Source of content for unit is:	Textbook	Life experiences and content areas, such as social studies, etc.
Source of information is:	Textbook	Books, periodicals, community, experiences, etc.
Learning is directed toward:	Mastery of facts	Needs and interests of children and well-adjusted child
Learning experiences are:	Formal	Varied and many
Tools of learning are mastered:	Through relatively meaningless drill	Through meaningful drill and through use in solving significant problems

SELECTION OF UNITS

The effectiveness of the unit method of teaching is determined in no small part by the selection of appropriate learning units. The suitability of a unit is dependent upon various factors which operate in a given learning situation. The most significant factors are the characteristics of children, particularly their abilities, educational status, interests, and social maturity. Other considerations are (1) its contribution to important educational outcomes (these outcomes should be expressed in terms of basic understandings, attitudes, appreciations, and skills); (2) its appeal to the interests of the children; and (3) the possibilities of developing desirable concomitant learnings.

In the process of selection, a careful analysis should be made to ascertain whether or not a unit possesses good teaching qualities as measured by the following criteria.

1. The learning unit should have a useful purpose.
2. It should reproduce actual life situations as nearly as possible.
3. It should utilize materials as they occur in life.
4. It should involve a variety of direct sense experiences.
5. It should provide a considerable amount of pupil activity.
6. It should provide for some free, informal association of the pupils.
7. It should provide a good opportunity for the pupil to originate, plan, and direct activity.

8. It should make an opportunity for manipulative or physical activity.
9. It should provide opportunities to judge, choose, and evaluate.
10. It should contain accurate information.
11. It should be possible to complete within the time available for the unit.
12. The exposition should be clear enough for a new teacher to reproduce the experience.
13. It should state exactly where materials may be obtained.
14. When references are given, they should be complete and exact.

The materials and activities of a learning unit may be selected on one of several bases.

1. In terms of textbook or subject-matter requirements
2. On the basis of interests, concerns, or needs of the students
3. In terms of significant current social problems
4. On the basis of suggested resource units
5. On the basis of suggestions contained in units used in other schools
6. On the basis of materials developed and distributed by commercial organizations

Teacher committee

The basic needs and interests of children at the various levels of development are known as are the various patterns of behavior that should be developed as the children mature. By using this information as a guide, many schools through teacher committees have set up a flexible program of sequential units for all elementary grades which provides for continuity and prevents repetition from grade to grade. Frequently, teachers are furnished with a course of study or an outline of several units which are to be developed during the year. From this list the teacher and children cooperatively select the unit or units which they wish to pursue.

Teacher and pupils

In other schools the teacher and children cooperatively choose the units out of the children's own areas of experience. To be effective, this type of activity requires expert guidance on the part of the teacher. Because of immaturity children may decide upon units which are too comprehensive or units which are limited in providing for the goals to be achieved. Or they may wish to repeat a unit of the preceding year and thus omit an experience needed for the development of skills, attitudes, and understandings which are needed for their present period of maturity.

Teacher

The individual teacher's responsibility for choosing units varies from one school system to another. She may be expected to make her selection from a list in the official course of study, or at least to adapt the units chosen from the course of study. In a few schools, teachers cooperate in the preparation of resource units (See Chapter 11). Ordinarily the individual teacher is not required to teach any resource unit or any part of one unless she believes that it serves the needs of the children, and in some schools she assumes full responsibility for the selection of units which she will teach. In an increasing number of schools, however, the choice of the unit represents the combined judgment of the teacher and children.

EXPERIENCE-TYPE UNITS

Experience-type units may be classified as activity units and projects. In the activity unit the learning activities are selected from areas of human living in which there are problems that all men must face. The essence of the project is the purposeful, wholehearted involvement of the learner in learning activities which are related to his felt needs or concerns.

Activity units

In the activity unit, the learning activities of elementary school pupils usually begin with the study of problems in their immediate environment, for example, the home and local community and a gradual expansion to more remote environments.

The following list illustrates a few activity units which may be studied in the different grades of the elementary school.

GRADE ONE

1. Living happily together at home and at school
2. Safety at home and at school
3. Helpers who prepare our food at home and at school

GRADE TWO

1. Community helpers in securing food, clothing
2. Having fun in our community
3. Safety community helpers

GRADE THREE

1. Means of bringing food into our community
2. Controlling traffic in our community
3. Controlling spread of colds and diseases

GRADE FOUR

1. Natural community resources that supply our needs, such as coal, oil, etc.
2. Elimination of hazards in our community
3. Cultural contributions of various national groups in our community

GRADE FIVE

1. Providing for the basic needs of people of other countries
2. Being friendly with our neighbors, Canada, Mexico
3. Strengthening interdependence with other countries

GRADE SIX

1. Maintaining health and safety among world neighbors
2. Considering our privileges and responsibilities in a democracy, as world citizens
3. Developing world unity based on scientific discoveries and inventions

In an activity unit, subject-matter lines may be abandoned, and children may draw on any source for information, such as books, experiences, community resources, creative arts. If the teacher recognizes that the skills in the three R's are not sufficiently developed incidentally, she provides periods in which the skills and abilities are presented and developed through practice and drill and perfected through use in the unit. Teacher and pupils cooperate in planning procedures to be used in solving problems, in setting up standards of accomplishment, and in evaluating results.

The following is an example of how an activity unit, designed to give the pupils in a sixth-grade class a better understanding of the people of India, was selected and developed in a democratic class context in which subject matter was organized around the pupils' interests.

A STUDY OF TODAY'S INDIA [1]

A group (sixth grade) of children in the George Gray School, Wilmington, Delaware, became much interested in India as they discussed the news together each morning. They asked, "Why are they saying that what happens to India will affect the whole world?"

After talking together about what was happening in India, the class decided that much more information about the people of India was needed to understand better what was happening and why it had meaning for us. The pupils made a list of the following questions they wanted to have answered:

1. In what kind of homes do the people of India live?
2. What do they eat?
3. Is it true that many children of India never have enough to eat?
4. What are their religious beliefs?

[1] Samuel Everett and Christian O. Arndt (eds.), *Teaching World Affairs in American Schools, A Case Book* (A Publication of the John Dewey Society, New York: Harper & Bros., 1956, pp. 22–24.

5. Is it true that they think cows are holy?
6. What educational advantages do Indians have?
7. What is their form of government?
8. What kind of work do they do for a living?

The next step was to decide where to find information that would help in answering these questions. Some members of the group had already gathered information from the television and radio. To this were added the following sources:

1. Maps and globes
2. Encyclopedias
3. Books and pictures from our classroom and the school library
4. Daily newspapers
5. The news and magazine sections of the Sunday papers
6. Weekly magazines
7. People who have lived in India

The children decided that someone who had recently lived in India could give a true picture of how the people lived. Through the school principal an exchange student was located who had spent the previous winter living with a farm family near Delhi, India.

With the aid of colored slides, which were taken during his stay in India, this student gave the class a vivid picture of the home life and the constant struggle for existence of the farming population of India, which comprises about 85 per cent of the population. The children asked many questions of their visitor about what they saw in the pictures and about his relationships with the people. They learned that because of primitive farming tools, and the dry and rainy seasons, the people of India failed to raise enough food to feed themselves and that, in consequence, many were hungry most of the time. As the visitor explained the American Point Four and Technical Assistance programs with which the United States is aiding India, these terms became more meaningful. When the illustrated talk was finished, many of the questions which had puzzled the children were answered. The children were beginning to understand why there is so much unrest in India.

An article in their Weekly Reader on India's objection to United States military aid to Pakistan was read, and posted on the bulletin board was an article from a morning paper on the same subject. After reading both, the class divided into Indians and Pakistanis. They debated whether the United States was right or wrong in the action taken, according to the viewpoint of the respective countries. During the debate, the world map was used to make clear the location of India and Pakistan. Their nearness to Communist China and Russia was noted. These places thus began to have real meaning to the children.

A newspaper article, about hundreds of Hindus being trampled to death rushing to bathe in the holy waters of the Ganges during a religious bathing festival, led the children to the encyclopedia to learn more about the religions of India. Discussion of the reports on the various religions, superstitions, and the high rate of illiteracy of the Indian people enhanced their understanding of India's needs.

A scrapbook of newspaper and magazine articles on India was made to use for later reference, or just to be re-read when needed. A large map of India was also constructed on which pupils showed the leading industries and the leading exports and imports, so that they could get a clearer picture of the kinds of work the people of India do, the food they eat, and the countries with which they trade.

Graphs were made showing the daily consumption of nourishing foods in India and in the United States, as well as of the yearly death rates in the United States and India. The relationship between a nourishing diet and the health of a people was thus clearly suggested. A chart was developed showing the ways in which the United States had helped India in her food production and health program. The class thought that what it had learned about India was important enough to share with other sixth-grade groups and they arranged a sharing program.

The children acquired many insights from these activities. They began to think of India as a country of 360,000,000 people rather than as a spot on the map. They became acquainted with the customs of these people, learning how they dressed, what they ate and what they wore, how they felt about other peoples, and how quickly Indian children had to grow up and accept responsibilities.

They began to understand that when people are hungry, unlearned, sick, and afraid, they are likely to have a kindly feeling toward those who help them overcome these difficulties.

They learned something of the moral obligation of the more fortunate toward those less fortunate.

They gained an appreciation of how rapidly the world is changing, as they found it difficult to find up-to-date material on India except from newscasts on television and radio and from daily newspapers, current magazines, and people who have recently visited India.

They acquired an increased interest in reading the daily papers and current magazines and in watching television newscasts to learn about what is happening in the United States as well as in other parts of the world.

They realized India's strength as a leader among the nations of Southeastern Asia, and that whether she remains a free, democratic nation or falls under the domination of Communism, will greatly influence all of Southeast Asia and eventually the entire world.

The project

The project is a unit of activity carried on by the learner in a natural and lifelike manner and in a spirit of purpose to accomplish a definite, attractive, and seemingly attainable goal. Projects may be classified as *individual* or *group* on the basis of the number of pupils involved. In the study of a comprehensive unit an individual pupil may make an intensive study of one of the aspects of the unit. In the group project the entire class may develop the unit cooperatively. In the latter case the terms "project" and "experience unit" are often used synonymously.

The following are examples of learning projects:

1. Writing a song to be sung by the class
2. Writing and staging a play by the class
3. Writing letters to local newspapers presenting viewpoints on current issues

4. Carrying on correspondence with students in other states or countries
5. Studying ways in which the local community attempts to protect the health of its citizens
6. Making a study of local housing conditions
7. Making a survey of the provisions for traffic safety in the local community
8. Making a mural portraying the history of transportation
9. Getting out a school newspaper
10. Planning a girl's wardrobe
11. Caring for a small brother or sister after school for a period of one month
12. Making posters for school events
13. Designing and making book ends, book covers, Christmas cards, billfolds, etc.

Characteristics. The project possesses the following characteristics:

1. The project is a learning unit. Its unity depends upon pupil purpose rather than upon the logical arrangement of subject matter.
2. The project is a self-imposed or willingly accepted task growing out of an awareness on the part of the pupil of its significance. Along with the acceptance of the challenge of the task goes the acceptance of responsibility for "following through" until its completion.
3. The project grows out of the pupil's experiential background, thus enabling him to discover clues for planning and organizing his own activities.
4. The project retains its identity only as long as the pupil has freedom to pursue his purpose unrestrained by the barrier of subject-matter boundaries or teacher domination.
5. The project invokes a wholehearted effort on the part of the pupil to achieve an attainable and desirable goal.
6. The project leads to goals which are recognizable by the pupil, thereby enabling him to evaluate his own progress in achieving his objectives.

Values. There is little objective evidence which reveals the superiority of the project over other methods of teaching. The use of projects does not automatically insure that optimum learning will be achieved. It appears clear, however, that the philosophy and psychology underlying the project method are related more closely to the conditions essential for effective learning than are those of many other widely used methods of teaching. Properly used, the project method reveals the following values:

1. The relationship between the pupil and the teacher is conducive to effective learning, in that provision is made for guided self-activity on the part of the learner.
2. The attitude of the pupil is more favorable for learning as the result of his responsible participation in establishing and planing the goals of the learning activity.
3. The participation of pupils in learning activities which they have accepted as vital and significant to themselves tends to reduce the causes of misbehavior.
4. In the group project the child becomes a helpful co-worker in a common and significant social task.
5. The use of the individual project is one of the most effective means of providing for individual differences. The group project also provides learning activities of many kinds suited to different capacities and interests.
6. The similarity of the technique of problem solving utilized in the project method to that involved in dealing with problem situations in life facilitates the application of school learning to life situations.
7. The possibilities of achieving desirable concomitant learning are enhanced by the project method. Among the attitudes which may be developed are open-mindedness and tolerance. More ample provision is also made for the acquisition of certain skills, such as study and work habits, techniques of cooperative effort, etc.

Sample class project. A second-grade class in reading "Mr. Hurry Changes Things" in one of their readers *More Friends and Neighbors* (Chicago: Scott, Foresman & Co.) became interested in all the trouble Mr. Hurry had because he did not *listen* to all the directions for running the digging machine. Using the pupils' interest as a lead, the class engaged in a group project on *Learn to Listen*.

Marjorie Wright, the teacher of the class, describes the development of the project in the following extract:[2]

First we talked about WHY we listen. We listen to learn, we decided—to learn how to play games, how to make things, how to do our work. We listen for entertainment—to stories, TV, movies, radio. We listen for safety's sake to the sound of cars and trains approaching.

HOW to listen was our next subject for discussion. When we had reached some conclusions we wrote them down on a group chart:

Stop what we are doing.
Look at the speaker.
Keep very quiet—hands, feet, and lips.
Listen to the WHOLE THING.

[2] From "Chiefs, Learn to Listen—and Like It" by Marjorie K. Wright; *Primary Activities,* March 1957. Copyright © 1957 by Scott, Foresman & Co., and used with their permission.

We also decided that we LIKE to listen (1) when the speaker talks clearly and in a loud enough voice, (2) when the speaker tells something interesting, (3) when the speaker sticks to his subject, (4) when the rest of the audience is listening attentively.

To help the youngsters become aware of the sounds around us, I suggested that they listen each morning on the way to school. During conversation time they shared their listening experiences. The variety of sounds reported was ear-opening, indeed:

Sandra heard the wires singing. Tony heard her own footsteps on the sidewalk. John heard the creak of branches as the wind moved them. Steven heard a baby crying, Julie heard road machinery rattle and bang. All these experiences and many more we recorded on charts with illustrations made by the children.

A "listening" field trip was our next project. With tongues quiet and ears alert, we took a walk together. Besides mechanical sounds such as the ring of a telephone and the whistle of a train, we heard a squirrel chattering, leaves rustling, a cricket chirping, a woodpecker hammering, a bee buzzing. Our walk turned out to be an excellent nature-study trip, for our ears helped our eyes locate the little creatures we would have passed by unnoticing, had we not been listening so acutely.

Mr. Hurry's experiences, as you can see, had really taught us a lesson. To help us remember, we drew illustrations of the story to make a movie reel for our homemade projector. Producing our show pointed up all over again the importance of listening. The movie operators had to listen to know when to turn to the next picture; the readers had to listen to keep the place; and the audience had to listen to share in the fun.

Katherine summed up all our experiences with a slogan which we thought was a good one to remember: "A good listener is a good learner."

TEACHING A UNIT

The activities of the teacher and the pupils in the teaching and study of a unit may be divided into four phases: the preparatory, the initiatory, the developmental, and the culminating.

Preparatory activities

In order to develop a working plan for unit teaching, the teacher must have information pertaining to the children, the content to be covered, the materials on hand, and the available community resources. The outline below suggests how a teacher might secure the information she needs to develop her working plan.

1. Discover interests of children
   a) Observe them at their play, in the classroom, on the streets, in their homes
   b) Listen to their conversation, discussions, suggestions
   c) Check books read during free time
   d) Check on hobbies, leisure time activities

    e) Study their drawings and paintings
    f) Note materials which they bring to school on their own initiative
  2. Ascertain the needs and abilities of children
    a) Observe them at their play, at their work, in the classroom, on the playground
    b) Listen to their conversations, discussions, suggestions
    c) Study their drawings and paintings
    d) Study cumulative records
    e) Hold conferences with parents
    f) Diagnose basic skills
  3. Determine the activities and interests of the community
    a) Make a survey of the community
    b) Converse with citizens
    c) Attend civic functions, such as forums, concerts
    d) Observe community activities
    e) Take part in a community group or organization, such as church activities
    f) Study major occupations
    g) Study local newspapers
  4. Locate natural resources, community resources, human resources as sources for profitable experiences for children
    a) Make a survey of the community
    b) Note industries
    c) Note museums
    d) Note libraries
    e) Note parks, playgrounds, swimming pools
    f) Keep a file of newspaper clippings pertaining to persons who have visited other countries, etc.
    g) Make a survey of homes for materials, such as pictures, models, exhibits
  5. Locate source materials available in school
    a) Books, children's encyclopedias, magazines, bulletins
    b) Audio-visual aids
    c) Construction materials and art materials, such as clay, paints, paper, saws, nails, scissors, etc.
    d) Microscopes, magnets, electric plate, work bench, easels, etc.

In preplanning, the teacher should formulate a list of the outcomes which may be achieved by the study of each of the units. Taking, for example, a unit on "Conservation of Our Forests as a Source of Lumber," a few of the desired outcomes might include:

  1. Attitudes and appreciations: To develop—
    a) Appreciation for our natural resources
    b) Appreciation for the benefits derived through conservation projects

  c) Appreciation for the efforts of our leaders in science and in the government who were or are interested in lumbering and in conservation of our forests
  d) Appreciation for the needs of future generations
  e) Appreciation of our independence
2. Understanding: To gain better understandings of—
  a) The necessity to conserve our forests
  b) The effects of one industry upon daily living of many persons
  c) Best measures to use in lumbering and in conservation of our forests
  d) The life of lumber men
  e) Our responsibilities in cooperating with government and with private organizations interested in conservation
  f) Responsibilities of those who are in charge of the conservation of our forests
3. Abilities in using tools of learning: To develop increased ability to—
  a) Locate and organize information
  b) Use reference materials
  c) Read and interpret maps and graphs
  d) Read critically and analytically
  e) Creative work, such as writing, self-expression, and art
4. Habits and skills: Learn to—
  a) Plan before executing
  b) Stick to the job until it is completed
  c) Listen to learn
  d) Practice neatness and accuracy
  e) Learn cooperation
  f) Practice courtesy in classroom and while on trips
  g) Use reference material intelligently

Initiatory activities

The tone and quality of the work of a unit are established in the introductory phase. The first impression the child receives of the unit largely determines his attitude toward all his subsequent work on it.

In instituting a unit, the teacher should seek to achieve the following purposes: (1) create pupil interest in the unit, (2) reveal the significance of the unit to the pupils, (3) reveal the main features of the unit, and (4) assist the children in formulating their objectives of the unit.

Creating an interest. It is not unusual to find a small percentage of children in a group who will admit that they are not interested in the unit. These children frequently have a limited background of experiences; when they begin to realize what is in store for them, their attitude may change. If children have been motivated previously for the unit by means of another unit or through experiences, it is advisable to move immediately into the exploration and problem-stating period. In organizing the approach period of a unit, the teacher must take into consideration the purposes of the unit and the interests, capacities, and needs of the children.

The major techniques that are employed in introducing a unit are experiencing situations that are real to the children or experiencing situations in vicarious ways and then sharing those experiences in a discussion period. Following are a number of ways of conducting an approach period:

Planned Classroom Environment. It is very important that the teacher create the proper classroom climate for stimulating an interest in the unit. This may be accomplished by directing the children's attention to interesting incidents or situations of the unit by means of materials which are displayed in the classroom, such as a display of pictures, graphs, and charts on the bulletin board; an exhibit of products, models, specimens; and books on the reading table.

Motion Pictures, Slides, Excursion or Field Trip. Motion pictures and slides which are shown in the classroom are very effective in motivating children for study of a unit, as indeed is an excursion or field trip somewhere in the community. Occasionally a movie (that is, if it comes at the psychological time) and the reviews of the movie in magazines may be used.

Radio. The radio is an effective technique to use in arousing the interest of children in the intermediate grades. News broadcasts, dramatizations of historical events, round-table discussions of controversial issues, speeches by prominent leaders in economics, and science and musical programs may be used. The major problems in using the radio are that the desired program is not on the air during school hours; in the home there are many interruptions, or probably another member of the family prefers to listen to another program; and often the radio program does not come at the time of year when it is needed for the unit. In order to overcome these difficulties, teachers may make tape recordings of the programs and then use them when they are needed.

Reading a Story or a Book. Frequently a story or book that is read during the story hour or during the literature period becomes the motivation for a unit. For example, a fourth-grade class that had listened to a story about a child who lived in a jungle asked if they might have a unit based on "Life in the Jungle." Several books based on a specific unit may be placed on the reading table after the teacher has read selected passages to the children. If this reading is interspersed with remarks by the teacher and children, the children will read the books on their own initiative and during a free discussion period will comment on the story or stories which may serve as a lead into the exploration period.

Exploration Period. The main purposes of the exploration are to—

1. Discover what the children know and do not know about the unit.
2. Discover incorrect concepts.
3. Discover particular needs of children.
4. Extend the interest of the children in the unit.

Exploratory Discussion Period. Exploratory discussion periods are intended to reveal what the children know and do not know about the unit. During these periods the teacher and children ask general questions which give direction to the discussions. While the children are discussing issues, offering explanations, and giving information, the teacher evaluates each contribution and records understandings and concepts which are not clear to the children, skills that must be developed, attitudes that must be strengthened, and those which must be developed. This information is used as a guide throughout the study of the unit. Pretests of the essay type are not recommended for elementary grade children. If a teacher desires to use a test, it is recommended that she prepare her own materials.

Stating the problems. After the interests of the children have been aroused and they have learned what the unit holds for them, the formulation of problems becomes the main issue. These problems should be in the form of clear statements of the purposes or goals to be achieved in order to give the children a definite aim toward which to direct their efforts.

The discussions of the exploration period should lead into the problem-stating period. Often these periods overlap to such a degree that each loses its identity. The problem-solving period is introduced by the teacher asking the children what they should like to learn about the unit. As the children present their questions, the teacher writes them on the blackboard. Since the children do not have the background out of which all important problems should be developed, it is the teacher's responsibility to suggest and recommend those that the children omit. The teacher should mention these problems at the time when the children are making their suggestions. After the questions have been listed, the children and teacher evaluate them in order to discover relationships, avoid duplications, eliminate irrelevant material, and organize the problems so that they will be a sequential pattern of attack. Often it is necessary to restate questions, particularly if two are closely related and may be integrated so as to eliminate one question.

Questions based on the unit "Conservation of Our Forests as a Source of Lumber" might include the following:

1. Where are the forest regions of the United States?
2. What will we learn when we study this problem?
3. What are the enemies of our forests?
4. Mr. Brown worked in a saw mill. Could we ask him to tell us about a saw mill?
5. Is there a movie about lumbering or our forests?
6. Could we go to the lumber yard and see the different kinds of lumber?
7. How do we make use of our forests?

During this phase it is the responsibility of the teacher to see that all problems which are to be studied are—

1. Paced to the needs, interests, abilities, and experiences of the children.
2. Stated in the child's terminology.
3. Limited so that problems can be completed in a reasonable length of time.
4. Challenging to the children and at the same time possible for the children to solve.
5. Conducive to use of several activities capable of making a contribution to the major theme of the unit.

Developmental and evaluative activities

Although the formulation of the problem and the planning of pupil activities should involve pupil-teacher cooperation, it is necessary for the teacher to make a thorough preliminary plan for the conduct of activities in order that she may be able to guide the pupils in their study of the problem. The plan should include a formulation of the chief problems, a brief summary of the facts and principles involved, and suggested pupil activities, together with sources of information. This plan should, of course, be subject to change as the unit progresses and new pupil interests become evident.

Teacher-pupil planning. This planning period is a natural outgrowth of preceding periods. Frequently at this point the culminating activity is determined; it often is a factor in determining problems to be solved and activities to be used in solving the problems. As the children re-evaluate the orientation activities they make decisions in regard to: (1) finding ways for solving the problems;

(2) making provisions for solving the problems; (3) organizing committees for various activities; (4) noting those activities for which individuals may be responsible. Following are suggestions for solving two problems out of eight that were presented by sixth-grade pupils who worked on the unit "Conservation of Our Forests as a Source of Lumber":

Problem: Who owns and manages the forests? What are the specific problems of each type of ownership?
1. Locate the information in various sources by evaluating the titles of books and by using tables of contents, indexes.
2. Write to Forest Service of United States Department of Agriculture for information pertaining to the problem.
3. Appoint committees to solve specific problems.
4. Committees are to report their findings to the class.
5. Make a map of our state showing the National Parks of the state.
6. Make a graph showing public and private ownership of forest lands.

Problem: How may we conserve our forests?
1. Locate information in various sources.
2. Take notes on materials read.
3. Report information to class during a discussion period.
4. Ask a member of conservation agency in local community to speak to the class about the problem.
5. Make a frieze showing how our forests may be conserved.
6. Use motion picture "Forests and Men."

Supervised study. In the supervised study period the children and teacher put into effect plans on developmental activities which were made in the planning period. It is at this time that the problems are solved one at a time and in the sequence that seems feasible to the group. The real purposes are—

1. Put plans into effect.
2. Evaluate the work as it progresses.
3. Modify plans if necessary.
4. Develop in a functional way abilities and skills needed to solve the problems.
5. Provide opportunities in which children will learn to communicate their ideas to others.
6. Give children an opportunity to share information.
7. Develop attitudes and appreciations.
8. Develop cooperation and a sense of responsibility to the entire group.
9. Give children an opportunity to test results.
10. Summarize frequently and draw conclusions.

During this period activities will vary from day to day. There will be days when every child will be locating information, reading, and writing for materials. There will be periods in which groups of children will be working on various activities, such as clay modeling, weaving, painting, while on another day the class may go on an excursion. At another time one child may read to a group of children for whom the reading material is too difficult but who can understand the ideas and generalizations presented in the reading materials. During the study period, specific plans may be made for excursions, construction work, an experiment, and the culminating activity.

As the children progress in the solution of the problems, they will feel the need from time to time of adding new elements and of subtracting those elements which do not make a contribution at that particular time. During discussion periods, they will present to the class work which they wish to have criticized and will ask for help also. Activities of the study period should not be hurried. Children must think carefully and critically and evaluate the activities from time to time.

Evaluation. Evaluation is an important factor in every learning situation. It is important to know whether the objectives have been achieved, how the child is progressing, and how the environment and the teaching techniques are affecting the child. In a unit of work evaluation cannot be accomplished at a specific time. It is a continuous process and is going on during the planning period, problem-stating period, and study period.

In organizing an evaluation program, the objectives should be stated in behavior patterns and the instruments used in securing the information should be valid and reliable. Data for evaluative purposes may be obtained by means of tests, interviews, recorded accomplishments of children and of the group, and observations. Opportunities should be provided for each child to check his own progress, either individually or by presenting the results of his work to the group for criticism. This information is very valuable and should aid the teacher in—

1. Stimulating the children to do better work.
2. Discovering weak places in their work.
3. Pointing out better ways of doing the work.
4. Making it possible for the teacher to know what has not been accomplished.
5. Evaluating the worthwhileness of the activities.
6. Making home reports.
7. Preparing for individual conferences with parent and/or child.

Culminating activities

The culmination of a unit is very important, since it becomes the guidepost for many of the activities which are used in solving problems. Frequently during the planning period children decide upon the type of culminating activities; if they do not have enough background to do it at that time, the decision may be made later. Details of the culmination are planned as the unit progresses. The purposes of a culminating activity are to—

1. Provide a way of sharing experiences with others.
2. Provide group motivation for solving problems.
3. Give recognition to the efforts of every individual who has made a contribution to a group project.

The major characteristics of an effective culminating activity are—

1. Making it possible for each child to participate.
2. Making it possible for each child to identify himself with the activity.
3. Making it possible for each child to achieve.
4. Providing an audience situation.
5. Providing for the presentation of many understandings acquired during the study of the unit.
6. Bringing the unit to a satisfactory close.

In the elementary grades, culminating activities usually take the form of assembly programs, exhibits, or plays.

The culminating activity for the unit on "Conservation of Our Forests as a Source of Lumber" consisted of the following activities:

1. A film on conservation of our forests showed to the parents; the children answered the questions raised by the parents.
2. An exhibit of products and by-products of lumber, posters and frieze on conservation by the children, and pictures representing various facts which had been presented during the study of the unit were on display in the classroom. Each child was responsible for his guest at the exhibit and answered any questions that he asked.

QUESTIONS, PROBLEMS AND EXERCISES

1. What are the chief differences between instructional and resource units?
2. Defend the statement, "Elementary school children are capable of carrying on effective research activities."
3. Prepare a ten-minute talk on advantages and disadvantages of teacher preplanning.

4. Show how democratic teaching procedures function in a unit of work.

5. Construct a list of democratic procedures that function during teacher-pupil planning.

6. List and evaluate the chief objections to unit teaching.

7. How can a teacher know whether the objectives of a unit have been attained?

8. How may the objectives of a given unit of learning be interrelated?

9. Present various means of appraising the outcomes of a unit of learning.

10. What does educational research reveal in regard to the values of unit teaching?

SELECTED SUPPLEMENTARY READINGS

ADAMS, FAY. *Educating America's Children*, 2d ed. New York: The Ronald Press Co., 1954.

Chap. 5, "General Method: The Unit of Work Procedure." Contains outlines of several units of work for various grade levels.

HANNA, LAVONNE A., GLADYS L. POTTER, and NEVA HAGAMAN. *Unit Teaching in the Elementary School.* New York: Rinehart & Co., Inc., 1955.

Chap. vi, "Developing a Unit of Work." Describes procedures for selecting, initiating, developing, and culminating a unit of work.

LEE, J. M., and D. M. LEE. *The Child and His Curriculum*, 2d ed. New York: Appleton-Century-Crofts, Inc., 1950.

Chap. vii devoted to the unit of work.

MACOMBER, FREEMAN GLENN. *Principles of Teaching in the Elementary School.* New York: American Book Co., 1954.

Chap. v, "Selecting and Planning an Experience Unit." Suggests principles governing the selection and preplanning of units.

MOFFATT, MAURICE P., and HAZEL W. HOWELL. *Elementary Social Studies Instruction.* New York: Longmans, Green & Co., Inc., 1952.

Chap. viii, "The Unit of Work." Discussion of the types of units and sample of unit for sixth grade social studies class.

NATIONAL SOCIETY FOR THE STUDY OF EDUCATION. *Learning and Instruction. Part I, Forty-ninth Yearbook.* Chicago: University of Chicago Press, 1950.

Chap. ix, "Implications for Organization of Instruction and Instructional Adjuncts" (by William H. Burton). Section of chapter contains a general outline for planning and developing a unit.

OTTO, HENRY J., HAZEL FLOYD, and MARGARET ROUSE. *Principles of Elementary Education,* rev. ed. New York: Rinehart & Co., Inc., 1955.

Chap. xii, "Working with Children." Discussion of types of characteristics of different types of units, with suggestions for planning and developing them.

RAGAN, WILLIAM B., and CELIA BURNS STENDLER. *Modern Elementary Curriculum.* New York: The Dryden Press, Inc., 1953.

Chap. vi, "Organizing the Class for Living and for Learning." Discussion of the meaning, types, problems, and advantages of units.

11

ADAPTING AND USING
INSTRUCTIONAL MATERIALS

Instructional aids helpful to teachers in their planning of learning activities for children include courses of study, resource units, textbooks, workbooks, book lists, and children's books, among others. Problems and considerations related to adapting and using these materials are presented here.

COURSES OF STUDY

The terms "course of study" and "curriculum" are often regarded as synonymous. This confusion has resulted from failure to recognize their respective purposes and scopes. The curriculum consists of all the features of the school environment to which the student reacts. The course of study is the instrument designed to guide the teacher in selecting and arranging the elements of the curriculum so that the student's experiences with various aspects of the school environment will result in desirable learning. The curriculum is the means utilized to attain the objectives of education. The course of study is intended to assist the teacher in the effective use of the preplanned framework of the curriculum to achieve the desired outcomes of education. Their functional relationship can be indicated by a consideration of the purposes.

Courses of study are purported to—

1. Cause teachers to think through and be conscious of the aims and objectives of education in general and in every subject.

2. Suggest the content and sequence of the learning experiences of the pupils.
3. Provide a guide to local resources and approaches and to content and pupil activities in order to realize the aims and objectives.
4. Suggest good methods and procedures.
5. Set up standards of attainment and growth.
6. Orient the course in relation to instructional materials of other grade levels.
7. Assist in the coordination of the efforts of the school system.

The official course of study and that designed by the teacher for use in a particular grade differ in several important respects. The main differences may be summarized as follows:

OFFICIAL COURSE OF STUDY	TEACHER ADAPTED COURSE
Purpose	
To serve as a general guide for a typical teacher in a typical situation	To serve as a specific guide in teaching a particular class in a particular situation
Origin	
Teacher committee or outside authority	Adapted from official course of study by individual teacher
Educational Aims	
General aims of subject outlined	Specific aims of course listed in terms of changes in children's behavior
Content	
Suggested content of considerable variety and scope	Content selected in terms of abilities, maturity, and previous experiences of students to attain specific objectives of the course
Methods	
Variety of teaching procedures suggested which are suitable for typical students	Teaching procedures based upon teacher's knowledge of students in class and relative degree of success experienced with alternative procedures
Time Allotment	
In terms of average student and relative values of many elements	In terms of individual students and relative values of a selected list of topics
Evaluation	
Suggested evaluation in terms of general objectives of course	Evaluation of specific outcomes sought for a particular group of students

Procedures in adaptation

Course-of-study construction involves numerous important decisions. Judgments are required in regard to the most urgent needs of pupils and the relative values of different learning activities and materials in meeting these needs. Decisions on the inclusion or omission of certain items of content as well as their optimum time allotment and grade placement demand intelligent discrimination.

The teacher occupies an advantageous position in respect to many of these matters. Her close proximity to pupils in the process of learning, in addition to her familiarity with the subject matter, provides her with invaluable insights into the problems of course-of-study construction. Many programs of curriculum reconstruction have failed of fruition because the participants lacked firsthand knowledge of actual classroom conditions. Mere proximity to a problem, however, does not insure adequate comprehension of its implication.

In adapting a course of study to meet the needs of a particular group of students, the following steps are suggested.

1. *Obtain firsthand information in regard to the pupils and the social scene of which they are a part.* The most significant types of data are those concerning:

   A. The children to be taught, with particular reference to their—
      1. Needs—intellectual, physical, and social
      2. General experiential background, including the level of school achievement or previous preparation and out-of-school experiences
      3. General intelligence
      4. Individual and group concerns
      5. General and special interests
      6. Home conditions
      7. Community background
   B. The local community with particular reference to its—
      1. Resources—cultural, educational, recreational, and natural
      2. Population—characteristics, nationality, etc.
      3. Attitudes and mores—economic, political, and religious
      4. Adult vocational activities
      5. Recreational facilities for adults and youth
      6. Welfare and youth-serving agencies
   C. The social order, with particular reference to its—
      1. Characteristics
      2. Ideals
      3. Deficiencies
      4. Possibilities for improvement
      5. Trends
      6. Critical problems

Firsthand information on the subjects listed above should be obtained in advance, or as the teaching proceeds. Data concerning students may be revealed by an examination of school records, testing, interest questionnaires, interviews, and various observational techniques. Active participation in community affairs provides the teacher with the best primary source of knowledge with respect to community life. This may be supplemented by informal surveys of community conditions. A thorough knowledge of the local community, augmented by analyses and studies of the general social order, furnishes a basis for the understanding of the problems of society.

2. *Supplement these primary sources of information about individual and social needs with data from various other sources.* Teachers usually do not have sufficient time or facilities at their disposal to acquire at first hand all the data necessary for building a course of study. Hence they have to rely upon secondary sources of information such as:

A. Scientific education research on curriculum problems by individuals and educational institutions.
B. Studies of contemporary life by committees of national and regional organizations.
C. Studies of child growth and development.
D. Courses of study from other schools, representing the combined judgment of teachers who have given considerable study to curriculum problems. These courses of study may suggest techniques of obtaining data, as well as instructional materials, which may be adapted for use in a particular school. Too great reliance upon material from other schools should, however, be avoided. Without proper adaptation and modification, the inherent evils of the scissors-and-paste method of course-of-study construction manifest themselves.
E. The opinions of competent persons on economic, educational, and social problems. The considered judgments of "juries of experts" are usually more valid than the superficial opinions of large numbers of persons who have given little time or thought to the issues involved.

3. *Consider which educational needs are met by the home and other agencies.* The school is only one of several educational agencies in our society. The needs of children are so diversified and numerous that no one agency can serve all of them. The school can hardly be expected to assume exclusive responsibility for the total education of children unless it is given supervision over them for a much larger proportion of their time. Recent extensions of educational services downward and upward, as well as the trend toward a longer school day, week, and year, have increased the opportunities of the school to serve more of the needs of children.

The assertion is frequently made that the school should limit its activities to the intellectual development of the child. To accept this area of child development as the major responsibility of the school does not change the supplementary nature of the school. All aspects of the child's growth are so interrelated that his needs cannot adequately be provided for in any single area to the exclusion of needs in other areas.

There is no disposition on the part of thoughtful teachers to usurp the prerogatives of the home and the church in the important areas of education in which they are peculiarly fitted to serve. The limited resources of the school also make it imperative that the latter confine its activities to those matters which are neglected by other institutions.

4. *Ascertain the interests of the pupils who are to be taught.* A knowledge of children's interests can be acquired in informal conversations with them, classroom discussions, observation of their spontaneous activities, simple questionnaires, and conversations with parents. (See Chapter 3 for a partial list of elementary school pupil interests. Such a list needs to be supplemented and adapted for the individual group of pupils in the grade for which the course is being used.)

5. *Consider the areas of human experience from which the content of the curriculum should be selected.* The major experience areas which determine the scope of the elementary school curriculum may be classified as follows:

A. Social relationships—social studies, geography, history
B. Biological and physical science—nature study, animals, plants, rocks, soil, and other geological formations in local community, elementary concepts in general science
C. Arts
    Practical arts—woodwork, cooking, and sewing
    Language arts—reading, writing, art of communication, or speech
D. Aesthetics—fine arts, crafts, music, literature
E. Physical and mental health—physical education, health instruction
F. Computational experiences

It is essential that the elementary school child acquire basic understandings and skills in each of these areas. In some schools it may be feasible to break the broad areas into smaller divisions or subject areas such as social studies.

6. *Formulate objectives of divisions or subjects in terms of desirable child behavior, such as: attitudes, appreciations, ideals, understandings, habits, and skills.*

A good illustration of the type of statement of objectives in terms of child growth and development for a subject is found in the following course of study in the social studies for the primary grades. In the second grade the content covers the child and his relationships in the community. The objectives stated for the social studies in the second grade follow:

THROUGH THIS CONTENT THE SOCIAL STUDIES PROGRAM IN THE ELEMENTARY SCHOOL CAN HELP THE CHILD TO DEVELOP AND GROW IN	I. Persons who guard life and property (the policeman, the fireman) II. Persons who bring us news (the postman, the newspaper boy) III. Persons who supply us with food (the grocer, the baker, the milkman) IV. Persons who work to keep us in good health (the doctor, the druggist, the dentist, the school nurse) V. Places where we enjoy ourselves (the park, the theatre, the circus) VI. Places to which we may go to learn (the school, the church, the library)
UNDERSTANDINGS AND CONCEPTS	The program should provide opportunities for the child to understand— Who his neighbors are. Many aspects of home and business life in his neighborhood. The purposes of neighborhood institutions, public and private. The natural influences upon life in the community. Man's efforts to lighten his work. The results of man's attempts to spend his leisure time in pleasant and satisfying ways. The need for health and safety regulations.
HABITS AND SKILLS	The program should provide opportunities for the child to grow in the ability to— Use those skills begun in the first grade. Use the public library and its resources. Select and handle books. Use the beginning techniques of research reading. Travel about his neighborhood in safety. Give directions clearly and certainly. Welcome visitors in his home and in his classroom.
ATTITUDES, APPRECIATIONS, AND INTERESTS	The program should provide opportunities for the child to develop— An appreciation of his own worth to the community. A respect for public and private property. A desire to cooperate in community enterprise.

An appreciation of the contributions made to his welfare through the industry and efforts of his neighbors.

A desire to express his appreciation of courtesies shown and services rendered.

A desire to acquaint others with the benefits and pleasures his neighborhood affords.

7. *Consider what modifications are necessary because of limitations of time, equipment, and building facilities.* In some situations, one or more of these factors may impose serious restrictions upon the inclusion of many desirable learning materials and experiences. For example, the number and variety of field trips in connection with science instruction or school excursions by social studies classes will be limited by the proximity of the school to places of educational interest.

8. *Review the grade placement of activities and learning exercises suggested in the textbook and official course of study.* Recommendations of grade placement of materials in courses of study are usually made on the basis of experimentation or the judgments of teachers and experts in regard to the difficulty of the material and the interests of children at different grade levels. The logical arrangement of subject matter has usually been a factor in allocating many materials of instruction to different grade levels. These recommendations require the careful scrutiny of the teacher in adapting the course to her pupils. Many teachers report that a considerable amount of reading material recommended for certain grade levels is too difficult and does not appeal to the interests of students of those grades. The common learnings needed by all pupils have not been given sufficient consideration in many instances. Content of great social significance for all pupils should be introduced early in the educational program before large numbers of pupils have been eliminated.

The teacher should ascertain the mental and social maturity of the students in the class and not forget it when he selects materials. Since the vocabulary used is often the source of students' difficulty in the comprehension of learning exercises, "stepping down" or "stepping up" may be necessary.

9. *Time allotments should wherever possible be reasonably flexible so that learning and teaching activities are not forced into a rigid time and schedule but may have more or less time for a given subject as a particular learning activity seems to suggest.*

In the Denver Public Schools no rigid time schedule is provided, but a general allotment of proportions of total time in a grade is set up as guides for the teacher. For the primary and intermediate grades the proportion of total time recommended for the several subject areas and units of study follow:[2]

PRIMARY GRADES

Language Arts (units of study)		50–55%
Reading	35–40%	
Reading Skills and Phonics		
Literature		
Library		
Writing, Speaking, Listening	10–15%	
Composition (class chart stories)		
Spelling		
Penmanship		
Reporting		
Orientation		
Conversation		
Social Studies (units of study)		10–15%
Social Living		
Science		
Health		
Mathematics		10–15%
Arithmetic Skills		
Quantitative Understanding		
Number Concept		
Social Significance of Number		
Problem Solving		
Art		8–10%
Manipulative Activities		
Expressive Activities		
Appreciative Activities		
Music		5–8%
Singing Experiences		
Rhythmic Experiences		
Creative Experiences		
Listening Experiences		
Physical Education		5–8%
Physical Skills		
Social Skills		
Recess		as needed

INTERMEDIATE GRADES

Language Arts (units of study)		30–40%
Reading	15–20%	
Literature		
Basic Reading Skills		
Library Activities and Skills		
Reference Skills and Reading for Information in Social Studies		

[2] *Teachers' Manual,* Denver Public Schools, Denver, Colorado, 1953.

INTERMEDIATE GRADES (Cont.)

Writing, Speaking, Listening	15–20%
Composition	
Spelling	
Penmanship	
Orientation	
Oral and Written Reports	
Social Studies (units of study)	15–20%
History	
Geography	
Civics	
Economics	
Science	
Health	
Mathematics	15–20%
Arithmetic Skills	
Quantitative Understanding	
Number Concepts	
Social Significance of Numbers	
Problem Solving	
Art	8–10%
Manipulative Activities	
Expressive Activities	
Appreciative Activities	
Music	8–10%
Singing Experiences	
Rhythmic Experiences	
Creative Experiences	
Listening Experiences	
Physical Education	8–10%
Physical Skills	
Social Skills	
Recess	as needed

10. *Organize the content into units of instruction.* The crucial issue in respect to the organization of material is the proper unifying element. In most subject-matter-centered courses of study, the unifying principle lies within the body of subject matter itself. The chronological sequence of topics in a history course illustrates the type of organization which results from the use of this principle. An increasing number of teachers believe that the student's past experiences and present interests provide the proper integrating basis. With these present elements as a beginning point, the learning activities and experiences should flow out to encompass learning materials more remote in time and space. Thus the history of social organizations would evolve from a study of the present social situation, of which the student himself is a part. An analysis and under-

standing of the current social scene would be the first phase of study of society.

These two approaches represent the extremes of two points of view. There are many degrees of variation between the two extremes. Whichever approach to organization of content is made, sufficient flexibility should be provided to allow for the special interests and needs of students. In any form of organization, a distinction should be made between materials designed to meet the common needs of all pupils and those intended to serve individual needs. Another factor in organizing materials is the advisability of correlating them with materials from other fields. The relative value of the topic, the availability of instructional materials, and the possibilities of leading on into related topics should determine the size of the unit of instruction.

11. *Make a tentative time allotment to each unit on the basis of its relative significance in achieving the objectives of the course.* In making decisions with respect to the optimum time allotment for each phase of a subject, the teacher is confronted with a mass of important material and a very limited amount of time in which to present it. The teacher should therefore recognize the implications of each decision she makes with respect to time allotment. The time allotment cannot, however, be made solely on the basis of the content involved. The abilities and experiential backgrounds of the students are of paramount importance in every case where the element of time is involved.

12. *Select from the teaching and learning procedures suggested in the official course of study and resource units those which appear to be best adapted to the pupils concerned.* Consideration should be given to the way factors in the learning process operate in a given situation. Problems of pupil interest, motivation, recognition of the significance of various topics, and emotional factors which influence learning all vary considerably from one group of pupils to another. Teaching procedures should be governed by the principles of effective learning. For example, a student's reaction to a learning situation is greatly influenced by his past experiences of learning. New learning has to be built on previous learning. *Teachers must begin with children where they actually are.* Their present stock of knowledge, prejudices, and skills may be assets or liabilities, but these are the foundations on which present and future learnings must be built.

Since self-activity is essential in learning, provision should be made for pupils to become active participants in every learning situation. In the acquisition of skills, the need for self-activity is obvious. The principle of self-activity, however, is equally applicable to the higher mental processes such as analysis, organization, and reasoning. In most school subjects, many opportunities can be provided for self-expression in the form of discussions, planning study procedures, conversation, drawing, and writing.

13. *Evaluate outcomes in terms of the stated objectives.* Evaluation should be continuous throughout the course, but a summary of the outcomes achieved should be made in the final phases. Measurement provides one basis for evaluation. Until recently measurement was confined to the more tangible outcomes of instruction, such as mastery of factual material. In Chapter 20 there are descriptions of instruments for measuring some of the important outcomes, such as ability to apply knowledge, reasoning, etc. For purposes of evaluation, the data obtained from test scores should be supplemented by anecdotal records, examination of written and other original work, and the various observational techniques mentioned in Chapters 19 and 20.

RESOURCE UNITS

In many schools committees of teachers prepare resource units, for use by themselves and by other teachers in the same subjects or combinations of subjects. A resource unit differs materially from a course of study. It may be used to replace or to implement parts of a course of study (see page 197). A resource unit contains the objectives of the unit, a general framework or outline of the unit, suggested instructional materials from books, the community, the library, and elsewhere. In addition, a resource unit contains a wide variety of suggested learning activities involving projects, reading, conversations, things to make, questions to answer, problems to solve, and reports to prepare. The teacher is free to select and arrange the learning materials and the learning and teaching activities in whatever way she pleases in order to assist the pupils in her class to grow most effectively toward the goals and objectives set for the unit, for the course of study for the year, and for education in general.

There is a wide variation in the use of resource units. Some teachers employ them with little or no class discussion of the various alternatives. An increasing number of teachers discuss with the class the alternatives and develop cooperatively the decision as to what material should be used and what learning activities shall be engaged in. In many instances, there will be differences of opinion among individual pupils or among different small groups of pupils as to what learning materials and activities will be employed.

With respect to the use of resource units, the same fundamental principles and considerations apply as with the adaptation of courses of study.

TEXTBOOKS

In the modern elementary school, the curriculum includes a great variety of learning materials. One resource of learning experiences is printed materials. Elementary school pupils should be taught to use these materials effectively and helped to acquire strong interests in reading. The acquisition of these interests is largely dependent upon the intelligent selection and effective presentation of reading materials by the teacher. The teacher should be familiar with the available reading materials suitable for children of her age group. In some schools, the teacher is provided with suggested lists of books, from which she may select those which appear to be most appropriate to the concerns and needs of her class. A knowledge of the criteria for evaluating the materials and the best procedures for selecting the materials is essential.

Limitations

The unfortunate effects of overdependence upon textbooks are numerous and far-reaching. Most important of all, the reciting of words is considered as the index of understanding. It results in temporary, superficial results instead of permanent mastery. It is a deadening procedure devoid of interest for the great majority of pupils. It robs most school subjects of their richness and value. It does not result in ability to apply the subject to a variety of life situations. It does not encourage the teacher constantly to learn more about her subject and to plan better methods of teaching. It encourages verbalism—the learning of words without understanding —and finally it results in concentration upon information and the neglect of ideals, attitudes, interests, concepts, and tastes as objectives of learning.

In addition to these limitations, dependence upon *one* textbook possesses other dangers. The course of study is then limited largely to one author's theory of education and his abilities to devise effective learning materials. The class and the teacher are committed to the author's emphasis, improper or otherwise. They are also dependent upon various divisions or types of material in the subject as well as the author's ideas of the selection and arrangement of materials, regardless of the needs, backgrounds, and interest of the pupils of a given class or the needs of a given community.

Textbooks are restricted not only in point of view but also in scope. Because of price limitations they are small, condensed, and hence too often artificial and uninteresting. This is especially unfortunate in history, the sciences, and the social studies, where it is better to assign twenty or thirty pages a day of interesting material than four or five pages of material written in the encyclopedia style. Textbooks are also written so as to be "teachable" by mediocre teachers rather than to exercise the full powers of superior teachers, and hence are not of the highest type of learning materials. They are frequently censored, distorted, and incomplete so that they will not offend ignorant or selfish groups of laymen who would prevent their use in the schools. Furthermore, textbooks get out of date in a few years and are commonly used for five to ten years after they should have been discarded.

Advantages

Textbooks are not without values, particularly for beginning teachers and older ones whose knowledge of the subject is no longer adequate to the needs of modern life. The experienced teacher of good preparation and superior abilities may employ the textbook to advantage along with other aids—supplementary readings, discussions, and visual and auditory aids. This is especially true if a very superior textbook is employed.

In general a textbook—

1. Furnishes an outline which the teacher may use in planning the work of the semester or the year.
2. Brings together in one volume a great deal of the more important information in a given field.
3. Usually contains some serviceable teaching aids, such as pictures, charts, diagrams, questions, problems, maps, summaries, outlines, headings, exercises, and table of contents.
4. Serves as a permanent record for future exercises later in the course, e.g., reviews.
5. Saves the teacher much time in presenting material or finding material for students to read in the library.
6. Enables the learner to take home with him in convenient form some of the more important materials for study.
7. Facilitates the making of assignments—though often assignments of inferior grade.
8. Provides a uniformity in the learning materials of pupils which is desirable to some degree, particularly for the purposes of class discussion and testing.

9. Provides a logical organization, though by so doing it deprives the learner of the responsibility for organizing and hence of the educational training involved.
10. Relieves the teacher of responsibility for evaluating much of the material of the course; more time is thus made available in class for discussions, explanations, assignments, the use of visual aids, and other activities.
11. Unifies the study of the class around a definite specific topic.
12. Avoids the confusion which may result from the attempts of pupils to organize a mass of facts from various sources.

Use of the textbook

In the use of textbooks the following suggestions are important:

1. Select the best available textbook. (See page 211 for suggestions on selecting textbooks.)
2. Supplement its use by discussions, collateral readings, and pupil activities of a wide variety.
3. Avoid mere recitation of textual materials. In discussion time call on pupils for main ideas, applications to life, and general principles.
4. Teach pupils how to read the textbook critically and understandingly.
5. Teach pupils how to use the various aids included in the textbook, such as the table of contents, the index, marginal and other headings, study questions, visual material.
6. Make assignments which call for recitation, evaluation, criticism, interpretation, application, and supplementation.
7. In some classes, particularly in history, follow an introductory survey or rapid reading of the text with a more thorough, slower study of the text and collateral material.
8. Adapt the textbook and other materials to the individual and to the various levels of ability of the class.

Certain practices in the use of textbooks should be avoided in classes in history, the sciences, the social studies, and other content subjects. The one-book teacher in these subjects cannot possibly be a superior teacher. By relying exclusively upon one textbook, she fails to train pupils in the skills of comparison and of synthesis of materials from more than one source. The students will also lack training in library skills and habits and other important educational results which will remain long after most of the textbook content has been forgotten. The citizen of tomorrow must read current materials not only in books but in periodicals and newspapers and must know where to look for and how to interpret such materials.

The teacher in the content subjects should avoid overemphasis upon "recitation" of textbook materials. She should instead encourage the organization of material from textbooks and other sources around problems and questions, particularly those of current importance and interest. She should avoid using too much of the class period for oral testing over the textbook material and instead leave the majority of the time for socialized discussions, telling by the teacher, pupil reports, supervised study, and other effective learning activities.

In all subjects the teacher should subordinate "textbook covering" to efforts to achieve the objectives of the course in terms of learning or child growth. She should not make the error of having pupils "learn" the textbook, trusting thereby to achieve the objectives. The textbook is not the course itself but only one valuable instrument for teaching and must be used intelligently. It must be supplemented daily by one or more of a wide variety of teaching and learning materials and devices.

Selection of textbooks

While theoretically the classroom teacher makes the course of study for the subjects she teaches, in many instances her principal role in making the course consists of selecting the textbook. Once the textbook is selected the general pattern of the course is determined, at least to the extent that the textbook is emphasized. This is true whether the textbook is the student's only aid or is used as a reference book along with other textbooks, references, and collateral readings or is supplemented with workbooks, field trips, visual aids, and other instructional materials and methods.

Because of the degree to which the textbook determines or constitutes the course of study, great care and intelligence should be exercised in selecting it. In the following rating scale[3] is a list of items which should be taken into consideration in the selection of textbooks.

		Points
I. Authorship		170
A. The author's scholarship in subject field	50	
B. The author's familiarity with pertinent research findings and scientific investigation	20	
1. In this subject-matter field	5	
2. In reading which is basic to proper use of any text	5	
3. In graded words lists (vocabulary)	5	

[3] Samuel E. Burr, Jr., *The Journal of Education,* CXXXII (May, 1949), pp. 138–39.

Points

      4. In the use of appropriate technical vocabulary . . .   5

      5. In techniques of textbook construction   5

   C. The author's classroom or other teaching experience . . 25

   D. The author's ability to reflect his scholarship and experience through the pages of his book 50

II. General Considerations 125

   A. Recency of copyright date 20

   B. Correlation of material with general objectives of the school 20

   C. Suitability of author's style for pupils of this grade level 25

   D. Evidence that this text helps to build active citizenship in a democracy 25

   E. Availability of book in desired quantities 25

   F. Comparative cost per copy 10

III. Mechanical Features 100

   A. Waterproof binding 10

   B. Durability of binding 10

   C. Type of cover 5

   D. Color of cover 10

   E. Design of cover 5

   F. Quality and clearness of illustrations 20

   G. Size and shape of page and of book 10

   H. Size and design of type 10

    I. Color and tint of paper 5

   J. Texture and surface of paper 10

   K. Color of ink 5

IV. Selection of Subject Matter 150

   A. Scientific grading of material 20

   B. Adaptability of material to class needs 20

   C. Adaptability of material to community needs 20

   D. Basic value of material 25

   E. Variety of practical applications to life situations 20

   F. Abundance and grading of material to meet individual and group abilities and needs 25

   G. Sufficiency of detail in presenting materials 20

V. Organization and Presentation 125

   A. Adaptability to a pragmatic program 20

   B. Psychological sequence 15

   C. Possibility of omissions without destroying sequence . . 15

   D. Degree of emphasis on variety of topics 15

   E. Plan for problem solution 15

   F. Systematic development of reasoning power 15

   G. Distribution, amount, and balance of drill 15

   H. Variety and effectiveness of diagnostic testing materials 15

Points

VI. Techniques or Features 100

  A. Attractiveness of book and contents 20
  B. Recognition of psychological principles 20
  C. Provisions for meeting individual differences 20
  D. Use of life situations for motivation 20
  E. Inclusion of desirable project materials 20

VII. Proper Documentation 80

  A. For textual material 20
  B. For charts 10
  C. For maps 10
  D. For diagrams 10
  E. For tabulations 10
  F. For illustrations (pictures) 20

VIII. Teaching Helps 150

  A. A preface of information for the teacher 10
  B. Teacher's manual or guide book 10
  C. Adequacy of table of contents 10
  D. Adequacy of index 10
  E. Adequacy of glossary 10
  F. Adequacy of appendixes 10
  G. Adequacy of illustrations 10
  H. Adequacy of charts or maps 10
  I. Appropriateness of illustrations and charts or maps . . 10
  J. Effectiveness and appeal of illustrations 10
  K. Summaries and previews 10
  L. Study helps for pupils 10
  M. Norms for tests 10
  N. Norms recognize ability grouping 10
  O. Suitable and adequate forms 10

Total possible evaluation   1000

WORKBOOKS AND SUPPLEMENTARY
READING MATERIALS

The workbook provides "work" for the student to do—questions to answer, problems to solve, projects to undertake, drill and practice materials, tests, and remedial assignments. Although controlled experimentation in the use of workbooks has not definitely established the degree of their value, some of the experiments have indicated that pupils' performance on written tests was more satisfactory in classes in which workbooks were used than in those where they were not used. The experiments, however, throw little light on the matter of how much time of teachers was saved for other work by the use of workbooks. Most of the experiments were conducted years ago when the workbooks available were not generally of superior quality and often not coordinated with the textbook and other phases of the course.

Advantages

The workbook is helpful because it—

1. Provides definite assignment of supplementary material.
2. Makes practice and review materials readily available.
3. Provides wider variety of learning activities.
4. Supplies student with copy of assignments.
5. Provides for individual differences by:
   a. Variety of tasks for different interests.
   b. Diagnostic tests—some for self-diagnosis.
   c. Remedial materials keyed to diagnostic tests.
6. Furnishes study materials for homework and study halls.
7. Saves time in class period ordinarily used in copying exercises.
8. Provides training in self-direction and independent study.
9. Provides a simple means by which pupils can study while absent from school and thus make up work missed.
10. Saves time of teacher for other work.

Not all workbooks offer all these advantages.

The workbook does not relieve the teacher of the responsibility of planning the daily work, including use of the workbook. She must plan to use it as a supplement to the textbook, coordinating the two. She must plan assignments in advance in terms of differences among the learners in ability, interest, and need. Most workbooks should not be followed closely. Skill in the use of the workbook will probably have to be developed through study and experience.

Limitations

The lack of positive experimental results markedly favorable to the use of the workbook is indicative of the limitations inherent in its use. The following limitations should be recognized and kept to a minimum by careful planning:

1. Lack of coordination with the textbook
2. Some material not adapted to interests or abilities of class with which workbook is used
3. Materials not well graded
4. Failure of some materials to contribute much to the objectives of the course ("busy-work," blank-filling, petty questions, etc.)
5. Lack of sufficient choice in the references to books and periodicals to take care of lack of library materials in the local school

6. Failure to provide materials especially for bright pupils and for slow or dull pupils
7. Abuses in use of workbooks:
    a) Lack of careful planning by teacher
    b) Acceptance as self-teaching devices
    c) Lack of adaptation and correlation with course
    d) Overemphasis upon nonessential outcomes

In view of these weaknesses and dangers, the teacher should employ workbooks as possible resources and weave them into the rest of the activities of the class, rather than rely upon them steadily as assignments.

Selection of the workbook

In selecting workbooks for use in elementary school classes the teacher should remember that—

1. The workbook should be used as a supplement to and not as a substitute for the textbook.
2. The workbook should provide amply for reading of references on each of the topics and units.
3. Because the readings, problems, exercises, and other materials should be systematically correlated with the textbook and should supplement it intelligently, a workbook specially constructed for use with the adopted textbook is preferable.
4. The vocabulary and style of writing of the workbook and the references included in it should be appropriate for the pupils who will use it.
5. The learning activities included should be adapted to the interests, abilities, and previous background of the students.
6. The learning activities should include some adapted to the interests and abilities of weaker students and some appropriate for the abler ones. Variation in interests should be provided for.
7. The learning activities should be appropriately distributed with respect to the different objectives of the course, including ideals, attitudes, interests, and tastes as well as information and skills.
8. There should be ample provision for diagnostic checking on possible failure of individual pupils in any of the more important outcomes of the course.
9. There should be optional material (in most subjects) for drill upon weak points of individual pupils as discovered by the diagnostic devices.
10. If checking or grading by the teacher is contemplated, it should be provided for in such a way as to be economical of the teacher's time.

11. The learning activities should for the most part be self-explanatory or at least require a minimum of explanation by the teacher.
12. There should be some "shutoff" device to avoid the continuance of study and learning activities far beyond the point of adequate learning.
13. The contents should be in attractive form.
14. The workbook should be mechanically sound, that is,
    a. sufficiently well bound to last through the course.
    b. printed in a type size appropriate for its users.
15. Where materials are to be handed in or checked by the teacher, the pages involved should be readily detachable and should provide a blank for the student's name.

School library materials

One of the most significant developments in elementary education within recent years has been the school library. The need for adequate libraries for high schools was recognized many years ago, and considerable impetus was given by accrediting agencies. In elementary schools the development has been largely the result of the recognition by teachers of the need for enriching the school and other life experiences of the elementary school pupil. In the better elementary schools of today, the library is considered an important resource in the education of pupils.

The classroom teacher in one of these schools has the opportunity and responsibility of recommending books for the use of her class. She may wish also to supplement the central library collection with books for her classroom library. Thus it is essential that the elementary teacher know the books available for children and plan to use them wisely and intelligently.

Many schools make booklists available to teachers. These lists can be supplemented by those from book publishers and book sections of magazines and newspapers.

Many interesting and valuable children's books are available for use in elementary schools. Although many of these books can be used to supplement textbooks in the content subjects, they have other important values. Because of their wide variety and interesting style, these books can serve to broaden and enrich children's experiences. New interests may be developed and old ones reinforced by wide reading of properly chosen books. The teacher's effort in stimulating and guiding her pupils is a rich and rewarding activity. Some of the methods which teachers have found useful in stimulating and extending children's interests in books are shown in the following examples.

1. Arranging book displays
2. Making trips with children (beginning in third grade) to public libraries
3. Discussing favorite books of individual pupils with class
4. Organizing informal book clubs in class
5. Having book talks by persons interested in children's books
6. Having class illustrate and dramatize stories in books
7. Discussing stories in class
8. Making scrapbooks of favorite books

The teacher can obtain information in regard to children's books by reading the reviews in such publications as:

The Booklist, published regularly by the American Library Association
Childhood Education

Collateral and supplementary reading materials

Since most textbooks contain only a limited amount of material, highly condensed, there is a need for additional reading materials, especially in the content subjects. Among the most important types are:

1. Materials which develop more intensively and thoroughly one or more phases or units briefly treated in the textbook
2. Materials relating to topics omitted from the textbook which the teacher may think best to assign to one or more of the students
3. Materials which differ in point of view from those in the textbook
4. Materials written in a different and perhaps more interesting or attractive style

While it is frequently useful to assign *collateral* readings in other textbooks, they are usually not sufficient. *Supplementary* readings are also needed. Supplementary readings are materials which fall into the first three categories mentioned above—materials which do not merely parallel the textbook but extend beyond its scope.

Among the ways in which collateral and supplementary readings may be used to advantage are the following.

1. The class may be given definite assignments by title and page for which all are to be held responsible. This extension of textbook teaching is often useful in widening the scope of material and in introducing new or different viewpoints or treatments.
2. The class may be given, from time to time, a list of supplementary materials from which they may select what they wish, being responsible not for pages but for the mastery of topics, problems, or questions. This plan is very much to be commended in in-

stances where the subject is of sufficient interest to insure that a considerable portion of the class will search in the extra-text materials. The value of the contribution of material the student has found for himself and the pride engendered in the contributor add greatly to the interest and life of the class.

3. Individual and group reports may be used to advantage. This additional challenge need not be given to the brighter individuals alone. Frequently an average student may be asked to do something with collateral readings and report back to the class, as a means to developing interest on his part.

4. Collateral reading may be employed in planning flexible or differentiated assignments.

5. Where the problem or project method of teaching is employed, collateral reading in connection with the problem or project is not only desirable but essential.

QUESTIONS, PROBLEMS, AND EXERCISES

1. What factors should be considered by a teacher in the selection of learning activities for a given age group of children?

2. Formulate a list of objectives which should serve as guideposts in the construction of a course of study.

3. How may the classroom teacher assist in the selection of textbooks?

4. What supplementary materials may be used to supplement textbooks in the grade you plan to teach?

5. Examine one or more resource units which may be available in the curriculum collection. Be able to describe them in class and to explain how they could be used.

6. What changes in the use of textbooks have resulted from changes in classroom methods and curricular reorganization?

7. Select the three criteria which are of the greatest importance in selecting a textbook. Justify your selection.

8. Evaluate two standard textbooks of recent publication upon the basis of the suggested criteria.

9. Outline a plan for the effective use of textbooks in one of the subjects you plan to teach.

10. Discuss the advantages and disadvantages of free textbooks.

11. What factors should be considered by the teacher in making a decision to use a workbook in her course?

SELECTED SUPPLEMENTARY READINGS

ADAMS, FAY. *Educating America's Children*, 2d ed. New York: The Ronald Press Co., 1954.

Chap. 4, "The Child, the Teacher, and the Curriculum: The Broader View of Method." The unit of work is described with a presentation of the steps in unit construction. The disadvantages of units of work are listed.

ADAMS, HAROLD P., and FRANK G. DICKEY. *Basic Principles of Student Teaching.* New York: American Book Co., 1956.

Chap. vii, "Selecting and Using Materials of Instruction," pp. 178–96. The action approach to the selection and use of materials of instruction is presented. Questions that teachers might ask about selection and use of materials and suggested answers make this chapter practical reading for the teacher.

BURR, JAMES B., LOWRY W. HARDING, and LELAND B. JACOBS. *Student Teaching in the Elementary School.* New York: Appleton-Century-Crofts, Inc., 1950.

Chap. ix, "Utilizing Learning Materials With Children." A very excellent listing of various audio-visual materials and how they can be used in the classroom. An annotated bibliography at the end of the chapter is very helpful.

EDUCATIONAL POLICIES COMMISSION. *Education for All American Children.* Washington, D.C.: National Education Association, 1948.

Chap. iii, "The Curriculum." Who should plan the curriculum, what it should include, and the important position of the teacher in curriculum planning are presented.

KLAUSMEIER, HERBERT J., KATHARINE DRESDEN, HELEN C. DAVIS, and WALTER ARNO WITTICH. *Teaching in the Elementary School.* New York: Harper & Bros., 1956.

Chap. 4, "Curriculum Organization."

MELVIN, A. GORDON. *General Methods of Teachings.* New York: McGraw-Hill Book Co., Inc., 1952.

Chap. 4, "Forecasting the Class Program." Daily, weekly, and long-term plans are discussed with many types of schedules presented which should prove helpful to the classroom teacher.

OTTO, HENRY J., HAZEL FLOYD, and MARGARET ROUSE. *Principles of Elementary Education,* rev. ed. New York: Rinehart & Co., Inc., 1955.

Chap. ix, "Organizing the School Program." This chapter contains a description of the various forms that curricula take such as correlated and broad fields. The organized-synthesized program is defined and an excellent sample program of this type is given.

SAYLOR, J. GALEN, and WILLIAM M. ALEXANDER. "Newer Approaches to Curriculum Design," *Curriculum Planning for Better Teaching and Learning.* New York: Rinehart & Co., Inc., 1954. Pp. 277–305.

The major social functions of living approach to curriculum design is defined and the curriculum designed on the basis of interests, need, and abilities of the learners included.

———. "Using Resource Units and Unit Plans," *Curriculum Planning for Better Teaching and Learning.* New York: Rinehart and Co., Inc., 1954. Pp. 391–425.

A very good description is given in this chapter on the resource unit with a sample unit of this type provided.

12

USING AUDIO-VISUAL MATERIALS

The building of accurate concepts is essential to learning. Unless the learner can associate the written or spoken word with some past or present experience, the resulting concept is likely to be vague and meaningless. The effective use of books is dependent upon numerous rich and meaningful experiences of elementary school children in their natural and social environment. The multiple approach through ear, eye, and touch contributes to more effective initial learning and greater retention.

In order to assist pupils in acquiring an experiential background for reading and vocabulary, elementary school teachers utilize many types of audio-visual materials. Recent research reveals that (with the exception of films) audio-visual materials are more extensively used in the elementary school than in either the high school or college.

In many elementary schools objects are brought into the classroom, identified, and used. Elementary science laboratories have been established. Dramatizations and construction projects represent important pupil activities. Firsthand acquaintance with the children's immediate environment is acquired by observing individuals at work, talking with the postman and fireman, and making trips to gardens, parks, and stores.

While firsthand experiences provide, no doubt, the soundest foundation for learning, the practical limitations on the scope and variety of these experiences make it necessary for the teacher to utilize many audio-visual materials in the classroom. Fortunately there are many valuable and inexpensive materials available for classroom instruction.

VALUES OF AUDIO-VISUAL MATERIALS

On the basis of results obtained by the use of audio-visual materials in classrooms over a considerable number of years, sufficient evidence is available to reveal clearly their effectiveness in teaching. This conclusion is supported by the findings of educational experimentation. Among the most significant values of audio-visual aids as revealed by educational research and actual classroom use, are the following. Not all of them are equally applicable to all types of audio-visual instruction materials.

1. *Arousing interest.* Reference has been made to the technical difficulties which students encounter in making verbal experience meaningful. Another obstacle to effective learning is the student's attitude toward certain materials of instruction. A literary classic as presented in a printed volume may be very unimpressive or even forbidding to a pupil. A good screen or radio version of the classic is likely not only to contribute to understanding and retention but also to arouse a compelling desire to read the book.

2. *Supplementing other sources.* Knowledge for its own sake is unimportant. As the basis of sound judgment and appreciation it is fundamental. To be well informed is to possess the first essential of effective, intelligent action. Audio-visual materials not only enable the student to see information from books in a new light, but they also add to his fund of knowledge and in this way help him to see the facts gleaned from textbooks in their proper relationships.

3. *Enlarging the individual's environment.* By the proper use of audio-visual aids, a student may live realistically and vicariously in environments remote in time and space from his immediate surroundings. A motion picture makes him realize that rivers on maps are no longer mere verbal or diagrammatic abstractions. In history, films portraying the struggles of our forefathers in establishing this nation give the student a vivid understanding of early American history which cannot be gained from verbal descriptions.

4. *Promoting intellectual curiosity.* A well-chosen photograph or film of a scene of historical significance is most likely to arouse an interest in the study of the event. Pictures of places of geographical interest serve to promote the reading of books on the subject or to create a desire to visit the place. The curiosity aroused in a schoolboy by a photograph in a geography textbook may become the source of his interest in the people of another country. It is far from the truth that children's interests are necessarily limited to their immediate environment. While students should be interested in living conditions in their immediate neighborhoods, it is

likewise important for them to desire to know how people live in other parts of the world.

5. *Contributing to faster acquisition and longer retention of learning.* The intensity and accuracy of impressions received through the eye or ear are conducive to more lasting imagery. The relative effectiveness of concrete experience as compared to verbal instruction is dependent upon the nature of the instruction and the student's previous experience with the visual aids used in instruction.

6. *Fostering favorable attitudes for learning.* Novelty and variety may be introduced into classroom situations by means of audio-visual materials. Monotony promotes boredom, which is detrimental to the formation of favorable attitudes toward learning activities. While entertainment is seldom the main outcome to be sought in the presentation of audio-visual materials, joyous attitudes are desirable concomitants of any educational activity.

TYPES AND SELECTION OF VISUAL MATERIALS

One of the most notable contributions of science to the development of visual materials has been the motion picture. As a result of its spectacular characteristics and wide general acceptance, it has been considered as synonymous with visual education. This, however, is an erroneous conception, as there are various types of visual materials, each possessing its own distinctive value. Among the most readily available and usable are projected pictures, unprojected pictures, graphic materials, objects, models, and specimens.

Dramatizations, demonstrations, experiments, and school excursions are sometimes considered as types of visual materials. They are, in reality, *techniques* of making available some of the visual aids in the foregoing list. Exhibits, collections, bulletin boards, and sand tables also are referred to as visual materials. These terms pertain to the plan of arrangement or instrument used in the display of various types of visual materials. Because of the extensive use of bulletin boards, charts, chalkboards, and sand tables in the elementary school, reference will be made to their use later in this chapter.

When it appears that some type of visual material will serve a useful purpose in a particular classroom situation, the teacher must decide what type of material to use. The type most suitable in a given situation depends on several factors. The standards for selection of a particular visual material are more specific. They will be considered later in this chapter in the discussion of each type of visual material. The factors which should be considered in selection of the type of visual material include the following.

1. *The degree to which the type of material is adapted to the objectives and problems of the course.* For example, if the desired outcome is the understanding of a process involving motion, the motion picture is particularly suitable; in the physical sciences, demonstrations of the action of objects or materials are valuable; in nature study, field trips for the purpose of observing and studying animals and plants in their natural habitat are important; maps and globes assist in the formation of accurate concepts of the relationships of places.

2. *The relative effectiveness of the available types of visual materials.* A considerable amount of educational research has been devoted to the relative values of different types of visual materials. The evidence is clear that different types of aids serve different purposes. In many instances the decision in regard to what aid to use is not in terms of the relative superiority of one type of material over another, but rather of what combination of materials is the most desirable.

3. *Proper balance and variety of materials.* Not all types of visual materials are equally effective in different types of classroom activities. For example, stereograph views are well adapted for individual pupil study, whereas projected pictures are appropriate for group activity. The interests of an individual pupil may be more adequately served by a variety of materials than by a single one. A model may arouse the interest of one pupil, while the dramatic quality of a film may make a strong appeal to another. The selection of visual materials should be made on an objective basis, thereby avoiding overemphasis on those types which may have a particular fascination for the teacher or for a few members of the class.

4. *The extent to which the type of materials is adaptable to the pupil's mental abilities.* Visual teaching materials appropriate for one group of pupils may appear to be "kid stuff" to another group.

5. *Availability and cost of materials and time required for presentation in the classroom.*

6. *If the visual material has been used previously by the teacher, the evaluation she and her pupils have made of it.* In an increasing number of schools, the expert opinion of the director of visual education is available to teachers.

PROJECTED PICTURES

Films

The crucial issue involved in the selection of a film for classroom use is the purpose to be served by the film. Important considerations in the selection of films include the following.

1. Availability of the film (possibility of obtaining the film when needed)
2. Mechanical and technical quality of the film
3. Possibilities of correlating film with the topic being studied
4. Appropriateness of film to mental and social maturity of the pupils
5. Distinctive contribution to be made by the use of the film, e.g., motivation, providing information, culminating activity
6. Opportunities for follow-up procedures

It should be understood that films are *supplementary* teaching aids. They are not designed to replace books or the teacher. They cannot serve all the purposes of instruction. In fact, except in cases where an understanding of processes is involved, films may be inferior to other types of visual aids, such as film strips. Good teaching techniques based upon sound educational principles are as essential in the use of films as of any other type of instructional materials.

The effective use of films requires careful planning, not only in terms of the outcomes sought but also in regard to the proper facilities. Excessive and indiscriminate use of films hinders rather than promotes the learning process.

After the film has been selected on the basis of the foregoing criteria, the teacher should plan a definite procedure for the teaching of the film. The following steps may be suggestive.

1. The teacher should preview the film for the purpose of becoming familiar with its content and organization.
2. The teacher should prepare a brief list of the main features of the films which are emphasized in the lesson.
3. The pupils should be given an assignment which includes:
   a) Reading materials giving information in brief story form in regard to the general nature of the film.
   b) If a sound film is used, a list of the unfamiliar words to study in order to understand the sound track.
   c) A list of questions pertaining to the main points of information included in the film.
   d) A list of suggestions to pupils in regard to what to look for in the film.
4. Have the class view the entire film without interruption.
5. Follow up the showing of the film with a class discussion of the main points presented in the film.
6. Repeat showing of film if class discussion reveals misconceptions or lack of understanding on part of pupils.
7. Have the class read textbook and supplementary materials related to the subject of the film.

8. Have individual pupils read and give reports to the class on special problems suggested by the film.
9. Give a test based upon the film, related readings, and class discussion.

Film strips

Film strips are also known as slide films, film rolls, stereopticon films, and film slides. They are still pictures, printed on short strips of standard-width, noninflammable motion picture film and may be used in place of glass slides. They can be projected serially or singly, and forward or backward as desired. Both silent and sound types are available. They cost only a fraction as much as regular motion pictures and are convenient to handle. Another advantage is that a picture can be held on the screen for any length of time desired and pictures can be reshown. A disadvantage is that the pictures have to be shown in a predetermined order. The silent slide films possess great flexibility in teaching: the teacher can emphasize certain pictures by explanations as they are held on the screen. The sound film strips which reproduce sound from disc records can be run without sound in the event the teacher wishes to supply the explanation or have the class discuss the picture. Since the slide films do not move, stronger impressions can be gained by closer attention to details than the moving film permits. The projection equipment is relatively simple and inexpensive.

Slides and opaque projections

Glass slides of photographs and diagrams are well adapted to group instruction. Both the slides and the necessary projection equipment are inexpensive. The equipment is relatively simple and easy to operate. In comparison with film strips, glass slides are more durable and less likely to be damaged by heat. Another advantage of slides is that it is not necessary to show them in any fixed sequence.

Many slide projectors have an adjustment feature which makes it possible to show either slides or opaque materials. Regular opaque projectors are also available. By means of these projectors postcards, materials from the pages of a textbook, or geology specimens can be shown on a screen. A dark room and a good screen are absolutely essential. Light-projected maps are also widely used, and it is claimed that they have much greater teaching force than the traditional wall map, because they can be more easily seen and are easier to handle than a series of wall maps. Map slides in color are now available. Perhaps the most satisfactory slides are those prepared by experts in photographic work; however, many teachers add to their list of slides by having students assist in making them.

Like other visual materials, slides should be selected carefully for classroom use. Among the criteria for selection are relevancy, technical quality, maturity of pupils, and contribution to the work at hand.

UNPROJECTED PICTURES

Unprojected pictures are often referred to as still pictures or merely as pictures. The various kinds of unprojected pictures include actual photographs, prints, paintings, murals, and illustrations in textbooks, magazines, and other publications. They can be obtained from photographers, school supply companies, and many other sources. From the standpoint of pupil interest, excellent sources are the pupil's and teacher's own collections. Still pictures are inexpensive and abundant in variety and scope.

The unique value of this form of pictorial material lies in its possibilities for detailed analysis and study. Mountains, other geographical features, and many constructed works lend themselves to more effective portrayal by still pictures than by motion pictures because of their natural immobility.

The first essential in the effective use of pictures is that each pupil be able to see the picture clearly and distinctly. Many teachers, however, fail to devise adequate methods of showing pictures. A single large picture may be utilized satisfactorily for group study. In the case of smaller pictures, it is desirable to provide a sufficient number of duplicate copies of each picture so that each pupil may have a copy for individual study. If duplicates are impossible to obtain, it will be necessary to rearrange the seating so that all may see a single picture or one of a limited number of pictures. A common error is to distribute a large number of more or less unrelated pictures to be passed along hurriedly from one pupil to another.

Better results are usually obtained if the members of a class concentrate on a few pictures during a given class period. When it is necessary to pass pictures around in the class, they should be arranged in some logical sequence. The chief value of pictures of this type depends largely upon thorough analysis and study, which require time and involve guiding pupils in observing the various features of the picture. Individual and group discussion based on the objects and their relationships in the picture are often fruitful.

Pictures can be clipped from various types of publications and can be mounted very easily. Mounted pictures can be shown to greater advantage and retained for future reference more easily than unmounted ones. When not in use, they should be filed according to subject and topic. Proper labeling for purposes of identification is also desirable.

Many textbooks and supplementary reading materials are well illustrated. These illustrations can serve a useful purpose in contributing to the pupil's understanding and appreciation of a topic. The teacher can relate them to the reading material by directing attention to the meanings they convey. Investigations have revealed that, unless this is done, children often fail to understand the full significance of pictures in books.

A few well-chosen pictures of artistic merit add to the attractiveness of classroom walls. They also may become the basis of or a supplement to classroom study. Pictorial bulletins, many in color, suitable for bulletin boards are available from commercial organizations. Many current bulletins pertain to historical, scientific, or industrial themes. As is true of other bulletin board materials, only a few should be displayed at any one time, and they should be changed from time to time.

Many state libraries have a variety of pictorial materials available for use in schools, which can be obtained on a free rental basis except for transportation costs. These materials, particularly valuable for the study of state geography and history, consist of mounted pictures and periodicals containing pictures, magazine and newspaper clippings, and photographs of pictorial materials.

The postage stamp collection has great educational significance in these days of increased attention to world geography and foreign countries. The stamps of many countries have considerable artistic merit, but it is in the fields of geography, history, and international relations rather than art that postage stamp collections have their greatest value. Many issues of United States stamps commemorate significant historical events and the achievements of leaders in art, education, music, science and government. Stamps of foreign countries depict the geographical features, products, history, and peoples of those countries. Stamp collecting in school often becomes the basis of a life-long hobby.

GRAPHIC MATERIALS

Graphic materials depict ideas by emphasizing certain elements in a situation and subordinating others. They are not designed to reveal details as other types of visual aids do. In this respect they are the most abstract of all visual materials. They arrest the attention by exaggeration or unusual arrangement of line and color.

Their power lies in their ability to convey meanings dramatically and instantaneously. Their direct and forthright treatment and their simplicity of form enable them to portray an idea of light humor or one of great social significance.

Cartoons and posters

The degree of interest which can be developed in commonplace objects or events by graphic representation is disclosed by the popularity of the newspaper comic strips. Recently an effort has been made to capitalize for educational purposes on the appeal that comics make to children. Several series of cartoon books designed to teach history, literature, science, and religious subjects are now available. The artistic quality and potential interest value appear to be satisfactory.

The comics, however, represent only one of several forms of cartoons. Magazines, newspapers, and books contain many cartoons of considerable political and social significance. These offer many possibilities for supplementing numerous areas of the school curriculum.

The quick initial impression which a good cartoon makes may be superficial and fleeting unless it is accompanied by further reflection. Students can be guided in their study of cartoons by discussions which assist them to understand the symbolism and to interpret the meanings. A comparison of cartoons representing different points of view may serve to stimulate an interest in reading leading to the development of an unbiased interpretation of the issue or subject depicted.

By line, composition, or color, the poster emphasizes one dominant theme. It is designed to convey one idea directly and forcefully. The strong impression it makes may be utilized to impart information or to develop attitudes.

As one of the culminating activities of a unit of instruction, students may summarize attitudes and knowledge they have acquired in the study of the topic by designing and making posters. Thus training in techniques of drawing and in the use of color and other materials is provided in a purposeful situation.

Maps and globes

The function of the map is to give a graphic representation of the abstract concepts of distance, direction, location, and size. Maps were among the first types of visual aids to be used in schools. Recent developments in the preparation of maps have made them much more useful in teaching than they formerly were. In comparison with the older types, the newer maps give a far more accurate representation of the relative positions of places on the earth. The globe, however, is the only true map because it shows the roundness of the earth.

On the basis of form, maps may be classified as globes, relief maps, and flat maps. An understanding of the wide range of topics which are encompassed by maps can be gained by attempting to classify flat maps according to content. Now available are airline maps, contour current events maps, political maps, political-physical maps, product maps, rainfall maps, temperature maps, soil maps, vegetation maps, military maps, literary maps, population maps, road maps, and many more—some showing location by nationality, religion, or institutions.

The mechanical features of maps for school purposes have been greatly improved in the last generation. More consideration is given to proper arrangement and balance of materials. Color is used more effectively, and useless detail is omitted. Maps should be selected with reference to the maturity of pupils, purposes to be served, and type of learning activities involved. For example, in group instruction large or projected maps are necessary. If individual study of maps appears desirable, smaller maps for individual use should be available. If pupil activity in the making of maps appears feasible, outline maps should be obtained.

The effective use of maps as visual aids is more dependent upon classroom arrangement and other routine matters than is true of most instructional materials. As part of the preparation for teaching a topic with the aid of maps, the teacher should examine the available maps pertinent to the topic, select the types and sizes best suited to her purposes, and arrange the maps in advance for optimum use.

One purpose of the study of maps in schools is to teach pupils to use them effectively in their own study. It is no compliment to elementary and high schools that students come to college without a knowledge of directions as indicated on maps.

The teacher can assist elementary school pupils to utilize maps and globes effectively in their learning, by means of the following activities:

1. Pupils point out the cardinal directions inside and outside the classroom.
2. Teacher and pupils locate cardinal directions on maps.
3. Pupils make simple sketches of the classroom floor plan and diagrams of streets in the neighborhood of the school.
4. Teacher explains what maps and globes are for and how they differ.

5. Teacher explains the different types of information which can be obtained from maps and globes.
6. Pupils use simple maps in the beginning to find answers to questions or supply information concerning topics being studied.
7. Teacher explains common map terms (e.g., conventional symbolism, rivers, lakes, mountains, etc.)
8. Pupils locate simple geographic features on a large map and later on individual outline maps.
9. Pupils use maps and globes in study of unit or project.
10. Pupil committee prepares a wall map as one of culminating activities of the study of a unit.

OBJECTS, MODELS, AND SPECIMENS

The study of objects in their natural surroundings provides the best basis for understanding of their functions and relationships to other objects. Not all objects included in the curriculum can be studied in their native habitat. Children can be afforded firsthand experience with many objects by bringing them into the school. When they are studied against the pupils' background of experience with similar objects, they become an important aid to learning. The dual approach to learning—by sight and by touch—which is provided by this type of visual material adds meaning and realism to school work.

Models which are representations (not reproductions) of objects have certain distinct values. A model may represent in miniature an object which is too large for complete study. For example, more significant relationships can be revealed by studying a model of the earth than by scanning the horizon. On the other hand, a model may be made much larger than the actual object and so permit more detailed study. In using models in teaching, the teacher should be certain that students obtain a clear understanding of the relative sizes of model and object. Working models with moving parts are of great value in developing understanding of mechanical devices.

Objects can be arranged to reveal certain relationships in an effective manner. For example, relics of the American Indian can be grouped in the chronological order of their origin and use. By combining paintings and models or objects, the diorama creates realistic impressions. The realism of a foreign coin collection arouses interest and motivates children's study far better than a series of drawings and verbal descriptions of the objects. Newspapers or reprints published on the dates of significant historical events are quite effective in giving children a sense of reality in regard to the events.

The construction of models by pupils presents excellent opportunities for creative, meaningful work. Specimens suitable for use in science classes can be collected, mounted, and labeled by the pupils. Many objects which enrich and vitalize learning in various subjects can be obtained free or borrowed from people in the local community. Commercially made models are also available at a nominal cost.

In using materials of this type as teaching aids, the teacher should be certain that the aids are relevant to the topic and can be closely correlated with other instructional materials. The novelty of an aid may arouse initial general interest. It should do more. The attention of the class should be focused on the aspects of the object which bear a direct relationship to the study topic. The possibilities of relating these aids to other activities in connection with a subject include further reading about the object, writing reports on it, making diagrams or drawings of it, and individual and group discussions based upon it.

Many objects, models, and specimens collected for class use have permanent values. They can be used time and again if properly preserved and stored. The objects collected by a class might well become the nucleus of a school museum.

USING BULLETIN BOARDS, CHALKBOARDS, CHARTS AND SAND TABLES

Bulletin boards serve two purposes in the elementary classroom. They can be used to display items of interest to pupils, such as announcements, displays of the work of individual pupils and class committees. The items displayed at any one time should be organized around some central theme or idea. The number of items should be limited and should be changed frequently. Perhaps the chief value in the use of the bulletin board is in the opportunity for pupil participation in the selection and arrangement of the materials to be placed on it.

The chalkboard remains one of the most practical and functional of teaching aids. It is always convenient and available to give ideas visual representation. In chalkboard work the teacher can use ideas and information suggested by pupils, thus enhancing learning because of pupil participation. In the development of a lesson, the teacher can use the chalkboard to make notes of the main ideas, thus contributing to clearer understanding and greater retention by pupils. The chalkboard is useful in explaining new processes and illustrating new ideas presented in discussions.

Charts and posters may be collected from various sources for use in arousing pupil interest and providing information about various topics. In many schools pupils make their own charts and posters in connection with their study of a topic or unit. In the planning and making of charts and posters, pupils not only develop valuable skills in the use of several types of materials but the activity is an important form of creative self-expression.

Sand tables are used extensively in the study of various projects. They are excellent for use in developing concepts of physical surroundings, relief features of a locality, and models of historical objects.

SELECTION AND USE OF AUDIO MATERIALS

Until recently the number of practical auditory materials available for classroom use has been very limited. The record player has been the chief supplementary teaching aid which makes its appeal to the auditory sense. For many years after the invention of the radio, technical difficulties (as well as teachers' lack of awareness of its instructional possibilities) hindered its acceptance as a classroom teaching aid.

Recent scientific progress has eliminated many of the technical obstacles. The effectiveness of the radio in inculcating ideas and developing attitudes of persons outside the school has been amply demonstrated. Still another cause of the increased interest in radio in teaching has been recognition of the fact that radio listening has become an important leisure-time activity of youth. As a result of these developments, teachers have given consideration to two questions:

1. How can teachers assist pupils in making their leisure-time radio listening more beneficial?
2. How can audio materials, including the radio, serve to reinforce classroom instruction in achieving the desired outcomes of education?

Faced with the challenge inherent in these two questions, teachers have employed various forms of audio materials to supplement their classroom instruction. At present audio materials have taken their place beside the textbook and supplementary reading materials as an integral part of the course of study. Chief among these aids are:

Public address systems and sound amplifiers
The radio

Integration of quantitative ideas in social studies.

Using multi-sensory aids in social studies.
(Denver, Colorado, Public Schools)

Record players
Tape recordings
Sound pictures
Television

RADIO

The only justification for using a particular teaching aid is that it possesses, singly or in combination with other aids, certain unique values. In other words, its use must contribute more effectively to a process or an outcome than does any other available medium. The potential value of radio as an instrumentality of teaching is tremendous; its actual significance is dependent upon the manner in which it is utilized in the attainment of worthy educational objectives. The chief general values of radio as a teaching medium are discussed in the following paragraphs.

The radio can be used to motivate pupils. The radio program possesses several characteristics which are significant for purposes of pupil motivation. One of the most important is *timeliness*. Radio broadcasts of important events tend to eliminate feelings of remoteness which pupils attach to many topics presented in the classroom. One of the difficulties teachers encounter in motivating pupils in their study is the haze of unreality surrounding many classroom activities. A great deal of our teaching has been in terms of "long ago and far away." Firsthand accounts of significant happenings have a touch of reality which makes a strong appeal to children. Interests aroused by the broadcasts can be used as a point of departure for further study and reading on the broadcast topic, as well as related topics. Another motivating factor is that the radio *eliminates barriers of space,* bringing the world to the classroom. Broadcasts of significant current events taking place in the United States and elsewhere help to create real, lifelike classroom situations. Great personalities from every walk of life share their knowledge and enthusiasm with pupils in the schoolroom. Descriptions of historical events, forums, and the discussions of challenging problems by authorities serve to stimulate and inspire pupils.

The radio can be used to invigorate knowledge. The greatest contribution of radio to education lies in the inherent dramatic power of the spoken word. It can give vital meaning to instructional materials which otherwise may appear abstract and impersonal. Radio broadcasts, therefore, may serve to provide students with vicarious experiences having much of the force of actual experience. Authentic information, presented by well-informed radio speakers, also supplements knowledge obtained by pupils from books and other sources. As an integral part of the course of study, the radio is one of the determinants of the pupils' school experiences.

The radio can be used to establish standards in language usage. The standards of diction and pronunciation set by many radio speakers are worthy models for pupils. The extent to which faulty diction, careless pronunciation, and other errors in language hinder effective presentation of ideas on the radio becomes apparent to the children. This awareness of the significance of correct language usage becomes a motivating force for improvement of their own standards of speech.

The radio can be used to develop and increase worthy interests. New interests in drama and music may grow out of guided radio listening in the classroom. Until the advent of radio, good musical programs and theatrical performances were not available to most children. If given the opportunity to hear and the ability to interpret good music, many pupils may develop noteworthy recreational or vocational interests. Dramatizations of good books may lead to more extensive reading of significant material by children. The radio may also enable pupils to pursue worthwhile interests which have their origins in other situations.

The radio can be used to create desirable attitudes. World-mindedness should characterize the good citizen of the present and the future. Basic to this attitude is an understanding of the different peoples of the earth. By means of the radio, the elementary school pupil can acquire a knowledge of the characteristics, needs, and aspirations of the inhabitants of other countries. A sensitivity to the problems of human beings in our own country can be heightened by radio discussions of domestic, social, and economic issues.

Sources for programs

There are several means by which radio programs may be made available in the classroom. In considering the advisability of utilizing one or more of the different facilities, the committee on audio materials should consider not only comparative costs but relative advantages. The chief types of facilities are school-owned broadcasting stations and commercial broadcasting stations.

School-owned stations. Several of the larger school systems own broadcasting stations. Under this plan a school system acquires and operates its own transmitter and other necessary equipment. A license from the federal government is required to operate this type of station. It is necessary also to employ skilled and licensed operators. Programs are transmitted directly to an antenna in a school and then relayed to the classrooms, or the program may be transmitted to separate antennae for each classroom. If a radio studio is owned by the school, its equipment may be used for instructional purposes in science classes. The students install, maintain, and operate radio stations in many schools. The studio may also be useful for auditions of student announcers, vocalists, and instrumentalists.

Commercial broadcasting stations. The use of this facility requires equipping the school with receiving sets in each classroom, or a central receiving system with outlets in the various rooms through which regular radio programs are received. Schools with limited funds have made fairly effective use of the radio by shifting a single receiving set from one classroom to another as needed. The school may also purchase radio time for the purpose of giving broadcasts by students or school authorities. In many communities, schools have been able to obtain radio time gratis or at a nominal rate as a feature of the commercial station's public service program.

One of the difficulties in using commercial radio programs has been that of adjusting the time of the broadcast to class schedules. The differences in the standard time zones are partly responsible for this problem. Some radio programs are now being broadcast at different times for the different zones. Tape recorders and other recording devices and equipment for playing back programs to classes whenever desired serve to overcome this obstacle. With the advent of school-owned frequency modulation broadcasting stations, teachers will be able to use programs at times when they will best serve the purposes of classroom instruction.

Another objection to the use of commercial radio programs has been the limited number designed for juvenile listeners. Formerly programs for children were characterized by a tone of excitement and a flair for the sensational. The charge was frequently made that the general quality of many children's programs was low and in some cases vulgar. Broadcasters have begun to recognize the evils inherent in this type of program, with the result that the number of them is decreasing.

A third limitation is the amount and degree of misleading information in the form of advertising, and of statements of news commentators on questions of public interest.

Another handicap under which teachers have worked in their efforts to use programs of commercial stations has been their inability to obtain specific, detailed information about the program in advance. Listener's guides and teacher's manuals are now being provided for several programs by the broadcasting companies or sponsors.

Selection of programs

From the vast number of commercial radio programs available, a careful selection should be made of those programs which are most appropriate for classroom use. In many schools a radio committee consisting of classroom teachers obtains information in advance and recommends to the faculty the use of certain programs. If the members of the committee understand the educational possibilities of radio, and especially if they have among their members a radio enthusiast, they can render an important service to the teachers in school in advising on the selection of radio programs for classroom purposes.

In the event the teacher has the responsibility of selecting programs for her classes, she may not be able to obtain information in advance in regard to every radio broadcast. The major broadcasting companies will send schedules of programs upon request from the teacher. Information about various programs can likewise be obtained from the local broadcasting station. Radio magazines and bulletins also may be used as sources of information. The main factors which should be taken into consideration in selecting radio programs for classroom use are as follows.

1. *Are the purposes of the program in keeping with the objectives of the unit or course?* In an English class in which correct pronunciation or good diction is one of the outcomes, the ability of the speaker or actors in these matters is important. If appreciation of drama or music is one of the outcomes sought, the nature of the production and the quality of the performance are essential criteria for selection.

2. *Is the program relevant to the immediate learning activities of the class?* If the class is in the initial stages of the study of a topic, the chief value of the program may be that of motivation. In the study stage of the topic on which students are assembling information, a radio program which presents factual material pertaining to the topic is desirable. In the culminating stages of the study of a topic, the radio program may serve as a climax to the student's activities.

3. *Are the content and the manner of presentation such as will appeal to the interests of the class?* The vocabulary and style of the presentation should be adapted to the abilities of the students. The character of the material should be such that it can be adapted

to effective presentation on the radio. The presentation of the program should meet a high standard of excellence. The use of maps and supplementary reading materials and the study of unfamiliar words in the broadcast are effective methods of adapting the program to the abilities of students.

4. *Is the length of the program appropriate?* The age and maturity of pupils are important considerations in making this decision. If the broadcast is too long in terms of the attention span of the class, many of the important values of the program will be lost. The length of the program in relation to the length of the class period also should be considered. In many instances the optimum value of a radio program can be attained only when it is followed by a discussion in which the pupils and the teacher participate.

5. *Is the time of the broadcast suitable?* Except in the case of a spot program of considerable current significance, radio programs should be selected which will not interrupt the daily schedule too seriously. However, the value of the program, rather than its adjustment to a fixed schedule, should be the determinate factor in regard to the use of a broadcast in the classroom.

Preparation for the broadcast

The amount and kind of preparation depend upon the purpose and type of the broadcast. If the program is selected well in advance of the actual broadcast, the teacher may give a preview of the topic in the form of a discussion in which dramatic episodes related to the subject are included to arouse pupil interest. Sufficient information should be given in the presentation to provide pupils with enough of the background of the program to enable them to appreciate it. It may be advisable for the children to engage in some prebroadcast study of the topic. If, for example, the radio program is about the people of some foreign country, an assignment might be given which would involve:

1. Preparation of a list of books on the country by a committee of the class
2. Class study of a map of the country
3. Study of the meanings of words which are peculiar to the country
4. Study of pictures of the country
5. Brief reports by individual pupils on different aspects of life in the country

It is essential that the physical environment be conducive to effective listening. In most instances the schoolroom is the most desirable place for pupils to hear radio programs. Assembling a large number of children in a school auditorium is not a satisfactory arrangement for hearing most radio programs. The receiving equipment should be adjusted for maximum clarity and tonal quality. Distractions of all kinds should be reduced to the minimum.

Any reference materials to be used in connection with the broadcast should be readily available. The pupils may be expected to make brief notes of items for further study or discussion, or if the teacher feels that note-taking distracts the attention of children from the program, she may wish to make brief notations of topics for later consideration by the class. In some types of broadcasts, the use of maps and pictures during the program may be desirable. In teaching music by radio the use of the score when listening to a selection of music is often helpful.

The maximum benefits from most radio programs can best be achieved by follow-up activities related to the broadcasts. Depending on the type of program and its contribution to the specific objectives of the course, the follow-up procedures may take one or more of the following forms.

1. Class discussions of challenging problems suggested by the broadcast
2. Club activities stimulated by the program
3. Experiments following up a broadcast
4. Slides or films related to the broadcast
5. Reports by individual pupils to the class on topics related to the broadcast
6. Reading of books stimulated by the program
7. Test of basic understandings, information, and terminology

Critical and intelligent radio listening, both in and out of school, should be one of the outcomes of the use of the radio in school. Children should be guided in formulating a set of criteria for judging radio broadcasts. Class discussions of some of the programs in terms of the criteria are held in many schools. Some of the matters which may serve as a basis of the discussion are:

1. Objectionable advertising
2. Propaganda
3. Undesirable emotional appeal
4. Aesthetic value
5. Reliable and unprejudiced source of information
6. Craftsmanship in music, acting, speech, and synchronization

Out-of-school listening

Teachers are becoming increasingly aware of the power of the radio to influence the lives of individuals: the radio has become a great social force. Will it become an instrument in aiding man to achieve the good life or just another device for "pushing him around" by telling him what to think and what to buy, as well as whom to follow, whom to hate, and whom to fight? The answer to this question depends to some extent upon the ability of the millions of listeners to become discriminating, intelligent listeners.

There is little gained from a teacher's merely condemning the programs to which pupils listen. She should be in a position to suggest more desirable programs. Any such recommendation, however, should be based upon an understanding of individual pupil's interests and tastes. Assignments can be made occasionally directing pupils to listen to significant radio programs at home and be prepared to discuss them in class.

In the event the pupils are expected to listen to radio broadcasts during out-of-school hours, assignment should be as clear and definite as that of any other lesson. An assignment based upon a radio program should provide for:

1. Proper motivation through relation of the program to the pupils' past experiences, telling interesting incidents, or the like.
2. Definite information in regard to the time of the broadcast and the name of the station broadcasting the program.
3. Sufficient basis for understanding the program, such as information in regard to the characters or speakers, something about the play or musical composition.
4. Clear understanding of why the pupil should listen to the program.
5. A knowledge of what post-broadcast activities will be expected by the teacher, e.g., class discussion, individual reports, tests.

RECORDS

The phonograph is the most adaptable of all the audio aids for classroom use. A record can be played as many times as necessary to insure proper understanding and appreciation. Records of the best in music, literature, and English language are available at a nominal price. Phonographs with three speeds, operating at $33\frac{1}{3}$, 45, or 78 revolutions per minute, can be used to play both ordinary records and radio transcriptions. Transcriptions of many programs can be obtained from local broadcasting stations.

The teacher should listen to all the records to ascertain their suitability and to discover cues for their use before they are played for the class. Records should be selected in terms of specific objectives. In one instance the purpose may be analysis of form and content. In another case the record may be played for mere enjoyment or to give local color to a subject.

Many schools maintain a central record library, which has the advantage of making the records more readily available to all teachers as well as providing a safe place for filing. Unless records are stored properly, they may become warped or broken. Even the nonbreakable plastic records are subject to warping unless they are carefully protected when not in use.

Phonograph records can be more satisfactorily stored by an experienced librarian than by classroom teachers. Separate soundproof booths in the school library can be provided where pupils may listen to records. The booths may be fitted with glass doors, making it possible for the librarian to supervise the students' activities.

As an integrated classroom teaching aid, the phonograph record can serve to arouse pupil interest, illuminate and interpret what is read, and stimulate good reading and speaking habits. The following suggestions for the use of phonograph records apply particularly to the teaching of English literature, in this case a play, but the same plan may be followed in using phonograph records in other subjects.

1. Preparatory work of the teacher:
   a) Listen to the record in order to familiarize yourself with its content and organization.
   b) Prepare a brief outline of the main points to be emphasized in the lesson.
2. Preparing the pupils for hearing the record:
   a) Have the pupils read the printed text of the play, with particular emphasis on the scenes included in the record.
   b) Hold a general discussion of the play in which you or one of your pupils gives an overview of the story of the play.
   c) Have pupils read aloud the parts of the play presented on the record.
   d) Suggest to the class before playing the record that they give particular attention to the inflections, pronunciation, and dramatic qualities of the voices recorded.
3. Play the record through the first time without interruption.
4. Follow-up work:
   a) Have the students discuss the main points of the recorded version of the play.
   b) Give pupils questions to answer in regard to the main characters, plot, and action of the play as revealed by the recording.
   c) Ask pupils to mention and repeat selections or sentences of outstanding beauty or importance.
   d) Have pupils dramatize some of the most important scenes in the play. In the original dramatizations encourage pupils to make an effort to rival the recorded dramatization.
   e) Have pupils prepare written character sketches of the leading roles in the play.

f) Play the record again, stopping it at any time to clarify questions raised by the class.

TAPE RECORDINGS

Recent technical developments have made recording devices practicable for school purposes. By means of the tape recorder, inexpensive recordings can be made, played back for study, and then erased, after which new recordings may be made on the same tape. Other equipment is available for recordings of a more permanent form.

Schools utilize these recordings in a variety of ways. In some schools, radio programs are recorded for later use. Teachers of music make recordings of the solo and group singing of their pupils and play them back to the children for analysis and study. Instrumental music work lends itself to similar treatment. The distorted impression which a child may get of the contribution made by his own voice or instrument in group singing or playing can be corrected by listening to the recorded version, and the class can make an objective diagnosis of their rendition of a musical composition. Teachers of speech have found recordings valuable for the diagnosis of students' speech defects. In many schools dramatic productions and programs of special local interest are recorded for their historical value. In addition, tape recordings may be used—

1. As a practical aid in evaluating reading performance. As the children listen to the record they can recognize their mistakes in oral reading.
2. To play back to children their oral reading or speaking to show various patterns of enunciation and pronunciation, modulation of voice ideas, flexibility of voice.
3. For recordings of telephone conversations, social introductions, interviews, and announcements in which children have participated in order to help them detect their weaknesses.
4. To record an explanation which it may be necessary to give several times.
5. For music appreciation programs, broadcasting those that have come in over radio or television.
6. To prepare programs for broadcast.
7. To help blind, partially sighted, and hard-of-hearing children. The latter may use earphones for loud playback.
8. To record some parts of the lessons for the homebound student.
9. To record a counseling session. The counselor can substitute the record for notetaking.

TELEVISION PROGRAMS

Most of the educational values claimed for the use of the radio and the sound motion picture are potential in the use of television. One of the distinctive features of television which enhances its value for educational purposes is the combination of verbal and visual content of learning materials.

The verbal content of the radio program may appear as abstract symbols to the learner unless he has the background of experiences which enable him to visualize what is being described and explained. Like television, the sound motion picture combines visual and verbal materials. However, in sound pictures the learner is aware that what he is viewing has already happened. In a live television program, he knows that he is witnessing events as they are actually happening. This sense of "living reality" enhances the program's power to attract and hold the interest of the learner.

In a comprehensive study of pupils' TV habits made in southern California under the auspices of the Ford Foundation, Lazarus [1] reported that the median televiewing time for elementary school pupils is 20 hours per week, with a low of 13 hours in homes of high cultural levels to a high of 24 hours in homes of lowest socio-economic areas.

On the basis of his study, Lazarus states that television is *not* displacing reading. School and public libraries reported that both elementary and secondary students are reading more than ever before. However, studies have revealed that "*creative* activities" in the home, such as playing musical instruments, singing, acting, working in theater arts, painting, photography, and the like have been displaced by television. Lazarus suggests that the school therefore provide more opportunities and motivations for creative activities.

The majority of television programs are broadcast from commercial stations. Since commercial stations are dependent upon sponsors who measure the success of the program by the size of the viewing audience, the emphasis is upon entertainment rather than on educational values in most cases. A number of programs are highly regarded by teachers and parents, but one of the main criticisms of television programs is their lack of balance and their overemphasis on entertainment.

Many teachers and parents fear that some of the ideas children obtain from viewing television programs may be detrimental to them. Some health authorities have expressed the fear that tele-

[1] Arnold Leslie Lazarus, "Pupils' TV Habits," *Educational Leadership,* XIII (January, 1956), 241–42.

vision viewing will reduce the amount of time that the children will spend in outdoor play. Teachers also have been concerned lest the time spent watching television be lost from the time given to home-work and to sleep. The concern of parents about the kind of pro-grams provided has resulted in their willingness to contribute money or to approve the use of tax funds for establishing educational television broadcasting stations.

The educational value of television programs is largely dependent on the teacher's skill in assisting students to discriminate in their choice of programs. There are some programs each week which most teachers and parents can approve.

Many educators have expressed the opinion that better programs can be assured if teachers and parents will make their voices heard in the effort to raise the standards of taste of the broadcasts, the range of information supplied by them, and the educational value of the broadcasts.

The Division of Radio and Television Education, in cooperation with the Curriculum Office and special divisions of the Philadelphia public schools, prepares programs for the classrooms. The follow-ing copy of one week of the program shows the scope of the material.

DAY	TIME (A.M.)	PROGRAM	GRADE
Monday	10:45–11	We Play Melody Flutes	1–6
	11–11:15	Skin Care	4–9
Tuesday	10:45–11	Storybook Friends (Continued)	4–6
	11–11:15	People Collect Them	3–8
Wednesday	10:45–11	Structural Analysis	2
	11–11:15	"Mail Call"	8–12
Thursday	10:45–11	The Academy of Vocal Arts Presents	7–12
	11–11:15	Zoo Visitors	K–1–2
Friday	10:45–11	With Byrd at the South Pole	4–9
	11–11:15	Springtime Friends	1–3

The suggestions for the effective use of films and radio in the preceding sections of this chapter are applicable to television in the classroom. Special attention should be given to the selection of the programs, preparation of the pupils for viewing the program, and the follow-up activities.

QUESTIONS, PROBLEMS, AND EXERCISES

1. Monitor the radio and television programs broadcast in your city and list those which you think suitable for use in the elementary school.

2. Indicate how radio and television programs may be correlated with the various subjects in the elementary school.

3. How may the teacher assist elementary school pupils in developing powers of discrimination in the selection of television and radio programs?

4. Make a collection of cartoons from current magazines and newspapers for use in teaching an elementary school class.

5. List some objects, models, or specimens which might be used effectively in teaching one of your classes. From what sources could each of the items on your list be obtained?

6. How may elementary school pupils be taught to evaluate and appreciate good motion pictures?

7. Make a list of the abilities and skills elementary school pupils should acquire in the use of maps. Outline in some detail a plan of teaching designed to assist a class in the acquisition of four of the skills on your list.

8. Suggest methods of evaluating the outcomes of learning achieved by the use of a motion picture in classroom instruction.

SELECTED SUPPLEMENTARY READINGS

DALE, EDGAR. *Audio-Visual Methods in Teaching.* Rev. ed. New York: The Dryden Press, Inc., 1954.

An excellent treatment of the "why," the "what," and the "how" of audio-visual materials in teaching.

DE KIEFFER, ROBERT, and LEE W. COCHRAN. *Manual of Audio-Visual Techniques.* Englewood Cliffs, N. J.: Prentice-Hall, Inc., 1955.

Practical hints for using audio-visual materials in the classroom.

LEVENSON, WILLIAM B., and EDWARD STASHEFF. *Teaching Through Radio and Television.* New York: Rinehart & Co., Inc., 1952.

Describes values and procedures in the use of radio and television in teaching.

SANDS, LESTER B. *Audio-Visual Procedures in Teaching.* New York: The Ronald Press Co., 1956.

A comprehensive and thorough treatment of procedures in the use of audio-visual materials in teaching.

TARBET, DONALD G. "The Televiewing Habits of Pupils," *The Clearing House,* XXX (April, 1956), pp. 485-87.

Report of a survey of televiewing habits of sixth-grade children in four schools in a twelve-mile radius of Chapel Hill, N. C.

WILLEY, ROY DE VERL, and HELEN ANN YOUNG. *Radio in Elementary Education.* Boston: D. C. Heath & Co., 1948.

Contains suggestions for the use of the radio in teaching various subjects in the elementary school.

WINGO, G. MAX, and RALEIGH SCHORLING. *Elementary-School Student Teaching,* 2d ed. New York: McGraw-Hill Book Co., Inc., 1955.

Chap. x, "Audio-Visual Materials." Discussion of values, types, and suggestions for use of audio-visual materials.

WITTICH, WALTER ARNO, and CHARLES FRANCIS SCHULLER. *Audio-Visual Materials: Their Nature and Use.* New York: Harper & Bros., 1953.

Chap. xi, "Educational Recordings." Characteristics of these materials with suggestions for use in the classroom.

13

USING COMMUNITY RESOURCES

Teachers are likely to forget that the child's school experiences and learnings are only a part of his total education. Indeed, the significance of school experiences for the child is determined in no small degree by the teacher's ability to increase and to unify the stimuli to learning which the pupil encounters in the various areas of his social and natural environment. If properly integrated, in-school and out-of-school learnings supplement and reinforce each other. If, on the other hand, they are permitted to remain unrelated and isolated, the learnings in the different situations may hinder the full development of the individual.

In every community, however small, the major social processes are in operation. The community is the basic unit in the performance of many of the major social functions of life, such as making a living, obtaining an education, engaging in recreational activities, and pursuing religious interests. A firsthand study of the problems arising out of these processes in the community gives the child an insight into other social needs. In seeking to achieve this social objective of the school it is imperative that the culture and its fundamental structure and problems become increasingly the integrating element of the curriculum.

VALUES AND TYPES OF COMMUNITY STUDY

Since the community is a significant part of the elementary school pupil's total environment, the appropriate point of departure for the study of the society is the significant problems of the child's immediate social environment. The values of relating the program of the school to the community may be briefly summarized as follows:

1. The interests of the pupil in his immediate environment can be utilized to make school learning more meaningful to him.
2. Community study serves to vitalize and enrich the child's school experiences by practical application to actual situations.
3. Community study contributes to the realization of one of the school's major responsibilities, namely, that of introducing children to the life of their communities.
4. Community study contributes to habits of observation in children.
5. Community study develops pupil's appreciation and understanding of the social services of his community.
6. Community study counteracts isolation of the school from the realities of life, thereby enabling it to become a more effective agency of human welfare.
7. Study of community problems may become the antecedent for subsequent action to improve the quality of community life.
8. Community study provides opportunities for children to participate in socially useful, cooperative group endeavors.
9. Community study fosters cooperation of individuals and agencies interested in making community life more wholesome.

Obviously the realization of these values is dependent upon intelligent selection and utilization of community resources. Students of curriculum construction, seeking to reduce the social lag of education, have incorporated instructional materials pertaining to the community into various courses. Some curriculum committees have accepted the point of view that "the community is the curriculum." More conservative leaders in curriculum reconstruction, aware not only of the unique characteristics of each community but also of the *common factors of living in all communities*, have urged the adaptation of curricular materials to local community conditions. In the utilization of community resources and in student participation in community affairs it is essential that a proper balance be maintained with other educative activities.

The ability to understand and apply in life things learned in school depends upon how closely the school materials are related, in teaching and learning, to their uses in life. This is the modern, and apparently the correct, interpretation of the phenomenon commonly referred to as "transfer of training." A recent tendency has been to make less effort to cover all details of subjects including the minor ones and to take time to learn the more important information, skills, habits, ideals, attitudes, interests, and understandings in connection with their uses in everyday life. This has been found to be especially effective for young people of average intelligence or less.

Retention and use of learnings depend upon understanding; understanding depends upon having acquired meaning; acquiring meaning depends upon seeing the relationships with uses and related areas. Consequently, learning becomes real and valuable as it is associated with use and application in the home, in industry, at play, and indeed in all aspects of living at home and in the community.

Many teachers are handicapped by not having readily available suggestions of resources which can be used in constructing school activities around community topics. A valuable in-service education program for teachers carried on by a considerable number of school systems is the compilation of a list of community educational resources which could be utilized in various subjects and classes. In many schools teachers have planned community excursions for the purpose of becoming better acquainted with their local environment and listing materials available for classroom use.

Types of community study

The techniques of using community resources vary considerably. Many materials gathered in the community may be brought into the classroom. Among these are exhibits and visual aids. Speakers from some community organizations may be invited to the school. Frequently it is necessary to send individual pupils, committees of the group, or the whole group for interviews and observations. The findings should be reported to and shared with all members of the class by means of oral reports and the utilization of pictures, charts, and graphs.

Another device is to have the children draw a map of the city, using a color chart in which different colors represent such things as public parks and recreational facilities, industrial plants, schools, churches, libraries, post offices, municipal buildings, courthouses, and other points of interest. In connection with the use of community resources, care should be taken to employ only those which seem to have the greatest direct bearing on the problem in hand.

There are four approaches to the problem of utilization of community resources of teaching and learning that deserve some detailed discussion in this chapter. The following sections of the chapter will include discussions of community surveys, educational excursions, resource persons, and school camping.

Using community resources in teaching

The selection of community resources for use in school should be made for very definite educational purposes. The value of relating the work of the school to community life as a method of enriching the curriculum and motivating pupils has been emphasized in previous sections of this chapter. The use of community resources has, however, a broader implication. If, through contact with the community, teachers are able to instill in pupils the recognition of community problems along with a desire and a plan to improve conditions, one of the major objectives of education, namely, *social* sensitivity, will be achieved.

Ideally the information gained from various subjects and from observation of the community would be fused and utilized in the study of any problem. In schools in which the curriculum is still divided into separate subjects, however, teachers have been able, within the boundaries of each subject, to utilize various community resources in an effective manner. The first requisite for the successful utilization of community resources is for the teacher to know the interests, activities, and resource materials of the local community. The teacher can obtain this information through local newspapers, conversations with citizens, observation of community activities, and participation in community life.

Increasing teacher orientation

In smaller villages and cities as well as in those larger cities where citywide inventories of available out-of-school educational materials have not been made, the individual teacher should make such an inventory for the subjects she teaches. In doing this, she should employ the cooperative efforts of the pupils in her classes, using as the criterion the value of the contribution to educational needs and the purposes of each subject.

While the number and type of resources available vary from one community to another, any community has numerous usable materials but many teachers do not know that such educational opportunities exist in their immediate environments.

COMMUNITY SURVEYS

Community surveys may be divided into (1) broad, general surveys of community conditions to obtain a general overview of the community, and (2) study of some specific problem of major concern to the group.

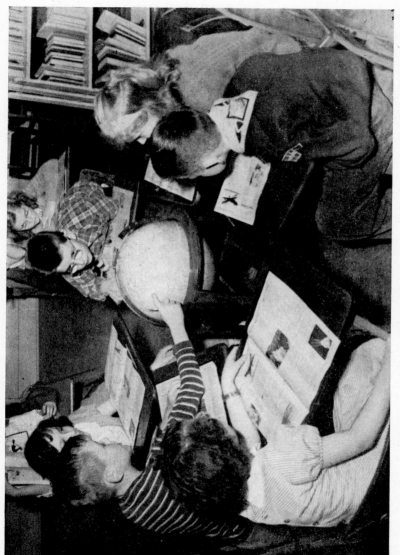

A fourth-grade group working with visual aids and supplementary reading materials. (Boulder, Colorado, Public Schools)

Neighborhood map. Many quantitative concepts were clarified in constructing the map by second-grade children. (Denver, Colorado, Public Schools)

Properly planned and conducted, both surveys have great educational possibilities. While the main purpose of a survey is to obtain information relevant to community understanding, its chief educational value is the way the information is related to other significant learning activities. Doing this demands intelligent analysis and interpretation. Merely to assemble information by means of surveys without a definite objective is educational profligacy under the guise of progressiveness.

In most cases the limited type of community survey in which data are obtained on one community problem or area is the most suitable for elementary school groups. A definite problem or need which directly affects the pupils as members of a community, such as health, recreation, or traffic safety, may well be the basis of an investigation. The problem is even more appropriate if it is such that the pupils can take definite action resulting in discernible community improvement.

General survey

The survey should arise out of the curriculum and return to enrich and vitalize it. The purpose should be clearly understood by the teacher and the pupils. The kinds of information and the methods of obtaining it should be determined by a process of democratic group planning. The pupils may be organized into various committees, each having definite responsibility for some phase of the survey. The committee findings should be reported to the entire class for evaluation and interpretation. The total results of the survey should be organized into an appropriate form for presentation to the class and interested adult groups.

To insure the maximum educational values, the actual survey should be preceded and accompanied by a study of library materials on the subject. The details of making the survey should also be carefully considered in advance. Plans should be made with due regard to the maturity of the pupils who are to participate as well as with regard to the probable reactions of the adult citizens of the community.

Among the outcomes of the general community survey may be the development of a desire on the part of the members of a class to make an intensive analysis and study of one or more community institutions or activities. In the typical community there are several types of institutions suitable for special study by elementary school classes, for example, factories, personal and professional services, social agencies and organizations, city and county agencies, cultural, educational, and religious organizations, and homes.

The factors which determine the choice of an institution for study are the kinds of institutions represented in the community, the objectives of the curriculum or course, the adaptability of the institutional materials to the abilities of students, and the interests of pupils.

Scope of the survey

The nature and scope of a community survey by elementary school pupils will depend upon the age and grade level of the pupils. Nevertheless, the scope of the survey may be fairly wide even in the lower grades, though it should not be too intensive or complicated.

Among the important aspects of the community which may be included in the community survey are those indicated below. Which of these should be employed and how many aspects of any should be included depends upon the maturity of the pupils.

People: racial and national backgrounds, birth rate in the community and its trends, size and growth of the community with respect to geographical area and population, social structure including the types of people who live in the community.

Homes: overcrowding, presence of slums, zoning regulations.

Employment: diversity of occupations, wages or salaries in occupations employing a considerable number of people.

Industries: types of industries, trends in change in the nature of the industries.

Geographical Backgrounds: geography of the community, factors affecting the economic growth of the community, such as opportunities for water transportation, geographical features which now or may in the future influence the location of residences and business and industrial buildings.

Historical Background: folklore, places of special historic interest, historical development of the community.

Government: the various governmental services, such as those rendered by the fire and police departments, how much they cost, how they are supported, and how they operate, the people employed by the government and how they get their positions in the government.

Health: hospital facilities, provisions for an adequate and pure water supply, safeguards for purity of milk and food, and methods of sewage and garbage disposal.

Recreation: public and commercial or privately sponsored programs and equipment.

Welfare Services: governmental and nonpublic welfare agencies such as the Salvation Army, the Red Cross, churches, missions, settlement houses, the Community Chest and its activities, welfare agencies for veterans, public assistance, and public medical care.

Religious Agencies: the churches represented and the services churches render in a community.

Educational Services: the public schools—number, type, control, and support, private schools, educational agencies of church, local government, and voluntary educational organizations.

Other Community Organizations: civic groups, including men's and women's service clubs, League of Women Voters, Consumer's League, and Junior League; patriotic groups, including the American Legion, AMVETS, Veterans of Foreign Wars, the Daughters of the American Revolution, and the Colonial Dames; fraternal organizations, such as the Masons, Odd Fellows, Elks, Eagles, and Moose; cultural groups promoting enjoyment of art, music, drama, literature, gardening, local history, etc.; business and industrial organizations, including the Chamber of Commerce, trade organizations, labor unions, and cooperatives; organizations for young people, such as Boy and Girl Scouts, "Y" groups, Camp Fire Girls, Junior Red Cross, Junior Achievement, and various interest groups such as junior music clubs.

EDUCATIONAL EXCURSIONS

The school excursion, when utilized as a learning activity, is an effective method of providing direct experiences with the realities of social living. Guided school trips can be planned to achieve the development of new interests and the intensification of old ones, the observation of objects and processes in their functional relationships, the clarification of concepts, the development of keenness of observation in particular fields, the supplementing and verification of information obtained from books and other sources, the illustration of abstract ideas, the enrichment and expansion of pupils' experiential background, and the acquisition of certain social abilities such as acceptance of responsibility and willingness to cooperate in group undertakings.

Community resources

The following table lists possible destinations of trips for purposes of observation by the class, small groups, or individuals and shows the purposes and major contributions to be achieved.

Destination	Specific Purpose	Primary Emphasis
Historical museum	for general exploration of materials available	on pioneer life
Wholesale house	to answer specific questions	about how bananas are brought to wholesale houses, cared for, and distributed to retailers

Destination	Specific Purpose	Primary Emphasis
Cannery	to observe the process	by which whole ears of corn become cans of corn
Railroad station	for general exploration	of the kinds of work necessary in railroad transportation
Dairy farm	to answer specific questions	about how cows are cared for and milked
Lumber yard	to answer specific questions	about different kinds of building materials
Stone quarry	for general exploration	of excavation, and of how the stone is obtained
Railroad station	to answer specific questions	about diesel engines
Print shop	for general exploration	of how printing is done
Art museum	to answer specific questions	about Chinese culture: metal work; ceramics; paintings; stone carvings
Post office	to observe processes	by which letters and packages are received and prepared for distribution
Model home	for general exploration	of modern improvements made possible by technological progress
Department store	for general exploration	of various departments and workers
Radio station	to answer specific questions	about how broadcasts take place
Farm	to answer specific questions	about how baby animals are born and raised
Wharf	to answer specific questions	about freighters: from where they came; products; how unloaded
Dairy	to observe the process	by which ice cream is made
Flour mill	to observe the process	by which grain becomes flour
House under construction	to answer specific questions	about what various construction workers do
Supermarket	for general exploration	of products sold
Shoe factory	to observe the process	by which leather is made into shoes
Water works	to answer specific questions	about source and quantity of water, and how purified
Farm	to answer specific questions	about modern methods of preventing soil erosion
Apartment building	for general exploration	of construction, arrangement of living space, and maintenance [1]

[1] James B. Burr, Lowry W. Harding and Leland B. Jacobs, *Student Teaching in the Elementary School* (New York: Appleton-Century-Crofts, Inc., 1950), pp. 297-98.

Other places in the community which may be used as curriculum resources follow:

Brick yard
Packing plant
Rubber factory
Candy factory
Thermometer factory
Hydroelectric plant
Cotton gin
Mill
Tapestry weaving shop
Newspaper plant
Bakery
Photographer's studio
Steel plant
Road under construction
Building under construction
Coffee company
Automobile assembly plant
Warehouse terminal
Oil well
Church
Freight yard
Airport
City hall
Courthouse
Iron mine
Coal mine
Bank
Hotel
Summer resort

Chicken hatchery
Apiary
Greenhouse
Art gallery
Library
Voting polls
Political meeting
Police station
Court
Assessor's office
Flower garden
Vegetable garden
Fair
Dog kennels
Grain elevator
Interesting natural scenes
Various types of houses
Telephone exchange
Theater
Zoo
Planetarium
Park
Cemetery
Monument
Historical sites
Fire department
Business college
High school
University

Program planning

Considerable preparatory work is essential if the time and expense involved in school trips are to be justified in terms of desirable educative outcomes. The process of cooperative planning and preparing for a trip by pupils and teachers presents an unparalleled opportunity for democratic school activity.

One of the first steps to be taken in planning a program of school excursions in larger cities is to make a community-wide survey of all available places of educational interest and value. A central committee of teachers in each school should prepare a list of places appropriate for visitation. Individual members or subcommittees should then visit different places on the list to ascertain their educational potentialities. The information thus obtained may be recorded on cards to be filed in the school for reference. Each card should record the following information:

1. Name of person, place, or thing visited
2. Location

3. Possible value of visit
4. Transportation needed
5. Time appropriate for visit
6. Names of persons to be contacted and necessary preliminary notification

A committee of pupils and the teacher in each class should be formed to examine the information on file, select trips appropriate to their classwork, and report a tentative schedule of their trips to the central committee, which in turn prepares a schedule of trips for the entire school. Extreme care is necessary in planning the routine details of the trip—transportation facilities, time schedules, food, and liability insurance.

Each teacher who is to serve as leader of a group has the responsibility of making pupils cognizant of the educational implications of each trip. Reading materials, films, pictures, and discussions relating to the trip assist in orientation.

Other suggestions for successful organized community excursions are the following: (1) Investigate the unusual dangers or hazards of the trip. (2) See that the trip is taken at the appropriate time, especially with respect to (a) its fitting into the work of the school and (b) its convenience to the people at the place visited. (3) Make careful arrangements for the transportation and see that the expense is adequately taken care of. If private cars are to be employed, unusual care must be taken to see that there are safe drivers and that cars stay close together or follow a common route. (4) Obtain permission from the principal and get written permission of parents for students to take the trip especially in cases where transportation employed is not that furnished by the school with adequate insurance against injury. (5) Arrange for appropriate aides and guides at the destination of the trip if possible. If not possible in some instances, have at least one or two parents or other adults assist with the trip and with the care of children. (6) Anticipate difficulties or unusual developments such as unfavorable weather conditions, sudden illness of a child, misbehavior of children, or a misunderstanding with those who are to assist in supervising the trip.

The trip should be closely correlated with the actual flow of instruction in the classroom. Classes functioning along pupil activity principles encounter little difficulty in expanding their units of work to include school trips related to the various units. Each trip should be followed by class discussions in which questions which arise out of the trip can be cleared up and significant facts emphasized. The information obtained by pupils on a school trip should be organized, synthesized, and presented in the form of oral or written reports to other school or adult groups, thus providing experience in oral and written English composition. Trips to rural areas may be correlated with the study of the poetry and fiction of farm life. Students may be inspired to express their reactions to the places visited by drawings and sketches, thereby using them as the basis of creative exercises in art. The work in the practical arts takes on added significance when pupils observe related activities in carpentry, masonry, and machine shop work in the community.

RESOURCE PERSONS

Increasingly, in recent years, use has been made of people in the local community as resources for information, understandings, and assistance in the development of certain skills, ideals, attitudes, and tastes. Two ways to use a local lay person as a resource person are as a visitor to the class where he may speak, present audio-visual aids, and answer questions raised by the pupils and teacher and, secondly, as a person who may be interviewed by an individual pupil or a small committee who will then report the results of the interview to the class.

Among the types of resource persons that may be employed advantageously by the school are:

1. Individuals who have recently made journeys to interesting parts of the country or to interesting foreign countries including, of course, individuals who have recently come to this country to live.
2. Persons who have unusual information by reason of specialized experience, for example, a forester who is familiar with the wildlife of the country, particularly the local flora and fauna.
3. Individuals who are familiar with the history of the community, and indeed anyone who is well informed along the lines of any of the areas mentioned for study under community survey.
4. Citizens engaged in occupations which may be of interest to the school, for example, an attorney, nurse, architect, farmer, stock raiser, or mail carrier.
5. Persons with interesting or unusual hobbies or collections such as those who have made a hobby of model railroad trains, a collection of dolls, a collection of stamps, a collection of handiwork of some particular tribe of Indians, or some foreign country.
6. School staff members employed to render some sort of service in connection with projects in the schools—carpenters, electricians, cooks.
7. Individuals who may give educational entertainment, such as a musician, magician, ventriloquist.

8. Possible assistant teachers, for example, in connection with play-ing baseball or other games.
9. Individuals to assist teachers in training youngsters in chorus work or choral readings or in marionettes and puppets.
10. Parents. A publication of the United States Office of Education [2] reports how parents helped in enriching the school experiences of children.

A father takes the class. While Mr. M. chatted with his child's teacher after a PTA meeting he asked if the class would enjoy some colored movies he had taken of a deep-sea fishing trip off the coast of Florida. A time was arranged and Mr. M. brought his films, staying to give explanations and richer meaning to the pictures.

The children valued the experience, and these movies became a "community resource" to be filed for future use. The film is also listed under "available movies" in the file. The following year another teacher and group will find the same films valuable and appropriate.

Parents help with transportation. Much of the work on social studies for the fifth grade is centered on a study of their state and city. Trips are made by the children to many places of historic interest. Parents assist on problems of transportation.

A father sends an invitation. A father sends a message by his child offering their darkroom to the eighth-grade photography club. The same family donates month-old photography magazines to the school.

A mother invites a visitor from China. A classroom study of China brings forth many authentic Chinese pieces from homes. They become objects of study and entertainment and things to be shared together with other groups. A mother knows a lecturer on China and invites him to come to school. A child in the group remembers that her music teacher had taught in China. Both of these persons who knew China intimately come to talk to the group. Thus firsthand experiences are related to the children in a way that makes China a live and real place to them.

Preplanning for the visits

The educational value resulting from the use of resource visitors from the community is very much dependent upon the quality of the preplanning for the visits. Burr, Harding, and Jacobs give the following practical and useful suggestions: [3]

1. *Clarification of the purpose of the visit.* Children profit fully from a visit only when they are quite clear about its purpose. A large part of this clarification emerges from their participation in the decision to have the adult come. Sometimes special research

[2] Federal Security Agency, Office of Education, *Working with Parents Handbook,* Bulletin, 1948, No. 7, pp. 19-20.
[3] James B. Burr, Lowry W. Harding, and Leland B. Jacobs, *Student Teaching in the Elementary School* (New York: Appleton-Century-Crofts, Inc., 1950), p. 312.

activities may precede the visit. In any case, it is advisable shortly before the visit to devote time to review and further discussion of the reasons for the visit.

2. *Planning with children their roles in receiving the visitor.* Children should have the opportunity for the social learnings involved in being hosts. They can share responsibility for meeting the visitor, bringing him to the classroom, caring for his wraps, helping with his equipment, introducing him to the group, and getting him started. Since these are learning experiences for children, they will need help in planning their roles.

3. *Planning to be a receptive audience.* As is always necessary with novel situations at school, there must be discussion with children of appropriate behavior, and agreements made. How can we indicate that we are appreciating and understanding? When might we talk to each other? Should we applaud? There should be preplanning for the handling of possible disruptions, such as messengers from other teachers, ventilation problems, and the like.

4. *Planning with children their roles in helping the visitor.* Children sometimes participate directly in the presentation. They may help by handling equipment, assisting with a demonstration, following directions in learning a new process or skill, asking questions, or sharing information at appropriate times. The group can consider, without rigid preplanning, how to assume their active roles during the visit, preparing to adapt to the situation as it emerges.

5. *Planning for the termination of the visit.* Social learnings are involved, also, in gracefully bringing the visit to a close. Certain children can be delegated to express orally appreciation for the group, to invite the visitor to stay longer to watch other school work, or to return later for another visit.

Planning for interviews

Interviewing of people as resource persons of the community by individual pupils or committees must be planned, and the youngsters must be given definite instructions if not some demonstration of good techniques by having a pupil interview the teacher who takes the role of some specified person in the community with a specified and described background of experiences. The interviewer should learn a great deal about the interviewee beforehand as a basis for planning questions and conducting the interview so as to obtain information which may be brought back to the class. The interviewer should plan in advance and perhaps discuss with the teacher, if not with the entire class, some of the questions he expects to ask the particular interviewee.

In the elementary school, the teacher has the responsibility usually for making the first contact with the interviewee, and if there must be a conveyance provided for the committee or group of students attending the interview, the teacher should make the usual arrangements for the transportation. Furthermore, the teacher must coach the students with respect to what would be regarded as good social behavior during the interview.

Among the points which the interviewers should observe, and perhaps receive some coaching from the instructor or from suggestions coming from the cooperative discussions of the class, are the following:

1. Students must do or say nothing which would indicate anything but keen interest in the interview and what the interviewee says in answer to the questions.

2. In general, the interviewee should be permitted to carry on the conversation as he sees fit without too much interruption. On the other hand, in order that the full benefit of the time may be realized, the interviewer or the teacher may wish to raise a question and, perhaps in some instances, to indicate the desirability of getting on to some other aspect of the interview before the limited time available is consumed.

3. In some instances, it may be well to give to the interviewee in advance a set of questions which he will be expected to answer. The interview, however, need not be confined entirely to these questions, as there may develop other very important questions which might well be asked.

4. In general, not too much attention should be given to the taking of notes, especially if there are several students present at the interview. The interviewer should take notes on points which he is likely to forget, for example, specific dates, specific names, etc.

5. As soon after the interview as possible, the student interviewer or the recorder and reporter for the group should sit down while the interview is fresh in his memory and make notes for report to the class.

6. The interviewers should not drag out the interview beyond the time the interviewee wishes to give to it. They should have a sense of time and attempt to get the ground covered during the time originally allocated to the interview. Shortly after that time is up, if not immediately, the interview must be ended, rather than have the interviewee feel that he has been imposed upon.

7. Before too much time has elapsed, a report to the class should be planned in some detail.[4]

[4] E. G. Olson and others, "People as Resources," *School and Community* (2d ed. Englewood Cliffs, N.J.: Prentice-Hall, Inc., 1954), VII.

In the use of personal observations and interviews with people in the community, there is a splendid opportunity to train pupils, particularly in the upper grades. In this connection, perhaps there should be some preliminary training in the classroom with some staged interviews in which the teacher may be the person interviewed or in which some person in the community may be asked to come and be interviewed by one of the more alert, intelligent students.

Furthermore, this type of educational experience affords a splendid practical opportunity, in a relatively real-life situation, for training in oral expression and in writing reports. Students or committees of students who have interviewed individuals and who have taken notes may be asked to study their notes and to prepare, plan, and give oral reports in class about their interviews, and/or they may write up reports to be turned in to the teacher in good English and correct form.

SCHOOL CAMP

Effective living in the world of today requires the development of cooperative skills in living and solving problems together. One of the major difficulties encountered by teachers has been that of integrating many portions of the school curriculum with the life experiences of pupils.

In boarding schools, an adequate opportunity is afforded for training young people to live together in a community under the direction of trained leaders. For pupils who do not attend boarding schools, summer camps and school camps afford to some degree a substitute and provide opportunity for a training which is different from and superior to any community experience available within the walls of a school building. Summer camps sponsored by schools, churches, commercial camp institutions, and philanthropic and social agencies have multiplied rapidly in recent decades and now reach several million young people annually.

In a school camp, children are placed in an environment favorable for learning to live together, to assume responsibility, and to explore source materials of the curriculum.

Planning camp experiences

Prior to the camping trip, the teacher and pupils should make tentative plans as follows:

1. Discuss reasons for camping
2. Plan the trip to camp, exploring interesting places en route

3. Study history of the camp area
4. Compile a list of articles the pupils will need at camp
5. Work out a tentative camp program

Plans should be made to insure that the pupils may participate effectively in such camp experiences as the following:

1. Getting acquainted with the camp area and the other campers
2. Observing trees, flowers, rocks, and birds in the area
3. Making things to be used in the area
4. Sharing responsibility for camp chores
5. Preparing programs of an inspirational nature
6. Taking special exploratory trips
7. Having evening get-togethers
   a. Campfires
   b. Songfests
   c. Story-telling
   d. Games
8. Planning leisure-time activities
   a. Hobbies
   b. Crafts
   c. Swimming
   d. Reading
   e. Hiking
   f. Dramatics

Among the more important types of follow-up activities educationally valuable are these:

1. Computing camp expenses
2. Writing letters of appreciation to camp officials
3. Holding class discussions of camp experiences
4. Making plans to continue experiences begun in camp

There are many indications that camping is coming to be recognized as a vital educational experience for all children and youth. Notable among camp programs are those conducted by the schools of Atlanta, Georgia; Catskill, New York; Battle Creek, Michigan; and San Diego County, California.

The teacher has an important role in promoting the development of the school camp movement. In the activities of the camp, the teacher serves as leader of her pupils and utilizes the camp counselors as resource leaders. Since the camp experience should be an integral part of the pupil's total educative experience, the teacher is responsible for assistance in planning, evaluating, and integrating the camp program along with that of the school.

Criteria for school camps

The following criteria [5] are proposed for a good school camp.

[5] Adapted from *Toward a New Curriculum*, Yearbook, Department of Supervision and Curriculum Development, National Education Association, 1944, pp. 102-104.

School Camp Purposes and Philosophy

The school camp should have, as its central objective, helping young people to understand the democratic way of life and to practice it in their relationships with others.

   a. The school camp should treat each youngster as an individual. It should guide him, help him face his problems, help him develop his potentialities, and open up new interests to him.
   b. The school camp should help youngsters to live with others, giving and taking, sharing and accepting responsibilities, constantly learning to widen the area of shared interests through partaking in enterprises with others for objectives commonly agreed upon by the participants.
   c. The school camp should stress problem solving involving the process of critical thinking.
   d. The school camp should teach youngsters to be concerned for human welfare, inside and outside the camp.

Programs to Achieve Purposes

   1. The school camp should fully utilize its environment for educative ends, whether that setting be the field, forest, and stars of the organized out-of-doors summer camp, or the community setting of the work camp.
   2. The school camp should teach social living and citizenship, using as the raw materials of education those situations and problems which arise in the everyday life of the camp. (Democratic values should be applied not only to the present camp problem which serves as the source but also to larger social issues related to the immediate problem.)
   3. The school camp should involve camper and staff joint planning and cooperative conduct of the program.
   4. The school camp should be an informal experience in which fun and joy are cherished and promoted.
   5. The school camp should be a place where health and vigor are improved, where health, nutrition, and safety practices are taught by the demands of camp living, with direction by educationally alert adults.
   6. The school camp should encourage and develop work experiences of a variety of kinds teaching the dignity of labor and the significance of shared responsibility in democratic living.
   7. The school camp should continuously evaluate and appraise its program and periodically report its findings to interested groups.
   8. While the school camp should fully utilize work experience, forest living, crafts, hikes, athletics, dramatics, and similar activities, it should not conceive its function to be that of a noneducative, nonintellectual agency devoted simply to recreation and physical culture.
   9. While the school camp should fully utilize such activities as discussion, reading, forms of self-government, community visitation and study, speakers, radio and motion pictures, it should not conceive its function to be that of a nonsocial, nonemotional agency concerned with developing the mind of the child through the traditional curriculum centered on assuring college entrance for the few.

In short, the school camp may well become an integral part of the youngster's year-round educational experience, blending what is best in camping with what is best in schooling to foster democratic living.

QUESTIONS, PROBLEMS, AND EXERCISES

1. To what factors do you attribute the increasing use of community resources in elementary schools?

2. Suggest a list of criteria which should be used in selecting community resources for study in an elementary school grade.

3. Present arguments for and against the school's assuming responsibility for improving present community life.

4. A major problem in utilizing community resources in teaching is that of coordinating them with other curricular materials. Select a community resource and describe how it can be related to the grade you teach.

5. Outline a community service project in which it might be feasible for elementary school pupils to engage.

6. How may a teacher appraise the educational value of an excursion which her class has made?

7. What contribution can educational films make to a study of local community life?

8. Describe in some detail the methods of utilizing a community resource in your teaching.

9. What factors should be considered before taking a class to observe an industrial plant, coal mine, or museum?

10. What are some of the differences to be recognized in making a general community survey in the rural area and in the urban community?

SELECTED SUPPLEMENTARY READINGS

ASSOCIATION FOR SUPERVISION AND CURRICULUM DEVELOPMENT. *Organizing the Elementary School for Living and Learning. 1947 Yearbook.* Washington, D.C., National Education Association, 1947.

Chap. iii presents an excellent treatment of many aspects of school and community relationships, including guides for service planning, projects, coordinating, and councils. Descriptions of outstanding programs.

BECK, ROBERT H., WALTER W. COOK, and NOLAN C. KEARNEY. *Curriculum in the Modern Elementary School.* Englewood Cliffs, N.J.: Prentice-Hall, Inc., 1953.

Chap. vii, "Communities and Children." Types of communities. The rural and urban community are described with a section on how teachers can build good community morale.

DEPARTMENT OF ELEMENTARY SCHOOL PRINCIPALS, *Community Living and the Elementary School. 24th Yearbook.* Washington, D.C., National Education Association, 1945.

Broad and inclusive coverage of community resources, with descriptive examples.

GRINNELL, J. E., and RAYMOND J. YOUNG. *The School and the Community.* New York: The Ronald Press Co., 1955.

Chap. 2, "Community and Curriculum Correlation," by Albert I. Oliver, pp. 19-45. Historical survey of community-school cooperation and suggestions for insuring good relations. Chap. 3, "Learning About the Community," by Albert I. Oliver, pp. 46-68. The community survey and what should be included in it. Chap. 4, "The Learner, Learning, and the Community," by Lloyd H. Elliott, pp. 69-87. Camping, field trips, and work experience are described. Chap. 8, "The Parent Teachers Association and Other Parent Groups," by Raymond J. Young, pp. 140-58. Historical survey of P.T.A. and its many ramifications in school-community cooperation. Chap. 15, "Cocurricular Activities as Public Relations," by J. E. Grinnell, pp. 274-96. The emphasis given to various school activities and the problems encountered. Chap. 16, "School and Home Communications," by Lloyd H. Elliott, pp. 297-324. How to improve school-home relations, with concrete examples. Chap. 18, "The Pupil in Community Relations," by Hubert H. Mills, pp. 346-62. Specific suggestions on how to improve school-home relations by working through the pupil.

HERRICK, VIRGIL E., JOHN I. GOODLAD, FRANK J. ESTVAN, and PAUL W. EBERMAN. *The Elementary School.* Englewood Cliffs, N.J.: Prentice-Hall, Inc., 1956.

Chap. 3, "The Elementary School in its Community," pp. 42-68. The school as a community institution and as a community center; the community council; the school program; and the community. Chap. 6, "Planning and Organizing the Curriculum," pp. 125-54. Common denominator; different approach; suggested ways.

MICHAELIS, JOHN U. *Social Studies for Children in a Democracy,* 2d ed. Englewood Cliffs, N.J.: Prentice-Hall, Inc., 1956.

Chap. ix discusses principles, techniques, and services of the community in relationship to the elementary school.

OLSEN, EDWARD G., and OTHERS. *School and Community.* Englewood Cliffs, N.J.: Prentice-Hall, Inc., 1954.

Chap. 5, "Planning Community Experiences." Chap. 6, "Community Materials." Chap. 7, "People as Resources." Chap. 8, "Field Trips." Chap. 9, "Surveys." Chap. 10, "School Camping." Chap. 11, "Work Experiences." Chap. 12, "Community Service Projects." Chap. 13, "Cataloging Community Resources."

WESLEY, EDGAR BRUCE, and MARY A. ADAMS. *Teaching Social Studies in Elementary Schools,* rev. ed. Boston: D. C. Heath & Co., 1952.

Chap. xxii presents techniques for community study, with illustrations of good programs. Comprehensive lists of possible resources and places to visit on field trips. Many helps for exercising good judgment in the use of community resources.

WOFFORD, KATE V. *Teaching in Small Schools.* New York: The Macmillan Co., 1946.

Chap. xiv, "Taking Excursions." Chap. xv, "Understanding the Community." The community survey is defined and a variety of techniques in making a survey are suggested.

14

SUPERVISING LEARNING AND STUDY ACTIVITIES

Supervising the learning activities of pupils in the classroom is a complex process. As the director of learning, the teacher has the responsibility of providing a balanced program of individual and group activities which contribute to the development of constructive attitudes, basic understandings, and effective skills. In guiding a group of children toward these outcomes, the teacher must incorporate a great variety of learning experiences into each day's program.

Opportunities must be provided for the pupils to engage in many individual and group learning activities, such as reading, writing, listening, observing, group planning, using reference materials, making charts, preparing bulletin boards, practicing various skills, conferring with the teacher, engaging in group discussions, acquiring information about their study topics, exchanging ideas with other pupils, evaluating their achievement, and keeping their classroom in proper order. The teacher who exercises effective leadership in the supervision of such a multitude of learning activities needs a thorough knowledge of the practical operation of the laws of learning.

A knowledge of the general characteristics of children and an understanding of the specific abilities and needs of children under her supervision are essential to the teacher in supervising study. Information obtained by careful diagnosis of the difficulties encountered by individual children should be utilized in planning study procedures. Obviously, it is impossible to remove the obstacles

264

without a clear understanding of the causes of their existence. Teachers who have never experienced serious frustration in their own learning frequently are unable to realize that their children have problems in this respect. The gap caused by the different viewpoints and degrees of maturity of children and adults also is not easy to bridge.

The directed study situation presents many opportunities for the observation and analysis of study techniques. However, the observations may be superficial and meaningless unless the teacher uses the insights thus gained as leads in assisting children in the formation of effective study habits.

Perhaps the best point of departure in organizing and directing learning activities is the immediate needs and concerns of the members of the class. The needs of the individual members of a class in the elementary school vary greatly in kind and degree. There are, however, certain common developmental tasks of children at each grade level in the elementary school which can serve as the central core of the learning activities. An adequate program of learning activities must be sufficiently flexible to meet the needs of the individual pupils in the class. Approaches to ways of meeting the needs of individuals within a group include helping the individual to belong, giving the individual special help, promoting individual self-evaluation, providing opportunity for individual planning, and using the group to help the individual.

FACTORS IN DEVELOPING PLANS FOR STUDY

These needs of pupils cannot be met by confining the activities of the school day to a series of oral recitations. In an endeavor to provide pupils with the learning experiences necessary to satisfy their needs, many schools have designed plans in which supervised study activities are combined with other learning activities in each day's program. In these plans the study activities and environment are supervised by the teachers as carefully as are the other aspects of the pupils' learning activities. Several factors have contributed to the recent development of plans for supervised study. These will be discussed in the following paragraphs.

Teaching procedures

When the contents of a textbook constituted the sole basis of instruction, a pupil who took his book home with him had all the study materials necessary for what was at that time considered adequate preparation of an assignment. The introduction of the unit and project methods has altered the procedures of study. These methods require the use not only of textbooks, but also of other supplementary materials and library references. Few homes are adequately supplied with these materials. The facilities of the school afford the best opportunity for extensive use of a great variety of study materials.

The new teaching procedures have injected another element into the study activities of children. Formerly preparation for a recitation was strictly an individual task. In the modern school much cooperative effort of children and teachers is considered essential to the successful operation of many learning activities. This involves a group attack upon many of the problems. The solution of these group problems does not lend itself to individual study at home. Cooperative study under the direction of the teacher is essential. The necessity for self-activity in the form of independent study, however, is still present. The two types of study are complementary.

Home study. It would be very unwise to say that there should be no homework. There are situations in which the home is the most important source of information. There are also learning situations which can be met only in the classroom. Little or no homework should be assigned to pupils in the primary grades. Lessons, which have been formally organized with the major objectives of introducing and developing new abilities and new skills, should be studied under the direction of the teacher. Parents often do not understand the techniques used by teachers and, in an attempt to help the child, perform the task for him. Individual projects and some group projects for which information may be obtained in the home or in the community must be done outside of the classroom. The following questions should be considered in connection with homework.

1. Is the home environment conducive to study?
2. Are parents favorably inclined to homework?
3. Is the child learning to do things alone?
4. Can the child do the work independently?
5. Will good work habits be developed?

While physical conditions are not as significant as pupil purpose in effective study, distracting elements are not conducive to satisfactory pupil study. In many homes the competition provided by the radio, television, conversation of members of the family, movies, and games is detrimental to the formation of proper study habits.

The assignments given by teachers have contributed to the difficulty of pupils in doing effective homework. Too frequently the assignments have been too indefinite to present a clear challenge to children in their study. Equally serious has been the poor judgment exercised in regard to the amount of time required of the children to prepare each assignment.

Certain types of homework have great potential values for making the pupil's learning a continuous and unitary experience in which the home and the school cooperate. Homework which involves the study of real life problems has a much greater appeal than does that based upon abstract problems in a textbook. A list of homework assignments of this type adapted from the pamphlet entitled *It Starts in the Classroom* [2] follows:

Mathematics	In the study of budgets the teacher asked each pupil to keep a weekly cash account of his spending money for one month, according to a form set up in class. Each week, before the forms are handed in, parents are asked to audit and initial the accounts.
Arithmetic	Figure out with your mother the number of dishes and silverware she washes in a year.
English	Take one walk thru your house, from room to room, and see how long it takes you to list twenty-five common nouns which are suggested to you by what you see.
Mathematics	Find the area of your front room, and the lot upon which your house stands.
Art	Draw a pencil sketch of your father or mother.

SUPERVISING CLASSROOM STUDY

The teacher's role

In the modern school the teacher is considered a director of learning of a variety of types having as objectives a variety of types of behavior outcomes, information, habits, skills, interests, attitudes, and ideals. The teacher is responsible for arranging situations which provide suitable stimuli for learning. The skilful teacher performs her role without resorting to the artificial stimulation of warnings of failure, low marks, and coming examinations. Some psychologists suggest the need of disturbing the mental and emotional equilibrium of the child. The only defensible method of creating this condition in the mind of the child is by assisting him in gaining a clear recognition of the need of acquiring desirable behavior patterns which he does not possess. The child's under-

[2] *It Starts in the Classroom* (Washington, D.C.: National Education Association, 1951), pp. 31-32.

standing of the value of learning, together with participation in learning activities which are for the most part satisfactory to the learner, is sufficient incentive. The good teacher does not often find it necessary to disturb the mental equilibrium of the child by instilling fears of grade failure.

The teacher has the responsibility not only of providing interest-developing situations which compel to action but also of leadership in directing the learning activity into channels which result in improved habits of action. The teacher should perform the task of maneuvering the abundant energies of children into approved ways of human endeavor. Assignments should be developed in class and made clear to the learners in a way which excites interest—exploiting the better qualities and personality of the teacher.

The teacher's role in directing study activities is that of leadership, guidance, stimulation, encouragement, and evaluation. The specific duties vary with the nature of the subject and the maturity of the children. While each directed study situation calls for a great range of teacher activities, self-direction should rest as largely as possible with the children at all times. A positive program of teacher guidance in pupil self-direction is indispensable. No policy of negative inaction will suffice.

In supervising pupil study most teachers tend to devote too much time to slow-learning children and neglect the more intelligent ones. In directing study and in all other phases of teaching, sound judgment is required to maintain the proper balance between all the various activities. There is no reason why the judgment of teachers should not be as good in respect to pupil study as in other aspects of their work.

Some children have a tendency to observe the activities of other children and of the teacher and so fail to concentrate on their own problems. If a pupil is wholeheartedly engaged in a piece of challenging work, the chances are slight that he will be distracted by the activities of others.

The teacher who supervises study on a part-time basis rarely if ever acquires proficiency in supervising study. The study period is not the proper time for the teacher to score papers or bring her correspondence up to date. She should devote the entire period to helping, guiding, and encouraging children in their work. It will not suffice to give children the opportunity to come to the teacher's desk for assistance. Those who need help the most may not avail themselves of this privilege. The teacher should move quietly about the room observing and conferring in a subdued tone of voice with individuals or groups of children who need assistance. Whenever the same difficulty is encountered by several children, the teacher may conduct a group discussion for the purpose of removing the source of the trouble.

There is frequently too little checking of results to ascertain the effectiveness of child study. This is an important and difficult matter. Supervised study in comparison with other types of child study presents the best opportunity for the teacher to learn the child's method of study.

Children need encouragement. A word of praise often gives the child who is about to give up trying the "second wind" which he needs in order to get over the hard spot or to complete the assignment. Such comments as "You are doing all right" and "You are on the right track" are effective tonics for the child who is struggling with his work. The teacher's praise and encouragement should not convey to the child the idea that he is doing it to please her, but that he is doing it well.

Often children are discouraged by the many red checks on their papers in spelling, arithmetic, written reports, etc. If the errors must be checked with a red pencil, wouldn't it be wise to check correct responses with a blue pencil? It would encourage the child to see on his spelling paper the word "good" written after three words that have been spelling demons for him and which he spelled correctly. Then the five red checks would not appear nearly so hopeless—for he knows that he has had power to correct his errors. Scientific studies show that accomplishment is a great motivating factor. The child should know that he is one step ahead of where he was yesterday.

The study environment

Psychologists have emphasized the importance of the "psychology of place" in connection with the establishment of desirable study habits. There has been some doubt expressed as to whether the classrooms in the typical school can be arranged in a manner suitable for pupil study. Little consideration has been given to provision for pupil study in planning school buildings. Eventually as much attention must be given to the proper study environment as is given to plans for the auditorium and the gymnasium.

Many classrooms have insufficient light. This condition may result from too few windows or improper location of a sufficient number. In the case of artificial lighting, the difficulty may result from the use of light bulbs of low candle power or from placing them too far from the desks. Too often the fact is overlooked that the intensity of the light decreases in inverse ratio to the distance.

For example, a bulb which gives light of adequate intensity for reading at a distance of six feet from the child's desk is only 25 per cent adequate at a distance of twelve feet. As the distance is doubled, the strength of the light must be quadrupled to give the same illumination. Light meters should be used to measure the intensity of the light in all parts of all rooms at frequent intervals. Since dirt decreases the efficiency of incandescent lamps to a remarkable degree, bulbs and reflectors should be kept clean at all times. Cross lighting and glares also contribute to unsatisfactory conditions for pupil study.

Essential study materials such as reading charts, workbooks, and paper should be readily available. Each classroom should have its own library. Many of the books should be kept in the room permanently. These books should be supplemented by other books pertaining to the work materials but on easier reading levels than the books used by the average children in the room, and also by books on a higher reading level.

Distractions should be kept at a minimum at all times. Noise caused by children passing or talking in adjacent halls may be eliminated by the simple measure of keeping classroom doors closed. Within the classroom every child or group should be taught to respect the right of other individuals or groups to pursue their study without interference. The teacher should be certain that her own activities in directing study do not constitute a source of disturbance.

The assignment

The assignment, whether teacher imposed or cooperatively planned, represents one of the most important phases of teaching. It should be recognized as an aspect of teaching rather than as a step preparatory to teaching. The assignment has been referred to as the key to the learning process, the heart of the problem of pupil direction, the beginning point in teaching, the guide necessary to effective work in the study period, the stimulus to the learning activity, and a means of directing study. These characterizations represent attempts by various authors to emphasize the significance of the assignment in the study process. Despite this emphasis, the full potentialities of the assignment have not been realized in actual classroom practice. The most encouraging trends in assignments and assignment making are manifest in connection with the unit and project methods of teaching. Additional trends are those toward the cooperative development of the assignment by pupils and teacher and toward greater flexibility in terms of the varying abilities and needs of the different members of the class.

Progress has been slow in making the daily assignment an effective instrument in promoting learning. However, in many schools in which the daily recitation is still predominant the page-to-page textbook assignment is being replaced by the topic and problem types.

Functions. Broadly conceived, the main function of the assignment is to serve as a guide to the pupil in his learning activities. More specifically the functions are (1) to establish a motive or develop interest for engaging in learning activity, (2) to institute worthy and significant objectives which give direction to learning activities, and (3) to give the child a clear understanding of how the purposes of his activities may be accomplished in an economical and effective manner.

Learning is satisfactory when it operates toward a definite goal. A goal lends an interest motive and a direction toward which a child can direct learning, eliminating the nonessential and choosing and developing the essential elements. Motives which are drives to action are deep-seated in human nature. They cannot, however, be taken for granted. They may lie dormant in regard to intellectual matters unless the teacher is successful in relating school learning to the child's basic needs in such a manner that he is able to associate the activity with himself. While the sources of motivation may reside in the subintellectual life of man, the direction of his activities is dependent upon his intellectual discrimination. (Learning and motivation have been more completely discussed in Chapter 6.) In order to arouse a genuine interest in a topic, it should be related to interests previously acquired. In addition the utilization of native impulses, such as curiosity and manipulation, is often quite effective.

Characteristics. The effectiveness of the planned learning activities is dependent upon the degree to which its functions are clearly perceived. As the assignment is a guide for the child it should, like all good guideposts, point unerringly straight to the goal. Plans and directions should be understood fully by the learner. Allowing for appropriate initiative and self-direction, they should be sufficiently detailed and explicit to indicate to the class how to use materials efficiently, thereby preventing children from wasting time in their search for materials.

The character and purpose of the learning activities should be entirely clear to each child in the sense that he knows rather definitely *what* he is to do and *why*. The activity in which the child is expected to engage should be of sufficient value to him to justify the time and effort required for it. Emphasis upon clearness, definiteness, and specificity should not be disturbing to those teachers who believe in the freedom of the child in directing his own activities. There is no real conflict between the two concepts. Where freedom and definiteness are combined, each child has the responsibility for studying his methods of work and analyzing his progress in terms of the factors which hinder or further it. The dangers which might be perceived in a system of definite tasks and goals are offset by freedom in the choice of various activities.

Since children's needs, abilities, and interests vary markedly, flexibility of assignments is essential. A sufficient degree of difficulty is needed to challenge the pupil to his best efforts. The materials of the assignment and the manner in which it is made should serve to arouse a genuine interest in the following class discussion.

Appraisal. The effectiveness of the assignment should be measured in terms of the outcomes of the learning activities likely to be engendered by it. The new concept of learning considers the individual as an organism in interaction with his environment. Since these reactions are numerous, the outcomes are multiple. Evaluation of these outcomes is more adequate when observational techniques for recording behavior are employed. The instruments and techniques for measuring the outcomes of learning will be discussed in Chapters 19 and 20.

The most common and least satisfactory of all the methods of appraising the assignment is that of devoting the entire recitation to oral testing of the pupil's preparation. Data obtained from the measurement of the pupil's mastery of factual material should be supplemented by information gained from a consideration of the following questions:

1. Did the activities invoked by the assignment contribute to the social maturity of pupils?
2. Did the children's study have educative value?
3. Did the assignment lead to activities which contributed to growth in total child personality?
4. Did the work result in new and improved aspects of behavior, such as desirable understandings, attitudes, and appreciations?
5. Did learning activities originate in the purposes of the children?
6. Were the learning materials interesting and challenging to the child?
7. Was provision made for wise use of source materials, choice of values, and solving problems?
8. Were vocabulary and other difficulties anticipated?
9. Did the assignment give proper consideration to different abilities and past experiences of the children in the class?

10. Were initiative, originality, and creative activity on the part of children permitted to emerge?
11. Were the children free from unnecessary tension?
12. Were the pupils able to discover the relationships between the assignment and other assignments?
13. Did the assignment guide the study activities in an economical and effective manner?
14. Was there pupil participation in developing the assignment?
15. Did the assignment induce critical thinking on the part of the children?
16. Were the goals established attained by the children?
17. How many children experienced the satisfaction of success?

Work-study period

One of the most significant developments in instructional procedures has been the elimination of the separate recitation and study period in favor of a "working period." Under this plan, longer continuous periods of varied activity have replaced the shorter periods devoted to separate subjects. In the longer periods children engage in the study of related subjects. Spelling, writing, and written communication may be combined. Work-type reading will include word analysis, concept building, development of reading abilities. Story hour or literature may be combined with oral language at one time and at another with social studies. The content of work-study periods will vary from time to time, depending upon objectives to be achieved at the time.

Pupil-teacher planning of topics and procedures functions also. A wide variety of source materials may be utilized. Textbooks, magazines, general reference books, pamphlets, models, and films are made available. Guided trips outside the school are undertaken to obtain firsthand information concerning the topic under consideration. While the work usually centers around some general theme or topic, opportunity is provided for individual children to engage in different activities which contribute to the main purpose.

Individual and small-group projects are carried on as well as those involving the entire class. Individual work is characteristic of certain phases of the work-study period. The formality which characterized the older study plans and procedures is dispensed with under the work-study plan. Time schedules, processes, and standards should be tentative and flexible. Under the intelligent guidance and stimulation of capable teachers, the possibility of achieving the multiple outcomes of modern education are perhaps greater in this procedure than in any of the older directed study plans.

Individual conferences

The use of the individual conference as a means of guidance, encouragement, and establishing rapport with the child is a desirable practice. The conference should ordinarily not be a matter of chance. It should be planned upon the basis of the immediate needs of the child and the more real the purpose the more valuable the conference will be. The technique of a conversation should be employed. The teacher may put the child at ease when opening the conversation by telling him about interests and problems that she faced at his age, always keeping in mind that the incident which she relates is similar to the problem which the child is facing. Then cooperatively teacher and child analyze the problem, plan procedures for solving the problem, and make agreements in regard to remedial work. Just to tell the child that he must improve and to get him to promise that he will do better will not produce results; neither will advice without knowing what the difficulty is be effective.

The sincerity of the teacher and the informality of the conference will help the child to know that the teacher is taking a personal interest in him which will provide the "personal touch" that promotes desirable human relationships and mutual understandings. The ultimate outcome of a conference should be that the child has acquired a better understanding of himself, that he has decided to do something about the problem, and that he knows that someone understands him and is interested in his welfare.

Small-group study plan

Many teachers have found that the formation of several small groups within the class is frequently desirable for study of different phases of a problem. While large-group discussion may be prompted by the heterogeneity of the group, since the presence of members with different points of view contributes to complete consideration of a topic, the basis of membership in a small group may well be the common need among a few pupils to acquire greater proficiency in a particular skill, such as accuracy in computation of numbers. They are therefore grouped together and given an assignment involving practice on that skill, while another group of the class may be given experiences to enable them to acquire greater reading comprehension. A small group also may be formed upon the basis of a common interest in a problem. Groups of this type should be given assignments which will enable them to pursue their interests. Small-group activity within a class may help provide for individual differences in mental abilities of the pupils. Groups of superior children may be given learning tasks of sufficient difficulty and of such a nature as to challenge their capabilities, while a slow-learning group may be encouraged to engage in some less abstract activity. The membership of the group does not remain intact at all times. As different topics emerge or new interests and needs are revealed, regrouping of pupils should be made. The teacher may assist each of the groups in their study, or she may conduct a recitation for one group while the other groups study their assignments. Individual pupils may engage in various types of independent study activities, such as reading, working with clay, or drilling themselves with self-help arithmetic cards.

SUPERVISING COOPERATIVE PROBLEM-SOLVING ACTIVITIES

In modern teaching there is a tendency to reorganize both content and methods of instruction on the basis of units presenting psychological challenges, called variously activity units, contracts, problems, and projects. In the study of a problem more of the planning and oversight of the work is left to the learner and his fellow learners in the group. Problem-solving produces learning situations in which the efforts of the pupils are stimulated by a felt need, difficulty, or desire, rather than by the arbitrary assignment of tasks by the teacher.

The problem as a unit of educational activity is probably the best adapted of all teaching situations to arouse genuine interest and purposeful, wholehearted activity on the part of the pupil. The traditional procedure lacks the values and points of strength which appear when study of educational materials and participation in educational activity are the logical and self-chosen procedures for solving problems which present themselves to the learner.

John Dewey called attention to the fact that thinking originates in some problematical situation. After a detailed discussion of the point, he continues:

We may recapitulate by saying that the origin of thinking is some perplexity, confusion, or doubt. Thinking is not a case of spontaneous combustion; it does not occur just on "general principles." There is something specific which occasions and evokes it. General appeals to a child (or to a grown-up) to think, irrespective of the existence in his experience of some difficulty that troubles him and disturbs his equilibrium, are as futile as advice to lift himself by his bootstraps.[3]

[3] John Dewey, *How We Think* (Quoted by permission of Boston: D. C. Heath and Company, publishers, 1933).

Dissatisfaction with things causes one to start thinking about them in an attempt to find a solution. The starting point of thinking is the recognition of an unsatisfactory state of affairs, the unpleasantness of things as they are, or of desires and how they may be attained. There are enough situations demanding adjustment, for which instinctive tendencies and habits have no ready-made solution, to occupy us in all our waking moments.

Problem-solving teaching consists of raising perplexity, confusion, or doubt in the minds of pupils in a manner such as to challenge solution and then supervising their efforts at solution.

Many topics can be presented in an elementary school course which are of common concern to all members of the class. In the study of these problems the combined efforts of all members are desirable.

Selection of the problem

The essence of cooperative group thinking is the presence of a problem about which the pupils are concerned. Pupils' interest in a problem is dependent upon its identity with reality and the extent to which they share decisions with the teacher in regard to selecting and planning procedures for the study of the problem. It is not realistic to expect a group of students to enter wholeheartedly into the study or discussion of a problem for which they have no concern and have had no voice in selecting.

Pupils' initial interest in a problem may grow out of a field trip, radio programs, newspaper accounts, or the presentation by the teacher of a significant and timely topic. The final selection of the topic should be made by the pupils and teacher upon the basis of previously accepted criteria. In one school, a teacher, with the assistance of the pupils in her class, developed the following criteria for problems for class study.

1. Is it a significant problem?
2. Is it timely?
3. Is it of some concern to each of us as individuals and to the people of the community?
4. Does the nature of the problem lend itself to solution by group attack procedures?
5. Is the problem such that the maturity of the pupils permits some success in its solution?
6. Is the problem sufficiently limited in scope to permit progress toward its solution in the time and with the resources available?

The study of the problem

After the selection of the problem, a cooperative plan for its study should be made by the pupils and the teacher. *There should be a clear understanding that group discussion is usually futile unless it is preceded by a careful examination and study of all the facts involved.* The mere expression of superficial or biased opinions by a group may be detrimental. It certainly does not contribute to the pupils' understanding of effective group work. In planning the study, there should be discussions of sources of information, points of emphasis, allocation of responsibility for various phases of the study, and procedures in conducting the study. On the basis of preliminary research of an elementary nature, each member of the class may be expected to suggest materials pertaining to the problem. School library materials, field trips, films, and outside speakers may be suggested. The entire class may participate in a study of some parts of the topic, while individual pupils or small committees may be held responsible for the study of other phases.

Group decisions should be made also in respect to the form of presentation of the results of the study. Some preliminary thought should be given by the group to the means of evaluating their study.

Various approaches may be made to the solution of a problem by a class. Study of textbooks and library reading materials by individual pupils under the guidance of the teacher is essential. Directed study by the class, with occasional discussions of common difficulties by the teacher, promotes economy of time and greater understanding. If the problem requires firsthand information obtained by means of field trips, the teacher acts as leader of the group. She should be available at all times as a consultant and resource person for individual pupils and for the group as a whole. She should be alert to the learning difficulties and progress of the group. Of paramount importance is the teacher's role as a learner along with the other members of the group. She is responsible for keeping the problem clearly before the pupils, thus preventing wasted time and effort. By her attitude and assistance she can help pupils to sustain interest in completing the task of solving the problem they have set for themselves.

Group discussion. The initial stages of group work described in the preceding paragraphs should serve as the basis of group discussions by (1) providing the members of the class with knowledge about the topic, and (2) unifying them into a group as a result of their cooperative endeavors in obtaining the needed information.

The group discussion can add to both of these outcomes. If the members of a class are immature and inexperienced, it may be necessary for the teacher to assume leadership in the early stages of the discussion. The teacher's role at this point may be to act as temporary discussion leader until the purposes and procedures of the discussion are clearly understood by the group. The teacher may find it desirable to encourage the group to state the goals of the discussion by writing them on the blackboard as they are suggested. If the initial discussion is conducted in a permissive manner, student leadership will emerge and should be given an opportunity at the earliest moment to take responsibility. In the course of the discussion, as various matters are considered, different student leaders may emerge and take turns in heading the discussion.

Pupil leadership in group discussion does not relieve the teacher of responsible leadership; it merely shifts the emphasis of her responsibility. The teacher is not *above* or *outside* the group, but *within* it. As a member of the group, she is obligated to contribute her knowledge and ideas to the solution of the problem. Beyond this function, however, the teacher has certain unique functions. It is of chief importance that the teacher do the following:

Assist the class in sticking to the problem. Good group thinking is characterized by adherence to the problem under consideration. Most problems do not exist in isolation from other problems. This interrelatedness may make a particular problem of greater practical value than if it were entirely separate from other problems, but it makes more difficult the task of the individual or the group to identify the data which are relevant to its solution. Some of the rambling discussions of a group may result from the deliberate efforts of individuals to inject their personal views into the discussion. In many cases the diversion may result from confusion as to what knowledges or ideas have a direct bearing upon the problem. Some of the most effective means of keeping the discussion on the subject are:

1. Asking a question in regard to what the problem is may serve to refocus the attention of the class upon the main theme of the discussion.
2. Having a summary of the discussion given by one of the members or the leader of the group may serve to keep the discussion moving toward the goals of the group.
3. Listing the main points of the discussion on the blackboard may suggest the proper direction for subsequent discussion.

Assist the class to include all relevant data on the problem. A consideration of all the facts pertaining to the problem is necessary to reach sound conclusions. One of the chief values of socialized procedures is a recognition by the participants of the compelling need for a consideration of *all* the facts before arriving at conclusions. The teacher should call attention to sources of materials which the pupils may have overlooked. Suggestions of a more careful analysis of some materials tend to insure that these materials will be given the weight they deserve.

While pupils should be expected to exercise their initiative in carrying on elementary research in regard to the location, collection, and relative value of data, the teacher should provide needed guidance and reassurance at times to prevent confusion and discouragement. Even though the pupils may have obtained the essential data in their study or in the course of the discussion, they may fail to give sufficient attention to some important material unless reminded by the teacher.

Help obtain the participation of all members of the class in the discussion. Two considerations are involved in this matter: encouraging the timid pupil, and preventing monopolization of the discussion by the more extroverted pupils. Shy pupils may be encouraged to participate in the discussion by directing questions to them in line with their special interests or asking them to state their opinions in regard to the topic. Expressions of appreciation of their contributions can be given in such a manner as to reassure them, thus building up self-confidence. It may be suggested to pupils who tend to monopolize the discussion that every member of the class should be given a chance to participate. As the timid pupils are drawn into the discussion, there is less danger of anyone dominating the discussion.

Keep the discussion moving toward the group-accepted goals. The pace of the discussion should not be too rapid to discourage deliberate and thoughtful consideration of the implications and interrelationships of the data. On the other hand, lagging discussions may threaten the attainment of important outcomes. In the consideration of a point, it may become evident that further discussion is futile until additional information is obtained. In such cases, the discussion should be deferred until further study has been made.

When a topic has been adequately covered, it may become necessary for the group leader to suggest that the discussion move on promptly to other topics. If the discussion flounders or loses its sense of direction, a summary of the points discussed may serve to indicate the course to be taken.

Help the group to evaluate their progress. Evaluation by the pupils of the procedures and the results of their work can be made a valuable learning experience. During the progress of their work on a problem, the pupils should make continuous appraisal of the success of their efforts as a basis for modification of objectives and plans. A final evaluation of the results of the work can be made by pupils' asking themselves such questions as: Were the source materials adequate and reliable? Did the group achieve the goals it set out to accomplish? Was there participation by all members of the group? What modifications in procedure might have been desirable?

Class committees. As a concomitant activity of cooperative group work, various committees may be formed for an intensive study of different aspects of a topic, problem, or unit. The committees may be appointed by the teacher or suggested by members of the class, or individual pupils may volunteer for work on a committee. Regardless of the method used in selecting committee members, it is feasible to distribute membership widely to include, at one time or another, all the members of the class. The membership of committees should change as the work proceeds, thus avoiding the formation of cliques in the class. The interests, abilities, and needs of individual pupils should be taken into account in forming committees. This is not to suggest that homogeneity of membership should always be sought. Working as a member of a heterogeneous group can be a valuable learning experience for an individual.

After a committee is formed, the members should clarify their learning task and develop their study plans on a cooperative basis. All committee decisions should be made not only with a view to an equitable distribution of duties for the committee members, but also in terms of their responsibility to the entire class to whom they are to report the results of their learning endeavors.

Supervision of the activity

In order to achieve economy of pupil effort and to produce effectiveness in problem-solving, the teacher must facilitate the steps in problem-solving with considerable skill. Cooperative pupil-teacher procedures are appropriate in the study of many problems in the elementary school classroom. The teacher may find some of the following suggestions useful in supervising problem-solving activities of pupils.

Creative learnings.

First independent seat work. These children are identifying phonetic sounds by means of pictures while the teacher is working with another group of children. (Madison, Wisconsin, Public Schools)

1. Identify actual problems present in the environment or experiences of the pupils which are suitable and worthy of study.
2. Permit pupils to select one of the problems in which they have a real interest.
3. Help pupils clarify the problem clearly.
4. Formulate with the pupils a set of attainable goals for studying the problem.
5. Involve the pupils in planning the procedure for the study of the problem.
6. Organize the class into groups for division of labor and responsibility in the study of the problem.
7. Provide for the acquisition of study abilities and skills as needed in the solution of the problem.
8. Allow for individual pupil initiative and participation in the study of the problem.
9. Assist pupils to keep problems and conditions of each problem in mind and prevent digression in their study.
10. Provide for periodic appraisal of progress toward the goals.
11. Assist pupils to find or recall data which will contribute to the solution of the problem, offering hints, suggestions, and references but being careful to give no more assistance than is necessary and thereby avoid depriving the pupil of any educational opportunity.
12. Encourage pupils to evaluate carefully each suggested conclusion and to maintain an attitude of suspended final judgment.
13. Insist that pupils be systematic in the consideration of hypotheses and their evaluation, to follow some order, and to complete the consideration of one before digressing to another.
14. Assist pupils to formulate their conclusions on cooperative bases.
15. Provide for continuous and final evaluation and verification.
16. Fix solutions in mind by drill, application, memory work, or exercises.

SUPERVISING CREATIVE LEARNING

Any new and novel experience is a creative learning, regardless of how many have experienced it before. For example, many children have constructed airplanes by nailing together two boards crosswise, but this does not deprive another child of having a similar creative experience, provided he has discovered the idea and put it into its external form.

Creative learnings can be included in practically every subject. In social studies the culture of a people can be clarified by studying their creations in paintings, poetry, dancing, pottery, weaving, music

—this often serving as a motivation for children to create with the same media. In arithmetic some children may create a device in order to clarify the meaning of tens in our number system. Letters and written compositions should be creations of the child through which he projects himself. In oral language, the child communicates to others his pleasures, his anticipations, his appreciations, by inventing a phrase or an expression. Through spontaneous play, many children unravel tangled experiences and vague concepts. An experience either real or vicarious may be expressed in a picture, in a clay model, in a soap carving, and if the child has not copied too completely from another model, the object expressing the experience will be his own creation.

The creative environment

An atmosphere conducive to a child's interest must be developed by the teacher so that a child's potentialities toward creativeness will be uncovered and will grow. The physical environment, as well as the psychological, affects the development of a child's abilities. The classroom should be airy and light; the activities should be appropriate to the age, sex, and skill level of the children and to the facilities and equipment available. Especially should the activities stimulate, challenge, and permit success so that the child's self-confidence will be assured. The teacher must integrate the emotional climate she creates with the physical surroundings so that conditions which are conducive to creative growth and development will result.

The process of creative learning is difficult to analyze. Many creative productions develop spontaneously, such as dancing, acting, singing, playing, while others need direction in the initial stages and will gradually merge into an original production. Often old ideas are revised and reorganized from an abundance of accumulated information, and a new concept comes forth. Children in primary grades are free from conventionalities in their activities while in the intermediate grades children are more realistic.

In directing creative learnings, the thing essential to keep in mind is to make it possible for children to use their imagination and reasoning, and through their own efforts solve problems and put things together in a way which is new and different for them, even though it has been done many times by others. All standards must be the standards of the creator—to force upon him the standards of another person would remove the basic characteristic, which is *genuineness.*

The teacher's role

In a creative learning situation the teacher's role is that of guide, not dictator or protective benefactor. Through guidance she provides opportunities for children to determine their own purposes, to direct their own planning and acting toward the achievement of their own purposes, and to profit from their successes and failures through their own evaluations. Authoritative or benevolent control will unduly influence children's thinking and acting. The function of the teacher consists of developing in herself certain characteristics, of providing both atmosphere and situations in which children may learn to be creative, and of utilizing methods which are conducive to continuous growth in the process of learning. Children create when they explain, describe, and interpret what they have seen, heard, touched, or constructed. The teacher guides when she gives a child assistance by having him answer questions, such as experiential questions, imaginative questions, recall of factual information, and suggestive questions. In no case should a teacher discourage creative activity by too much technical criticism. As children develop and gain confidence in themselves, the skills which function in the creative work will improve.

To function effectively in the guidance of creative learnings the teacher must establish herself with the children as an acceptable and active member of the class group. In this role she can provide opportunity and stimulation for the members of the group to work freely. Only the efforts of an accepted guide will stimulate growth. The teacher must enthusiastically and sincerely share the children's interests and purposes and work with them on their level of maturity. As a guide she should lead the children toward developing their interests and accomplishing their purposes. She should provide the opportunity for the children to rely on their own self-direction for the success of their plans, insofar as possible.

In the primary grades the teacher must assume responsibility for procedures if the child is to approach success in his creative endeavors. She must help little children toward the ability to assume responsibilities for themselves and to make choices. She must provide activities that stimulate group interest and give promise of satisfaction and success. Then, one situation at a time, she can attempt the transfer from teacher control to pupil planning and assumption of responsibility for creativity. In the upper grades children begin to have a feeling of responsibility for directing their own actions in the light of their purposes and plans. Guidance in these grades is concerned with affording children the opportunity to develop their creative abilities to their full potentialities.

QUESTIONS, PROBLEMS, AND EXERCISES

1. What is the modern conception of the teacher's responsibility in supervising learning activity?

2. In what respects do the more recent plans for supervised study differ from the older plans?

3. Indicate the activities of the teacher in supervising the study of pupils.

4. Formulate three problems about which the work of a class might center for several days or more.

5. Suggest a list of from six to eight dangers to avoid in employing a problem-solving type of teaching.

6. How may the special abilities and interests of individual pupils be utilized in cooperative problem-solving activities?

7. Suggest five ways of fostering creativity of pupils in the classroom.

SELECTED SUPPLEMENTARY READINGS

ASSOCIATION FOR SUPERVISION AND CURRICULUM DEVELOPMENT. *Creating a Good Environment for Learning, 1954 Yearbook.* Washington, D.C.: National Education Association, 1954.

Chap. ix, "Learning Experiences Are Important." Suggestions for planning and guiding pupils' school experiences.

————. *Toward Better Teaching. Forty-ninth Yearbook.* Washington, D.C.: National Education Association, 1949.

Chap. v, "Fostering Creativity." Describes classroom activities designed to foster creativity.

HANNA, LAVONNE A., GLADYS L. POTTER, and NEVA HAGAMAN. *Unit Teaching in the Elementary School.* New York: Rinehart & Co., Inc., 1955.

Chap. viii, "Problem Solving." Application of the problem-solving technique to the study of a problem by a third-grade class.

LANE, HOWARD, and MARY BEAUCHAMP. *Human Relations in Teaching.* Englewood Cliffs, N.J.: Prentice-Hall, Inc., 1955.

Chap. xvii, "Using Group Discussion and Role-playing." Describes techniques of utilizing these activities in the classroom.

MACOMBER, FREEMAN GLENN. *Principles of Teaching in the Elementary School.* New York: American Book Co., 1954.

Chap. xi, "Developing Appreciations and Creativeness." Discussion of the factors essential to creative expression.

MIEL, ALICE and ASSOCIATES. *Cooperative Procedures in Learning.* New York: Bureau of Publications, Teachers College, Columbia University, 1952.

Chap. x, "Getting Started with Cooperative Procedures in Schools." Describes prerequisites for getting started in using cooperative procedures.

REED, CALVIN H. "Developing Creative Thinking in Arithmetic," *The Arithmetic Teacher,* IV, 1 (February, 1957), 10-2.

Suggests teaching procedures to help pupils develop creative thinking in arithmetic.

STEPHENS, ADA DAWSON. *Providing Developmental Experiences for Young Children.* New York: Bureau of Publications, Teachers College, Columbia University, 1952.

Suggests many kinds of learning experiences with language, music, and science.

STRANG, RUTH. *Guided Study and Homework—What Research Says to the Teacher.* Washington, D.C.: National Education Association, Department of Classroom Teachers and American Educational Research Association, 1955.

Report of research, practices, and expert opinions concerning homework and guided study.

15

MANAGING THE CLASSROOM
LEARNING ENVIRONMENT

The classroom is an organized aspect of the elementary school environment designed to promote desirable pupil growth and development. It is a controlled environment in that the activities are directed toward the attainment of certain educational objectives. The nature of the controls determines in large measure the extent to which it is a good learning environment. In a good classroom environment, pupils are challenged and stimulated to participate in a variety of meaningful learning activities. In seeking their goals, learners engage in activities which contribute to their feelings of security and satisfaction.

There are many aspects of the classroom situation which influence the quantity and quality of pupil learning. Among the important factors are the teacher, the interpersonal relationships of the members of the class, the learning materials and equipment, and the general conditions and arrangement of the classroom.

The general objective of class management is to facilitate the multitude of pupil learning activities in the complex social, emotional, and intellectual environment of the classroom. More specifically, classroom learning activities are organized and managed to:

1. Establish conditions conducive to the formation of proper individual work and study habits.
2. Create a social climate in which individual pupils can gain satisfaction in wholesome group living.
3. Maintain conditions conducive to the establishment of proper habits of pupil behavior.

4. Develop proficiency on the part of pupils in the use of the tools of learning.
5. Help each child experience optimum intellectual growth and development in terms of his abilities and potentialities.
6. Assist each pupil to achieve an ever-increasing emotional maturity.
7. Contribute to the acquisition of desirable concomitant or related learnings, i.e., attitudes, appreciations, etc.

In achieving these objectives the teacher has two closely related responsibilities, namely, (1) maintaining a satisfactory physical environment, and (2) directing the intellectual and social processes of the class. The management of both the physical environment and the intellectual and social activities of pupils should be considered not only as a means to learning but also as an end in promoting the formation of effective habits of work and study on the part of pupils.

PHYSICAL ENVIRONMENT

The physical conditions under which pupils do their schoolwork greatly affect their physical well-being, learning efficiency, and conduct. Important features of the physical environment include the classroom, the furniture, and the instructional materials and equipment. In planning new elementary school buildings, considerable effort is being made to provide attractive, comfortable classrooms. Greater emphasis also is being placed upon custodian services. Despite these improvements, the teacher can do many things to make the physical features of the learning environment more pleasant and challenging to pupils.

General classroom conditions

The learning efficiency of pupils is greatly influenced by the lighting, ventilation, temperature, and appearance of the classroom. Inadequate lighting represents a serious danger of eye strain. The large windows in the newer school buildings may permit too much light to enter the classroom at certain times during the day for pupils seated near the windows. In an endeavor to correct this condition, teachers frequently adjust the window shades in such a manner as to reduce the light too much for pupils in other parts of the room.

If there is sufficient glass window surface (one-sixth to one-fourth of the floor surface of the room) natural lighting is perhaps the most satisfactory type under normal conditions. However, on cloudy days or other times when artificial lighting is necessary, the standards for lighting suggested by the Illuminating Engineering Society of 30-foot-candles for desks and study tables in a classroom should be observed. The teacher should verify the adequacy of the light periodically by means of a light meter.

The type of the reading materials should not be smaller than 4 mm. in height for first-grade pupils and 3 mm. for older children. Chalkboard letters should not be less than 50 mm. in height. The teacher should group pupils so they can see the chalkboard without difficulty. Pupils with visual defects should usually be seated near the front of the room.

The temperature generally recommended for classrooms is from 68° to 72° F. Closely related to temperature is the humidity of the air which should be from 40–60 per cent in the classroom. In a school building ventilated by a central fan system, the windows should be kept closed. In classrooms not ventilated by this system, windows should be equipped with window boards to prevent drafts on pupils, and the windows should be opened during intermissions and during periods of physical exercises.

The size of the desks should be adjusted to that of the pupils to prevent discomfort and bad posture. The teacher should assume responsibility for checking on various health and safety factors which affect her pupils. Pupils should be given clear instructions and practice in fire drills. A sufficient number of fire extinguishers should be properly placed and kept in condition for instantaneous use at all times. Storage spaces in the classroom should be kept free of combustible material. First-aid equipment should be readily available.

Playground activities should be selected, organized, and supervised to provide the maximum safety for the pupils who participate. The teacher should be on the alert for evidences of low physical vitality and ill health in directing pupils' playground and classroom activities. Pupil traffic safety patrols can be used in the effective control of moving traffic while pupils are crossing streets near the school.

Proper lunchroom management contributes not only to the physical well-being of pupils but also to their social development. In many schools, pupils take turns serving as hosts or hostesses for their lunch tables. These students act as leaders in the practice of good table manners. In the health classes, instruction is given in the proper selection of foods and proper eating habits.

Instructional equipment and supplies

Modern methods of teaching in the elementary school require the use of a great variety of equipment and instructional materials. The

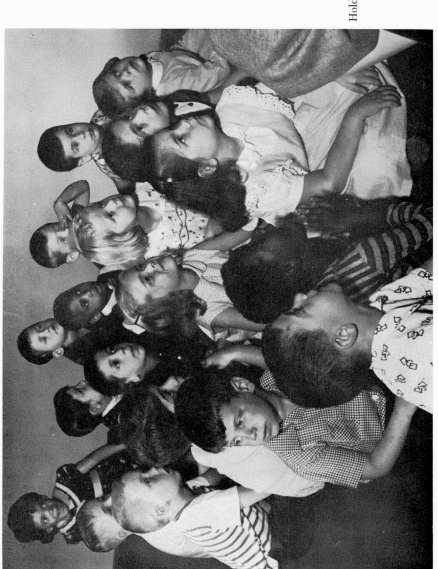

Holding the attention of children is an art.

Application of language skills in independent writing.
(Des Moines, Iowa, Public Schools)

Integration of reading and numbers in social studies unit.
(Denver, Colorado, Public Schools)

manner in which these are handled determines their effectiveness in pupil learning. The cooperation of pupils and the teacher in the arrangement, care, and use of these materials contributes greatly to their value. Pupils who share in the management of this aspect of their classroom environment acquire a greater respect for and pride in their school buildings, school grounds, furniture, equipment, and books.

Many teachers form rotating committees of pupils who assume responsibility for keeping maps, globes, and charts in proper order. These committees (sometimes referred to as "service committees") keep the various materials systematically arranged on shelves and storage closets. When the materials are needed, the members of the committee provide for their proper distribution to the members of the class. Various groups of pupils are given the task of assembling and arranging reading and other learning materials for the center of interest tables.

Many teachers encourage pupils to use their initiative in planning different arrangements of pictures, vases, and statuary in the classroom. The selection and arrangement of items on bulletin boards foster creativity in pupils. The members of elementary school classes have responded readily to the collection of resource materials for use in connection with the study of various topics.

Pupils enjoy the opportunity to keep their classroom as attractive as possible. They enjoy planning interesting displays of their drawings and written work. In keeping the classroom tidy, each pupil accepts responsibility for keeping the area around his desk free of waste paper. Flag raising and lowering ceremonies are conducted in many schools by pupils.

Light, movable furniture is desirable for multiple-group work; however, in classrooms with desks fastened to the floor, it is possible to place sheets of plywood on the desks to provide working spaces for pupil committees.

Bulletin boards, and more recently flannel boards, are standard equipment in most classrooms. The bulletin boards should contain items showing the interests and achievements of pupils. The materials should be displayed without crowding. They should be well-organized and arranged attractively. The items should be centered around one theme and should be changed frequently. If a table is placed beneath the bulletin board, models, specimens, and pupil-made dioramas may be arranged and attached by ribbons or strings to the labels, pictures, and printed accounts of the objects on the board to which they refer. Pupils should be largely responsible for these details. The delegation of these matters frees the teacher for the performance of other important duties and provides valuable learning experiences for pupils.

Audio-visual instructional materials are used extensively in elementary schools. These materials should be procured and arranged in advance of their use. (See Chapter 12.) Pupils can assist in the care of many of these materials. However, the use of some of the materials requires rather expensive equipment. Film projectors and television receiving sets should have careful use. The teacher should learn to operate and take proper care of film projectors. She should also know how to store films properly.

The teacher can set an excellent example of orderliness in the classroom by keeping the materials on her desk neatly arranged. Teachers should share with pupils the task of erasing the chalkboard at the end of each class period and keeping the chairs or desks properly arranged around work tables or in rows. Permitting pupils to share responsibility for the appearance of their classroom contributes to their feeling of belongingness. They acquire the feeling that "it is our classroom". The extent to which pupil participation in "good school housekeeping" is a valuable educative experience depends upon the leadership of the teacher in creating and maintaining a permissive classroom atmosphere in which pupils feel free to exercise their initiative and assume responsibility in the performance of their duties. Pupil participation in these matters should be planned to enable every pupil to have an important job at one time or another.

ROUTINE MATTERS

One of the problems a teacher encounters in class management is determining the extent to which certain aspects of the class situation should be routinized. Certain types of recurring activities in the classroom can be systematized thereby providing more time for the teachers and the members of the class to engage in group and individual learning activities. One of the advantages of routinizing certain class activities is economy of time. However, its main value is in the development of stronger feelings of security on the part of the pupils who know what to expect in a given situation and the experience they gain in making habitual certain types of their behavior.

The number and kind of desirable routine procedures in class management are dependent upon the size of the class, the type of activities, and the maturity of the pupils. In large classes it is necessary to employ more routine procedures in order to insure the effective operation of group and individual activities than in small classes. Class exercises in a formal classroom are characterized by a more highly organized plan of classroom procedures in contrast to the permissive type of situation in which pupils feel they have freedom of choice (within limits) concerning many of their activities. The children in the lower grades usually need to establish more regular responses in some of their personal habits than do older children.

In the traditional school there was a tendency of teachers to overemphasize routine matters at the expense of a more permissive atmosphere. Teachers of today are aware of the advantage of using certain routine procedures especially if the pupils help establish and carry out the routines. When any routine is adopted, it should be clearly understood and rigidly adhered to by the pupils and teacher. Group discussion and decision are used to establish group routines in many schools. The pupils not only share in making decisions concerning the need for routine procedures but they assume responsibility for their execution.

Types of classroom routines

Effective learning can be fostered by routinizing some of the following classroom activities: (1) checking attendance of pupils; (2) distributing and collecting pupils' written work; (3) distributing and collecting books and other learning materials; (4) engaging in fire drills; (5) keeping the floor free of paper (each pupil accepting responsibility for keeping space around his desk free of paper); (6) keeping chalkboards and erasers clean; (7) watering flowers and plants in the classroom; (8) taking care of the aquarium; (9) returning books and equipment to shelves and storage rooms; (10) emptying wastebaskets; (11) keeping materials properly arranged on reading and work tables; (12) leaving and entering the classroom by individual pupils during the work-study period; (13) keeping desks and study tables tidy and attractive; (14) storing wraps and lunch boxes; and (15) entering and leaving the classroom by the entire class.

Use of classroom routines

In large classes each pupil may be assigned to a definite seat and a chart prepared to show the position of each member of the class. Taking attendance can be expedited by noting the vacant seats. The seating chart also enables the teacher to learn the names of the pupils more promptly. If pupils are grouped informally around tables or centers of interest, attendance may be checked according to groups. A pupil may be designated to check the attendance, thus enabling the teacher to begin the learning activities more promptly.

When a pupil returns to class after being absent from school, he is usually expected to present a class admission permit from the principal or school nurse. In some schools, tardy pupils are also required to obtain class admission slips from the principal's office. Unnecessary tardiness can be reduced by beginning the day's work promptly with interesting activities. Discussions of the importance of punctuality with individuals and the class also may be helpful in reducing tardiness. Plans should be made with pupils who have been absent to enable them to resume the regular work of their class.

Time can be saved and disorder avoided in the distribution and collection of pupils' written work by following a systematic plan. In collecting papers, pupils may pass the papers to one side of the room; the papers are then passed to the front by pupils on the end seats. If test papers are numbered in accordance with each pupil's seat and row numbers, they can be returned without waste of time and unnecessary confusion.

Pupils in the present-day elementary school use a great variety of study and work materials. A well-organized plan for the distribution, collection, and storage of these supplies should be followed in terms of the kind of materials and the seating arrangements of the pupils. In the primary grades, it may be advantageous to have the materials placed on the work tables before the pupils come into the classroom. In the upper grades, pupil assistants can help in the distribution and collection of materials. Each pupil, however, should be instructed concerning the proper use and care of the materials.

Ideally, pupils should be permitted to sit where they wish. The nature of the learning activity in which a pupil may be engaged at a particular time determines where he should be seated. He may be seated with a group engaged in the study of a particular problem. In a free period, he may be seated at a reading table. If he has defective vision or hearing, he should be placed near the chalkboard or where he can hear the discussions of the teacher.

Except in large classes, there is a trend away from the row-on-row seating of pupils in classrooms. Regardless of the plan, it is advantageous for each pupil to have a definite desk or place to work which he can call his own. It may be necessary to change the seating of an individual pupil because of problems of behavior when he is near certain other individuals. Some teachers have discovered that placing some pupils near their friends facilitates their study habits. When sociograms of the class reveal a change in pupil relationships, their seating is changed.

What each child does in a classroom affects all the other members of the class. This is especially true in fire drills. The welfare of the group demands that all the individuals follow the rules which are invariable. Pupils should clearly understand the plan for leaving the school building from their classroom and be required to follow the plan without any exceptions.

In entering and passing from the classroom on other occasions, pupils should have the opportunity to exercise greater initiative and self-control. Rather than require pupils to march in and out of classrooms in military order, a more natural plan with general suggestions such as, "keep to the right" is more desirable.

When groups of pupils work at the chalkboard, disorder may be avoided by assigning them to definite places at the board. It is also advantageous to use certain sections of the chalkboard for pupils' work and reserve other sections for writing announcements, daily schedules, etc.

The pupils should be aware of the order of daily events including any variation in the usual schedule. In many classrooms the teacher and pupils share in planning the activities of the day. As the daily schedule is developed it should be written on the chalkboard for reference by the pupils.

In making the daily schedule of events, it is necessary for the teacher and the pupils to consider specifically how each block of time should be used. Decisions should be made concerning the activities to be included in the various work periods and the free activities period. The plans should not only provide for group activities but also those of individual pupils.

In addition to making a schedule for the day, the teacher and pupils should share in the formulation of long-term plans for the week and for the activities to be included in the study of a unit. This involves making a list of the activities and considering their relative values in the study of a unit. Making a tentative timetable for the completion of certain tasks is of great value in getting the job done and in giving pupils an understanding of the importance of budgeting their time.

LEARNING ACTIVITIES

There are two general types of classroom organizations in the elementary schools of this country. The most common type is the self-contained classroom in which one teacher directs the learning activities of her pupils in all the subjects. In the other plan, the classroom teacher assumes responsibility for teaching the regular subjects and teachers of special subjects such as art, music, and physical education teach those subjects.

Policies concerning the extent to which the classroom teacher has the responsibility for planning the daily program in her classroom varies considerably from one school system to another. In some of the small schools, the teacher constructs her own program. In other school systems, general suggestions for the guidance of the individual teacher are prepared by administrative officers or committees of teachers. For example, suggestions for the time allotment for subjects and activities in the upper grades were formulated by one school system [1] as follows:

Routine Activities	4 per cent.	Mathematics . . . . 10 per cent.
Language Arts	60 per cent.	Music . . . . 5 per cent.
Physical Education	8 per cent.	Industrial Arts and
		Homemaking . . . . . . 8 per cent.
	Daily evaluation. . . . . 5 per cent.	

(A more detailed time allotment is included in Chapter 11.)

Within the general framework of the suggested daily program, the teacher decides what group and individual learning activities should be conducted. While many of the group exercises involve all the pupils at a given time, good class management makes provision for small group and independent pupil activities while the teacher works with other groups of pupils in the room.

Centers of interest

Managing the independent activities of pupils calls for considerable teacher skill and ingenuity. Many elementary school teachers establish centers of interest in the classroom with enough space and materials for a few pupils to work at each center. Centers of interest (sometimes referred to as work centers) most commonly found in classrooms are a reading or library corner, arts and crafts center, science center, sand tables, and games centers.

As independent reading constitutes a major part of the free activities program, the classroom library corner should have a variety of supplementary readers, picture books, and stories on its tables, with attractive book jackets on the bulletin boards. For the primary grade children, names of books and page numbers of

[1] Department of Curriculum and Instruction, *Instructional Guide, Upper Grades* (2d ed. Portland, Oregon: Portland Public Schools, 1953), p. 22.

stories may be posted on the bulletin board by the teacher. In the upper grades, individual pupils can use the bulletin board to suggest stories for other pupils to read. Individual pupils can make a drawing to tell the stories they have read for display and group discussion. Pupils can put on a shadow show in which scenes from a story can be projected behind a bed sheet with the pupil actors between it and an electric light. Pupils may also take turns in reading their favorite stories to one another.

Young children enjoy working with clay. They can use clay at their own desks by placing pieces of oilcloth over the desks. The materials needed for arts and crafts such as colored paper, scissors, paste, newsprint, wall paper books, etc., should be assembled in one area of the room. The area should contain work tables and storage shelves.

The sand table is another good center for independent activities. Pupils can make models of characters in stories they read or miniatures to illustrate projects they are studying. Building blocks, cardboard, papier-maché, and paper for cut-outs should be available for use in making various objects. Pupils are usually pleased to bring toys from home for use in some of their sand table displays. Self-drill materials in arithmetic and vocabulary building can be made by the teacher or purchased. These drill materials should not be used until the pupils acquire an understanding of the concepts.

Guiding the activities

In managing the learning environment of the classroom, the teacher must make ample provision each day for various periods of study and work in which the entire class engages. The purposes of these periods is to assist all the pupils in the class in acquiring command of basic abilities and skills essential for effective living. These include mastery of language—speaking, writing, spelling, listening, and reading efficiently; ability to perform number computations; and techniques of social living.

Provision should be made in the daily program for the mastery of these skills as useful tools in the study of all the subjects. The skills should be taught with due regard to the maturation and ability of pupils to understand their use. After a basic skill has been acquired, it is necessary to maintain it at a functional level by continuous practice.

Research reveals that many of the basic patterns of oral expression are established in the early years of an individual's life. In directing the learning activities of elementary school pupils, the teacher should arrange numerous opportunities for them to talk about their personal experiences, such as taking trips, viewing television, and listening to the radio. Topics in the social studies, science, and literature also provide opportunities for explaining, discussing, and reporting, in which fluency of expression and ability to organize ideas are increased.

Oral presentations also contribute to good listening habits. A considerable amount of the instruction in correct language usage can be based on the needs of pupils as revealed in their oral expression work.

The total daily program presents numerous opportunities for the practice of the social skills. Instruction in the social studies, science, and health contributes directly to the child's understanding of civic and social relationships. In these courses and in various group endeavors, pupils should engage in activities which promote self-direction, concern for the welfare of others, respect for self and others, appreciation of interdependence of people, respect for public property, responsibility of individual for completion of tasks, and ability necessary for the solution of group problems.

In directing the daily program, the teacher should be aware of certain guiding principles, as follows:

1. There should be provision in the program for a great variety of learning experiences.
2. There should be considerable flexibility in the time allotment by providing large blocks of time for many of the activities.
3. There should be sufficient stability in the program to give pupils needed feelings of security in their work.
4. There should be a balance between individual and cooperative learning activities.
5. The daily program should provide alternate periods of study, rest, and play.
6. Pupils should obtain experience in self-direction by sharing with each other and the teacher responsibility for many aspects of the daily work.

PUPIL BEHAVIOR

An important managerial responsibility of the teacher is that of guiding the day-by-day experiences of pupils toward self-directed behavior. One of the characteristics of good class management is an ever-decreasing dependence of pupils upon the teacher in directing their activities. Learning self-control and other forms of self-directed behavior is a slow, gradual process. As in other types of learning, self-direction is learned by self-activity on the part of the learner.

In moving toward desirable self-directed behavior, pupils need numerous opportunities under the guidance of the teacher to plan, analyze, and judge the effects of their actions. They must understand *why* certain types of behavior are desirable. In guiding pupils to assume responsibility for their activities, it is feasible to involve them in relatively simple matters, such as the orderly arrangement of their learning materials. It is fairly easy to lead pupils to see the importance of the proper arrangement of these materials in doing their work in an economical and satisfactory manner. From their experiences in accepting responsibility for more obvious matters, pupils can move toward self-direction in more complex individual and group activities.

There is a growing awareness among students of child growth and development that child behavior is the resultant of the interaction between the individual and his environment. The effect of environmental factors upon the behavior of the individual is revealed in Chapter 8.

There are many features of the classroom situation which contribute directly to the objective of guiding pupils toward increasingly higher levels of self-directed intelligent behavior. An attractive, comfortable classroom provides a favorable setting for the development of desirable conduct. The organization and management of the various learning activities greatly affect the attitudes and actions of pupils. A type of organization that is so formal that it unduly restricts the initiative of the pupils may cause dissatisfaction and unrest. On the other hand, the organization may be so informal that feelings of insecurity and futility may be generated.

Instructional procedures which are adapted to the maturity and interests of the members of the class are of paramount importance in promoting good class morale. Pupil boredom and restlessness may occur if they are not kept actively engaged in challenging tasks. A child's attitude toward school is greatly influenced by the degree to which he finds his learning activities meaningful and interesting and the extent to which he is capable of doing them well. The maintenance of high standards of conduct is dependent upon provisions for learning experiences of considerable variety and different degrees of difficulty which are appropriate to various levels of intelligence. Good class management avoids having pupils work too long at one type of learning activity without rest periods.

Many problems of pupil behavior have their origins in the interpersonal relationships of the members of a class. Tensions growing out of strong animosities among pupils may become sources of emotional disturbances and may supersede work interests. If a pupil feels rejected by other pupils, his reaction may be one of hostility toward them and the school. The traditional recitation tended to promote the spirit of competition rather than cooperation. The effective use of cooperative problem-solving learning procedures which are described in Chapter 14 contributes to the development of skills essential for group work and living, resulting in the release of personal tensions and the satisfaction of sharing in group action. The successful use of cooperative group work in the elementary school is dependent upon the following:

1. The study of a significant problem about which the pupils are concerned.
2. The nature of the problem lends itself to solution by group study.
3. The maturity of the pupils permits some success in the solution of the problem.
4. The problem is sufficiently limited in scope to permit progress toward its solution in the time and with the resources available.

Cooperative learning is facilitated by the teacher serving as an active participant and leader in maintaining an atmosphere conducive to satisfactory classroom relationships. The teacher acts as resource person for ideas and learning materials. Her control is exercised on a friendly, helpful basis rather than by authority. Pupil relationships vary for different types of activities. In some of the activities each pupil may work quietly at his desk. If the class is divided in small groups or committees, provision must be made for the pupils to move freely about the room and consult with other members of their group. In general, class discussions of the behavior of pupils should be based upon mutual respect and courtesy toward each other and the teacher.

The teacher's success in class management is dependent upon various personal traits and professional abilities. Skill in the efficient operation of a classroom can be acquired by careful, intelligent planning and practice. Mere efficiency and technical skill, however, are not sufficient for the creation and maintenance of a satisfactory learning situation. The tone and quality of classroom procedures are determined largely by the teacher's personality. Personal qualities of the teacher (see Chapter 1) such as sincerity, fairness, sense of humor, and tact loom large in the thinking of elementary school pupils about their school. More basic, however, is a sympathetic understanding and interest in each pupil. Pupils' feelings of satisfaction are revealed in statements such as, "Teacher likes us."

The teacher must not only be aware of differences in the learning abilities of children but also of the great variation in their social and emotional maturity. At any given grade level, many children are not ready to assume responsibility for their learning or behavior. Assisting pupils in acquiring this readiness requires great patience and understanding on the part of the teacher. In the process of achieving a degree of maturity in these matters, it is essential that the teacher become sensitive to the feelings of each pupil and accept him emotionally. The pupil's expressions of hostility toward the school should not be considered as personal affronts by the teacher. Many of the frustrations of pupils which lead to misbehavior in school have their origins in the home or elsewhere. These frustrations can best be resolved by providing opportunities for the release of pent-up feelings through participation in satisfying and productive learning activities rather than by restrictive measures.

The teacher can evaluate her success in creating a favorable learning environment by observing the degree to which each pupil is motivated to set and work toward appropriate learning goals and the extent to which the class is growing in their ability to plan and direct their own learning and conduct.

QUESTIONS, PROBLEMS, AND EXERCISES

1. Describe the characteristics of a good learning environment.

2. In what aspects of class management can a fourth-grade class be guided to participate effectively?

3. Study the descriptions of the centers of interest mentioned in this chapter and suggest other desirable centers of interest that might be established in a first-grade classroom.

4. Outline a plan for the establishment of a new center of interest in a classroom.

5. What information concerning pupils in her class does a teacher need in order to adapt the class organization to their maturity and needs?

6. Analyze the daily programs in Chapters 11 and 15 and suggest desirable pupil-teacher activities in each of the main divisions of the programs.

7. Suggest the advantages and disadvantages of the multiple small-group type of class organization.

8. How may the teacher assist individual pupils in achieving success by participation in cooperative learning enterprises in the classroom?

SELECTED SUPPLEMENTARY READINGS

ADAMS, FAY. *Educating America's Children*, 2d ed. New York: The Ronald Press Co., 1954.

    Chap. ii, "The Function of Classroom Organization and Management: Learning the American Way." Contains general principles for guiding the daily program.

300 TEACHING IN ELEMENTARY SCHOOL

ASSOCIATION FOR SUPERVISION AND CURRICULUM DEVELOPMENT. *Creating a Good Environment for Learning. 1954 Yearbook.* Washington, D.C.: National Education Association, 1954.

A challenging discussion of techniques for improving learning environments.

BUHLER, CHARLOTTE, FAITH SMITTER, SYBIL RICHARDSON, and FRANKLYN BRADSHAW. *Childhood Problems and the Teacher.* New York: Henry Holt & Co., Inc., 1952.

Chap. xi, "The Teacher's Management of Situational Difficulties." Suggestions for overcoming some of the difficulties in class management caused by pupil maladjustment.

GARRISON, NOBLE LEE. *The Improvement of Teaching.* New York: The Dryden Press, Inc., 1955.

Chap. vi, "Environments Favorable for Teaching and Learning." Describes the physical, social, intellectual, and emotional environments in which learning occurs.

HERRICK, VIRGIL E., JOHN I. GOODLAD, FRANK J. ESTVAN, and PAUL W. EBERMAN. *The Elementary School.* Englewood Cliffs, N.J.: Prentice-Hall, Inc., 1956.

Chap. xiv, "The Learning-Teaching Day." Discussion of the factors which influence the quality of the learning-teaching day.

MELVIN, A. GORDON. *General Methods of Teaching.* New York: McGraw-Hill Book Co., Inc., 1952.

Chap. vi, "Peace and Order." Deals with the causes and the ways to prevent disorder in the classroom.

OTTO, HENRY J., HAZEL FLOYD, and MARGARET ROUSE. *Principles of Elementary Education.* New York: Rinehart & Co., Inc., 1955.

Chap. xii, "Living with Children." Contains practical suggestions for controlling the classroom environment.

WINGO, G. MAX, and RALEIGH SCHORLING. *Elementary-School Student Teaching,* 2d ed. New York: McGraw-Hill Book Co., Inc., 1955.

Chap. vi, "Managing the Classroom." Discussion of the importance of classroom management and suggestions for handling routine matters.

16

DIRECTING LEARNING IN
PRIMARY GRADES

It is the purpose of this and the following chapter to present the instructional program in the elementary school. Grades one, two, and three are designated as primary; grades four, five, and six as intermediate; and grades seven and eight as upper. Major emphasis will be placed upon the way in which modern teaching is being geared toward functional living of children. For example, in teaching children how to make introductions, teachers utilize real situations, as a child bringing his mother or friend to school. Children learn to read so as to solve problems in social studies, to enjoy books and stories written for children, and also to give pleasure or information to others who are listening. It is imperative that teachers stress this point of view as they discuss educational problems with parents.

Every learning area is an integration of many skills and abilities. For example, in learning to spell, children must listen to the pronunciation of the word and understand how it will be used in order to convey the meaning desired by the writer. They must also appreciate the fact that if they learn how to write the word correctly the first time, they will save effort and time.

Units of work in content subjects provide many real experiences for planning, discussing, reading, and writing. In order to clarify the idea in social studies that improved transportation has progressively made the United States relatively smaller (intermediate grade project) the following facts and abilities are essential: knowledge of how long it took to go from coast to coast by stage coach, pony express, transcontinental railway, streamliner, and plane; knowledge of where and how to locate the information needed, which requires the use of an encyclopedia or table of contents of a book; knowledge of presenting the information graphically by means of pictorial map and/or graph. But at no time should necessary habits or skills overshadow the major learnings in any area.

READING

The activity of reading involves very complex skills. In silent and oral reading, symbols to which specific meanings have been attached must be interpreted. The essential organ is the eye through which we perceive the printed symbols during the pauses as it moves from left to right across the printed line. The ear and voice aid in acquiring the meaning of the printed symbols. The vocabularies which the child brings to school are his speaking and listening vocabularies, and with these he puts meaning into the printed symbols by associating experiences with the reading materials. The act of reading is physically fatiguing to a child from the very fact that sitting quietly and putting forth effort to remember and to recall are in conflict with his natural activity impulses. In the following section, the discussion will consider problems related to guiding primary children in learning to read which are factors related to reading, reading readiness, grouping for reading, beginning reading, and expanding reading.

Reading readiness

A child cannot make much progress in learning to read until he is ready for it. Not all children are ready at the same chronological age; some may be ready at four years of age, others at eight. Girls frequently are more mature than boys of the same age and therefore learn to read at an earlier age. Nothing is gained if children are subjected to a reading program before they are ready for it. Factors that influence readiness for reading may be organized as intellectual or mental, physical, social, and emotional. These factors are interdependent and their interaction varies from child to child. Some children are not handicapped in any of the factors; others are limited in several; and a few individuals in all. Teachers must understand the factors that influence readiness for reading and also must plan activities for the development of those factors which are weak.

Factors pertaining to the intellectual development are very important because learning to read is an intellectual process. Before the child begins to read he must have wide speaking and listening vocabularies, be an intelligent listener, able to retain ideas, be able to think, be able to recall and retell stories and experiences, and be able to see likenesses and differences in abstract forms. Some say that a mental age of six and a half years is essential to success in learning to read; others have shown that children with M.A. of a little less than six and a half years can learn to read. Mental development is an important factor, but there are other factors.

Physically the child must be in general good health, have good vision and hearing, and possess good speech patterns. Frequently, adjustments can be made in the classroom to take care of these needs. Extreme cases should be referred to the nurse and/or parents, who should obtain the help of an expert in making needed adjustments.

The child who feels secure with his classmates and teachers, who has confidence in himself and who is eager and interested in learning to read (providing all other factors are equal) usually will succeed in learning to read. Children who are not happy, who are afraid to attempt new things, and who are not at ease with other children must be helped in making satisfactory adjustments to school living before subjecting them to reading.

During the first weeks of school and after the children are adjusted to the school environment the teacher should learn all that she can about the reading readiness status of each child. Much information can be acquired by studying the child's home and community environment, his out-of-school experiences, his vocabulary and sentence structure during discussions and conversation periods, and by administering intelligence and reading readiness tests.

A careful analysis should be made of all available information and of results obtained from tests. If the analysis shows that the child is strong in the majority of the readiness factors, has a mental age of six and a half years, and is physically and emotionally adjusted to the school situation, he may be placed in a group which is learning to read. Should the analysis show that the child is weak in a composite of readiness factors, he should first be placed in a nonreading or prereading group.

Instructional program for beginning readers

The program for the prereading or nonreading group should be remedial and should be adjusted to fit the needs of the children. Probably they will need many new experiences so as to enrich their understandings and their vocabulary. They may put together puzzles, match pictures, match words (without being expected to recognize the letters), thus developing the ability to recognize likenesses and differences. Teachers should read and reread stories and poems and give the children an opportunity to tell the stories. As the teacher records experiences on the chalkboard, children may observe the movement from left to right. The readiness workbook also is a good device if it has been carefully analyzed to see whether it meets the children's specific needs.

An effective instructional program for beginning reading requires careful planning on the part of the teacher. She should be cognizant of the following purposes: further development of readiness factors; developing an understanding that reading is a process of thought-getting and a means of getting information and of enjoying stories, maintaining an interest in reading. Mechanical and technical factors with which the teacher is concerned are developing a sight vocabulary; developing ability to identify and recognize words; developing proper eye-movements; diagnosing children's needs; removing difficulties as soon as they appear; and using preprimers, workbooks, and worksheets effectively. These are discussed in the following paragraphs.

Basic principles. Today teachers are using an eclectic approach in the teaching of reading. The competent teacher understands the values of different methods (as experience method or experience chart, units of work, basal series), selects factors from various methods, and recombines them to fit the needs of individual children or groups.

One essential factor in any method is that of maintaining the child's interest in reading. Most children have had their interest in reading aroused before they enter the first grade. They have observed the pleasure that daddy has in reading the newspaper. They have enjoyed having the "funnies" or stories read to them by adults and older children. Many are eager to learn to read when they come to school. This interest may be maintained by providing reading experiences in which children see a purpose, obtain meaning from the context read, and experience a feeling of accomplishment and pleasure.

Since many books have been written about various methods, and since authors or reading series provide manuals with very detailed descriptions of teaching techniques, it is not necessary to present here the details of various methods. However, certain basic principles must be observed in all methods so as to have an effective beginning reading program. Among the basic principles which all teachers of beginning reading should observe are the following:

Learning in primary grades. Listening in story period.
(George R. Balling)

Elementary science interests in primary grades.
(Corcoran School, Minneapolis, Minnesota)

1. The environment should be attractive and stimulate a desire to read; physical conditions should be comfortable; and emotional climate calm and pleasant. The classroom should have centers of interest such as picture and reading table, number table, science table, painting center, etc.

2. Modern methods recognize the fact that "learning is experiencing." Reading experiences are provided by means of experience charts, chalkboard records of duties, bulletin board devoted to class news items, preprimers, and primers.

3. First reading activities should be based on children's experiences. Children enjoy reading about themselves, their plans, and trips.

4. The teacher recognizes individual differences in intelligence, motivation, etc., by pacing materials and methods to fit the needs of each child.

5. The primary grades are not considered as three separate grades with definite standards to be reached in each grade. The reading program is an ongoing process. The level of achievement of each child at the end of the year is what he has been capable of doing during that year and continuing from that point the following year.

6. Many teachers are using flexible grouping, the typical classroom having three or four groups. Frequently children are transferred from one group to another. Some teachers use the individual approach and find that children enjoy that very much.

7. Slow, halting reading should be prevented by preparing children to meet vocabulary difficulties.

8. An effective sight vocabulary is a basic reading tool. The teacher should be familiar with the vocabularies of the first books that children will read and as nearly as possible use these words in the early reading experiences. Words will be used in experience charts, etc., that are not in preprimers, primers, first readers, but little or no drill should be used in an attempt to have children recognize them.

9. Children should reread materials for different purposes, some of which are reading the part of the story he liked best; finding the part that tells about a specific incident or answers a question; planning a dramatization of the story.

10. To be independent readers, children must acquire some means whereby they can identify or analyze words that are not sight words but are in the child's listening or speaking vocabulary. The instructional program in the first grade provides for the identification of words through the development of the following skills: use of pictures, reading context, picture and reading context combined, general configuration of words, comparison of likenesses and differences of new word with similar use of sight word, phonics, and noting of word structure.

11. The teacher should not ask too many factual questions. Instead ask questions that will require children to think as, "Why did John know where to look for his ball?"

12. The high achiever should be encouraged to extend his reading interests.

13. A continuous evaluation of the abilities which function in reading day by day. A few of the most widely used methods are as follows: (a) observing the child daily as he reads orally and silently; (b) teacher-made tests or checks, such as word recognition from flash cards, classifying words under appropriate headings, completing incomplete statements, arranging in proper sequence statements about story read, answering Yes and No statements; (c) standardized tests, such as Gray's Oral Reading Paragraphs, Gates' Primary Reading Tests.

Guiding children in reading

Reading materials—primers and first readers—may be presented in several ways. Attacking the material page by page and discussing each page in sequence is the procedure used in the earliest stages of reading and frequently with slow learners. Average groups usually have the power to read the story or selection as a unit. The following steps may be used in guiding children in reading selections:

1. Arouse their interest by asking questions, by showing pictures pertaining to the theme of the story, by discussing experiences of the children that parallel those of the story.

2. Remove anticipated difficulties, such as new concepts, new words.

3. State purposes for reading the story, such as to learn what the story is about; to answer questions by the teacher and/or children; to find out what happened to certain characters in the story, etc.

4. Read the story orally and/or silently. At this time the teacher observes the children at their work, checks to note progress, and gives individual or group help.

5. Discuss the content after the story has been read. At this time children should feel free to ask questions in regard to anything not clear to them or to make a comment pertinent to the story read.

6. Present seat work related to abilities being developed as a check in order to learn if children can work independently and may be used also to fix new learnings. Suggested activities for seat work are: (a) draw pictures in proper sequence of incidents in story; (b) match sentences and words with pictures; (c) select from several possible endings the correct ending for sentences; (d) use workbooks.

A creative teacher will think of many other types of activities that will parallel the learnings at any level of development. By providing independent work for one group, the teacher will have an opportunity to work with another group.

Recreational reading. As the child grows in reading power, he should be able to read much easy material other than books read during the instructional period. A center may be provided so that the child may go to the reading table when he has free reading time, make his own selection, and read to satisfy his own individual interests. On a low reading shelf may be placed preprimers and primers not used in the instructional program, picture books, story books, jingles, and science and social studies reading materials.

Instructional program in second and third grades

Children entering the second and third grades will be on different reading levels. In the second grade a few children may be at the reading readiness level; others will be beginning to read; and some will have reached the level at which they can begin to expand on their own power. In the third grade many children will have developed their reading skills to such a degree that they can study independently, but there will be some who will be working at levels indicated for grade two. Consequently, it will be necessary to have multiple grouping so as to guide children according to their needs and to provide appropriate materials. *It is very important that no child should be frustrated by reading materials definitely beyond his ability.* Care must be exercised that the materials are not too easy or too difficult. At the instructional level, the child should comprehend approximately 75 per cent of material read, should be able to anticipate the meaning, should be at ease in a reading situation, and should recognize at least 95 per cent of the running words.

Reading for comprehension

At this level major emphasis is placed upon comprehension—reading to learn, remember, organize and use information, and recognize words. One of the most important skills to be emphasized is the ability to read critically and to think while reading. Critical reading is more than reproducing details, outlining materials, or accumulating ideas. To think while reading, the individual must evaluate; he must decide what is important or not important as related to the purpose of reading and determine relevant and irrelevant ideas. The ability to do critical thinking actually could begin to be developed during the reading-readiness period. Children are capable of solving many problems which they face. For example, the teacher can help the child know what he is thinking by repeating what he has said. By listening, the child can hear the words that he used and decide whether that was what he intended to say. During a discussion period in reading, the teacher could list suggestions related to the problem and then ask the children whether the suggestions are sensible. In answering, children will begin to understand what is meant by "thinking carefully."

At about the third grade level of reading children will begin to encounter unfamiliar words. In developing independence in comprehending meaning of words, children must be guided in discovering how the author often clarifies concepts through the context of the reading material by using punctuation marks, figures of speech, pictures, and diagrams. Another skill to be developed in acquiring meaning is to list several meanings of a word; as each meaning is applied to the context, children must think in deciding which meaning makes sense in a particular situation.

Word analysis introduced in the first grade should be continued, and additional emphasis should be placed on phonics and structure of words. Skills to be developed in identifying words will be determined by the child's need and based upon materials being read by the children. Manuals which accompany the readers present excellent programs for the development and application of various techniques used in identifying words.

The content subjects constitute a fertile field in which reading functions as a tool of acquiring information. Intelligent guidance on the part of the teacher in having children apply their reading skills and abilities will pay great dividends in improving the fundamentals of reading. It can also develop a desire on the part of the child to understand what he is reading. The content subjects may be considered as a basis for functional reading in that the child must read critically in solving problems, must be aware of the ways in which the author or writer has attempted to clarify the meaning of new words and new ideas, and must apply his knowledge in analyzing unknown words.

Leisure reading

Teachers who understand children know that they enjoy reading stories for pleasure. Often excited or fatigued children will relax while reading a story. Stories of kindness, truthfulness, and fairness are of special value for leisure reading. Such stories should present the incidents so vividly that there should be no need for any moralizing on the part of the teacher.

Oral reading

Most children enjoy reading orally to give information or to entertain others. Third-grade children enjoy reading stories to lower primary grades, who in turn derive a great pleasure by reading to kindergarten groups or to an interested adult. The child who reads aloud effectively has learned to read in meaningful thought groups, pronounce words correctly, speak in a natural and pleasing voice, and use the proper voice intonation so as to make the meaning clear. Planned developmental lessons in oral reading will help children in acquiring effective oral reading habits.

LISTENING

Listening is essential not only in the classroom, but also in adult society. Much of the value derived from conversations, attendance at the movie or church, and using the radio, television, and telephone depends upon effective listening.

Today many teachers are concerned in helping children listen effectively. They are helping children understand that listening is a way of finding out what another person is trying to tell them. This does not imply that additional learning situations must be added to a day that is filled with many and varied experiences. By utilizing the existing learning situations to better advantage, effective listening can be developed.

Factors affecting listening readiness

Several factors have a great effect upon listening. The relationship of hearing and health to listening ability is easily recognized. The physical condition of the listener often is the determining factor in what is heard. The child who is undernourished, fatigued, or ill has neither the energy nor the drive needed for attentive listening. A child who has defective hearing often does not hear accurately what is being said; after several unsuccessful attempts, he becomes discouraged and eventually never pays attention to the speaker.

A *physical environment* favorable for effective listening has no disturbing or loud noises, no distracting activities, a comfortable temperature ranging from sixty-eight degrees to seventy-two degrees, and good ventilation. Research shows that dullness and inattentiveness often are the result of excessive humidity and a lack of air movement and that fatigue frequently is due to noise. Frequently the speaker or the listeners may be the disturbing elements in the situation. A speaker who has an unpleasant voice, does not pronounce his words clearly, and uses distracting mannerisms often disturbs his listeners to such a degree that they do not hear what is being said. Listeners also may distract the attention of others by engaging in another activity while listening, by shifting positions frequently, or by moving about the room.

The *emotional atmosphere* of an environment is as important as the physical atmosphere. Factors which create a climate or an emotional tone that stimulate listening are interest in what is being presented, openmindedness and willingness to listen to the other person's point of view, unobtrusiveness and unselfishness, favorable attitudes toward each other in the group, and a pleasant participation. Often the greatest obstacle to overcome is a great difference between the teacher and children with reference to background, cultural level, and word usage. The teacher must assume the responsibility to correct any unfavorable factors in the environment.

An effective *listening vocabulary* is essential since the word is the medium through which ideas are conveyed from speaker to listener. The accuracy of mental response to the spoken language of another person depends upon the listener's ability to understand the meaning of the words as intended by the speaker. If the listener has a very narrow and limited vocabulary much of what he hears is not comprehended. The experiential background is a great factor in determining the kind of listening vocabulary that a person possesses.

A child who has lived in an environment in which a very limited vocabulary is used will have a meager listening vocabulary whereas a child who has had many interesting experiences and has talked with and listened to others discuss these experiences will have a rich listening vocabulary. If interest is maintained in sharing experiences with others and in enjoying the experiences of others by means of the spoken word, the listening vocabulary will grow year by year.

Firsthand experiences are the grassroots of prejudices, attitudes, and interests which often influence in a negative or positive way the reactions of a listener. A limited number of experiences narrows the individual's range of view and often results in little or no interest in those ideas which are being discussed. Because of a lack of interest, listeners simply tune out what is being said. Happy and pleasant experiences are the source of friendly feelings toward others, respect for the feelings of others, fair mindedness, appreciation for the contributions of others—all of which may affect listening favorably.

Listening readiness cannot be attributed to a single item. Readiness is a developmental condition which depends upon the combination of several factors. Differences in the degree of readiness will vary from child to child. For example, the out-of-school experiences of the children differ, and major interests also vary. Furthermore, listening readiness cannot be prescribed for a specific grade. Every child at any grade level must possess those abilities and understandings which will make it possible for him to comprehend what he hears. It is as important for the child in the sixth grade to have a clear concept of ideas or words that are being used in a discussion period as it is for the primary child to have a good listening vocabulary. Teachers who are interested in listening readiness must consider the listening needs of each child and must prepare the child for success in listening. Factors which should be considered in determining listening readiness may be stated in the form of questions as follows:

1. Does the child have good hearing?
2. Does the child have an effective listening vocabulary?
3. Does the child understand the concepts which will be used?
4. Is the child interested in the topic or topics which will be discussed?
5. Does the child have adequate informational background or experiences?
6. Does the child have any misconceptions which should be clarified before he listens?
7. Does the child have a purpose for listening?
8. Is the environment favorable for good listening?

Aspects affecting listening development

In guiding children in acquiring effective listening teachers should—

1. Provide an environment that is conducive to good listening.
2. Integrate listening with all curricular areas.
3. Provide purposes for listening, such as finding answers to questions, enjoying the story.
4. Fit the listening context to previous experiences of children.
5. Guide children in explaining what they have read.
6. Help children in understanding the importance of being a courteous listener.
7. Have children do something with the information that they acquire through listening.
8. Help children evaluate radio programs to which they listen.
9. Pace materials and method to the maturity and needs of children.

COMMUNICATION

There is much current criticism of children's inability to speak, write, and spell. One cause of the existing situation may be found in methods employed by teachers. When language, spelling, and writing are taught as separate subjects, thus keeping the skills and habits of each in its own separate compartment, no provision is made for the children to integrate all skills in a functional situation. Therefore, the application of compartmentalized learning in a real life situation is most ineffective. When a teacher is not aware that it is her responsibility to guide the child in developing a critical attitude toward correct usage and correct spelling whenever and wherever he speaks and writes, the learning will not be as effective as it should be.

Since speech is acquired largely by imitation, the teacher's speech patterns must be a model worthy of imitation. This is not to imply that the teacher should use a scholarly vocabulary that is not understood by the children, that an issue be made out of every trifling point, or that there should be rigid adherence to every rule. Good language patterns include such points as the following: speaking clearly and distinctly, using words so that they make sense, speaking in a tone that is appropriate for the occasion, and being courteous at all times.

Oral expression

In the primary grades the major objective of oral expression is to help the child to communicate orally. Children should learn to share with others their experiences, surprises, and disappointments. They also must know how to make their needs known. Oral language is a cooperative affair, there must be a speaker as well as a listener or listeners. In order to have a desirable situation, the speaker must be sincere in making his contributions and the listener must be sincerely interested in what is being said.

When young children come to school, they usually have much to talk about. The school must make it possible for them to continue to have many worthwhile and interesting experiences and to provide situations in which children can share their experiences and information. Seven- and eight-year-old children have made great progress in oral expression and therefore can begin to share their thoughts. They also can learn how to organize announcements and directions.

Real functional situations should be utilized, such as announcing a lost article in other classrooms or inviting another class to a

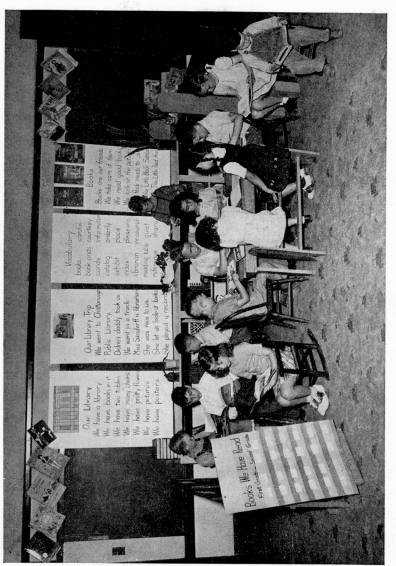

A functional reading center in a primary unit.
(Chattanooga, Tennessee, Public Schools)

Application in word analysis.

program. Most primary programs in oral language are built around spontaneous conversation, telling about personal experiences, telling and dramatizing simple stories, telling stories about pictures that they have drawn, planning activities, discussing various problems, introducing parents and friends, and fostering courtesies as "thank you" and "please."

Show-and-tell period is enjoyed by primary and intermediate children and is an excellent procedure of motivating a conversation. Many teachers use the first period in the morning for the show-and-tell activity. At this time children show some favorite object, collection, or hobby that they have brought from home and tell their classmates about it. They also enjoy telling about their toys, showing a new book, displaying a collection of coins, describing what they have made, such as a rabbit pen, a cradle for the doll, a picture that they have painted.

The purpose of show-and-tell activities is to help boys and girls to learn to talk with a group about things and activities in which they are interested. The teacher must provide an informal atmosphere (children often sit in a circle) and should encourage children to speak spontaneously and naturally. She also participates directly with the children, thus making them feel what they have to say is important. Listeners should be encouraged to listen courteously and to ask questions.

A discussion is generally more formal than a conversation and deals with such things as solving a problem, planning a trip, consideration of the results of a project in art, etc. In a discussion, the speaker must stick to the problem. Children should not be required to make a distinction between a conversation and a discussion, but the teacher must keep it in mind so that she can guide the work effectively.

In primary grades, oral language is functioning most of the time during the reading process, the creative period, and the play periods. In spite of this, it is advisable frequently to have a short period devoted to guidance in stating ideas clearly, correctly, and coherently, which will give children confidence in their ability to express themselves. During this period the teacher should provide opportunities in which children and teacher will set up the standards for various communicative situations. For conversation the standards might be: (1) to talk about things everyone will be interested in; (2) to talk only when no one else is talking; (3) to give others a chance to talk; (4) to listen carefully. Then, following a conversation, the children and teacher should evaluate it on the basis of the standards set up by the group.

Written communication

The first writing experiences in which children convey ideas by writing should be meaningful and serve a purpose. Purposeful writing situations for conveying messages or recording ideas are letters to children who are ill, thank-you notes to individuals who have made a contribution to the school program, outlines based upon observation trips, stories based upon experiences, and announcements of lost and found articles. Posters and pictures should have captions or legends. By using functional centers for writing experiences, the motivation grows out of the situation and children will learn to appreciate the value of legible handwriting.

The first real writing experience should be a group project in which the teacher and children decide what they wish to write. The teacher must be careful not to dominate the discussion and thus discourage the initiative of the children. Children must learn to select the important points of any written message. The teacher writes the word, sentence, or message on the chalkboard and calls attention to the correct formation of letters and the use of capital letters and periods. Soon many children will be able to copy the message and, toward the middle of the year, the more mature children will show a desire to write without being motivated by the teacher.

In the second grade some children, and in the third grade most children, should begin to see the necessity of observing certain forms for writing, such as comma in the heading of a letter and after the salutation, proper placement of the heading and salutation. The concept of the paragraph should be developed also. It must be remembered that in the primary grades the amount of time given to written expression is not nearly so great as that given to oral language.

HANDWRITING

Handwriting is a skill that is needed in written communication. Since written material must be read to serve its purpose, the goal to be attained in handwriting is legibility. In order to achieve and maintain this skill, it must be integrated with functional writing situations, supplemented with practice periods in which children receive special guidance as related to each child's need.

Today two types of handwriting are being used in schools—*manuscript* (printscript) and *cursive* (joining letters). Experiments, practice, and opinion reveal that manuscript or printscript is the most practical and effective writing for beginners. Cursive writing is preferable for the intermediate grades. The change from manuscript to cursive should be made in second half of grade two or in grade three, the development of the child determining the appropriate time for the child.

Handwriting readiness

An important factor in learning handwriting is that of maturation. A readiness program in handwriting consists of creating a desire to write, development of muscular coordination and of eye-hand coordination, and situations in which children understand that there is a need for writing and observe the teacher as she writes their dictated stories on the chalkboard. Primary teachers must acquire the skill of manuscript writing and should use it in writing the experience charts, notes, and invitations.

The teacher can determine a child's readiness for handwriting by noting the muscular development of the child, his ability to draw and color, his interest in and attitude toward writing, his ability to sit still for a short period of time, and his attempts to copy his name and labels.

The initial stage of writing

In the initial stage of learning to write, children should have a copy of everything that they write. As the teacher writes, the children observe closely. Whenever they copy the notes special guidance and instruction should be given (if needed) in how to form the various letters. The form of the letters will be learned quickly by the children as they are copying and writing the materials. All beginning handwriting situations must be supervised by the teacher. By guiding children in developing proper habits of placing the paper on the desk, holding the pencil, and forming the letters and numbers, many mistakes will be avoided.

Teachers should not expect perfect letter formation immediately, but gross errors such as backward letters must be corrected. Today we do not expect children's handwriting to conform in every detail to the copy which they are using; there will be individual differences in slant, height of letters, and the formation of some letters. Individual differences in handwriting are acceptable providing the written material is definitely legible. Day by day as the child matures, his handwriting should improve. As standards, children can use the handwriting of the teacher and the alphabet strip which is usually posted above the chalkboard.

The left-handed child should be permitted to use his left hand in handwriting. The roots of the "hook" or the twisted hand position of the intermediate grade child are started in the primary grades. It is the responsibility of every primary teacher to observe and guide very carefully the writing of the left-hander. The desk of the left-handed child should be turned around so that the light will come over the right shoulder. The left-handed child's normal slant will be to the left. Since this child's hand is apt to obscure his view of what he is writing, he should be trained to grip his pencil farther away from the writing point than a right-handed child would grip it and to keep his hand below what he is writing.

Transition from manuscript to cursive

Cursive handwriting should be introduced gradually. The cursive writing should be placed under the manuscript writing on the chalkboard in advance of its introduction; in this way the children become familiar with the appearance of the forms and joinings of cursive handwriting. After ten or twelve weeks of transitional experimentation, cursive handwriting should be used in all written expressions. Manuscript forms should be retained for labeling, captions, and any other situations in which manuscript writing is more suitable than cursive writing. The cursive letter forms in enlarged form should be kept before the children in a prominent place so that they may have an opportunity to study them.

The teacher who guides children in making the transition from manuscript to cursive must know the differences between them and make children aware of these. The major differences are noted in the chart [2] below.

Manuscript Writing	Cursive Writing
Letters are made separately; pencil is lifted after each stroke.	Letters are joined; pencil is lifted at the end of a word.
Letters are made with downstrokes and circles; they require fewer strokes and are easier to make.	Letters are made with upstrokes, downstrokes, ovals, and connecting strokes.
Writing is vertical. (Bottom edge of paper should lie parallel with lower desk edge.)	Writing is slanted from right to left. (For right-handed child lines on writing paper run almost parallel with a line drawn from upper right hand corner of desk to lower left hand corner of desk. For left-handed child paper is placed in position opposite that for right-handed child.)
Letters are bunched to form words; space between letters is controlled by the shape of the letter.	Spacing between letters is controlled by the slant and manner of making connective strokes.

[1] Division of Curriculum Research, *Practices and Problems in Handwriting* (New York: Board of Education of City of New York, 1947), p. 46.

Manuscript Writing	Cursive Writing
The *i* and *j* are dotted and the *t* is crossed immediately after the letters are written.	The *i* and *j* are dotted and the *t* is crossed after the completion of the word.
Letters resemble print and are therefore legible and easy to read.	Letters are unlike those on the printed page.
Small letters and capitals are very similar.	Some small letters and capitals are very different.

SPELLING

Writing and spelling are of value only when they function as means of communication. The major problem is to help children realize that when they wish to use a word in a writing situation, they must recall the letters and position of letters that make up the word. The ultimate goal is to automatically write words correctly, so that the writer may concentrate on the content which he is writing.

Spelling readiness

Building a readiness for spelling is the major problem in the first and early second grades. The child is ready to spell when he (1) has a need to write words, (2) has a fairly large sight vocabulary in reading, (3) understands need to write words correctly when copying an invitation, etc., (4) understands meaning of words used, (5) can see likenesses and differences in words, (6) pronounces words correctly, (7) hears words correctly, (8) recalls muscular movements required in copying words, (9) and attends thoughtfully to the job to be done. Great care must be exercised that in early primary grades the spelling skills do not interfere with the early reading habits which are being developed.

Steps in learning to spell

The spelling needs of children will vary. The more mature child and the fast learner usually will use more words in their writing than slower learners. Common words as "the," "what," "come," or words that all children use should be learned by every child. Words that are used consistently by the fast learner but are not needed by the majority of children should be mastered only by the superior child. If a school uses a spelling text or a standard list of words, teachers should note the words that children are using in their functional writing; the teachers should then give most practice to these words.

The process of using spelling functionally is an interaction of associating the sound of the word with form of the word and the motor habit of the hand in forming the letters, while the mind is creating what is to be written. Before the middle of the second grade, normal children can recall some words correctly for writing purposes. In many words they can recall part of the sounds and can write the letters representing the sounds. This should be accepted as a great accomplishment at this level, since it is the initial step in understanding the concept of the word "spelling." These partial learnings are the first steps in learning to spell, and a child should be encouraged to take this step rather than to be discouraged because he has made an error.

The growth pattern in acquiring ability to spell is a developmental process. Day by day, the teacher will help children in early primary grades in learning how to write or copy words that they need. By the end of the second grade, children will have acquired a basic writing vocabulary from copying invitations, short stories, etc., from a copy; from working on analysis of words by means of phonics in reading; by observing labels and signs in stores; and by making records of experiences in social studies, science, or health units.

In the third grade, children of average ability are beginning to write freely and independently and are ready to learn how to spell words in a systematic way. They can begin to note common characteristics in different words. For example: *cat, cap, can* have same beginning sounds; *night* and *light* look alike but begin with different letter sounds. The ability to make these discoveries and many others is an indication that the children are ready to make generalizations about the structure of words and to apply their generalizations to words as they are studying spelling. The plan for studying words in third grade is to have a short daily spelling period, with children studying only from one to three new words during each lesson under the supervision of the teacher. Teachers must be sure that—

1. Children understand the meaning of the word.
2. Children pronounce the word correctly.
3. Children watch the teacher write the word on the chalkboard.
4. With the help of the teacher, the children observe the word closely so as to detect aids, such as phonetic aids, endings, beginnings.
5. Children write the word and check with teacher's copy.
6. If the child has written the word correctly, he writes it again; if the word has been misspelled, he starts over again.

CONTENT SUBJECTS

The content fields in the elementary school curriculum consist of social studies, natural science, health, and safety. Instruction in these areas should utilize in an integrated way most of the abilities and skills developed in the language arts. In grades one and two, information is obtained by taking observational trips, experiencing activities such as caring for pets, studying pictures, exchanging ideas and understandings in a discussion period, and reading. Sometimes children may want to write about their experiences, make models out of clay, draw pictures that will tell a story about a trip. If the activities are properly planned, children also will have many experiences in social and civic living.

The usual procedure in teaching the content subjects is to develop *Units of Experience* within areas of children's interests and needs. In each unit children engage in many activities, one of which is solving problems. General principles of unit construction have been given in Chapter 10.

NUMBERS

When a child enters the first grade, he may be able to count and may understand several quantitative words, but these abilities are not sufficient to introduce the child to an abstract idea, such as $3 + 2 = 5$. There is no justification in delaying the development of a vocabulary having numerical concepts. Understandings of numbers, combinations, and measurement develop gradually and have their beginnings in the preschool years. Early in life, the child wants two cookies—one for a friend and one for himself. He measures the sand in the sand box with a spoon or a cup. Numerical concepts developed in this way are very concrete learnings.

The modern philosophy of teaching numbers or arithmetic stresses meaning and understanding of quantitative relationships. Children must see sense in what they are doing. Hence, abstract ideas of number facts must grow out of concrete situations or functional experiences. Since many primary grade experiences call for the use of numbers, it is essential that the teacher assume the responsibility of making numbers significant and meaningful for the children.

Numbers in the early primary grades should be taught informally and integrated with other learning activities. For example, numbers function during the story period: Pat sits on the *first* chair; *today* the story will be told *before* the milk period and *tomorrow after* the lunch hour. In the story of "The Three Bears," a *threeness* is developed through *three* bears, *three* chairs, *three* bowls, *three* spoons, and *three* beds. During the painting period, children need *large* sheets of paper. They use *small* paint brushes, and they may need a *half* glass of water for paints. If there are *nine* children in the reading group, *nine* books will be needed.

During classroom experiences the teacher may write on the chalkboard number symbols representing quantity. For example, if the group is planning a garden project many ideas should be recorded for future reference. If they need four packages of seed, record the fact as "4 packages of seed." Record three hoes as "3 hoes." A child may discover that two crayolas and two crayolas are four crayolas. The discovery would be written first as a story—two crayolas and two crayolas are four crayolas; later in the more abstract form, 2 and 2 are 4; finally, $2 + 2 = 4$.

Many problems arise daily and should be solved by the children under the guidance of the teacher. Concrete or manipulative materials should be used in discovering the answers. From the concrete the teacher moves to the use of pictures which represent ideas. This leads into the semiconcrete which is only one step removed from the last step, the abstract.

Problem-solving experiences in primary grades vary from group to group, and teachers should be alert for the natural experiences which arise in their own particular situation. It should not be a forced experience. Typical primary problematic experiences are bringing money to pay for milk and crackers, making a playhouse, building a train, building a store, playing school, planning a party. The reasoning ability needed for problem-solving develops in the natural process of growth; therefore, all learnings should be adjusted to the maturity of the child.

Many second-grade children are ready to learn about *tens* and *ones*. After children understand that individual digits stand for a collection of individual *ones*, the idea of *tens* can be developed by using slips of paper or tongue depressors bundling the materials into a group of *tens*, and holding them together by rubber bands. A pocket holder is very useful in arranging the material and in developing an understanding of place value—the individual units being kept in *ones* place and only structured or grouped materials of *tens* being in *tens* or second place.

Some second- and third-grade children are ready for work with addition and subtraction facts, and some third-graders for the processes of addition and subtraction. Children again manipulate counters during the initial period of learning and gradually move on to the abstract levels by using pictures and visualization materials which lead to the levels of seeing relationships and making generalizations. When the teacher feels that children understand the process, she should provide practice or drill to develop further the skill or skills and to maintain the same at the accepted level of accomplishment for each child, as disuse will result in forgetting or a deterioration of the behavior patterns that have been acquired.

QUESTIONS, PROBLEMS, AND EXERCISES

1. Suppose that you are a teacher of thirty first-grade children. Plan and illustrate how you would determine those who are ready to read preprimers.

2. Evaluate the preprimers and primers of three reading series in terms of their usefulness in helping children to read.

3. How may the instructional reading program contribute toward developing an understanding of the sentence and paragraph?

4. List situations that could be used for "thank-you" letters or notes.

5. Illustrate forms for letter writing in first grade, second grade, third grade.

6. Prepare a five-minute talk on "The relation of oral expression, writing, and spelling.

7. Write a paragraph on "The purposes of spelling."

8. Observe children at one grade level. Select one of the learning areas discussed in this chapter and note individual differences of ten children with respect to interest and achievement.

9. Prepare a panel discussion on the topic "The value of readiness in numbers" and present to the class.

10. Be prepared to present to the class the objectives of social studies and science in primary grades.

11. Examine four courses of study or curriculum guides in social studies. Note likenesses and differences in the emphasis of areas of learning for the grade level in which you are interested.

12. Arrange with a teacher to go on an excursion with her class. Analyze your guidance of children in terms of their responses.

SELECTED SUPPLEMENTARY READINGS

DAWSON, MILDRED A., and MARIAN ZOLLINGER. *Guiding Language Learning.* Yonkers, N.Y.: World Book Co., 1957.

Chapters pertinent for primary grade children are: chap. 6, "Developing the Basic Speech Skills"; chap. 11, "Oral Communication in the Primary Grades"; chap. 13, "Written Communication in the Primary Grades." The instructional program suggested is related to principles of child growth and development. Procedures for the improvement of functional communicative skills are presented clearly and effectively.

FREEMAN, FRANK N. *What Research Says to the Teacher; Teaching Handwriting.* Washington, D.C.: National Education Association, 1954.

Easy to read and to understand. Teachers will find that many questions relative to handwriting will be answered in this booklet.

HILDRETH, GERTRUDE. *Readiness for School Beginners.* Yonkers, N.Y.: World Book Co., 1950.

Emphasis is placed on the introductory period in schooling. Topics that are clarified are the concept of readiness, readiness for school beginners and for the three R's, and the transition from readiness to instruction in tool subjects. Several readiness tests are discussed. Primary grade teachers will find many useful suggestions for helping slow learners and bilingual children.

———. *Teaching Spelling.* New York: Henry Holt & Co., Inc., 1955.

Relevant chapters are chap. 3, "Beginning of Spelling"; chap. 5, "Practice for Spelling Through the Primary Grades." A clear presentation showing how oral communication, reading, and writing activities are related to spelling. Also shows how handwriting and spelling can be integrated. Excellent suggestions for an effective spelling program.

MCKEE, PAUL. *The Teaching of Reading.* Boston: Houghton Mifflin Co., 1948.

Part 1, "The Nature of the Process of Reading," focuses the reader's attention upon problems related to identifying and recognizing printed words, understanding the meaning intended by the writer, and using meanings acquired through reading. Chaps. 6 through 10 suggest an effective reading program for primary grades. Includes many practical illustrative exercises and suggested programs of instruction.

ROSENQUIST, LUCY. *Young Children Learn to Use Arithmetic.* Boston: Ginn & Co., 1949.

This book deals with arithmetic for kindergarten and grades one and two. In discussing the number learning process three levels of maturity are recognized: (1) discovering facts, (2) using known relationships between facts, (3) memorizing facts for automatic recall. Suggestions are based upon psychology of learning and are definite and practical for classroom purposes.

WILLCOCKSON, MARY. *Social Education of Young Children,* rev. ed. Washington, D.C.: National Council for the Social Studies, 1952.

A presentation of units and a description of techniques to be used in the primary grades.

17

DIRECTING LEARNING IN
INTERMEDIATE AND UPPER GRADES

READING

An important job in the middle grades is the development of reasonably mature reading skills and interests in reading. Since the child is living in a reading world and information is acquired through reading, it is imperative that he become a facile reader. Some children entering the intermediate grades have not acquired independence in analyzing words, comprehending materials read, and being able to read effectively materials in different areas of learning, such as science and social studies. The range of reading abilities within each grade is great. The poorest reader is likely to be at least one or maybe as much as three grades below the average child in any class and the best reader is likely to be able to read as well as the average child two or three grades above.

In the upper grades, most children should become proficient in attacking new words, be able to read for many and various understandings, be interested in understanding new concepts and ideas, and know how to use various reference resources, including library facilities. Great emphasis should be placed upon critical reading. Such reading may be motivated by an informal or formal debate in reading groups. In social studies and science, opinions can be verified or refuted by reading several authorities in the field.

Reading readiness

The importance of reading readiness is not confined to the beginning grades. The intermediate and upper grade teachers must guide children in seeing and hearing accurately, provide those experiences which will aid in clarifying concepts and in understanding what is read, and anticipate difficulties and clear misunderstandings in all reading situations.

During the first weeks of school, the teacher should learn at what level each child can read independently, how proficient he is in attacking new words and in discovering the meaning of words, and how well he can locate information. If the results reveal that the children are weak in many of the reading skills, special groups should be organized to take care of their needs. All groups should be flexible, so that any child may move to another as his needs and achievements become apparent.

Pronunciation and meaning of words

Identifying strange words and discovering the meaning of words in different contexts are skills that must be expanded as children read more difficult materials. In the intermediate and upper grades new words and new ideas are added more rapidly in reading materials than children are able to acquire as a speaking vocabulary. Therefore, children must be encouraged to become independent in methods of attacking the pronunciation and meaning of new words.

Many children are not ready to make and understand generalizations about various sounds until the fourth or fifth grade. Learning to divide words into syllables, to sense each syllable as a part of a whole word, and to pronounce the word will aid children at these levels to be more independent in their reading. In the fourth grade, children can discover the pronunciation of words by integrating phonics, structural analysis, and verbal context. In developing abilities to analyze words, teachers must help children in such a way that this skill does not become an end in itself, but instead a means toward the end of understanding what is being read.

The enrichment of a meaningful vocabulary is of great importance also. In these grades, word meanings are extended by real and vicarious experiences with people, concrete and semiconcrete materials, and by talking with adults about these experiences.

The dictionary is an aid in determining the pronunciation and meaning of words. Development of skills is usually begun in the fourth grade, the more complex skills being introduced in upper intermediate grades. After the skills have been introduced and specific practice has been provided at a given grade level, review must be provided throughout the following grades so as to maintain the skills. By the time children have reached the upper grades most of them should have mastered the skills and acquired the habit of using the dictionary efficiently for various purposes. If possible each child should have a dictionary, such as the *Winston Simplified Dictionary for Schools* or the *Thorndike Century Dictionary*.

The ability to use the dictionary intelligently should be taught as a result of a need in other work, for example, when words found in social studies or in reading are not understood. Children also need to learn the wide variety of information obtainable from a dictionary, such as synonyms and antonyms, and illustrations or examples for ideas.

Silent reading

Speed in reading is not a virtue in and of itself; speed without comprehension has no value. Indeed, the acquisition of those abilities which function in comprehension will itself speed up reading. Speed in reading is influenced by familiarity with material, difficulty of material, and purpose for reading. If a child is reading to remember, his speed will be slower than if he were reading only to get the general significance. If the ideas are unfamiliar and he must read carefully and critically to discover how the author is clarifying facts by having him turn to another page to study a diagram, picture, or map, or by directing him to refer to a footnote, speed in covering materials will be reduced. If he does not recognize words and must stop to analyze approximately four out of every hundred, his speed will be reduced.

But learning to read speedily is important because slow readers are handicapped in many ways. They cannot cover school assignments satisfactorily or acquire as much interesting information as they should like for the solution of problems in content subjects. Therefore, it is the teacher's responsibility to help children to improve their speed in reading by guiding them in gaining ability to identify words, to use meaning clues, and to understand how to adjust speed to various purposes.

In the intermediate and upper grades much of the information needed in solving problems in units of work in content subjects is acquired through silent reading. Effective reading in these grades requires not only the skills used in the mechanics of reading, but also skills and abilities needed in locating and selecting information relative to a specific problem, and abilities needed in interpreting many different kinds of materials read. Effective reading study requires abilities to locate information, organize materials read, follow directions, predict outcomes, note details, read critically, remember what has been read, skim when necessary, take notes, outline and summarize, and use the library.

Reading study period

A semiformal reading study period is very useful to introduce a new skill, develop word analysis techniques, introduce work-study skills, and provide practice in all new skills introduced. After the assignment has been clearly stated and anticipated class difficulties have been removed, the children go to work, and the teacher gives individual help to those who need it. Following the study period, children and the teacher discuss as a group the information that they have acquired, the skills and abilities which they have used, and how the information and abilities may be used in other experiences. During this period the teacher should also clarify ideas that children do not understand, correct wrong impressions, suggest other ways of doing things as well as other materials that could be used.

The laboratory for the reading skills is every reading experience which occurs during the day. In content subjects reading skills are used as the children locate information they need for the solution of problems. In preparing a social studies report, appropriate materials must be selected and organized. In performing an experiment in natural science, great care must be exercised in following instructions. Newspapers and advertisements must be read critically so as to detect propaganda, opinions, and facts.

Recreational reading

Definite periods should be planned in which children may read without being pressured by an assignment. This does not mean that free reading is unguided. Teachers must be aware of the capacities and interests of the children so as to guide them in selecting reading materials and in improving their tastes. The teacher and librarian publicize books and frequently should suggest books to the whole group. The teacher should have individual conferences with children whose reading interests are limited. Children should be encouraged to share some of their recreational reading with the class or to recommend books by means of posters, but such activities never should be regarded as an additional task. Occasionally the teacher may guide informal discussions about characters in literature so as to increase the children's insight into human behavior and human relationships.

Oral reading

In the intermediate and upper grades oral reading may be a part of the recreational reading program. The major objectives of this activity are to give pleasure to reader and listeners and occasionally to give information to others. The following basic principles are important.

1. Materials for oral reading should be easier than materials used in work-type reading.
2. Poor oral reading should not be permitted.
3. Children should be able to speak well.
4. Child should read selection silently before he reads it orally.
5. Teacher should help child immediately if he gets into difficulties in oral reading situation.
6. Teacher should help prepare children who need guidance in oral reading by having them meet with her for a rehearsal so that she can assist them with such problems as pitch of voice, volume, enunciation.

Reading materials

In order to control the various reading factors and reading skills when they are introduced, it is advisable to use a basic textbook. Slower children will use easier books, while superior children will read more difficult materials. In addition to readers and textbooks used in content subjects, children should use all types of supplementary reading materials, such as encyclopedias and books other than textbooks. Especially useful are magazines and other materials designed for children's interests in special fields: picture magazines such as *National Geographic,* bulletins and pamphlets, maps and graphs. Book lists, standard catalogs, and guides to periodical literature are an aid in locating reading material for children. Many book lists and bulletins have brief annotations on content, style, and the reading age level of the material listed.

Measurement of achievement

The measurement of reading achievement is a very complex problem, for it is essential to measure all skills and abilities that function in the process of reading. The appraisal should be done in a systematic manner, and as much information should be secured as possible. The data should include the child's chronological age, mental age, intelligence quotient, reading age, ability to use English effectively, interest in reading books other than textbooks, and emotional and social characteristics. Teachers can secure the information through observing children as they read, through individual conference, and by use of workbooks and tests, both standardized and teacher-made. It is useful for children to evaluate their reading by using standards that they have set up cooperatively with the teacher. All information of individual progress of each child should be recorded and kept in a cumulative folder for each child.

Standardized tests present no difficulties if instructions for each test are followed carefully. Standardized tests should be used periodically for the following reasons: (1) To construct a reading profile for each child over a period of years: thus making it possible to compare and evaluate achievement from one year to the next and to evaluate achievement at a given time in the developmental pattern of the child; (2) To locate difficulties; (3) To check techniques of teaching; (4) To motivate the child.

The teacher should be conscious of the following limitations involved in standardized tests: (1) No one test measures all reading factors; (2) Interests in and adjustments to various types of materials are not measured; (3) Since children may give the correct response by guessing, such responses do not necessarily mean that the child understands what he reads; (4) Reading ability in contextual material that is being used at that particular time may not be checked.

It should also be recognized that the grade score is not a good guide in determining a child's reading level. If a fourth-grade child scores seventh-grade reading level, he is comprehending that material as well as an average seventh grader would interpret it. But it does not necessarily follow that he can comprehend ideas presented in seventh-grade reading materials.

LISTENING

General considerations relative to listening presented in the preceding chapter are applicable also at intermediate and upper grade levels. In these grades the teachers are concerned with the problems of helping children to grow in the power to think. They also need to realize the importance of listening habits and their own needs for improvement in this area.

In the intermediate grades children can listen for at least thirty minutes and may remember facts and regulations that interest or impress them. Upper-grade children can listen for about an hour and understand and remember cause-and-effect relations and opinions.

Since today's listeners must be versatile, it is essential that children understand the requirements of the various types of listening:

1. Assimilative listening requires—
    a) Intensive and attentive listening.
    b) Noting and remembering major ideas, information, and details.

      c) Awareness of the organizational patterns of materials presented.
2. Critical listening requires—
      a) High degree of concentration.
      b) Concern about discovering the truth.
      c) Alertness to note inaccuracies, distorted facts, and pertinent facts that should have been presented but are omitted.
      d) Identification of loaded and colored words.
      e) Sensitivity to various emotional patterns.
      f) Objectivity and freedom from prejudice.
3. Conversational listening requires—
      a) Casual listening.
      b) Interest in what is being said.
      c) Sensing the psychological time to make pertinent remarks.
4. Appreciational listening requires—
      a) Casual listening.
      b) Sensitivity to pleasurable, sympathetic, and kind thoughts.
      c) Responsiveness to varying emotional patterns.

Typical classroom situations that involve listening are conversation, discussion, planning work, setting up standards, evaluating work, announcements, and explanations in assignments. Other in-school and out-of-school situations that require listening are telephoning, hearing musical selections and other types of entertainment over radio and television, news broadcasts, movies, and sound track films.

The teacher should guide children in defining their purposes for listening and in setting up standards for effective listening which should be used in evaluating their listening habits. Pupils should be encouraged to demand meaning when listening and urged to ask questions whenever they do not understand what they hear.

COMMUNICATION

In developing an instructional program for oral and written language, it must be remembered that the laboratory for these skills includes every experience in which communication is used as a means toward an end. Thus the content of the study experiences should be based on abilities and skills needed by the children to communicate intelligently in all situations in and out of school. There is no sharp break in the program of oral and written communication from primary grades into intermediate and upper grades. Learning to talk is not a series of skills to be developed, but rather a continuous growth in speaking and writing for each person as an

individual.   In any typical group of children at any grade level there
will be wide differences in all language abilities. Intermediate and
upper grade teachers will have pupils who use very simple sentences,
while others are very efficient in the use of cause and effect relations.   These differences are the result of different abilities of maturity, different experiential and home backgrounds, and materials and
methods used by teachers.   As a rule the range of differences within
a grade is greater in the later intermediate and upper grades than in
the primary grades.

The language program at any level or grade must be flexible so
that the needs of children with varying maturity levels and interests
may be met.   Educators realize that it is not possible to divide the
language abilities into logical groups and to try to teach these skills
at a specific time or in definitely stated grades.   If oral and written
language are related to many meaningful situations which directly
concern and have real meaning for the child, and if special developmental and practice activities are provided occasionally as the need
arises, the child will acquire at least some of the more effective
language patterns.

The teacher's responsibility

The first responsibility of the teacher is to discover the needs and
abilities of children in the use of oral and written language.   Some
information may be obtained by administering tests of vocabulary,
word usage, and sentence sense.   By observing children at work and
at play, it is possible to evaluate their word usage, sentence structure, control of vocabulary, self-assurance in expression, listening
abilities, and attitudes toward correct usage.   Particular needs will
vary from individual to individual.

After the teacher has discovered the needs of each child, it is her
responsibility to provide some time during the day for guidance in
the various abilities and skills.   Those children who are above the
standard in all language abilities should be excused from this activity and should use the period to prepare various contributions in
social studies, work on some creative project, engage in original
research based on a hobby, or act as critical listener for a group that
is preparing an oral report.   During this period the teacher may be
working with the class as a whole on class difficulties, such as presenting the form of an outline, outlining a selection, or constructing
a complex sentence out of several short sentences.   At another time,
small groups may require help in placing a comma in a series of
words, analyzing handwriting difficulties, or discussing misspelled
words.   If these experiences are to be effective, children must feel

the need for help, have the desire to improve, and be willing to put forth effort in making the corrections.

Oral expression

The language abilities necessary for effective oral communication are effective speech patterns, vocabulary development, and word usage. Because these abilities are not ends in themselves but means of effective expression, they should be taught functionally in situations where they are essential to accomplishing the purposes of communication.

Speech patterns. Effective speech patterns are very important in the development of the child's personality. The person who has a pleasant voice, good diction, and good rhythm usually can express himself well and easily. Through practice children should learn the requirements for using their voices effectively, such as sufficient volume to be heard, a natural pitch that is varied to express the tone or mood of words spoken, and a pleasant quality. Articulatory disorders tend to decrease in the intermediate grades, but those which persist often are more severe and more difficult to correct than those detected in primary grades; for extreme cases clinical help should be sought.

Vocabulary development. Expanding interests and experiences in the intermediate grades furnish many opportunities for learning new words and for expanding the meaning of known words. The majority of children usually have many ideas to share with others but often lack an adequate vocabulary to express these ideas. A characteristic of children at this level is a desire to be perfectionists. The teacher must help them in learning how to select words and how to express ideas clearly and in an orderly manner.

Children in the upper grades are beginning to be aware that words have different meanings for people with varying backgrounds and as a result are beginning to adjust their language accordingly. They also are ready to be guided into new experiences and therefore will need new words and new arrangement of words to express new ideas. At this level the language activities in which children engage grow more and more complex; frequently they find themselves in situations where they must assume responsibilities that demand originality and initiative. Even though pupils are becoming mentally more mature, more capable of thinking critically, and can assume greater responsibilities, they still need the sympathetic and understanding guidance of a teacher.

Word usage. Language authorities characterize speech patterns as being on three levels—*formal, colloquial,* and *illiterate.* In public speeches, certain business situations, and in diplomatic relations, the speaker will select a formal usage of words. Colloquial language is used in a general way and is the speech pattern used usually by the middle class. Schools are tending to use good colloquial usage as a standard of communication. Illiterate speech does not mean that the speaker cannot be understood, but that he is mispronouncing many words, using slang, and making grammatical errors.

Children have acquired their vocabulary through the ear, and the ear is the most important channel through which incorrect usage is corrected. It is the teacher's responsibility to create an environment in which children will hear good usage, feel free to use oral language, and have some means for self-evaluation. Many experiences can be planned in which children will gain group approval for having spoken well. Typical experiences in intermediate grades are telling about an actual experience, giving interesting book reports, or making a report of something of special interest to the children.

Oral exercises may be provided by having the children's corrected sentences read aloud and by taking part in language games. Children who need the practice should not be eliminated from the games because they made a mistake. Children may ask listeners for criticism on the effectiveness of their choice of words in expressing certain ideas. Much can be accomplished through personal conferences with children. The personalized interest of the teacher can be a great motivating factor, for if the child does not have the desire to improve, time and effort on the part of the teacher will bring very little progress on the part of the child. Making tape recordings of reports and conversations and playing them back so as to study and analyze speech patterns and word usage is a worthwhile activity, particularly if a series of records is made and children can actually hear their progress.

The most effective procedure for the development of effective oral language is to provide activities that have value for children. The situation must make it possible for them to talk sincerely and naturally. It is as important to have them work in smaller groups (perhaps as small as three children), as to carry on class discussion. Whenever children at this level form their own groups for spontaneous work the number usually is about six. It is not necessary that the child who has something to say should go to the front of the room. Frequently the situation may be such that he may make his contribution from where he is sitting.

In the intermediate grades several new forms of communicative activities may be added to those used at the primary level. Among them are interviewing business people and other individuals, giving reports based on research, announcing what a committee has decided to do, participating in meetings, such as clubs and/or school council, panel discussions, and choral speaking. Children may use outlines for presentation of material, but such outlines should consist only of brief reminders that will aid them in recalling ideas. The teacher must guide pupils in understanding that we do not copy directly from a book and then read that material for an oral report, but that the ideas must be assimilated and given in our own words.

Written communication

The purposes of writing are to communicate ideas to other people, express ideas for pleasure, and record information for future reference. Writing may be classified as *personal* and *practical*. Personal writing is creative writing—the child expresses his own ideas in his own unique way, as in stories, poems, plays, jokes, and riddles. In this writing, the teacher is concerned more about the ideas expressed than about the mechanics of the writing. Since the teacher is not critical about spelling or punctuation but enthusiastic about the ideas that are written, children will learn to like to write and gradually the mechanics that must be considered in practical writing will be transferred to their personal writing. (Personal writing will be treated in detail in the following chapter, "Directing Creative Learnings.")

Practical writing has the purpose of communicating ideas, as in letters, invitations, notices, reports, and outlines. Children must realize that the real purpose of practical writing is that others may share ideas by reading what has been written. Since other people will be reading much of this material, it is imperative that the writer be concerned about making his ideas clear by using clear sentences, organizing his ideas, using proper punctuation, spelling accurately, and having legible handwriting. Need for being understood will serve as a motivating factor for the practice periods in which the mechanics of writing are developed.

Mechanics. The teacher must guide children in recognizing a sentence and being aware of sentences in their reading materials and in materials written by friends. As children mature and their thinking process develops, they should improve in using sentences effectively. It is easy to see improvement in (1) avoiding run-on sentences, (2) using variety in beginning of sentences, (3) joining short, related sentences with proper connections, (4) having variety in sentence structure, and (5) avoiding misplacing modifiers.

Fourth-grade children should have acquired an understanding of the major characteristics of a paragraph and the following habits: indenting the first word of a paragraph, beginning every sentence with a capital letter, and using appropriate ending punctuating marks. The writer must understand that punctuation marks are an aid in communicating his ideas to persons who are reading what he has written: correct punctuation minimizes the possibility of misunderstanding ideas expressed by the writer. Punctuation marks and capital letters serve the same purposes in writing that voice inflections, pauses, and facial expressions do in talking. The question is, "Is what I have written expressing the idea that I intended to share with my reader?"

Teaching techniques. The mechanics of writing are taught most effectively through functional use. Correcting and punctuating workbook exercises is relatively easy, and the transfer to the child's own writing is not great. It is much more difficult for children to punctuate their own writing. Investigations have revealed that children do not learn a great deal when they rewrite their papers and copy the corrections made by the teacher. The teacher might write a comment on the paper stressing some of the good points and asking the child to check on words that should be capitalized, or she might suggest that the sentences are monotonous and would be more effective if the form were varied.

The teacher should help children as they write. She should have conferences with individual children and work with groups who are ready for learning how to use a certain punctuation mark or who are making the same mistakes and need special help. Errors that are common to the class may be used to form the basis for class instruction.

Children should be encouraged to proofread the materials that they write. They may read their first draft orally to the teacher, who points out some of the errors and guides each child in learning how to detect his own errors in punctuation, spelling, and sentence structure. Group compositions or letters and individual productions may be written on the chalkboard by the teacher, evaluated by children and teacher, corrected by the group with teacher guidance. This same process is then repeated by each child with his own productions. This technique helps children to understand the way to proofread their own writing.

Many schools adopt language textbooks and build their program around a specific series of books. Other schools use the textbooks as supplementary aids in developing communicative skills for which children display readiness. The textbook also may be used as a handbook to which children refer whenever they are in doubt about such problems as correct form for a business letter or an invitation, use of the colon, and the like.

In the intermediate grades, children can learn functionally as needed in their written work those rules or generalizations (grammar) that will help them in correcting errors in their speech as well as in their writing. As they are learning the meaning of materials used in reading classes, they learn how writers use capitalization and punctuation as well as variants of words to help them understand what they read. In selecting the proper meaning of words in the dictionary, children should understand that there are several classes of words which function in sentences as nouns, pronouns, verbs, and adjectives. By hearing the teacher use the new grammatical terms as they are working on discovering meanings in sentences and also in making their written work more interesting, children will acquire the concepts of the new terminology and will begin using the terms as they evaluate their work.

In grades four and five very little emphasis is placed upon rules that govern expression, but in grade six the children who are ready should become familiar with explanations or rules of correct usage and should use them as standards in evaluating the expressions of their oral and written work. Most of the functional technical grammar should be taught to the average and superior children in the upper grades, with less emphasis upon this phase to slower children. Grammar should never be taught for grammar's sake but always as a means for standards to be used in oral and written communication.

In the intermediate and upper grades average and superior children are capable of securing information from several sources for reports. Abilities needed in recording and organizing materials for effective use are outlining, taking notes, and writing a summary. In outlining and in taking notes children must be ready to note the main ideas (in about grade 4), the subordinate ideas of each main idea (in about grade 5), and details of subordinate ideas (in about grade 6). The form and terms to be used in an outline are those which best serve the children. In writing a paragraph that summarizes the ideas of an outline, or ideas in a selection of several paragraphs, children must understand that the characteristics of a good summary paragraph are—

1. The first sentence gives the main topic of report or reference read.
2. Each following sentence gives one of the ideas.
3. Sentences relating to main ideas follow same sequence as main ideas in the outline or in the selection read.

Real writing situations provide the motivation for writing. Many of the writing situations in primary grades are continued in intermediate and upper grades and on into adult life. In intermediate and upper grades teachers might have pupils write—

1. Business letters to various commercial firms, asking for materials and information.
2. Friendly letters to friends.
3. Letters or notes of appreciation.
4. Reports in units of work.
5. Minutes of meetings.
6. Outlines of materials read that will be used for panel discussions and reports.
7. Summaries.
8. Articles for school newspaper.

HANDWRITING

By the time the children reach the intermediate grades, they have mastered the formation of the small letters and capital letters in either manuscript or cursive writing and can write legibly; however, many children's writing can be improved. Occasionally children should exchange written work so as to check legibility and then devote some time to correcting their own errors. Writing efficiency may be evaluated by two criteria or standards: speed and quality.

As the child gains control over letter formation and masters the spelling of words, his speed will increase. Mass drill to increase speed is a waste of time. The major goal should be to write legibly, with speed a secondary objective. When speed is required in writing in vocational situations, the typewriter is used—not the pen or pencil.

Teachers and children should set up standards for handwriting which represent the average performance of a group—not the minimum or maximum goal to be achieved. The standard serves as a goal, but the child who does not achieve it should not feel that he has failed. Nor should the goal preclude even better performance. Standards should not be rigid; achievement of as good work as the individual is capable of mastering should be the requirement. Elements to be considered in setting up a standard are formation of letters, spacing, line quality, and uniformity in size and slant of letters.

Whenever children (or adults) are writing a story or are attempting to put their ideas into writing, the quality of handwriting is below the maximum handwriting skill of the individual. No teacher should ask a child who is creating a story to be more careful about his letter formation. In this situation, the recording of the new ideas is more important, and the standard is only that the writer should be able to read what he has written. If the child wishes to share his production with someone else, he can make a second draft legibly enough that others can read it. When children are doing a writing job that requires a great deal of careful handwriting, fatigue will set in and the handwriting will deteriorate. This situation may be remedied by having the children take a rest period, perhaps after they have written half a page, just long enough to examine the quality of their handwriting.

The real instructional purpose of handwriting is its application in all writing situations during the school day. Handwriting should be integrated with all instructional areas. The legibility and spacing of numbers should be stressed in the handwriting practice period (about fifteen minutes) as well as in arithmetic. Some activities in social studies require writing: this affords the teacher an opportunity to detect handwriting problems. The aim in spelling is to write words correctly and legibly; therefore, it is imperative to stress letter formation. Letter writing is a very practical situation in which to discuss details of handwriting.

SPELLING

The objectives of teaching and learning spelling in the intermediate and upper grades are to learn to spell the words used in primary grades which have not been learned; to learn to spell other words used frequently; to integrate habits so that children will not need to depend upon others when it is necessary to learn to spell new words. In these grades the need for new words in writing situations will increase rapidly. Since the interests and needs of these children are so varied, they must assume some responsibility in gaining control over spelling words. The achievement of this goal will depend upon the child's ability to write words that have not been included in the spelling program, by applying through reasoning the skills that have been developed during the spelling period.

Words which are studied during the spelling period should be selected with great care. In selecting, teachers must keep in mind these principles:

1. Common words needed by children in their writing not mastered during preceding year should be mastered.
2. Only words at child's reading level should be stressed.

3. "Demon" words, those words which are constantly misspelled by the child, should be given special attention.
4. Special words in subjects that are used frequently by children in writing should be mastered.
5. Modern spelling texts should be used as a guide.

Both the *incidental* and the *direct teaching* method should be used in teaching spelling. Incidental learning occurs in practical writing situations as children develop the ability to proofread written work so as to detect misspelled words. A good procedure is to lay aside the written material for a while so as to let it "get cold," and then reread it to detect misspelled words. Even material that is copied should be compared with the original.

For the direct teaching of spelling a specific period of about twenty or thirty minutes should be set aside. During this period emphasis is placed upon being attentive to correct spelling; learning efficient ways of studying words; developing word-study skills (applying word-analysis skills developed in reading period); learning to use the dictionary as related to spelling; diagnosing and correcting difficulties; and using enriching activities. Spelling authorities recognize two plans of instruction—*test-study* and *study-test*, the former being more practical for children having no difficulties in learning to spell and the latter for the slow or retarded learner. They also agree upon essential steps in study procedure, which are presented in any one of the modern spelling texts.

The true measure of the child's ability to spell is how well he spells when his attention is centered upon ideas that he is trying to express as he is writing. Standardized tests have a place in the spelling program if they include the words that children have studied. Tests including words that children have not studied will indicate how effectively they can apply those skills and rules that have been learned during the spelling periods.

CONTENT SUBJECTS

Through the content subjects—social studies, science, health— the life of the child is enriched. Children are curious about beliefs, conduct of people, national affairs, elements in nature, and man's control over environment. For example, children in Colorado are interested in the conservation of our forests, in wild life, etc. They are interested in the needs of children in other countries. They are concerned about problems of their nation and the world. Children are working on units as lumbering, coal, national parks. Intermediate grade children can understand that all peoples are interdependent socially and economically. They accept change and experiences in an ever-changing environment. By learning to understand the likenesses and differences in economic status and racial heritage within their community and state, children acquire wider and broader understandings.

Content subjects must be organized so that children will develop those patterns of behavior essential for living peacefully in the modern world. Most schools designate broad topics for units of work at each grade level and use the idea of the expanding world of the child in determining the units to be taught. Many school systems are in agreement as to the selection of units at the primary grade level, but in the intermediate and upper grades the variation is great. Since unit teaching is presented in Chapter 10, it is not necessary to elaborate on the topic at this point.

ARITHMETIC

Quantitative thinking is playing an increasingly important role in society. A command of numbers is as important as a command of words. When a person realizes and appreciates the fact that arithmetic is a useful tool in his life, he understands that arithmetic is socially significant. Concrete experiences will aid children in seeing the significance of numbers. Intermediate and upper grade children have many experiences, both in class and out of it, in which they realize that numbers are being used to further a social project. The *"meaning theory"* of arithmetic, or "seeing sense in what you are doing," calls for an understanding of the decimal number system, common fractions, denominate numbers, and the various processes used in solving problems.

Guided instruction

Even though children have had a good beginning in primary grades in understanding number ideas, they still will need help in the intermediate and upper grades in developing quantitative understandings and in acquiring those skills needed in solving quantitative problems related to life situations and textbooks.

To adapt learning activities to the individual in arithmetic is a very difficult problem. Children vary in mental ability, in the mastery of facts, in the understanding of skills that function in each process, etc. Effective procedures in providing for individual differences are (1) multiple grouping, (2) differentiated assignments, (3) individualizing the work, (4) reducing requirements for slower learners, and (5) increasing requirements for fast learners. All children will not reach the same level of achievement, but with the wise guidance of a teacher each child should reach that level of accomplishment which is possible within the limits of his ability. *Social significance* of numbers can be extended through units of work based on topics such as "Ways of Telling Time" and "Banking."

The subject matter to be stressed is outlined in Chapter 5. Approximately one period a day should be devoted to mastery of these concepts.

Multisensory aids

Concrete or manipulative materials to aid children in understanding arithmetic concepts should be used in intermediate and upper grades. When the ideas involved are experienced, meaning becomes clear. The idea of ten being the base in the decimal number system and the idea of place values may be clarified by using a place-value chart. In the fourth grade the place-value chart may have three pockets representing *ones, tens,* and *hundreds* places. In *ones* pocket will be 100 cards which are ungrouped. The teacher will count out ten cards, clip them together to make one group of ten, and place the group in *tens* pocket. She will continue to do this until all cards in *ones* place have been grouped as *tens* and have been placed in *tens* place. Since the base is ten, and there are ten groups in the second place, those must be grouped into a larger group of ten *tens* which will be equal to hundred and will be placed in *hundreds* place. In recording the final grouping numerically the

Hundreds	Tens	Ones
P O	C K E	T S

symbol *1* must be in the third place because the value is *hundred;* to hold it in third place a zero will be placed in *ones* place and another zero in *tens* place (zero becomes a place holder); thus we have the number 100 which is the same as we are showing in the place-value chart. By adding rows of pockets, the place-value pockets can be used in developing understandings of the processes of addition, subtraction, multiplication, and division.

Fraction concepts may be developed by using whole discs and discs cut into halves, fourths, and thirds. Thus it is fairly easy to demonstrate the concept that if the number of pieces into which the whole disc has been equally divided are each divided equally again, the number of pieces increases, but the value of each piece or unit fraction is decreased. Many other fractional concepts can be made clear by manipulative materials. The hundred-board is very helpful in developing the meaning of per cent. Every classroom should have an arithmetic table with concrete materials that may be used in arithmetic, so that children may clarify meanings by actually seeing what they are doing.

Drill and practice

There is a place for meaningful drill in the arithmetic program. After the child understands the process or procedure and the need for making correct responses quickly, he is ready to practice those skills which need to be mastered. Drill may be used to gain better control over a new skill or process, recall skills and processes, and maintain or keep a process alive. An effective drill or practice period is based upon the following principles.

1. Drill must follow understanding.
2. Children must have a felt need for the drill.
3. Children must go to work in an aggressive and attentive way.
4. Each child must be working on his own individual needs.
5. Children must know what the response pattern is to be.
6. Children must have a means of checking to see whether their responses have been correct.
7. A child should be able to correct the error immediately.
8. Periods must be short.

Problem-solving

For a child to be able to do any reflective thinking in solving an arithmetic problem, it must have meaning for him. Problems should make sense in terms of the learner's previous experience and should be within the interest and understanding of the child. When using a textbook, he should be able to read the material without being blocked by unfamiliar terms or concepts.

A very important factor in problem-solving is to have an environment in which the child can keep his mind on his work. No child should be emotionally upset by worrying about the grade that will appear on his paper or by having to miss his play period because he has not completed all problems provided that he has worked diligently during the study period. The major concern of the child should be, "What am I trying to find and how will I find it?"

Evaluation

The evaluation of children's ability to solve problems in arithmetic and the evaluation of the teacher's instruction are very complex jobs. Many factors must be considered such as reading ability, understanding of technical vocabulary, understanding of facts needed, understanding of process or processes used in solving the problem, and ability to organize information in problems. Problems that children have solved should be checked on two counts: procedure used and computation. It is very unfair and upsetting to children not to receive credit for having analyzed the problem correctly and having used the proper procedure. Problem-solving is more than getting a correct answer. The reflective thinking that the child has done is of great value.

Modern textbooks include a good testing program which usually is superior to the teacher's testing program. Authors of textbooks are conscious of many factors which should be considered in an evaluation program. They are making provisions to check the child's readiness for new work by presenting readiness tests before the new work is introduced, thus making it possible for the teacher to know which children can go ahead, which need experiences to clarify basic concepts, and which need to do some remedial work before they can take up the new work. Provisions also are made to discover individual needs by including diagnostic tests. Many texts provide tests for review and for recall, which is a part of the maintenance program.

Standardized tests are effective instruments in diagnosing needs of children (diagnostic tests) and in graphing the growth of children (achievement tests) over a period of time, thus making it possible to compare children's developmental patterns at different stages and to note how varying conditions influence the child.

QUESTIONS, PROBLEMS, AND EXERCISES

1. Discuss the purposes that reading serves in the schools.

2. Discuss the merits of having a separate daily period of instruction in reading in intermediate grades.

3. List the different types of materials that you read during the past week. What is your main reading problem?

4. Prepare a panel discussion on "Values of a library in a reading program" and present to the class.

5. Plan a reading program for either intermediate or upper grades that will be flexible enough to provide for the reading needs of the children.

6. List the situations that call for listening in a normal school day in the intermediate or upper grades.

7. Analyze your listening habits in three different situations during the past week.

8. Prepare a list of functional situations for written communication in a specific intermediate or upper grade.

9. Illustrate how the spelling program can be developed around functional writing situations.

10. List spelling aids suitable for use in the intermediate grades.

11. Evaluate your handwriting by measuring a specimen of it with the Ayres Handwriting Scale.

12. Analyze the spelling words missed by ten sixth-grade children to discover the types of errors made by the children.

13. Bring an abacus or a bead frame (ten counters or beads on a rod) to class and demonstrate how to clarify the meaning of place values. Also in what way is the rod on the abacus or bead frame comparable to the zero in a number, such as 308.

14. Prepare a list of arithmetic sensory aids and show how each may be used in clarifying at least one arithmetic concept at the intermediate or upper grade level.

SELECTED SUPPLEMENTARY READINGS

BETTS, EMMETT ALBERT. *Foundations of Reading Instruction.* New York: American Book Co., 1954.

A thorough treatment of modern techniques in teaching reading. Includes many procedures for teaching reading systematically and also for diagnosing reading difficulties.

BLOUGH, GLENN O., and ALBERT J. HUGGETT. *Elementary School Science and How to Teach It.* New York: The Dryden Press, Inc., 1951.

Information and teaching techniques are presented for topics in three broad areas: earth and the universe, living things, matter and energy. Teachers will find answers to many of their questions in this book. Many excellent illustrations.

BREUCKNER, LEO J., and FOSTER E. GROSSNICKLE. *Making Arithmetic Meaningful.* Philadelphia: John C. Winston Co., 1953.

A complete treatment of teaching arithmetic in elementary grades. Mathematical meanings and social applications are clarified very effectively. Emphasis is placed on teaching in a meaningful way the fundamental operations with integers, common fractions, and decimal fractions. Teachers will find the book most valuable and practical.

BURROWS, ALVINA TRENT. *Teaching Children in the Middle Grades.* Boston: D. C. Heath & Co., 1952.

This book provides a comprehensive and effective treatment of all learning situations in the intermediate grades. Emphasis is placed upon helping and guiding children as related to developmental patterns of children. Narrative accounts of teaching situations and learning patterns of specific children add interest and clarity to content presented.

FREEMAN, FRANK N. *What Research Says to the Teacher; Teaching Handwriting.* Washington, D.C.: National Education Association, 1954.

Findings of research are presented in a very concise and clear way. Teachers will find that the information will be a help in planning a handwriting program.

HATCHETT, ETHEL L. and DONALD H. HUGHES. *Teaching Language Arts in Elementary Schools.* New York: The Ronald Press Co., 1956.

An excellent treatment of the entire field of language arts. Major emphasis is placed upon functional-creative approach to language program. Many examples of concrete and tested techniques will suggest to teachers ways of meeting the needs of individuals and groups of children.

HILDRETH, GERTRUDE. *Teaching Spelling.* New York: Henry Holt & Co., Inc., 1955.

Emphasis is placed upon teaching spelling as a tool for written communication. Various study plans for intermediate and upper grades are analyzed. Chapter 9 presents many effective techniques for word study and word building; a section is devoted to word games and puzzles. A spelling vocabulary list of approximately 7200 words divided into ten levels based upon frequency use may be used by teachers to determine most suitable words for study, review, or achievement tests. A supplementary list provides additional words for fast learners.

McKee, Paul. *The Teaching of Reading.* Boston: Houghton Mifflin Co., 1948.

Chaps. 11 through 18 are devoted to teaching reading in intermediate grades. A thorough treatment on establishing independence in identifying words and on learning how to apply reading-study skills. Definite lessons and special exercises will aid teachers in planning an effective reading program.

Michaelis, John U. *Social Studies for Children in a Democracy,* 2d ed. Englewood Cliffs, N.J.: Prentice-Hall, Inc., 1956.

Very readable book. Democratic values, democratic behavior, and democratic processes are emphasized. Chap. 3 is an excellent discussion on pacing a social studies program to the developmental patterns and needs of children. Methods of developing units will be appreciated by teachers.

Creative learnings—using waste materials.

Creative learnings offering opportunities for self-expression and release of tensions.
(Muscogee County School District, Columbus, Georgia)

18

DIRECTING CREATIVE LEARNINGS

One of the hallmarks of modern education is its recognition that every child has creative ability and that the school is responsible for developing it. Creative activity is no longer defined solely in terms of producing a good poem, picture, or song. Instead it is realized that the housewife who rearranges the furniture so that the living room is more convenient for her family is being creative. So is the man who selects and plants shrubbery so as to make his home more beautiful. When a family works out plans for remodeling the house for greater convenience as well as attractiveness, this is creative activity.

But the values of creative activity do not lie in functional achievement alone. The major value lies less in the product itself than in its effect upon the creator. He experiences emotional satisfaction in achieving what he set out to do and acquires feelings of confidence that will aid him in meeting many other situations. Ability to express ideas and feelings in terms of his own level of maturity will help to prevent unnecessary tensions and frustrations. Through spontaneous play, many children unravel tangled experiences and vague concepts. The child who finds it very difficult to communicate ideas and feelings through language may achieve expression through pictures, music, or dances that contribute to the group as well as to his own satisfaction.

Children need guidance in developing their imaginative and creative abilities. Creative learnings can be included in almost every school subject. The social studies class which is trying to learn something about another people through their music, pottery, weaving, dancing, or pictures may well be motivated to try their own hands at using the same media. In arithmetic, a child may create a model or other device to clarify the meaning of the tens in our system of decimal numbers. Letters and written compositions can be made vehicles for children to express their own ideas and feelings. In the oral language period, a child may communicate his pleasure, appreciation, or anticipation by inventing a phrase or using an effective figure of speech.

In addition to this incidental encouragement of creativity in the various "courses," time should be set aside specifically for development of experiences and skills needed for self-expression that are not emphasized in other areas of learning. Such experiences and skills will differ with each type of activity and with each individual. Guidance is needed not only in learning the use of media but in helping every child to attain satisfaction from such use. It should always be remembered that any expression of creative ability which is new to the individual is creative, no matter how many individuals have had a similar experience before. That is, originality is to be judged in terms of the originator, not in terms of the experience of the race.

FACTORS INFLUENCING CREATIVENESS

It is not easy to identify those factors which influence and encourage children to be creative. Some teachers succeed by using certain techniques; others inspire children through entirely different approaches. Writers are in agreement, however, on several factors that aid creativeness.

Environment

In order to discover the creative powers of children, they must have an environment that will challenge those potentialities. The school should provide material and equipment with which the child should feel free to express himself. Many different kinds of materials must be provided, for not all will appeal to every child. In the primary grades there should be easels, a work bench, tools, scraps of various kinds of materials, clay, paints, blocks, dolls, and trucks. They also should have opportunities to run and jump, climb ladders, ride tricycles, play ball, turn somersaults, and teeter. In the intermediate grades all kinds of arts and crafts materials, mechanical and electrical devices, and work shops should be available. The playground should be equipped with materials which can be used in developing games. In the classroom and on the playground there are many sounds and movements which can become the basis for creative activities in music, poetry, and dancing.

Experiential background

In order to create, the imagination must have content. This content can be supplied through real and vicarious experiences which fit the pupil's maturity levels and needs. Often it is necessary to make the child aware of what the environment holds for him. Observational trips are planned so that children experience new sensations by seeing, hearing, touching, and smelling. Frequently these new experiences are immediate ignition points for creativity. At other times it is necessary to give a child some assistance by asking him experiential, imaginative, or suggestive questions. It must be remembered that children often do not react immediately in a creative way.

No definite statement can be made in regard to the optimum length and frequency of the experiential or creative period or whether it should be organized to provide experiences for a group or an individual. The occasion, type of work, and personnel all must be considered; hence the program must be flexible. In a group period, children often discuss discoveries which have been made, plan organization of materials, play with new experiences for new ideas, submit ideas for criticism, listen to poems and stories written by group members and by artists, and experiment with tools that they will use.

The teacher

The teacher's role in a creative learning situation is that of guidance. She should stimulate or draw out children's creative powers through suggestions, by being sympathetic with their efforts, and by refraining from adverse criticism. The teacher should provide a stimulating environment and surround children with examples of creative work by children. It is essential to provide the necessary time, for many new ideas and expressions come slowly and should not be rushed. The teacher's attitude toward creativity is far more important than ability to perform skilfully as a painter, sculptor, dancer, or writer.

The idea that the classroom teacher cannot teach the creative arts is being dispelled. Many teachers with little training through their enthusiasm and interest are stimulating children to create and to make new things. If a teacher is capable of diagnosing the needs of children in the three R's and of analyzing problems of conduct, she also is capable of discovering the latent creative power in children. If she can encourage and inspire children to master the skills in written and oral expression, she also can inspire them in developing their creative potentialities. The teacher knows from experience that as she diagnoses children's needs from year to year her ability and understanding of needs and achievements grow proportionately. As she teaches social studies and arithmetic, her teaching skills in those areas will improve from year to year. She should also understand that as she guides the creative activities of children she also will grow within that area. If the teacher plans and thinks as carefully about the creative activities of children as she does for the achievement of skills in the three R's, all normal children will learn to create according to their own individual growth patterns.

Principles

The process of creative learning is difficult to analyze. Many creative productions, such as dancing, acting, singing, and playing develop spontaneously while others need direction in the initial stages and will gradually merge into an original production. Often old ideas are revised and reorganized from an abundance of accumulated information, and a new concept comes forth. Children in primary grades are free from conventionalities in their activities, whereas in the intermediate grades children are more realistic. It is true that techniques used in various creative activities differ, but certain basic principles appear to be common in developing the creative urge in children. Teachers who are interested in creative guidance with children should—

1. Realize that creative growth may be fostered; maturity level of child determines creative growth.
2. Plan and vary the motivation for creative efforts.
3. Provide many opportunities for creative activity.
4. Refrain from forcing children to do creative work in areas in which they neither have the desire to create nor the talent to produce.
5. Allow children to choose their own ideas and themes.
6. Permit children to work on their creative projects if they choose to do so, at any time during the day when time is available.
7. Have the children feel that she appreciates their efforts and is eager to have them succeed.
8. Develop self-confidence in children by encouraging them and by approving their efforts.
9. Approve the honest, unique, original attempts, even though it is only a phrase and ignore the elements that are merely imitative.
10. Give children tactful suggestions as to how to manipulate the equipment or tool correctly.

11. Realize that on the part of the teacher patience is needed; first attempts may be poor and in some cases no meaning may be expressed in the product.
12. Help children to develop an appreciative attitude toward creative efforts of classmates.
13. Display the work of all the children.

CREATIVE ART

Art holds an important place in the program of nearly all elementary schools. Today there is less emphasis on perfection of drawing and a theoretical understanding of color than on emotional releases, imagination, and creativeness. For example, picture making is not what the teacher thinks it should be. It is the child's own expression of what he saw through his own eyes; felt with his hands, face, and feet; tasted with his tongue; and smelled with his nose; it is what he has experienced and drawn or painted as a child would draw or paint it.

Kindergarten and primary grades

It is essential that teachers understand the child's developmental growth patterns in art so as to effectively encourage him and also to know what to expect of him. In the kindergarten and primary grades children are passing through three developmental stages of self-expression in art that are designated as being manipulative, symbolic, and realistic. The young child enjoys manipulating materials such as clay, finger paints, crayons. This is a period of discovery; he learns that by pressing on his crayolas, the colors on his paper will be deeper and brighter, and that water colors will run. His results are very crude, but the child is happy in the activity and satisfied with whatever he produces.

At the symbolic stage, the child creates easily. The product is meaningful to the child, but not to others. The teacher must respect the child's work, for he is using his imagination, expressing his ideas with feeling, and has faith in his product. At this level children attempt to create forms that are related to something in their environment. From one day to the next, the same object may be represented in different ways and by different colors. The colors used are those that appeal to the child at the time that he is drawing. Children should not be required to use formal color combinations in their productions. The criterion to be used is, "Do the colors used bring pleasure to the creator?"

Ultimately, the child's creative product will be more realistic. His pictures will not only show a house, but also a child engaged in some activity in front of the house. He also has some appreciation for design which he uses quite effectively, for example, in decorating paper napkins or paper plates for a party.

Children are interested in things that they see around them. Therefore, the teacher should guide children in observing closely when they go on excursions, as they see pets at play, and when studying trees and birds in science. An excellent time for creative work is after children have had a vivid or new experience, particularly when they wish to express their experience by drawing a picture, painting at the easel, or probably cutting out objects.

Art materials must be selected to fit the needs and the activities of children at various developmental levels. The variety of materials is great; space will permit the presentation of only the most frequently used media. Large crayons are used at kindergarten and early primary level, while the smaller ones and colored chalk are used in later primary grades. Materials suitable for painting are large bristle paintbrushes, large sheets of absorbent paper (back side of wall paper in sample books is very absorbent), jars of poster paint or calcimine, and small pieces of sponge for painting (using one color to a sponge). For modeling there should be available plasticine and water clay. Scissors with blunt edge and colored paper are useful for designs or posters.

Young children enjoy printing with potato blocks; the sweet potato does not shrivel as quickly as the Irish potato. The potato blocks may be preserved for several days by putting them into water and keeping them in a cool place.

Waste materials often provoke an outlet for resourcefulness and imagination and also help children to see possibilities in discarded materials at home. The material should be organized, accessible, and available for immediate inspiration, so that children can create freely and undisturbed. Teachers may obtain an excellent booklet, "Uses for Waste Materials," by writing to the Association for Childhood Education, Washington, D.C.

Intermediate and upper grades

In the intermediate grades children still are interested in expressing their interests and emotions through the medium of art. They also are beginning to be more critical and as a result of this their products become more and more realistic. Frequently a child is dissatisfied with the creations that gave him so much satisfaction in the primary grades.

In the upper grades children are very much concerned about the finished product—whether it will be acceptable according to adult standards. They are very critical and often do not feel free to express their ideas in art form. The child who is visually minded will produce duplications of the actual appearance of the objects in nature; the productions of the nonvisually minded present the details that have emotional importance for the creator.

Teachers should guide children in making observations and in comparing things in their environment. Opportunities should be provided so that they can observe a painter or sculptor as he is creating a piece of work which will help them in attempting to express themselves. Mental images and imaginative and fantastic ideas should be encouraged.

Children in the upper grades are very much interested in practical arts. They use different crafts and decorative materials for purposes that have adult values. Even though practical arts and fine arts are separate fields of endeavor, they also are closely related. The making and designing of an article must be integrated into a single experience. By fusing construction and design of an object, emphasis is placed on creativeness.

Fine arts and practical arts should be integrated with units of work. In such projects practically all phases of art will be included, such as painting pictures, modeling, and crafts of many types. Free expression should be encouraged without sacrificing basic art principles. Copying a picture or a model should be discouraged. Children may be taught how to make thumbnail drawings of facts wanted and adapt them to their own compositions. By combining imagination and fact it is possible that a real work of art may be produced.

Suitable material and a convenient working place should be provided for creative work in fine and practical arts. Some of the materials and activities are (1) soap, wood, penknife with a slender blade or tenpenny nails sharpened into different shapes for cutting and carving; (2) potatoes, carrots, linoleum blocks, and penknife with slender blade for printing; (3) papier-maché for modeling masks and puppets; (4) water color, poster paints, easels, small plywood palette for poster- and oil-painting; (5) charcoal for sketching; (6) wood, wire, and metal for designing; (7) many kinds of textiles for stencils; (8) beautifully illustrated and readable art books and portfolios should be available. Teachers should select those materials that meet children's current needs. By the end of the intermediate grades children can handle each medium that seems most suitable for their product.

CREATIVE MUSIC

Music in the elementary school curriculum consists of singing, listening, playing instruments, rhythmic activities, and creative expression. In this section emphasis will be placed upon the creative activities.

No child should be hurried into responding with body movements to rhythm of music or into developing original compositions. Readiness for creative activities depends upon the social, emotional, physical, and mental development of the child and also upon his aptitudes and interests. No two children will respond to the rhythmic pattern and melody or mood of the music in the same way. In listening to a selection, some respond to the rhythm by moving about the room, slowly at first and then becoming more and more relaxed and free with their bodily movements. Other children may imitate the movements that they have observed. Still others will not respond at all.

Kindergarten and primary grades

Young children respond well to such experiences as dramatizing songs and rhythms; experimenting with sounds, tone, and rhythms; and various forms of composition. *Rhythmic experiences* give children an opportunity to express moods and feelings and aid them in handling their bodies gracefully. Before children are invited to interpret and to dramatize songs and rhythms, they should have experienced movements such as running and skipping; imitated rhythmic movements of animals, such as hopping rabbits, trotting horses; and listened to music that suggests movements such as hopping, trotting, and skipping.

Kindergarten and primary grade children enjoy acting out songs. As they sing "*Hickory Dickory Dock*" each child can be a mouse and do the actions of the song as they sing it. They also enjoy interpreting moods and rhythms of music through different kinds of body movements by varying steps as walking slowly, going on tiptoe, and by dances improvised by each child who feels like doing it.

In experimenting with *sounds, tone,* and *rhythm,* instruments of a toy orchestra should be used a few at a time. Children enjoy beating drums and listening to the thud. Nail kegs or wooden buckets with rubber or skin heads make excellent drums. Saucepan covers have many possibilities of producing various sounds and tones. The tones of bells and triangles thrill children. By experimenting with a few instruments or other materials at a time, children will become familiar with different sounds and also will learn how to handle various sound-producing materials. After they satisfy their curiosity they will want to play a piece of their own creation. Often they will select a certain instrument to reproduce a sound heard in the environment, such as a train approaching town, a road grader on the highway, or an animal at the zoo.

Spontaneous creative compositions begin early. Very young children create songs and rhythms at their play. They hum and sing, and chant words and tunes that accompany the activity in which they are absorbed. Whenever possible, the teacher should record the children's melodies, either by notation or by using a tape recorder. Then at an appropriate time, the teacher may allow the children to listen to the tunes and respond to the rhythm in their own way.

Frequently children will create melodies for poems. Whenever a group is developing a melody for a poem, the teacher should discuss with the children the meaning of the poem and ask them to try to think of a tune that fits the meaning. As the children suggest melodies, the teacher should write them on the chalkboard. After several tunes have been written on the board, the teacher should play each one on the piano or sing it. The children will listen attentively and decide which melody fits the meaning of the words in the poem. A clever teacher may then compose a piano accompaniment that will fit the children's melody.

Composing words for a song is another useful device for young children. Before the child can be expected to create a song, he must have enjoyed singing many songs. No single technique can be recommended for motivating children to experiment with musical expressions. The basic element is rhythm, and the most effective form of the expression is that of expressing the ideas in phrases. One technique is to have the children sing their first original song by answering a question sung by the teacher, as "Where is Jack?" (do, re, me), the child answering "I am here" (me, re, do). Another technique is for the teacher to be on the alert to pick up any rhythm or musical expression of a child that comes forth during a discussion in which some incident has inspired the group. As the children are learning songs by rote year after year, the teacher gradually will develop their understanding of the concepts, *unity in a song, variety in a song,* and *balance in a song.* As they grasp the meanings of these concepts, children will begin to apply the ideas to their own songs, the result being a creative production on a higher level of accomplishment.

Middle and upper grade

Children in this age range enjoy interpreting and composing songs. The method of approach is important. Middle and upper grade children are not interested in interpreting rhythmic actions that make us feel like snowflakes floating through the air or like galloping horses. At these levels pupils are more interested in the emotional and intellectual response to music, as in interpreting songs and instrumental pieces. The singing of a song or playing an instrumental selection is a creative production whenever a child makes it his own by interpreting the phrasing, rhythm, and mood of the composition to fit his own needs. Frequently children may become fascinated by the rhythm or melody of a selection and unconsciously will dramatize parts of it. This response is a type of creative expression that has been prompted by the musical composition.

When individuals let their imagination have free play as they are listening to music, they are *listening to music creatively*. To enjoy creative listening it is not necessary for the listener to know anything about the selection. The important factor for him is to interpret the music in his own way and to derive listening pleasure from his activity. It may be that the mood of the selection satisfies a need or that the melody fascinates him to such a degree that he will express these impressions in his own unique way, the result being an original composition.

Readiness factors for original compositions at the intermediate and upper grade levels are:

1. A rich background of rote songs.
2. A knowledge of do-re-me syllables.
3. A variety of interests.
4. Background of musical rhythmic activities.
5. Experience in composing little selections, as at the primary level.

Methods of approach to creative musical experience in these grades vary widely. Different interests may stimulate the desire to compose a song or musical selection. A child or several children may be inspired to write a song for some school event, such as programs at Christmas, Easter, birthdays, school parties, etc. Teachers should sense the situations when the enthusiasm of the class is high and suggest the possibility of creating a song. A poem with regular rhythm that is enjoyed by the children also may serve as the motivating factor to create a tune.

At this level children are interested in the songs, music, and dances of other peoples. By identifying themselves with the feelings of other people as represented in their musical activities during certain historical periods, children will learn to appreciate and understand other cultures. Reading about the fine arts of other cultures, studying pictures representing dance movements, and listening to various types of music of other peoples often inspire the creating of original compositions that interpret the understandings and feelings that children have experienced by studying another culture. If children are satisfied with their production (no matter how simple the motif, the musical phrases, or the bodily rhythmic pattern), then that production should be accepted and recorded as designed by the children.

INFORMAL CREATIVE DRAMATICS

Creative dramatics is playmaking; the child presents a story or an idea as he understands it in his own way. Reading the story of "Three Billy Goats Gruff" is one thing but when the children play the story it takes on different meanings. The major objective of informal creative dramatics is not to prepare and present a finished play for an audience. Instead the objective is to develop in children creative abilities, creative thinking, effective speech patterns, social relationships with other children, and self-confidence, and understanding of other people's problems, appreciation for efforts and contributions of others, and emotional behavior patterns.

To achieve these purposes, informal creative dramatics does not require memorization of a script or dialogues. The children remember the sequence of events, identify themselves with a specific character, and spontaneously say what they feel like saying in the various situations. Each time a story is dramatized, the various roles are enacted by different children; as a result, the speeches used to express ideas will vary. Much could be said about the many various activities related to creative dramatics. It is the purpose of this section to discuss briefly dramatic play, story dramatization, and pantomimes. Another form of dramatization, acting out songs and rhythms, was discussed in the preceding section.

Dramatic play

Dramatic play is the spontaneous activity of a child as he identified himself with another character in an activity. This activity does not have a plot. There is no real beginning, and it may end at any time. Dramatic play is usually associated with kindergarten and young primary grade children. As a way of learning about life, young children will play being mother, daddy, doctor, storekeeper, postman, going on a plane, driving a car, having a party, being a dog, being a car, etc. Older children will play cops and robbers, Indians, and cowboys.

Teachers are now providing an environment to encourage dramatic play. In visiting classrooms, teachers will see a clothing center or costume box with castoff adult clothing such as gay hats, high-heeled slippers, gloves, neckties, and purses that children may wear as they are playing the various roles of adults. There may be a housekeeping corner with stove, table, chairs, iron and ironboard, dishes, and doll-buggy. Another center has blocks that can be used to build a boat, airplane, train, or store. On the playground are planks, barrels, packing crates, wagons, old tires, short ladders, and sandbox supplied with pans, pails, sifters, and spoons. All of these things and many others will stimulate the imagination of the children to engage in dramatic play as they play.

Dramatic play offers many opportunities for gathering information about children. The teacher who is interested in keeping anecdotal records can secure information by observing children without their being aware of it, occasionally moving near enough to the various groups to see and hear what is happening. She can record speech patterns that a child uses as he expresses himself orally. She can discover pent-up feelings that are displayed in portraying the part of another person. She can observe his reactions to behavior patterns of other children. She can pick up some information about the home life. Whenever she discovers that children cannot settle their own problems or that some child cannot protect himself, she should help them in clearing the issue.

Story dramatization

The dramatization of stories is essentially creative. It grows out of the children's dramatic play and their interpretation of stories that they have heard and read. Dramatizations have a setting and a plot. They help the child grow in understanding how others feel and act, learn to think on his feet, develop poise, and release pent-up energy and emotions in an acceptable form. Story dramatization also develops those abilities that function when groups work harmoniously in solving problems.

In informal dramatization, the teacher does not do much directing; the children "just play the story." No planning is needed for simple stories, but as the stories become more complex and have several settings, some preplanning should be done. It may be advisable to decide who should play the parts of certain characters, number of settings needed, properties needed, and the place or places in the classroom appropriate for dramatization. The children keep in mind the sequence of the incidents in the story, but they create the dialogue and actions as they move along in the dramatization. The children who are not taking part in the play are the audience.

The major steps that teachers have found to be helpful in guiding children in creative dramatization are the same in primary, intermediate, and upper grades. These steps follow:

1. Stories must be selected with care. They must be on the interest level of the children and must have action.
2. The teacher must tell the story effectively so that children can identify themselves with the characters, scenes, and movements of the plot.
3. Since children cannot keep many events clearly in mind, they may select a specific part of the story to dramatize.
4. Children discuss the characters of the story and assign parts.
5. They discuss the setting and the sequence of events.
6. They act out the scene, improvising the dialogue as the dramatization progresses.
7. Children evaluate the dramatization in a kind way.
8. After the evaluation, other children will play the story and interpret the action as they understand it.
9. If children are working on specific parts of the story instead of the story as a whole, the teacher may retell the story before the children select another scene or setting. The culmination of this procedure would be to play the story as a whole.

In addition to stories in children's readers and story books, some stories that children create are excellent for dramatizations. No parts of a story should be assigned for memorization. Creative story dramatization should be a spontaneous production.

Pantomime

A pantomime is a dramatization or play in which the actors do not use words but express their ideas or meanings by body actions. Pantomimes are enjoyed by children and adults. The child with a limited vocabulary has a wonderful opportunity to express himself and to experience the satisfaction of doing something on his own initiative that is of great importance at a specific time.

The most effective way to familiarize primary children with this type of creative dramatization is for the teacher to demonstrate. She could say to the children, "I'm going to pretend that I am doing something and see if you can guess what it is." A first-grade teacher might pretend to be eating lunch, playing the piano, picking fruit. The next step could be to suggest a theme and have all the children pantomime it in their own way or allow an eager child to act out an idea of his own.

Favorite choices for primary children are Mother Goose rhymes. In the intermediate grades children enjoy pantomiming more complicated situations, such as making and flying a kite, playing football, acting out a part in a story. The wise teacher will have children whisper into her ear what they intend to pantomime. By doing this, she can eliminate those pantomimes that might cause embarrassments, hard feelings, and misunderstandings on the part of some children in the room and probably someone in the community.

CREATIVE EXPRESSION

Creative expression is not just speaking or writing words and training in the manipulation of words. It is the translation of experiences and ideas into effective words and phrases. In creative expression, a person is seeking to share his experiences, ideas, and interpretations with others. Whatever drives an individual comes from within himself; he feels something that he puts into words. This kind of creativeness gives the creator a great deal of satisfaction and makes him aware of the fact that he can do something on his own power.

Primary grades

Young children have creative experiences in hearing and composing stories and poems. Since children in the primary grades have not mastered the handwriting skills, much of their creative expression is oral. The major creative oral activity of a primary child is to tell about his experiences. Since experiences are the major source for creative expression at this level and since children can be led to see sights, hear sounds, feel emotions, and use words and phrases that tell what they see, hear, and feel, the teacher should be aware of experiences that children have had and also provide for new ones. She will guide children as they listen to others tell or read stories or poems and relate experiences in order to discover those words and colorful phrases that help them to respond vicariously to experiences and ideas that others have had. In this way they will realize that to have others enjoy their experiences as they relate them they also must use interesting, descriptive, and vivid words and phrases.

Children also enjoy creating make-believe or imaginative stories and will need guidance in developing an understanding of the difference between a funny, imaginative story and a senseless, silly story. Some children are very spontaneous and original, whereas others unconsciously incorporate and elaborate ideas from stories that they have heard. The teacher should accept these stories from young children for what they are and appreciate the imaginative touches that the child has given the story. It should be remembered that the stories of beginners usually are simple, spontaneous, and rambling statements.

Frequently the group may compose a story cooperatively. The theme of this story may be an excursion, a pet, or the first snow. As the children are composing the story, the teacher should write it on the chalkboard, so that the group may reread their creation and probably decide to replace some of the expressions with more descriptive words and phrases. At this time the teacher should have some specific goals in mind, such as using interesting words, having a simple plot, or reaching a definite ending.

As the children advance in the primary grades their stories will become longer and more complex. Many children at second-grade level are capable of writing short stories. A third-grade child of average ability has grown considerably, his interests have expanded, and his stories may have several paragraphs. Children may set up standards for writing their own stories and also may use the same standards for evaluative purposes. Emphasis will not be placed upon punctuation, spelling, or grammar but upon content, effective use of words, and originality. In this way, children will recognize and discover the qualities that make their stories good.

In this presentation, the concept of poetry will take on a broad meaning and include any style that a child uses. The terms "poem" and "verse" will be interchanged. Children enjoy creating poems that are characterized by sounds and rhythm, jingles, humor, a story, and verbal images.

In the primary grades children should listen to the reading of children's poems and verses written by adults and by other children. Some teachers deliberately choose poems that do not rhyme as well as poems that rhyme, so as to help children understand that rhyming is not necessary in creating verse. After children have listened to poems for several weeks, the teacher watches for the time when children are excited or thrilled about an experience and are apt to make spontaneous poetic remarks about their experience, so that she can concentrate for several minutes upon creative expressions.

Whatever moves a child deeply and means much to him is excellent material for creative verse or poetry. For example, some morning the children may be pleased and thrilled about their two rabbits that are having a good time hopping around and munching at lettuce and carrots in a large enclosure that the children have made by sitting in a circle on the floor. The teacher asks the children to watch the bunnies closely and see if a poem or a story comes to them about the pets. If it does, they are to share it quietly with the group. Whenever a child tells his thoughts, the teacher makes a record of it and then later in the day reads the poetic expressions and original phrases to the children.

When a group of children or a class have had the same experience, a cooperative poem may be developed. One child may offer a good beginning and another child add another idea. The teacher will record each contribution on the chalkboard so that the teacher or a child may orally read and reread ideas that have been offered. As the children are thinking and making contributions, they often will suggest a word or phrase that could replace one that has been recorded on the board. If the group accepts the suggestion, the teacher will make the substitution in the original expression.

Children enjoy assembling their creative stories and poems in a class booklet for the reading table. The booklet also may be checked out for a period or a day by children in other grades.

Intermediate grades

Stories written by intermediate grade children usually include much detail. Toward the end of this period, characters are important, and often the reactions of these characters and their conversations tell the story.

The creative oral and written activities as stories and poems should be continued in the intermediate grades. Emphasis also should be placed on original description, narration, diaries, articles, and editorials, perhaps for use in a school newspaper or children's magazines. Points that must be emphasized in this writing are originality, the need for having authentic information in voicing opinions, and being able to stick to the point. Children also must know how to give credit for borrowed ideas and understand what is meant by plagiarism.

Ways of stimulating creative writing at this level are to praise children for sincere efforts, read to them materials written by other children of similar maturity level, and have the children share their original work with their classmates. If a child does not wish to share his story with others he should not be forced to do so. Permitting children to select their own topics produces better results than to assign themes. It should be remembered that it is not necessary for all children to do creative writing and that not all creative work must be done at a specific time.

Upper grades

The creative activities involving oral and written expression of the intermediate grades are continued in the upper grades. There still is a need to seek and to play with words in expressing ideas. There also is a place for oral composition and group composition. If play writing is done, it should be introduced by studying plays. Usually when a class decides to write a play, it decides on a purpose for writing the play and also preliminary planning. The script is written by several committees, each committee working on a specific part of the play. Then the committees present their work to the class, which discusses the production and decides whether it is acceptable or must be revised. Material which can be turned into plays may be found in social studies units, in history, and in fiction. These plays may be used for assemblies or radio or television.

In the upper grades a creative writing club may be formed by a group of students who wish special help and guidance in creative writing. A requirement for membership should be a steady effort at writing and not the value of a written story or poem. Members who fail to make a written contribution during a specific period of time should be dropped. Materials should be turned in to the chairman of the group or the faculty sponsor in advance of a meeting, so that the material to be read aloud at the meeting may be selected beforehand. The material should be read aloud by the author when he is called upon to do so by the leader of the group. Then the group will make their comments. The faculty advisor serves as a guide rather than as director of the meetings.

QUESTIONS, PROBLEMS, AND EXERCISES

1. Prepare a five-minute discussion on "How can we give children complete freedom in the creative arts?"

2. How does an assignment in creative work differ from an assignment in a study period?

3. List several suggestions for encouraging children to be creative.

4. Collect the drawings of one child over a period of six months. Describe the progressive change in the quality of the drawings.

5. Make several finger paintings, using the motions of your hand and also making impressions by the use of the surface of your palm and fingers.

6. Collect the drawings of ten seventh-grade children. Group the drawings according to nonvisual expression and visual expression. How many drawings fall between the two extremes?

7. Start a card file for music. Label cards as *Marching, Waltzing, Songs,* etc., and on each card list appropriate records and songs.

8. Evaluate several music texts and the accompanying teacher's manuals. Which text would you select if you were teaching the grade, and why would you select that text?

9. Write several poems or a story at one specific grade level that you think children would enjoy. Share the writing with a group of children and evaluate your writing in terms of the reactions of the children.

10. Serve as a chairman of a panel discussion that will present to the class the best procedures for leading children to express their ideas through poetry.

SELECTED SUPPLEMENTARY READINGS

ASSOCIATION FOR SUPERVISION AND CURRICULUM DEVELOPMENT. *Toward Better Teaching, Forty-ninth Yearbook*. Washington, D.C.: National Education Association, 1950.

Chap. v, "Fostering Creativity." The content of creativity is clarified very effectively. An excellent discussion showing how creativity emerges out of experiences. Actual descriptions of how classroom teachers recognized possibilities for creativity in school experiences and how children carried through the creative activities.

BURROWS, ALVINA TRENT, JUNE D. FERBEE, and DORIS C. JACKSON. *They All Want to Write*, rev. ed. Englewood Cliffs, N.J.: Prentice-Hall, Inc., 1952.

Discusses practical ways of stimulating children to write stories and verse for the pleasure derived from creativity. Many illustrations of children's work show their growth in the techniques and mechanics of prose and poetry writing.

HATCHETT, ETHEL L., and DONALD H. HUGHES. *Teaching Language Arts in Elementary Schools*. New York: The Ronald Press Co., 1956.

Chaps. 12 and 13 present methods of stimulating creative prose and creative verse writing. Numerous examples of children's work illustrate content and form. An excellent presentation of planning and publishing a school newspaper.

LOWENFELD, VIKTOR. *Creative and Mental Growth*, rev. ed. New York: The Macmillan Co., 1952.

An excellent treatment showing how the child's growth is related to his creative development. Good descriptions of the developmental stages in art at various chronological age levels and clear illustrations of children's work clarifying concepts relative to the various developmental stages. Any teacher, not only the art teacher, will find answers to many questions relative to the child and his creative abilities.

MURSELL, JAMES L. *Music and the Classroom Teacher*. New York: Silver Burdett Co., 1951.

Music experiences of children which are emphasized are singing, listening, rhythmic responses, playing musical instruments, and participating in creating music.

RAGAN, WILLIAM B., and CELIA BURNS STENDLER. *Modern Elementary Curriculum*. New York: The Dryden Press, Inc., 1953.

Chapter xiii discusses the problem of enriching and beautifying life. The authors support the idea that in creative arts we are concerned with the finished product not for its own sake but how it is related to child growth. Emphasis is placed on creative music, art, and practical arts.

THOMAS, R. MURRAY. *Ways of Teaching in Elementary Schools*. New York: Longmans, Green & Co., Inc., 1955.

Modern classroom methods in creative activities are emphasized. Many examples show how teachers have successfully developed creativity in following areas: writing, art, music, dramatics.

19

EVALUATING PUPIL GROWTH

Measurement and evaluation in the schools used to be based very largely on daily class marks, oral and written tests and examinations, and scores on notebooks and papers to be handed in. Naturally, marks based upon such data measure only limited areas and certain kinds of pupil growth. In recent years, as education has been more and more thought of by more and more people as being the direction and acceleration of desirable growth of young people on all fronts—physical, social, intellectual, and emotional—the scope of measurement and evaluation has widened.

EVALUATION PROGRAMS

It seems quite logical that any complete program of evaluation should bring into relief any kind of growth that may take place while pupils are attending school. In other words, the aim of evaluation should be to discover what progress had been made in the achievement of objectives of education—in general and in restricted areas. An adequate program of evaluation covers not only school subject areas—reading, arithmetic, writing—but also growth in appreciations, work habits, health and physical conditions, cooperation, creativeness, social adjustment, mental health, and human relations.

There are two somewhat distinct and important aspects of evaluation. One of these is the measurement of status of growth at any particular time, for example, reading skill, computational skill, social adjustment, cooperativeness, and work habits. Perhaps even more important and necessary in an effective program of evaluation is the measurement of growth over a period of time. Such a program involves two evaluations stated in terms that will permit comparisons. For example, it is desirable to see what growth has taken place during a semester, a year, or a period of years in an individual or a class in various areas and types of growth and learning. Indeed, in recent years there has been a tendency to give marks as well as to make reports to parents in terms of growth between stated periods rather than merely in terms of status at the given marking or reporting.

Beginning teachers, and perhaps experienced teachers too, frequently think of evaluation as having one purpose only: to provide the basis for giving pupils marks on achievement. Although evaluation may be necessary as a basis for marking, this is only one of the purposes it may serve. Periodic evaluation of the progress which pupils are making should—

1. Provide information about the progress which the pupils are making as individuals toward the objectives which have been set for the learning activity concerned.
2. Provide information which can be used to develop further learning activities, both for the class as a whole and for the pupils individually.
3. Provide information which can be used by both teacher and pupils to ascertain each pupil's strengths, locate his difficulties, and suggest remedial activities.
4. Be used as a basis for motivating further learning by encouraging pupils through recognition of the progress they have made and by stimulating them to improve where they have fallen short.
5. Provide information on all aspects of each pupil's progress, not on subject-matter achievement alone, so that the teacher may help the child grow more effectively as a citizen and as a person.

Evaluation in terms of objectives of education, broadly conceived, is indispensable in determining the relative merit of various types of learning materials and of learning and teaching activities. The value of experimental research, either of the definitely scientific kind or of the action research, depends upon the measurement and evaluation at the beginning of the period of research and at the end.

Bases for an effective program

Teachers in the past attempted to discover whether children had reached specific goals in the learning process. Because they were concerned mainly with the intellectual growth, tests were devised to measure growth in the acquisition of factual information. The teacher of today is concerned with the evaluation of growth of the entire child in all aspects of his personality. Since the behavior patterns are of many types, devices of evaluation also must be of different types. An effective evaluative program which purports to meet the needs of today's children must embody the following:

1. Objectives defined in terms of learner growth and behavior patterns.
2. Situations which will foster the evaluation of behavior patterns.
3. Techniques which will be used in evaluating behavior patterns.
4. Interpretation of data obtained about growth and behavior patterns.
5. Records which facilitate evaluation.
6. Reports which are capable of adequate interpretation by those who are interested in the progress of children.

The following general principles underlying evaluation procedure are useful in developing ways of evaluating pupil progress.

1. Evaluation should be made in terms of progress toward recognized goals. These goals may be the objectives of the course, unit, daily lesson, or activity concerned.
2. Evaluation should be made in terms of some starting point from which the progress of the child is measured. That point is the achievement level of the individual pupil when he begins work on a learning activity.
3. Evaluation should recognize the backgrounds and potentialities of individual pupils. The superior pupil with favorable backgrounds should proceed more rapidly and more completely toward the fulfilment of the recognized objectives.
4. Evaluation should be continuous throughout the entire learning situation. In a unit of study, the evaluation should be so planned that teacher and pupils are continuously informed of the progress that the group as a whole and each individual child are making toward the objectives.
5. Many techniques and devices for evaluation should be employed, of which tests and examinations are only one. These devices should be made as objective as possible, but some of them may of necessity be highly subjective.
6. There should be self-evaluation by the pupils as well as evaluation by the teacher. Since the pupils are participating in the learning activity, they can contribute much to an evaluation of their progress. Furthermore, they should gain experience in evaluating themselves and their own individual growth.
7. Evaluation should be of a constructive nature, emphasizing ways in which the pupil might improve his progress. It should locate pupil shortcomings, not in order to pass judgment but to suggest ways for improvement.

Interpretation of data

In guiding and directing the "whole child," it is essential that all data be brought together. It may be necessary to isolate some factors in order to detect those which are influencing others, but each is evaluated and interpreted in terms of the whole child. Evaluative measures may be used to guide teachers, parents, and children in studying the behavior patterns of each individual, in finding causes for the behavior patterns, and in providing preventive measures and remedial measures. Information may be interpreted by teachers as individuals, by committees of teachers, by special teachers such as nurses, by staff, by teachers and parents, by teachers and children, by teachers, children, and parents. The type of problem, the policy of the school, the community—all are factors that function in determining the procedure to be followed in the interpretation of data.

An approach best adapted to the interpretation of data about a child is the clinical approach. In other words, the teacher should look at all of the data and see what relationships may be employed in interpretation. In many cases it will be discovered that useful information concerning the child grows not out of data of a particular type but in the interpretation of data of two or more types. In other words, by comparisons of data in several areas conclusions may be arrived at which would not develop from a single type of data.

Self-evaluation and cooperative evaluation

An increasing number of teachers believe that it is very desirable for learners to evaluate their own progress. Not only may this assist the child to improve his work in school, but it also is good training and preparation for self-evaluation in later years. Self-evaluation does not center so much around marks for a subject as it does about evaluation of activities and progress in various types of learning activities. While to some extent it may involve comparisons with the work of other children, they should be minimized rather than emphasized. Self-evaluation should be directed toward facilitating self-improvement; therefore each learner should be encouraged to analyze his learning activities and his achievements, focusing his points of strength and points of weakness.

The learner should be encouraged and directed to ask himself such questions as the following:

1. What are some of the things I have been trying to do in this subject or on this project?
2. How well have I succeeded in accomplishing my aim?

3. What are the important things I have learned?
4. How well did I complete the jobs the teacher set for me to do?
5. Where did I fall down most, and why?
6. How well did I cooperate with others in group learning activities?
7. How well did I manage my own time, and did I neglect my responsibilities too much occasionally?
8. How well am I growing up to greater self-control, better working with others, greater skills in the use of learning tools such as the dictionary, carrying out promptly my responsibilities in this class, including promptness and carefulness in doing my work?
9. What should I do now to improve my weaknesses?

Cooperative evaluation may be either one of two different types:

1. Cooperative evaluation of individuals' learning activities and progress; or
2. Group evaluation of group projects and group activities.

These evaluative activities should probably be done in a fairly informal way. Certainly they should not produce excessive embarrassment for any individual.

Cooperative evaluation should be introduced gradually so that children may develop skills and emotional objectiveness in what may seem to be minor and informal situations. Evaluation by a child's peers may cut and hurt, even more than evaluation by teachers. Very careful supervision is, therefore, necessary in cooperative evaluation. Children in the class should be trained and encouraged in concentrating upon constructive criticism and suggestions. Petty fault-finding and rudeness should be ruled out by the teacher. It should constantly be held before the class that the principal purpose of the evaluation is to assist the individuals or the group in improving their work and their learning.

Types of data

No classroom can provide possibilities for the development and evaluation of all behavior patterns. Intellectual skills and abilities may be developed and evaluated in a typical classroom. Social amenities are fostered and observed most satisfactorily on the playground, in the lunch room, on an excursion, at a birthday party. Attitudes and appreciations should be studied in situations which are characterized by an emotional tone; for example, an attitude of good sportsmanship is genuine when at a ball game the members of the losing team are "good sports." Mental and emotional disturbances may be evaluated through creative releases, such as finger painting, drawing pictures, and writing poems. Physical conditions, such as fatigue and listlessness, are observable in the classroom, on the playground, on excursions, and at home.

Techniques of evaluation are determined by the type of behavior pattern which is being evaluated. In determining growth in the tool subjects, such as reading and arithmetic, standardized achievement tests and teacher-made tests may be used. Readiness and diagnostic lists may be employed to advantage in discovering the degree of readiness of children in various areas of learning. Intelligence tests help to determine the power of the child to master intellectual skills. In order to measure the degree of human social relations, sociograms may be used.

In addition to "tests," teachers devise and use a great many situations in which the behavior of the learner may be observed as it brings into relief the degree of learning that has taken place in the specific areas. Among the types of data other than test scores which are most useful in evaluation are the following:

1. Evaluation of material things produced by learners, for example, drawings, clothing, foods, objects in arts and crafts work.
2. Evaluation of the development of skills by learners as observed by teachers, for example, in getting along with others, in singing, in speech, in personality.
3. Observations of pupils, in socially preferred ideals and attitudes, for example, honesty, responsibility, concern for the welfare of all.
4. Anecdotal records of behavior of children based upon observation.
5. Data concerning various aspects of child growth gathered from—
   a) Attitudes and conversation of other children.
   b) Conferences with the child himself.
   c) Conferences with parents.
   d) Sociograms and similar devices.
   e) Health records.
   f) Physical examination records.
6. Time spent in out-of-school activities including work experience.
7. The nature and quality of performance in extracurricular activities.
8. Amount of time spent in nature and the amount of time spent in leisure pursuits and associations.
9. Lists of problems and worries for students as a whole and for individual students.

CHARACTERISTICS OF EVALUATIVE DATA

Validity

Of most importance, of course, is the selection of evaluative devices and procedures which will afford a valid measure of what the instructor wishes to have measured. For example, if an instructor is concerned only with temporary acquisition of a limited body of subject information a good standard achievement test may be employed. If she is interested in diagnosis and identification of areas of weakness, a test especially built for that purpose and including some measure of all of the possible areas should be employed.

The degree of validity of an evaluative device or procedure is the degree to which it measures growth toward all of the objectives which it will be assumed are measured or evaluated. Most of the so-called objective tests today need to be supplemented either by additional tests or by informal observations made in a nontesting situation. Before employing a standard test, the teacher should read the accompanying description of its derivation—how it was devised. She should also examine carefully information relative to the validity of the test for the purpose for which the test will be used.

There are several ways to judge the validity of a test. The simplest way is to examine the material of the test and make a common-sense evaluation of it as a measuring instrument for the subject or function which it tests. In doing this, it is essential that the evaluator get in mind or on paper before him the objectives or the outcomes desired (for example, the information, understandings, ideals, attitudes, skills) and then see to what extent the test in question measures growth toward all the objectives in proportion to their relative importance.

Another procedure is to compare the subject matter of the test with studies or discussions of the objectives and essentials of the subject and with studies of the relative social utility of the items within the course. It is frequently helpful to construct test items as learning progresses and to organize the items into a balanced instrument of measurement.

The most effective method of determining the validity of a test, however, is to discover the amount of correlation between scores on the tests and scores made or some known valid criterion of the achievement or behavior pattern which the test is used to measure. The results obtained are usually indicated in the instructional materials that accompany the tests.

A test that may be valid for one group of children may not be valid for another. For example, a test that is given to a group of bilingual children who have difficulty in expressing themselves in the language in which the test is written will be invalid for that particular group of children because the scores measure language ability in addition to the other item the test was intended to measure.

Since instruments of evaluation may measure several different factors, the evaluator should have in mind clearly the behavior patterns which he is evaluating. An achievement test in arithmetic will indicate whether or not the child is having difficulty with the process of long division, but it may not show diagnostically what division facts and subtraction facts have not been mastered. A child scoring high in a recognition vocabulary test cannot always be considered as having a good comprehension in reading; in fact, his comprehension may not be great. A child possessing a wealth of information on the culture of a nation cannot be considered as having no prejudices toward its people.

Reliability

The potential validity of a test is realized only to the degree that the test is reliable. A measuring instrument is reliable if it gives consistently the same score when repeated under similar conditions and there is no variation in the score even though different individuals may score the paper. In addition, scores on reliable tests are not greatly influenced by chance fluctuations in the performance of the person being tested. Barring gross error on the part of the person doing the measuring, approximately the same result is obtained when a foot rule is employed to measure the width of a window, no matter how many individuals make the measurement or how many times it is made. This should likewise be true with school achievement tests. However, tests differ in the ability to call forth consistent responses from the student. On less reliable tests a pupil's score will vary appreciably from one testing to another for no apparent reason.

The reliability of a test depends greatly upon the *objectivity* with which the test may be scored. A test is objective if it is not subject to individual bias or idiosyncrasy of the scorer; hence two or more evaluators will arrive at the same score. Many tests are so devised that it makes no difference who scores the test; barring error, the score will be the same. Everything else being equal, tests which permit of no disagreement between scores are much to be preferred.

The *length* of a test also affects its reliability. Up to the limit of fatigue or varying attention, the more items included in the test, the greater is the reliability of the test. Administration procedures often affect the reliability of a test; if a child becomes disturbed and does not put forth his best effort, for him the measure is not reliable and hence not valid.

The coefficient of reliability of tests may vary all the way from a little above zero up to .90 or .95. (The coefficient of reliability is the coefficient of correlation between scores made on a test and the scores made on a very similar form of it.) In the very large majority of well made tests, the coefficient of reliability lies between .80 and .90 for a given grade, for example, the fifth grade. Tests having reliability coefficients of more than .85 for a single grade may be used with much confidence for measuring individual learners. When the reliability is below .80 two forms of the test should be combined if the test is to be used at all in order to get reliable scores of individuals. In general, tests having reliability of less than .70 for pupils in a single grade are hardly worthy of use even if two forms are used where the exact measures of individuals are desired.

For comparison of groups as large as 25 or 30, reliability of .65 to .70 is sufficient. Reliability coefficients based upon scores made by pupils in several grades should be naturally higher than those based upon the performance of children of one grade only. Therefore, for a test to be very useful, its reliability coefficients based upon the scores of pupils in three or more grades should be at least as high as .85 or .90, depending upon the number of grades for measurement individuals from .70 to .75 for comparisons between groups. It should be remembered that the reliability of an item or a section of the test is usually materially less than that indicated by the reliability coefficient for the entire test.

Practicability

Tests should not be long enough to develop fatigue or boredom on the part of children. Instructions and directions should be as short and simple and clear as possible. The case of administering an evaluative measure and of checking results is also important.

Various devices are employed to keep at a minimum the amount of time necessary to score tests. One device is to use strips of paper or cardboard with correct answers so spaced as to fall beside the blanks for the answers on the test. These may be placed edge to edge with the test paper, so that the correct answer is close to the pupil's answer, and can easily be seen. Another form is the cardboard answer key with apertures which, when the key is superimposed on the test paper, fit directly over the spaces provided for the pupil's answers, thus enabling the scorer to compare the answers on the pupil's test paper with the answers printed at the edge of the openings.

Instruments of evaluation which cannot be interpreted by classroom teachers with a minimum amount of effort are not practical. Data to be used effectively by teachers must be translatable into meaningful, descriptive language which makes possible an appraisal of growth that can be communicated to children as well as to parents.

Interpretation

Teachers need preservice or in-service training, preferably both, in interpretation of any kinds of test scores. This is especially true with respect to tests of intelligence, personality, temperament or disposition and aptitudes. A considerable amount of training, for example, is needed in interpretation of scores from Rorschach and Wechsler and other complex tests of personality.

With a few exceptions the teacher attempts to bring about as much growth as possible in view of the limitations of time available and the degree of intelligence and maturity of the learners. She is dissatisfied if nearly all pupils reach only a minimum level. Since this is so, she desires to construct or to select an evaluation device which will measure various degrees and amount of growth. She also wishes to use a measuring device with available data and techniques which will enable the teacher and learner to evaluate growth by means of its measurements.

Very useful for this purpose are data concerning the performance of other individuals on the same measuring instruments under the same conditions. With many standard tests such data are provided in the form of percentile norms, for example, the scores of ratings made by the pupils who rank 95th, 90th, 85th, and so on in a hundred, or proportionately in any smaller or larger group of persons. To be the most useful such norms—

1. Should be based upon at least several hundred cases, and preferably several thousand cases, of learners of comparable age and grade placement.
2. Should have been obtained under conditions similar to those under which the test is to be given, for example:
    a) At the same time in the course, that is, at the end of the first semester, in the middle of the second semester.
    b) From a group of the same general level and distribution of ability as the one to be tested; or if not, then from a group of known general level and distribution of ability so that appropriate allowances may be made.

In interpreting the test scores by means of norms, consideration should be given to such matters as:

1. The degree to which the teacher has emphasized the objectives or areas emphasized by the test
2. The amount and character of instruction the class may have received in previous years and in other areas likely to stimulate growth along the lines emphasized by the test
3. The general intelligence of the class or the particular individual

4. Any unusual distracting or motivating conditions attending the giving of the test

TYPES OF EVALUATION DEVICES

Many types of evaluation devices are employed to measure the growth of the learner in information, understandings, and skills. Those most often used at the elementary level are marks for classwork, oral and written tests, score cards and ratings, observations and anecdotal records, and culminating activities.

Marks

In schools in which the work is organized on the daily class period plan, some teachers record marks based upon pupils' participation in class discussion. These may be recorded once a week or even more frequently. Some teachers record marks daily while the class is in session. Some values claimed for use of class marks are these.

1. Marks serve as an immediate incentive for pupil study.
2. Marks provide a broad base upon which a final mark in the course can be determined.
3. The use of marks decreases the emphasis upon final examinations.
4. The use of marks makes pupil evaluation a continuous process throughout the course.
5. Marks serve as the basis of pupil diagnosis and remedial work.
6. The use of marks assists in establishing pupil habits of attention during the recitation.

Many teachers are convinced that when superior teaching is being done, the disadvantages of the daily marking procedure far outweigh the advantages. The teacher tends to become a bookkeeper intent upon recording a symbol opposite the name of each pupil. Elaboration and explanation by the teacher are necessarily reduced to a minimum, lest he invalidate a pupil's mark. Thus the recitation becomes only an oral testing period. The formality of the situation limits pupil discussion to the questions, whereas spontaneity and freedom of expression should be encouraged. Each pupil attempts to outwit the teacher by preparing the answers to the questions he thinks he is most likely to be asked. The inequality of the questions in respect to their difficulty and importance does not provide a common basis for evaluating responses of the different pupils. Since it is impossible to ask each pupil more than one or two questions, the sampling of his information on the lesson topic is so limited as to make it very unreliable. The forced attention of pupils is very likely to destroy genuine interest in the subject by focusing it upon the mark which is being recorded.

Oral vs. written tests

Considerable thought has been given by authorities on measurements to the relative values of oral and written tests in programs of evaluation of pupil achievement. In practice, the amount of time given and the significance attached to the two types of tests have varied greatly from school to school as well as from one classroom to another. While there is disagreement in regard to the comparative merits of oral and written tests, many teachers believe that both types have an important part to play in achieving the numerous purposes of measurement in teaching.

The advantages of the oral test in the classroom may be summarized as follows.

1. The test gives the pupil experience in oral expression.
2. Pupils derive certain benefits from listening to the responses of other pupils.
3. The total number of oral questions answered by a class is greater than those that pupils can write in a given class period.
4. Errors made by pupils can be discovered and corrected immediately in the class period.
5. The visual sense utilized in reading and writing about a subject is supplemented by the use of the auditory sense in an oral test on the same material.
6. The extraneous factors of handwriting and neatness of papers are absent.
7. There is less paper work for the teacher.

As an instrument of measurement, the written test is distinctly superior to the oral test in several important respects.

1. Since all the pupils of a class answer the same list of questions, the teacher has a fair basis for comparison of test results.
2. Written responses to written questions can be evaluated on a more objective basis than oral responses.
3. By the use of objective types of written tests, responses of each pupil to a large number of questions can be obtained in a class period, thus reducing the unreliability of limited sampling by means of the oral test, in which each pupil has the opportunity of answering only one or two questions.
4. The difficulty and importance of the questions answered by different pupils are equal, thus validating marks given on a comparative basis.

SCORE CARD FOR MEASURING HANDWRITING

By

C. Truman Gray

Pupil . . . . Age . . . . Date . . . .

Grade . . . . School . . . .

Sample Number . . . . Teacher . . . .

Sample	perfect score	1st mo.	2nd mo.	3rd mo.	4th mo.	5th mo.	6th mo.	7th mo.	8th mo.	9th mo.	10th mo.	
1. Heaviness 3		...	...	...	...	...	...	...	...	...	...	...
2. Slant . . . . 5 Uniformity Mixed		...	...	...	...	...	...	...	...	...	...	
3. Size . . . . 7 Uniformity Too large Too small		...	...	...	...	...	...	...	...	...	...	
4. Alignment 8		...	...	...	...	...	...	...	...	...	...	...
5. Spacing of lines . . . . . 9 Uniformity Too close Too far apart		...	...	...	...	...	...	...	...	...	...	...
6. Spacing words . . . . . . 11 Uniformity Too close Too far apart		...	...	...	...	...	...	...	...	...		...
7. Spacing of letters . . . . 18 Uniformity Too close Too far apart		...	...	...	...	...	...	...	...	...	...	...
8. Neatness . . . . 13 Blotches Carelessness		...	...	...	...	...	...	...	...	...	...	...
9. Formation of letters . . (29)		...	...	...	...	...	...	...	...	...	...	...
General form 8		...	...	...	...	...	...	...	...	...	...	...
Smoothness 6		...	...	...	...	...	...	...	...	...	...	...
Letters not closed . . 5		...	...	...	...	...	...	...	...	...	...	...
Parts omitted 5		...	...	...	...	...	...	...	...	...	...	...
Parts added 2		...	...	...	...	...	...	...	...	...	...	...
TOTAL SCORE		...	...	...	...	...	...	...	...	...	...	...

Scored by . . . .

Figure 2. Score Card for Measuring Handwriting.

375

5. The written test paper provides a record of the pupil's achievement which can be carefully analyzed for diagnostic purposes.
6. The influence of extraneous factors in testing, such as timidity and handicaps in oral expression, are minimized.

It appears probable that a combination of tests of considerable variety and scope is necessary in an adequate program of testing. Excessive use of the class period for formal evaluation, especially oral and written tests, is to be avoided. A current trend among teachers is in the direction of relying less upon recitation and quizzes and more upon observations of students at work in their learning situations. This trend is particularly marked in schools where the class period is as long as fifty minutes.

Score cards and ratings

In some subjects it is possible to employ score cards and ratings of a finished product which may be taken as a measure of the growth of the learner—not only of his information, but of his understandings and his skills. Ratings are particularly useful in the teaching of art, industrial arts, agriculture, household arts, and in health records. Typical of such rating devices is the penmanship scale (Figure 2) distributed by the Public School Publishing Company of Bloomington, Illinois.

Observations and anecdotal records

Teachers need not rely entirely for data concerning learner growth or status upon situations especially devised for measurement. The more intelligent and observant teacher will be looking constantly for evidences of growth, maladjustments, and failure to grow. She will constantly observe the written work of students at their desks, their participation in discussions, their questions, and their association and behavior with other people both in and out of the classroom with a view to gathering data concerning the growth of the individual pupil.

Informal observations and anecdotal records are particularly useful and the teacher should train herself to make informal observations of the status and growth of learners particularly with respect to character, personality, and social behavior. Almost daily she will wish to record her observations of evidences of growth or lack of it on the part of a few of her students. These may be entered in classbooks, in memo books, or in files of pupil data. These observations may occasionally take the form of brief anecdotes such as the following example.

In reading period today, Mildred did not work well even after receiving individual help in analyzing difficult words. She seems to be discouraged in learning to read and is attempting to gain admiration in her group by showing off. I think that the reading material is too difficult and that by locating her reader level, she will do satisfactory work and as a result gain the admiration of her friends because of her accomplishment.

Culminating activities

Teachers have come to employ a variety of special and culminating activities which have great potentialities for evaluation. Illustrative of these are the following.

1. *Displays of a large unit of work.* The children may arrange displays of their work, such as charts, pictures, and models, give demonstrations of processes, or present reports of their research and findings.

2. *Dramatizations of a favorite story or original idea.* The children may present their versions of stories read, adapt scenes from various books, or develop original plots. These might be presented as a series of informal, unmemorized dramatizations, productions of plays written by the children, or interpretative oral reading.

3. *Representative selections of creative work.* Representative selections of written creations may be offered by the children, including poems, short stories, descriptive sketches, and informal essays. Other forms of creative work which may be shared are roller-box movies, puppet shows, interpretations of murals, friezes, and pictures, explanations of clay figures, and original rhythms and dances.

4. *Presentations of accomplishments in special areas of the curriculum.* The children as a whole group, or as several smaller groups, may organize and present physical education activities such as folk dances, stunts, singing or group games, songs and instrumental selections from music, demonstrations and experiments from science, or materials illustrating mathematical concepts.

5. *Evaluations of important accomplishments.* In this type of program, the children share their evaluations of their schoolwork over a given period of time. The children review their purposes, present evidence of improvements and accomplishments, and share conclusions from their appraisals. To do this, they might use samples of written expression, handwriting, records of reading or physical development, examples of creative work, experience reading charts, anecdotal appraisals of group behavior, and the like.

6. *Celebrations of special occasions.* Occasionally, on special days, the children may invite their parents to celebrate with them. Arbor Day may be observed through utilizing the children's expe-

riences in nature study and science. For Halloween, community folklore and traditional customs may furnish the basis for a series of playlets. For Lincoln's Birthday, anecdotes about his youth, literary selections, and biographical sketches might be presented. Parents' visiting day, Mother's Day, and Father's Day may be suitably recognized through programs which emphasize appreciations and understanding of what Mother and Father contribute to the children and to the school.[1]

Evaluations in nonsubject areas

There are an increasing number of teachers who wish to measure types of growth other than subject-matter information, understandings, and skills. They are attempting more and more to measure other types of pupil growth: not only are teachers interested in contributing to it, but parents are interested in having more information about it. In arranging classroom experiences for children, teachers cannot help but influence growth in areas which may not be objectives of the particular subject being taught. Furthermore, an increasing number of teachers want to know much more about each individual pupil to assist in planning learning activities and in thinking about pupil-pupil and pupil-teacher relationships.

The more modern and practical teacher wants to have information concerning intelligence and mental age. The teacher also wants to know as much as possible at the beginning of the year and later about what information is available concerning aptitudes and interests of the individuals who compose her class. She also wishes to measure the development of work-study scales and ability to do independent and critical thinking. She wants to have information concerning health, both in respect to status and in respect to changes and growth. Of great importance and being employed more and more by teachers are data concerning status and growth or changes in personality and social adjustment, such as might result from pupil diaries, autobiographies, letters and compositions, sociograms and other sociometric devices, and character, personality, and social maturity in schools and other types of inventories. Teachers study other types of creative work by means of projection techniques and observation of the child's treatment of pets and toys, and through records of wishes, worries, and emotional behavior patterns. Daily informal observations are being applied more commonly and more effectively by classroom teachers for evaluation of social adjustment and emotional instability.

[1] James B. Burr, Lowry W. Harding, and Leland B. Jacobs, *Student Teaching in the Elementary School.* (New York: Appleton-Century-Crofts, Inc., 1950), pp. 327-28.

CONSTRUCTING, SCORING, AND INTERPRETING TESTS

The procedure in constructing an objective examination of considerable length (40 minutes or more) may be summarized as follows:

1. Get in mind the outcomes of teaching which constitute the chief objectives of the learning activities; that is, what information, what skills or habits, what ideals or attitudes are aimed at in presenting the material to be tested, and which of these is of most worth.

2. Decide how much time is to be given to the test, and estimate how many exercises may be completed by the pupils in the time available.

3. Select about one and one half times as many exercises that test the possession of information, understanding, skills, habits, ideals, or attitudes emphasized, as may be given in the time available, consciously attempting to distribute these over the course somewhat in proportion to the importance of each outcome in the ground covered.

4. Have all the test exercises of one type, true-false, completion, or multiple-response, or, make the examination up of different types. Ordinarily the latter procedure is preferable, since the most effective type of exercise for each item may be chosen on an individual basis. Formulate the items in the types most appropriate to the achievements to be tested. Items not of primary importance and difficult to fit into any form may be tentatively set aside to be used only in case they are needed to give balance or to complete the examination. The shorter the question or exercise, the better.

5. Take care to formulate exercises in such a way that something more than memory is tested. Provide some questions involving reasoning and attitudes.

6. Take care to include some questions which all pupils are likely to answer, and some which very few are likely to answer. The other questions should range in difficulty between these extremes, with a goodly percentage of questions of average or reasonable difficulty.

7. Go over the test exercises carefully, discarding those which are ambiguous or misleading, or which demand elaborate qualification. Reduce the number of test exercises to the desired number, being sure to retain such exercises as will give "range," to the test, and those testing important objectives. Discard those exercises which are least objective and which serve to test powers tested by other questions or exercises. Take care also to preserve proper distribution among the different parts of the material covered.

8. Rearrange the remaining exercises into groups by type; that is, group all the true-false exercises together, all the multiple-choice together, and so on.
9. Rearrange within the groups in the apparent order of difficulty, or in some other logical order. The most difficult exercises should not be placed toward the beginning of the test.
10. In preparing the blank forms for the test, control the position of the answers, allowing for them preferably along one side of the page to facilitate scoring.
11. Prepare a key of correct answers in such form that it may be laid alongside the pupil's paper and thus permit rapid scoring. A cardboard key is very convenient.

Objective tests

The construction of good objective tests requires care and considerable time. Teachers have discovered that there may be disagreement as to whether a statement is true or false and which is the best answer among several choices presented. They also have had difficulty in constructing objective test items which do not permit different interpretations by the pupils. The most serious of all limitations is that teachers employing objective test procedures have tended to include too many trivial items, too many isolated factual items (means and not ends of learning), to the neglect of items measuring understanding, mental skills, attitudes, interests, ideals, and habits. Only recently has anything like adequate attention been given to the matter of constructing objective test items which do measure other types of outcomes.

While in the upper grades objective tests may be used to excellent advantage, they should always constitute only a part of a comprehensive and varied evaluation program. Among the more commonly used types of objective test items are those discussed in the following paragraphs.

True-false items. The true-false test consists of a number of statements the truth of which the child is asked to affirm or deny. The testee is usually instructed to encircle or to check one of the two words *yes, no,* one of the two letters *T, F,* or one of the two words *True, False,* or the test may be set up so that the testee writes in the blanks provided either True or False, Yes or No, + or 0. The blanks, words, letters, or symbols should be placed in a column at the right or at the left of the respective statements. If placed at the right, the testee may write without having to place his hand over the test paper. On the next page is a portion of such an examination.

1. There is land on both sides of a strait.	Yes	No
2. An isthmus is a narrow strip of land that connects two large bodies of land.	Yes	No
3. An island is a small piece of land surrounded by water.	Yes	No

True-false tests have come somewhat into disrepute because they have often been poorly constructed or interpreted.

A true-false examination should contain at least fifty or sixty items to be reliable, although a smaller number may be employed when the true-false items form part of a test consisting of several types of exercises. The number of true and the number of false statements should not be exactly equal, or always approximately equal. It is better to vary procedure in this respect; otherwise, pupils will learn to adapt their answers in order to distribute them equally between true and false. However, not less than 25 or 30 per cent of the statements should be of one type. True and false statements should neither be bunched nor alternated; nor should they be arranged in any systematic order which would give any clues as to which are true and which false.

Care should be exercised to select false statements which are not obviously false, and which will not permit the pupil to identify the correct answers by eliminating the obviously incorrect ones or by any other process of reasoning which does not involve the possession of the knowledge or skill to be tested. The false statement should in every case be one which the pupil would be as likely to call true as false if he did not possess the knowledge or other educational outcome which the statement is designed to test. For example, the statement that "An ant has three legs" is not a good statement to use in a true-false exercise. Most pupils will identify it as false without any reference to how many legs an ant has, because they do not believe that any insect has an odd number of legs. Likewise the statement that "Chicago is the capital of Michigan" may be identified as false without knowing what the capital of Michigan or the capital of Illinois is, because the pupils know that Chicago is in Illinois.

The chance of guessing the correct answer in the true-false test is greater than in other types of tests. On the other hand in a given period of time a greater number of true-false items than of other types can be covered in a test and, if the number of items is great, pupils will tend to break even on bad and good guesses. Approximately one and a half times as many true-false items can be completed as five-choice, best-answer, or multiple-choice items. True-false tests are about as reliable as other types of objective tests that require the same amount of time.

Multiple-choice items. Among the most commonly used of all types of objective tests is the multiple-choice or best-answer exercise. It has been found that this type of test is, item for item, more valid and reliable than the true-false test and also checks on a large number of abilities, such as discrimination, judgment, and understanding. Teachers who construct multiple-choice tests must be aware that all responses deserve attention and require the reader to think critically as he makes his decisions. No item should contain any clues to the correct answers, nor should items be included which are obviously false. The task is to select, from three or more possible answers (four or five are probably best), the correct one or the best answer to the question or problem stated. Children may be instructed to check the correct response in any of several ways, such as to draw a line under the correct answer, or to write the number or letter of the responses on a blank or in a parenthesis placed at the beginning or end of the statement.

Multiple-choice tests take different forms as presented in the following examples:

Directions: Select the one correct spelling in each line, and underscore the correct spelling:

houce	hous	house	howse
city	sity	citi	cite
beleeve	believe	believ	beleive

Directions: Underline the correct words in the following sentence:

Temperature is measured with (a barometer, an anemometer, a speedometer, a thermometer)

Directions: Draw a line under the right ending for the sentence:

Beavers build their homes near the water
near a town
near the highway
near the mountains

Directions: Place an X before the best reason why the summers of Colorado are cooler than those of Kansas:

Much of the state has an elevation of at least 5,000 feet above sea level.
The prevailing winds blow from the west.
Colorado is on the fortieth parallel.
Colorado is in the West.

When preparing multiple-choice questions, the correct answer should not always occupy the same position (for example, third in the possible choices), nor should the location of it follow any consecutive pattern, such as fifth, fourth, third, and so on.

Matching items. Matching tests are not difficult to construct and are used to measure ability to see relationships, associate ideas, and understand concepts of symbols, such as words, numbers, abbreviations. Items are arranged in groups of three or more and are matched with terms grouped in a second column. A form of matching test is the ranking or arrangement test in which a given number of items are ranked in the order of time of occurrence, merit, or in accordance with some other criterion. For example, the child may be instructed to: "Arrange, in the order of their happening, the following events by writing the number 1 after the one happening first, the number 2 after that happening next, and so on." Illustrations of matching tests are given below:

Directions: Draw a line from the word to the picture that matches it.

House

Tree

Ball

Directions: Draw a line from the word in Column 1 to the word having an opposite meaning in Column 2.

1	2
right	sour
black	sad
sweet	left
happy	white

Directions: Write in the blank before each inventor the number which corresponds with his invention.

1. telephone   _____Edison
2. electric lamp   _____Morse
3. telegraph   _____Bell

Completion items. The completion item consists of a statement from which one or more key words have been omitted and enough data given to designate what is wanted. The child is asked to fill in the blanks with the correct words as indicated in the following items.

1. Cirrus clouds are composed of _____ particles.
2. Clouds are formed whenever there is _____ in the air.

Directions: Fill in the blanks with N, NE, S, SE, SW, W, etc.

1. Chicago is _____ of Detroit.
2. Philadelphia is _____ of New York City.
3. San Francisco is _____ of Denver.

The completion test exercise has one prominent advantage as compared with certain other types of objective examinations: it tends to keep guesswork at a minimum and calls for recall rather than merely for recognition of correct answers. But, as usually employed, it may not be entirely objective, because it may call for subjective judgment. It is also likely to encourage learning of exact wordings of statements rather than of the content of ideas.

Unless the items making up the test are chosen skilfully, they are likely to be somewhat indefinite, permit of more than one correct answer, or furnish insufficient data to stimulate the pupil to the correct response, even if he knows it. These pitfalls should be kept in mind when a completion test or check is being constructed.

In selecting completion exercises, care must be taken to leave only *key* words blank, and to furnish, in the portion of statement given, enough data to constitute a fair test—that is, to designate what is wanted. If this is not done effectively, the test may degenerate into a guessing contest.

Enumeration items. Many teachers have found enumerative exercises convenient and a fairly valid measure of certain types of educational growth. The weakness of enumerative exercises is that they may lack somewhat in objectivity particularly if they are of the evaluative or judgment type such as: Name the three principal causes of the War between the States; Name the five most important advantages of living in a democratic society; or, What do you think are the six most important foods to eat or drink in a balanced diet?

In an enumeration test one should attempt to formulate exercises which require a minimum of writing and for which there is only one correct answer, or at least exercises which will permit little difference in scoring between different teachers. Ordinarily it is better to avoid using exercises in the scoring of which it would be necessary to give partial credit for some answers.

Essay tests

The "essay" types of test materials possess certain limitations and weaknesses as well as unique value. Only a few essay items can be included in an examination; therefore the items should be selected with very great care in order to constitute a good sample of all the growth the test is intended to measure. Essay questions are often open to misinterpretation. Because of the small number of essay questions in any given examination, to misunderstand what is called for and write an answer to a question wrongly interpreted may result in a total test score which is a very misleading measure of the learner's status or growth.

In answering essay questions, children are likely to consume too much time in writing, wander from the main idea, and distribute their time unwisely. Marks in essay tests are quite likely to be measures of composition—of ability to interpret questions, write concisely, and distribute time wisely. These may not be the outcomes which the instructor has been attempting to achieve.

One of the most important ways to increase the objectivity, and hence the reliability and functional validity, of an essay test is to prepare for each question in advance an answer key covering all the more important points which an excellent or nearly perfect answer would include. With the key prepared carefully in advance, the teacher can then score each paper on a relatively objective basis, giving credit in proportion to the number of points adequately treated in the pupil's answer. Before starting to score the paper the teacher will find it useful to prescore answers of a few papers on each question, with a view to testing out his key. Frequently the key is revised after reading a few answers. Many teachers find it useful to provide some scale of points for evaluating qualities of answers such as allowing 3 for a nearly perfect answer, 2 for fairly good answers on the more important points, 2 for nearly perfect answers on all but one or two important points, and 1 for partial answers on less important points.

There is a great variation in the reliability and validity of essay examinations. Their quality depends very largely upon the amount of attention and skill devoted to application of the following principles and suggestions.

1. Be specific and clear in stating the topic and the instructions for dealing with it; for example, if learners are asked to "criticize" they should be told upon what basis or with respect to what. Frequently there should be subordinate or supplementing instructions, as in the following:

    Discuss farming in the lowlands of southern California with particular reference to the farmer's dependence on irrigation, to the irrigated crops that are grown there, and to the changes brought about in farming as a result of improved farming equipment.

    Rarely if ever should pupils be asked to "tell what you know about..."

2. State each question or make each statement so as to measure something besides recall of information, i.e., understanding of the information, its importance, its implications, etc.
3. Estimate the time required by a slow pupil to write out an excellent answer to the question and indicate that amount of time in parentheses after the question.
4. Attempt to keep at a minimum the time required for writing answers. It is of great value in essay examinations to call for short, concise answers so that more questions may be asked.
5. Prepare questions which will permit objective scoring as far as possible. Questions so planned can be scored against an inventory of the parts required in a perfect answer.

Standard achievement tests

The word "standardized" or "standard" as used in the phrase standard achievement tests indicates that it has been given at a considerable number of schools and that norms or average scores have been computed on the basis of test papers of a very large number of students from a large number of representative schools. Standard achievement tests are usually to be obtained only from commercial publishers. Among the principal publishers of standard tests of various kinds including achievement tests, prognostic tests, and personality tests, are the following from which catalogues may be obtained:

Benjamin A. Sanborn & Co., Chicago.
California Test Bureau, Los Angeles.
Educational Test Bureau, Educational Publishers, Inc., Minneapolis.
C. A. Gregory Co., Cincinnati, Ohio.
Houghton Mifflin Co., Boston.
Public School Publishing Co., Bloomington, Illinois.
World Book Co., Yonkers, N.Y.
Science Research Associates, Chicago.
Educational Test Service, Princeton, N.J.
Teachers College, Bureau of Publications, Columbia University, New York.
Bureau of Educational Research and Service, State University of Iowa, Iowa City.
Bureau of Educational Research and Service, Kansas State Teachers College, Emporia, Kansas.

Teachers using standardized achievement tests should use tests having equivalent forms. One form may be used in the fall in order to establish the basal evaluation; then by giving another form later comparisons may be drawn, thus making it possible for the child to see his progress in an objective way. By translating the raw scores into meaningful terms, such as age norms, percentiles, reading age, educational age, accomplishment quotient (depending on the construction of the test, the information of which will be conveyed to the teacher by means of the instruction sheet which accompanies every test), the teacher and child will detect those areas in which the children are low and high. If a child scores one or more years below grade and if his mental age is one or more years below the mental age to master the work, the work is too difficult for him.

QUESTIONS, PROBLEMS, AND EXERCISES

1. Explain why it is desirable to change the emphasis from measurement of learning to evaluation of learning.

2. Prepare a ten-minute talk on "The place tests and measurements in an evaluation program of learning."

3. Why is it important to evaluate growth in attitudes, appreciations, and social adjustment?

4. Clarify the following terms: educational age, intelligence quotient, chronological age, grade score, norm, reading age.

5. Prepare a five-minute talk on "The weaknesses of an intelligence test."

6. Select a good standardized achievement test at the primary level or the intermediate grade level. Give the test and interpret the results.

7. Outline a thorough medical inspection program for elementary school children.

8. Examine recent newspapers and magazines to determine the emphasis given to health topics.

9. Make a survey of available health agencies in your community in order to locate particular agencies.

SELECTED SUPPLEMENTARY READINGS

ADAMS, FAY. *Educating America's Children.* New York: The Ronald Press Co., 1954.

Chap. 6, "Evaluation: A Basic Tool in Pupil Guidance." Many types of evaluation techniques are given, many with excellent diagrams of pupil profiles, test record data, check lists, etc

BURR, JAMES B., LOWRY W. HARDING, and LELAND B. JACOBS. *Student Teaching in the Elementary School.* New York: Appleton-Century-Crofts, Inc., 1950.

Chap. viii, "Evaluating Your Work." This chapter contains a very fine section on evaluation by the student teacher. The practical aspects of evaluation are also discussed in this chapter.

CANTOR, NATHANIEL. "Measurement and the Quality of Learning," *The Teaching Learning Process.* New York: The Dryden Press, Inc., 1953. Pp. 198-221.

The how, what and why of evaluation, together with special emphasis on self-evaluation.

MICHAELIS, JOHN U. *The Student Teacher in the Elementary School.* Englewood Cliffs, N.J.: Prentice-Hall, Inc., 1953.

Chap. 12, "Evaluation of Children's Learning," describes nine guiding principles for evaluating pupil activities and is especially helpful in giving suggestions on the use of tests in the classroom.

MIEL, ALICE and ASSOCIATES. "Evaluating Group Processes and Achievements," *Cooperative Procedures in Learning.* New York: Bureau of Publications, Teachers College, Columbia University, 1952. Pp. 232-53.

Contains sections on how group plans work out, evaluating as a step in improving plans, taking stock periodically and a unique section on pupil participation in reports to parents.

MUDD, DOROTHY. "A Core Program Uses Evaluations," *Educational Leadership,* 8 (November, 1950), pp. 82-86.

Describes how one school attempted to evaluate behavior among school children.

SHANE, HAROLD G., and E. T. McSWAIN. *Evaluation and the Elementary Curriculum.* New York: Henry Holt & Co., Inc., 1951.

Chap. iii is especially helpful in defining the nature of evaluation and in showing its function in improving elementary education. Good annotated bibliography.

WILES, KIMBALL. *Teaching for Better Schools.* Englewood Cliffs, N.J.: Prentice-Hall, Inc., 1952.

Chap. ix discusses marks and evaluation, with a summary of specific suggestions essential to effective evaluation. Chap. x outlines specific techniques of evaluation.

WINGO, G. MAX, and RALEIGH SCHORLING. *Elementary-School Student Teaching.* 2d ed. New York: McGraw-Hill Book Co., Inc., 1955.

Chap. xiv, "The Broader Concept of Appraisal." Pupil-teacher role in appraisal techniques and reporting to parents are presented, as well as a very fine checklist for appraising the teacher's activity in the classroom.

20

RECORDING AND REPORTING PUPIL GROWTH

Modern programs of evaluating the growth of pupils now include many other measuring devices than the daily class mark and the written test. Furthermore, an increasing number of teachers now attempt to evaluate the degree of acquisition of learning activities such as understanding, attitudes, and mental and social skills. With this extension of measuring instruments and procedures and areas of measurement, new problems have arisen in how to record and report the total growth of the child.

MARKING SYSTEMS

Recent years have seen decreasing emphasis on marks as such. Educators have come to realize the bad effects of marks on some children and some parents. Less importance is being attached to the possibility of motivating effort by the use of traditional marking systems. Yet there remains the necessity for making assessment of pupils' growth in terms that will be meaningful to them and to their parents. And the school must have records of such assessments if the child is to be aided in his growth.

Literal system

The percentage system of marking is rapidly disappearing from American schools. Although a numerical system is used in scoring objective tests, it is almost impossible to report total growth, or even achievement, in such precise terms. In an attempt to do away with the impossibly fine distinctions required by the percentage system, most schools have devised a five-point literal system, with the interval between two points on a scale designated by a letter. Many literal systems are mere modifications of the percentage system; A equals 90 to 100, and B 80 to 89. More satisfactory is the system in which A represents superior work, B good work, C average achievement, D poor work, and F failure.

A clear understanding on the part of teachers of what the different letters represent will serve to decrease the variability of teachers' marks. Even so, a mark of A given by one teacher may be in respect to the quality and quantity of work the equivalent of a mark of B given by another teacher in the same school. Studies of marks given by teachers in the same school are almost certain to reveal that one teacher is very likely to give a small number of A's and a large number of D's, while another teacher gives a large number of A's and very few F's. This difference in the teachers' standards is very confusing and misleading to students and parents as well as to people making investigations of school problems in which marks are used as measures of educational status or educational growth.

A number of schools have adopted use of only two marks—U for unsatisfactory and S for satisfactory. This practice has not proved too successful, for many parents, quite rightly, want to know much more about their children's growth than merely a mark of "satisfactory" or "unsatisfactory." There is also great variation as to whether "satisfactory" means satisfactory in terms of a student's ability, or satisfactory in comparison with absolute or relative standards of achievement. In a great many schools in which the "U" and "S" system has been adopted without adequate supplementary marking and reporting, it has been discarded after a brief trial and protests by parents. Most of the schools where the system has persisted employ a third mark—H for honor. Under any circumstances, however, the use of only two or three categories for marks results in the necessity for more supplementary reporting.

Normal distribution

As deficiencies in the conventional marking systems have become more apparent because of the application of scientific methods to school measurement, new systems of recording pupil achievement have been suggested. A system based upon the normal distribution or normal probability curve has been adopted by a number of schools, some of which have subsequently discarded it.

The theory of probability is based upon the results of observations of the traits of large numbers of unselected human beings. These

observations reveal that in the measurement of any trait, the subjects are distributed by chance according to Figure 3.

It will be observed that a large number of cases cluster around the
average and a steadily decreasing number are found as the extremes
are approached.   Since the results of accurate measures of the school
achievement of unselected groups of children tend to be distributed
according to the normal probability curve, it seems logical to make
a comparable distribution of marks.

While no mathematical formula will indicate the *exact* number of
pupils who should receive A, B, C, D, or F, the normal distribution
curve provides a means of ascertaining the approximate expectan-
cies for the occurrence of each mark although the number of A's and
the number of B's, may be decided more or less arbitrarily.   In
general, a small number of A's and F's are given, a somewhat larger
number of B's and D's, and a still larger number of C's.

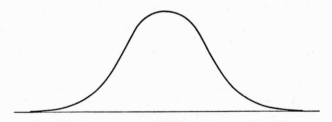

Figure 3.   The Normal Probability Curve

The normal distribution curve is sound precisely only in situations
in which there are a very large number of cases.   Hence the distribution of the marks of a small class into exact percentages as suggested by the curve is subject to a large error.   Similar divisions of
the marks of large classes are likewise liable to error.   The fact that
classes deviate from the normal injects another biasing factor into
the situation.   Some classes may have a large number of superior
students in them, whereas another class may have a disproportionate number of poor students.   In regard to the amount of deviation,
the teacher can verify his own judgment by the use of standardized
achievement tests.   However, the validity of standardized achievement test scores may not be great with respect to all of the objectives of the course or of educational growth.

It is extremely important for the teacher to understand that in the
use of the normal curve as a basis of marking it is not necessary to
give the mark of failure to any student or to any exact percentage

of the class. Neither is it likely, using a five-point marking system, that any exact percentages of the students, or for that matter any student, in a given class will receive a mark of A.

Allowances should and can be made for variations arising from small samplings of students. Various plans have been proposed which give a certain degree of latitude within each interval including the following:

A	B	C	D	F
0—15%	20%—30%	30%—40%	20%—30%	0—15%

While strict adherence to the normal probability curve is undesirable in the allocation of marks, extreme flexibility should likewise be avoided. One of the chief values of this type of marking system is that it promotes greater uniformity in the distribution of marks among teachers within a school. Preconceived ideas cause some teachers to consider all pupils in their classes as inferior or as superior. This bias is often revealed in the assignment of a large number of either high or low marks by a teacher over a period of years. Accurate evaluation of the achievement of a large number of classes, having a total enrollment of several hundred students, will very closely approach a normal distribution of marks. In most schools, intelligence tests scores of all the pupils are available. These scores provide a sound check on the teacher's judgment in regard to the extent to which a class deviates from the normal.

Despite the difficulties involved in the proper use of this type of marking system, it possesses certain distinct values which may be summarized as follows.

1. It serves to prevent misunderstandings among the teachers in regard to marks.
2. It affords a more satisfactory basis for an understanding of the meaning of school marks by pupils and their parents.
3. It provides marks of greater significance for guidance and other educational uses, since the subjective elements in marking are reduced.

Effective use of the system serves to minimize the opportunity of the teacher who wishes to establish a reputation for high standards by giving an unreasonable number of low marks. Likewise restrained is the teacher who appears oblivious of accepted standards to the extent of giving unearned high marks to students in order to win their approval. The pupils and schools deserve to be protected from both these types of teachers.

Achievement and potentiality

Increasingly there has been a trend to attempt to evaluate a child's achievement in relation to his capacity. Indeed in some schools marks put on report cards and sent home to parents are based on the ratio of achievement to supposed potentiality. For example, an A might be made by a student with a low I.Q. and average achievement, while a D might be made by a youngster who has a high I.Q. and a mediocre achievement.

While much may be said of its advantages, there are several limitations to determining marks on the basis of ratio of achievement to potentiality:

1. It is very difficult to determine with any degree of accuracy the potentiality or possible achievement of any individual youngster in any field.
2. Parents insist upon what they believe to be absolute marks rather than ratios or relative marks.
3. For the purposes of investigation and for the needs of colleges and prospective employers, marks in terms of achievement rather than in terms of ratio of achievement to capacity need to be used ordinarily.

In some schools both absolute marks and marks of achievement which are based upon achievement in relation to the learner's potentialities are sent to parents. Relative achievement is made the basis of encouragement, commendations, and criticisms of youngsters by teachers, and in discussions with parents about the work the youngsters are doing in the schools.

RECORDS

Today there are certain very important trends and newer practices in respect to school records. Among the most important may be mentioned the following:

1. Phrases and sentences are employed instead of letters and numbers to indicate the quality of growth or status.
2. More comprehensive records are employed including records of many things other than school achievement and school citizenship, for example, various aspects of personality, status and growth, social adjustment, health and citizenship.
3. Modern class record books do not have little squares in which a teacher records a numerical grade, but they have larger spaces in which descriptive accounts may be written.

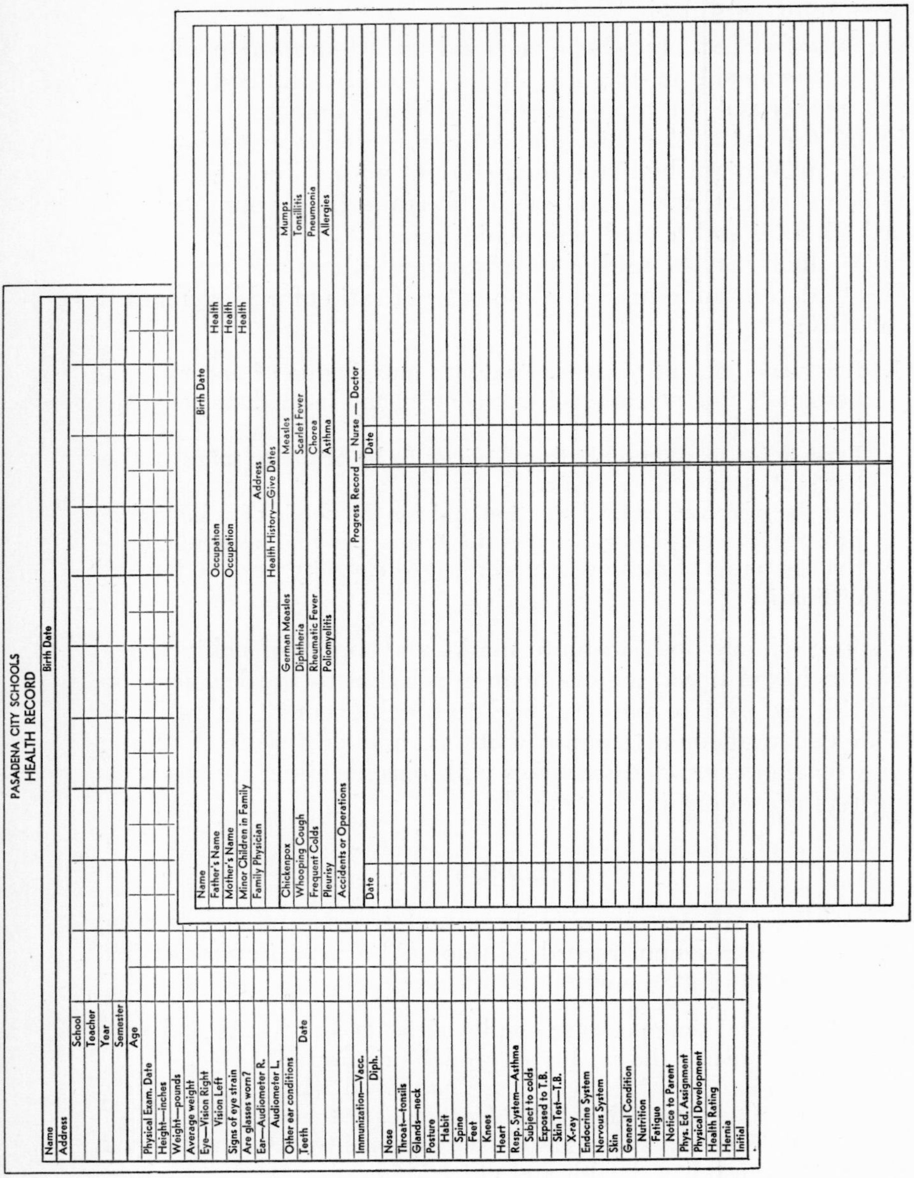

PASADENA CITY SCHOOLS
HEALTH RECORD

Name
Address

| School |
| Teacher |
| Year |
| Semester |
| Age |

Physical Exam. Date
Height—inches
Weight—pounds
Average weight
Eye—Vision Right
Eye—Vision Left
Signs of eye strain
Are glasses worn?
Ear—Audiometer R.
Ear—Audiometer L.
Other ear conditions
Teeth ... Date
Nose
Throat—tonsils
Glands—neck
Posture
Habit
Spine
Feet
Knees
Heart
Resp. System—Asthma
Subject to colds
Exposed to T.B.
Skin Test—T.B.
X-ray
Endocrine System
Nervous System
Skin
General Condition
Nutrition
Fatigue
Notice to Parent
Phys. Ed. Assignment
Physical Development
Health Rating
Hernia
Initial

Immunization—Vacc.
Diph.

Birth Date

Name
Father's Name ... Occupation ... Birth Date ... Health
Mother's Name ... Occupation ... Health
Minor Children in Family ... Health
Family Physician ... Address

Health History—Give Dates

Chickenpox	German Measles	Measles	Mumps
Whooping Cough	Diphtheria	Scarlet Fever	Tonsillitis
Frequent Colds	Rheumatic Fever	Chorea	Pneumonia
Pleurisy	Poliomyelitis	Asthma	Allergies

Accidents or Operations

Progress Record — Nurse — Doctor

Date ... Date

Figure 4. Health Record Card

4. Graphs are used to present a picture of the child's growth.
5. Anecdotal records reveal what the child has done or said.
6. Cumulative records show the child's developmental pattern.

These records are constructed cooperatively by the teacher, parents, and children—the teacher giving information pertaining to the child's patterns of behavior in school; parents presenting information pertaining to the home life of the child; and the children assisting in setting up goals of accomplishment against which they evaluate their behavior patterns.

The schools are concerned with the problem of devising new record forms which describe child growth and which record information obtained by means of the new evaluative techniques. The new record forms are assuming the characteristic of objectivity, thus making it possible for any one who reads the record to understand the information which is recorded. The forms of the records are simple. The mechanics of keeping the record should not take too much time, but must be sufficiently complete to be of practical value to the teacher.

Health record

Many classroom teachers are expected to assume the major responsibility in making observations pertaining to the health of the child, in checking periodically on such factors as weight, in administering screening tests in hearing and vision, and in keeping the records up to date. Schools use various types of health records—a separate health card, a part of permanent record card, or an anecdotal record. One health record (Figure 4) is presented in order to show specifically the information which is generally requested.

Achievement profile

An achievement profile represents the status of a child in various areas of learnings. An achievement profile may show (1) years or months retarded or accelerated at a given period and/or (2) growth in terms of years or months obtained by comparing profiles of two tests given several months apart. Teachers and children often construct their own profiles and fit them to their specific problems which they wish to study. Of the following profiles one is based on a standardized achievement test and the other was constructed by a teacher. The Stanford Achievement Test profile (Figure 5) shows that George was ahead of his class in all subjects, especially in language, word meaning, and arithmetic computation, and that his weakest areas were paragraph meaning and arithmetic reasoning.

Elementary Battery   FORM J

STANFORD ACHIEVEMENT TEST

Name *George Jensen*   Age *9*   Grade *4*   Boy or girl *B*

Teacher *J. Kelley*   School *Whittier*   Date of birth *1949 Nov. 16*
                                                                 Year   Month   Day

City or Town *Marshalltown*   State *New York*   Date *October, 1958*

	1 PAR. MEAN.	2 WORD MEAN.	AVER. READ.	3 SPELL.	4 LANG.	5 ARITH. REAS.	6 ARITH. COMP.	AVER. ARITH.	BATTERY MEDIAN
Grade Equiv.	4.4	5.0	4.8	4.8	5.3	4.5	5.0	4.8	4.8
Age Equiv.	9-5	10-0	9-10	9-10	10-4	9-6	10-0	9-10	9-10
%-ile Rank									

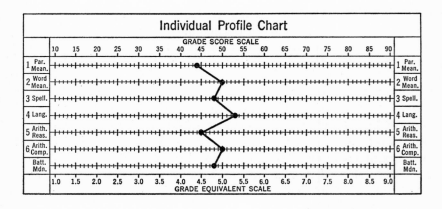

Issued 1953 by World Book Company, Yonkers-on-Hudson, New York, and Chicago, Illinois
Copyright 1952 by World Book Company. Copyright in Great Britain. All rights reserved.
PRINTED IN U.S.A.   SAT.: ELEM.: J-8

Figure 5. Stanford Achievement Test

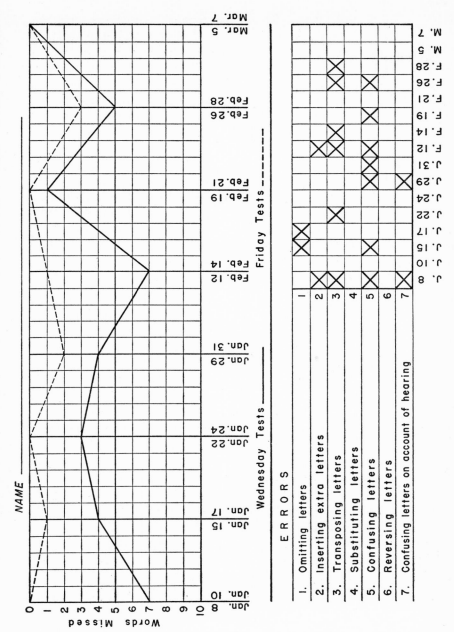

Figure 6. Evaluation of Spelling Ability

The spelling profile (Figure 6), taken from a teacher's records, shows number of words missed on Wednesday's and Friday's tests with type of errors made on each test. By knowing the type of errors made, it was possible for the child to direct his study efforts in order to remove spelling errors. In comparing the profiles, it is evident that the child improved as a result of study on Thursday. It is also shown that the number of types of errors is decreasing gradually.

Sociogram

Data can be obtained in regard to the status of the individual in different roles in the group by constructing a sociogram based upon the responses to questions pertaining to various matters. For example, an individual may be chosen as the one with whom other children may wish to work but he may be rejected as the best friend. Since social status is not fixed, sociograms based upon different questions may reveal varying types of acceptance or rejection of an individual. Various degrees of social acceptance of an individual in regard to the same matter may be ascertained by asking the members of a group to express first, second, and third choices: write the names of your *best* friend, the name of your *next best* friend, and the name of your *third best* friend.

One way to construct a sociogram is as follows: First, write the name of each pupil on a piece of paper. The name of each girl is usually encircled while the name of each boy is usually placed in a rectangle. (See Figure 1, Chapter 3, page 45.) The response of each pupil is indicated by an arrow drawn to the name of the classmate or classmates chosen. If more than one choice is requested, the different choices of each child may be indicated by the use of differently colored ink (or pencil) or by solid lines for first choices, broken lines for second choices, and dotted lines for third choices. Mutual choices of pupils may be indicated by lines with arrows at both ends drawn between the names of two children. Many teachers construct sociograms of their classes at the beginning of the school year. The children whom the sociogram reveals are not accepted by the class (usually designated as isolates) are assisted by the teacher in more effective participation in the activities of the class. If the presence of cliques within the class is revealed by the sociogram, wider participation by members of the clique in activities involving the whole class is encouraged. Near the end of the school year another sociogram of the class can be constructed to reveal the progress in social relationships made during the year.

Anecdotal record

The anecdotal record, sometimes called the journal record, is a record of anecdotes which recount a student's behavior and therefore indicate his status or growth in respect to some trait or achievement. In many schools the single anecdote is not considered to be of great validity and a cumulative record is kept in which teachers record a series of anecdotal and other records concerning positive and negative behavior patterns of children in varying situations and in different activities over a certain period of time with the date of each incident. These records may contain information pertaining to activities in and out of school, such as observations of behavior patterns; accurate accounts of statements made by children either orally or in written work; contributions made to work or play activities; responsibilities assumed; creative accomplishments in art and music. In order to avoid self-consciousness on the part of the individual for whom a record is being kept, no recording should be done in his presence. All entries must be made as soon as possible in order to avoid omitting important items which might be forgotten. A place may be provided on the record for interpretive data and suggested recommendations. Since the characteristics and an illustrative example of a good anecdotal record have been presented on pages 41–42, it will not be necessary to discuss them at this point. Only important information should be recorded on the record. The following incomplete record illustrates one type of journal record of a child who was a reading problem.

Name of Child			
Date	Activity	Accomplishment	Behavior Modified by
Jan. 27	Group reading	Read poorly	Not interested
Jan. 28	Silent reading	Sat and dreamed	Not interested
Jan. 30	Silent reading	Very little done	"I don't want to"
Feb. 4	Group reading	None	Inattentive
Feb. 6	Individual reading	Read well, enjoyed reading	Individual attention received
Mar. 5	Group reading	Contribution based on own efforts	Interested in sharing information

Cumulative record

Permanent records are a summary of the child's growth from year to year and show the progress which he is making as he matures. These records usually contain the following information: health rec-

| 1A | Name—(Last-First-Middle) | | | | | | Birth Date | |

FAMILY RECORD (To be entered whenever change occurs)

3	Date					
4	Family Status					
5	Occupation of Father					
6	Occupation of Mother					
7	Number of Children					
8	Position of Child					
9	Comments					
10	Teacher's Signature					

SPEECH AND READING DISABILITIES

	Date	Explanation
11		
12		
13		
14		
15		
16		
17		
18		

	Date	REMARKS ON MENTAL AND PHYSICAL HEALTH	HEALTH RECORD—YEARLY RE
19			Date
20			Height
21			Weight
22			Orthopedic
23			Posture
24			Nutrition
25			Anemia
26			Uncleanliness
27			Skin
28			Speech
29			Mouth Breathing
30			Nasal
31			Tonsils
32			Adenoids
33			Thyroid

34	Mother's Health		Home Conditions		Measles		Mumps
35	Father's Health				Scarlet Fever		Smallpox
36	Child's Health				Influenza		Tonsilitis
37	Operations						
38							

| 39 | Date—First Enrollment | School | Grade | Last School Attended (If from another system) | City |

| 40 | Father | Birthplace | Mother | |

| 1 | Name—(Last—First—Middle) | Birthdate | Sex | Race |

Figure 7. School Record Card

400

Sex	Race	Change in Name

ADDRESS—WITHDRAWALS—READMISSIONS

Date	Address or Reason for Withdrawal	School

Comments

PORT

HEALTH RECORD—YEARLY REPORT

Glands	
Teeth	
Hearing Ear Disease	
Vision (c)	
Vision (s) Eye Disease	
Headache	
Respiratory	
Cardiac	
Nervous	
T.B. Signs Acute Illness	
Habits	

Whooping Cough	Chicken Pox	Rheumatism
Diphtheria	Pneumonia	Date-Vaccination
Bronchitis	Poliomyelitis	Date-Diph Immun

FAMILY PHYSICIAN

State	Religion	Transcripts Mailed

Birthplace	Language Spoken—Home	Guardian—Name	Card 2 Made

Birthplace	Address (Use Pencil)
	Duluth Public Schools—Form 14A

Used in Duluth Public Schools (*face*).

401

| 41A | Name—(Last-First-Middle) | | | | Father | | | | |

Form 14B

ELEMENTARY GRADES (Kindergarten—One—Two—Three—Four)

_42_	Year
_43_	Grade
_44_	Schools

| _45_ | Days Attended | | | | | | | | | |
| 46 | Absent—Tardy | Abs. | | Tardy | | Abs. | | Tardy | | Abs. | | Tardy |

		SUBJECT	S.T.	Av.	SUBJECT	S.T.	Av.	SUBJECT		
_47_	Marks in School	Reading Readiness			Reading			Reading		
_48_	Subjects	English			English			English		
_49_	and				Spelling			Spelling		
_50_	Standardized	Numbers			Arithmetic			Arithmetic		
_51_	Achievement	Social Studies			Social Studies			Social Studies		
_52_	Tests	Natural Science			Natural Science			Natural Science		
_53_										
_54_					Penmanship			Penmanship		
_55_		Art			Art			Art		
_56_		Music			Music			Music		
57		Rhythms			Physical Education			Physical Education		

		NAME	Date	CA	MA	IQ	NAME	Date	CA	MA	IQ	NAME	Date	CA
_58_	School Ability													
59	Tests													

		Gr.	TEST		Date	Gr E	Gr.	TEST		Date	Gr E	Gr.	TEST	
_60_	Educational													
_61_	Tests—													
_62_	Standardized													
_63_														
64														

_65_	SOCIAL	POSITIVE	1-Adaptable	3-Aggressive	5-Conformist	7-Cooperative	9-Courteous	11-Dependable
_66_	QUALITIES	NEGATIVE	2-Stubborn	4-Retiring	6-Individualist	8-Uncooperative	10-Rude	12-Errotic

_67_	Social Qualities Rating			
_68_	Individual Development			
_69_	Special Abilities and Interests			
_70_	Personality Assets			
_71_	Needs Help With			
_72_	Behavior Modified By			
_73_	Referred to			
_74_	Teacher's Signature			
_41_	Name		Father	

Figure 8. School Record Card Used in

Mother				Birthdate			Sex		Race	

Abs.		Tardy		Abs.		Tardy		Abs.		Tardy	

S. T.	Av.	SUBJECT		S. T.	Av.	SUBJECT		S. T.	Av.	SUBJECT		S. T.	Av.
		Reading				Reading				Reading			
		English				English				English			
		Spelling				Spelling				Spelling			
		Arithmetic				Arithmetic				Arithmetic			
		Social Studies				Social Studies				Social Studies			
		Natural Science				Natural Science				Natural Science			
		Penmanship				Penmanship				Penmanship			
		Art				Art				Art			
		Music				Music				Music			
		Physical Education				Physical Education				Physical Education			

MA	IQ	NAME	Date	CA	MA	IQ	NAME	Date	CA	MA	IQ	NAME	Date	CA	MA	IQ

Date	Gr E	Gr.	TEST		Date	Gr E	Gr.	TEST		Date	Gr E	Gr.	TEST		Date	Gr E

13-Diplomatic	15-Friendly	17-Industrious	19-Leadership	21-Obedient	23-Respectful	25-Self-confident	27 Self-controlled
14-Tactless	16-Aloof	18-Lazy	20-Followership	22-Disobedient	24-Disrespectful	26-Timid	28-Uncontrolled

Mother		Address (Use Pencil)		Phone	

Duluth Public Schools (*reverse*).

ord, interests, scores made on achievement and intelligence tests, social qualities, frequently a profile. These records are usually recorded on cardboard or in booklets and are filed in the superintendent's or principal's offices. Figures 7 and 8 present a permanent cumulative record form.

In order to discern the growth pattern of a child, it is essential that a record of his development be kept over a period of years by the teachers under whose guidance the child happens to be at a specific time. Each teacher should study the previous records and add to the records. Information which is filed in cumulative folders should include the following: health record, achievement profiles and achievement test results, typical art work, records of daily work, teacher-made tests which have been taken by the child, individual sociograms, anecdotal records, questionnaires filled in by parents and children, records of conferences with children and parents.

An increasing number of teachers are following the practice of making and placing in the cumulative record folder brief informal notes about the behavior of youngsters which would give some indication of weaknesses of personality, social adjustment, clear thinking, emotional stability, character and citizenship, and other such characteristics, as well as of important changes for better or worse in the behavior of the youngster in these areas. A number of such comments may be very revealing as to what is going on in the growth of the individual child in these areas. This, of course, is not done for every child but only those who seem to have somewhat unusual behavior of which a record should be made.

A manila folder may be used to accumulate the information and can be filed in a wooden box made by manual training classes or in a box obtained from a merchant. Since the folders are likely to become bulky and difficult to manage, they should be "weeded out" several times during the year. At this time the teacher should summarize the information in a descriptive statement which tells about the child in various areas of learning and social activities. Cumulative records must be adjusted to fit each school system as school systems vary in regard to administrative policies, type of curriculum used, evaluative techniques used, and content that goes into the folder.

Since records include both positive and negative data, it is imperative that every teacher use the information professionally and should not permit herself to be prejudiced toward any child. In every record there also will be data which will reveal the worth of each individual. These cumulative folders should be passed on with the youngster to the teacher who will have him the next year.

REPORTING TO PARENTS

It is important to send reports to parents in order to (1) obtain parent cooperation and understanding of instructional goals and general principles of procedure; (2) motivate the children to greater and more intense learning activities; to (3) inform the parents of the child's status, improvement, and growth in school subjects and other important areas of education growth; and to (4) assist the pupils in self-evaluation of their status and growth to their school subjects and other important areas.

Trends in reporting

As records change and take into account the fact that the whole child goes to school, reports to parents should also stress the fact that the child is growing as a "whole." The traditional card with its marks of 70, 95, or A, B, C on subjects and other marks or ratings on a limited number of specific points of education and citizenship gives very little indication of the type of broad behavior patterns that are being developed or whether the child is growing according to his level of ability.

Report cards have been deservedly criticized for not being accurate records of pupil growth. This criticism is the result in part of the limitations of the traditional marking systems. It is also objected that teachers tend to allow good or bad behavior, personal likes and dislikes, personal appearance, "apple-polishing," and other extraneous influences to affect the marks. Some of the main limitations of the traditional report card are:

1. The temptation to use marking as a device to coerce children into doing better work
2. Probability of unsatisfactory competitive comparisons by parents and children
3. Misunderstandings of objectives of the school and of education in general on the part of parents
4. Concern of children with the grade rather than with the desire to improve and to grow in the acquisition of knowledges and understanding of all types of learnings
5. Tendency to overemphasize memorization of facts
6. Possibility of discouraging child who receives low grades to point of giving up trying
7. Probability of developing undesirable attitudes, such as superiority complexes, selfish pride, or snobbery, of children who receive high grades
8. Encouragement of resort to undesirable means of securing information by cheating or lying

There is a growing belief that parents are entitled to a much fuller report about the growth of their children than the mere marking of letters or numbers on report cards. There has also been a definite trend in the direction of reporting through letters, telephone conversations, and interviews with parents at school or at home. Another trend is that of having reports to parents made at various times during the year, rather than reports to all parents made at certain stated intervals such as at the end of every six weeks. In fact, in some schools the teacher makes it a point to report to several parents each week, the parents being chosen on the basis of those to whom reports would seem to be more appropriate in view of the student's growth or lack of growth. Each parent gets at least one report each semester.

In recent years reports to parents have become much more comprehensive. They now commonly include such matters as citizenship in various situations, social adjustment with other youngsters, emotional balance or behavior, degree of interests, initiative, creative work, cooperation or lack of cooperation, ethics and other ideals, etc. Experience with this type of reporting indicates that it is not always satisfactory to have a list of traits on a report card and with a grade comment made at every reported period. Some reporting periods offer insufficient basis for making any remark at all on some traits. Indeed, it is better for a teacher to have a list of traits before her which has been worked out by the teachers of the school and to report only on those traits on which she has something definite to report. There should be sufficient room on report cards so that something more than a mere mark may be made on one or more of the traits.

Types and forms of reporting

Illustrative of the types of information which may be given to parents is the following report on the work of a third-grade boy during his third month in a new school.[1]

Sam has a fine quality of honesty in dealing with himself and with others. It helps him meet problems squarely. He is coming to find his place in the group. He is showing some willingness to allow others their turns and to act, himself, as follower at times as well as to take leadership.

He seems to be happy and he is much more willing to accept suggestions.

Sam can work quite independently. He can stick to a piece of work until it is finished. He plans and he can work by these plans.

[1] Kimball Wiles, *Teaching for Better Schools* (Englewood Cliffs, N.J.: Prentice-Hall, Inc., 1952), pp. 232-34.

He is not particularly thrifty nor does he show much concern about caring for materials. However, he will join a group which is caring for materials and do a moderate share of it willingly, if asked.

He has high standards for most types of work. He holds himself to these standards.

He is doing quite mature work in all subject matter. He reads well and avidly. He has wide interests.

There are days when arithmetic seems uninteresting to him until we get well into it; then he seems to forget he preferred something else and loses himself in trying out his skill.

He has a fine speaking vocabulary, expresses himself well, and enjoys sharing his experiences.

He has fine sense of drama and contributes richly to group situations of this nature.

He enjoys music as a usual thing. He is interested in sound production as well as in the music itself.

Sam has a very fine curiosity. He is alert and asks many highly intelligent questions. He is learning to use the library.

It is easy to see how much more such a report tells the parent than the typical report card.

A second report, sent home in the eighth month, stated:

Sam has continued his growth in reading ability, he knows all the addition facts, most of the subtraction facts, and several multiplication facts. He has a beginning understanding of multiplication. He is showing more interest and more carefulness in penmanship. Spelling seems to him quite unimportant and hardly worth the bother, since one can express ideas through other means. However, he works on spelling with his small group of closest friends when they try themselves out on it. He has written some good letters, one brief story, and directions for puppet plays.

He has grown in consideration of others. He is more willing to allow others their turns with tools, privileges, and play things.

Sam is deeply concerned about the war situation to the point of worrying about whether it is going "to get me when I get big." This has shown up in puppet plays, dramatizations, and paintings.

Written statements should be phrased so that the parents will understand reports of the child's progress. In writing appraisals—

1. Favorable comments should begin and close the letter.
2. Items pertaining to growth socially, physically, intellectually, and emotionally should be included.
3. Comparisons with child's own previous accomplishments should be made.
4. Evaluations should be made on the basis of child's ability.
5. Causes should be cited for nonprogress.
6. Suggestions should be included for home guidance, with comments that they may or may not work.

Pupil growth is evaluated (1) in school subjects and (2) in social relationships. The Teacher's estimate of your child's growth is recorded each quarter. The report is an individual one; it is not intended as a comparison of your child with another, or with the class.

GROWTH IN FUNDAMENTALS	FIRST QUARTER		SECOND QUARTER		THIRD QUARTER		FOURTH QUARTER	
	Satisfactory	Needs to Improve	Satisfactory	Needs to Improve	Satisfactory	Needs to Improve	Satisfactory	Needs to Improve
LANGUAGE ARTS								
Reading								
Comprehension								
Vocabulary								
Oral Reading								
Language								
Written expression								
Oral expression								
Spelling								
Required words								
Practical use								
Handwriting								
Directed lessons								
Practical use								
Listening								
SOCIAL STUDIES — SCIENCE								
Skill in gathering facts								
Skill in using facts								
Participation in group activities								
Growth in understandings								
ARITHMETIC								
Knowledge of number facts								
Skill in solving problems								
THE ARTS								
Participation in music								
Participation in art								
PHYSICAL EDUCATION								
Cooperation in organized games								
Use of free play								

Figure 9. Progress Report Form Used

A check is placed in the appropriate column each quarter, indicating satisfactory progress or a need for improvement on the part of your child. Spaces for teacher comments are provided on this form and, when necessary, on additional insert sheets. Parent-teacher conferences supplement the written report.

PROGRESS IN SOCIAL RELATIONSHIPS	FIRST QUARTER		SECOND QUARTER		THIRD QUARTER		FOURTH QUARTER	
	Satisfactory	Needs to Improve	Satisfactory	Needs to Improve	Satisfactory	Needs to Improve	Satisfactory	Needs to Improve
HEALTH HABITS								
Personal cleanliness								
Posture								
Observation of safety rules .								
SOCIAL HABITS								
Working independently . . .								
Working with others								
Finishing work undertaken . .								
Use of time								
Use of materials								
Responsibility								
Self-control								
Promptness								
Neatness								
Consideration of others . . .								
Respect for property								
GROWTH IN OTHER AREAS								

Your attention is called to:

SECOND QUARTER	FOURTH QUARTER

in Palo Alto, California, Public Schools.

It may be objected that it takes much time to write appraisals and that it is very difficult to convey information to parents through the written word. With large classes letters may become stereotyped; if they do, they would not justify the expending of time and effort by the teacher.

Ways and means of reporting the progress of children to parents through reports have taken several different forms. The Progress Report form used in the Palo Alto, California, schools (Figure 9), is a typical illustration of a new type of form for reporting to parents.

Change from traditional to modern reports

Two procedures may be followed in making a change from the traditional report card to the modern report. In the *evolutionary* method the change is made first from the numerical to the letter system. In the second stage of development the letter system is changed to U (unsatisfactory) and S (satisfactory) according to the ability of the child. The final step involves the use of statements indicating behavior patterns. The latter system may be confusing to parents and children. With each change, a program of parent education must be developed in order to obtain the approval of those who are interested in the school program. Constant changing is not conducive to satisfactory parent-teacher-pupil relationships.

Another approach is to make the change in an *experimental* way. In this program the traditional card is used in the majority of the grades and the new reporting system is used in one or two grades. A good place to start the new plan is in the primary grades. In this way a smaller percentage of the parents would be affected by the immediate change to the new plan and an interested curiosity might be aroused on the part of many who are not directly affected by the change. Then as the primary children advance in the grades, the new program can expand; over a period of six or eight years, the new methods of reporting will be accepted by the public without public relations being strained. The speed with which a new reporting system is introduced into a school system must be determined by the nature of the community, the personnel of the faculty, and the status of home-school relationships.

Reporting through parent conferences

Modern schools are stressing parent-teacher conferences as a means of reporting the child's progress. These conferences may be held on a certain afternoon during the week, or two entire days in each five- or six-week period may be devoted to the work. In order to have a satisfactory conference with a parent, it is essential that the teacher prepare for the meeting by becoming familiar with the child's cumulative record and by considering the following points:

1. Favorable behavior patterns, which should be reported first
2. Unfavorable behavior problems
3. Attendance record
4. Special difficulties in basic tools
5. Child's ability to do school work
6. Select parts of record which will be shown to parent
7. Study those phases in which the child is apt to make most improvement
8. The degree to which the child is achieving in terms of his capacity
9. Anticipate questions which the parent may ask and prepare answers to them

During the conference the teacher should not ask too many questions, but she should be an attentive and sympathetic listener and give suggestions and advice in a kind and tactful way. It is not advisable to take extensive notes, but after the parent has gone, the teacher should make a memorandum of major points discussed.

An increasing number of elementary school systems are providing for teachers' office hours, usually about once a week for an hour or an hour and a half. All parents are urged to feel free to come. In some instances parents are invited to come at a specific time to discuss the work, growth, achievements, and problems of their youngsters.

Furthermore, an increasing number of teachers in schools and school systems are providing for visits to the home. In addition to reporting to the parent, the home visit usually results in increased understanding on the part of the teacher of the home conditions of particular youngsters and of the home life and problems of youngsters and their parents in general. Furthermore, when skillfully done, home visitation may not only increase parents' understanding of the school—its objectives, its work, the particular class and pupil —but also improve their attitudes toward the school and the teacher.

It is very desirable for teachers to study individually and collectively the principles and techniques of conferences with parents, particularly conferences in the home. Sometimes at a series of meetings teachers who are especially skillful and experienced in these matters (or government employees who have had experience in home calling and home conferences) may be used to help teachers acquire skill in this type of activity.

Following is a list of ten helpful suggestions for conferences with parents.

1. Rarely begin a conference with complaints about the child. Try to find some good things to say. Have the parent realize that you are trying to help the child.
2. Cultivate a relationship of friendliness and helpfulness.
3. Do not try to cover too much. Each parent thinks in terms of his own experiences.
4. Try not to "out-talk" a parent.
5. Listen to what the parent has to say. Try to understand his point of view.
6. Avoid discussing other children and making comparisons with brother and sister.
7. Avoid arguments. Hear criticisms objectively and make or receive suggestions for solutions.
8. Never repeat any matter of a personal nature to other persons, except when it is necessary professionally. Conferences are confidential school activities.
9. Accept and respect the personality of the parent.
10. Be completely honest in matters of fact. Look forward to each conference. Expect it to be interesting, pleasant, and a new adventure in understanding parents.

Reporting class activities

An increasing number of teachers, particularly those in the primary grades, send to the home of their pupils several times a year a summary of the more important activities in which all members of the class have been engaged.

An example of such a report follows:[2]

Dear Mother and Daddy:
I have been in kindergarten 45 days.

I have enjoyed learning:

    16 finger plays
    18 songs
    17 stories
    22 games

I know my way to:

    The school cafeteria
    The bus garage
    The school office

We have been learning to use:
    Easel paint
    Modeling clay
    Paste and scissors
    Crayons
    Woodwork tools
    Large building blocks
    Rhythm band instruments

Most of us know how to:
    Skip
    Tie our shoes
    Count to ten

[2] *It Starts in the Classroom* (Washington, D.C.: N.E.A., National School Public Relations Association, 1951).

Have you noticed that:	We are learning:
We know some new words	The names of the colors
We are trying to talk softly indoors	To know the numbers when we see them
We can "share" easier	The names of the days of the week
We know new things about the fall season	Names of the months
We are more aware of the world about us	Things that are "alike" and "different"
	Things that are "big" and "little"

Have you heard that our class won the prize for getting the most parent-teacher association members?

A great big thank you for helping us!

You are invited to our room Wednesday, November 19, from 9:30 to 10:00 A.M. We want you to see our art work, hear our songs and finger plays, and watch our games.

Tea will be served in Room 13 in the Primary Building at 10:00 A.M. We hope you will be able to visit our room on Wednesday.

Miss Howard's Kindergarten Class

QUESTIONS, PROBLEMS, AND EXERCISES

1. What are the relative merits and disadvantages of (a) the percentage marking system, (b) use of letters A, B, C, D, and F, (c) the use of Satisfactory and Unsatisfactory?

2. Select a child and develop a permanent record for him.

3. Why is it important to develop ways of measuring growth in appreciations, attitudes, work habits?

4. Write a letter to parents informing them of some particular accomplishment of their child in school.

5. Make a set of notes in preparation for a conference with a parent of a "problem child."

6. Review research in regard to the effects that traditional marking systems have had upon children and report findings to the class.

7. Prepare notes for a 10-minute talk on "Marking Systems" and be prepared to give the talk in class.

8. Prepare notes for an 8- to 10-minute talk on "Modern Reporting to Parents," and be prepared to give the talk in class.

SELECTED SUPPLEMENTARY READINGS

ADAMS, HAROLD P., and FRANK G. DICKEY. *Basic Principles of Student Teaching.* New York: American Book Co., 1956.

Chap. x, "Evaluating and Reporting Pupil Progress," pp. 254-310. Pp. 282-302: Good discussion of modern theory, trends and practices in recording and reporting marks.

BURTON, WILLIAM H. *The Guidance of Learning Activities.* New York: Appleton-Century-Crofts, Inc., 1952.

Chap. 21, "Marking and Reporting Progress."

GANS, ROMA, CELIA BURNS STENDLER, and MILLIE ALMY. *Teaching Young Children.* Yonkers, N.Y.: World Book Co., 1952.

Pp. 147-50 and 419-26: Good discussion of informal reporting; teacher-parent experiences.

HAGMAN, HARLAN L. *Administration of Elementary Schools.* New York: McGraw-Hill Book Co., Inc., 1956.

Pp. 192-99: Modern trends in records and reporting.

HUGGETT, ALBERT, and CECIL V. MILLARD. *Growth and Learning in the Elementary School.* Boston: D. C. Heath & Co., 1946.

Chap. xv, "Reporting to Parents."

KLAUSMEIER, HERBERT J., KATHERINE DRESDEN, HELEN C. DAVIS, and WALTER ARNO WITTICH. *Teaching in the Elementary School.* New York: Harper & Bros., 1956.

Chap. 16, "Reporting Pupil Progress."

SPAIN, CHARLES R., HAROLD D. DRUMMOND, and JOHN I. GOODLAD. *Educational Leadership and the Elementary School Principal.* New York: Rinehart & Co., Inc., 1956.

Pp. 262-74: Attendance accounting. Illustrative modern record forms.

UMBERGER, WILLIS H. "Refining the Report Card," *Clearing House,* 25 (November, 1950), pp. 162-64.

WILES, KIMBALL. *Teaching for Better Schools.* Englewood Cliffs, N.J.: Prentice-Hall, Inc., 1952.

Chap. 10, "How Do We Use the Evaluative Process?" Individual and group records; records kept by pupils; suggestions in reporting to pupils and parents.

21

GUIDING AND TEACHING
THE INDIVIDUAL

Guidance is one of the services of elementary schools designed to assist *all* pupils in solving their numerous personal, social, and educational problems. In the earlier phases of the guidance movement, emphasis was placed largely upon vocational guidance for high school students. Insights afforded by recent research into the nature of child growth and development in a complex society have revealed that many problems of young people originate long before they reach high school age. Many minor maladjustments can be overcome in their early stages. If these difficulties are not removed, they frequently become major problems later.

Many of the concerns of pupils attending elementary schools are personal and social in nature. These problems arise out of the pupil's transition from a highly protective home situation to the wider and more complex school environment. Elementary school children vary widely in their ability to make this adjustment, depending upon the type of child-parent relationship.

The numerous adjustments that the young child has to make to the strange environment of the school with its larger group of his age-peers, and schedule of activities quite different from those he has previously encountered in the home or informal play groups are very confusing and disconcerting. The pupil's lack of experience in living in such complex situations frequently forces him to seek solutions to his problems on an emotional basis with attendant emotional upsets and disturbances.

The emotions of elementary school children color their attitudes toward themselves, other children, and teachers. Some emotional states, such as a sense of belongingness, self-confidence, and security, reinforce learning. Emotions of fear and anxiety, which block learning, frequently grow out of the home and school situations. Deep feelings of insecurity and rejection acquired at home may seriously impair the ability to do school work.

The child's previous social experiences and his limited mental maturity may not have prepared him to meet the requirements of the educational tasks he is expected to perform. This is particularly true in reading. The difficulties encountered in respect to these matters further add to his confusion and unhappiness. The child's physical development and health may also be an important factor in determining his school adjustment.

ATTRIBUTES OF TEACHER COUNSELORS

Most of the guidance activities of elementary schools are conducted in the classrooms. Since the teacher is the key person in providing these guidance services, it is essential that she possess certain characteristics, attitudes, and professional skills. Among the most important are:

1. Good personal and social adjustment.
2. Emotional acceptance of children, including their shortcomings.
3. Deep concern for the welfare of pupils.
4. Keen insight into the causes of human behavior.
5. Clear insight into the conditions and forces of American community life.
6. Skill in the techniques for identifying pupil concerns, interests, abilities, and needs.
7. Recognition of the inherent worth of the individual.
8. Ability to win the respect and cooperation of pupils.
9. Ability to work effectively with other persons.
10. Understanding of the values and limitations of modern instruments for measuring pupil ability, achievement, personality, and interests.
11. Practical knowledge of child, adolescent, and social psychology.
12. Ability to apply present knowledge of psychology of learning.
13. Understanding of the social and economic forces which help shape the lives of men.
14. A grasp of the relationships of her teaching subject to the lives of her students.
15. Insight into ways in which men earn their living.
16. Some proficiency in the nondirective technique of counseling.

FUNCTIONS OF THE ELEMENTARY SCHOOL TEACHER

Instruction and guidance are very closely related in the elementary school. Elementary classroom activities are a combination of guidance and instructional activities, with the teacher serving as counselor and instructor.

In the performance of her guidance functions, the teacher works directly with pupils in the classroom, with other guidance personnel, and with parents.

Pupils

In carrying out her guidance function in the classroom the elementary school teacher can:

1. Create a good emotional atmosphere so that boys and girls feel free to express their ideas and put forth their best efforts as individuals and as groups.
2. Know her pupils—their backgrounds, abilities, personalities, and aspirations.
3. Realize that behavior is caused, that misbehavior as a deviation from normal behavior is due to factors in the home, school, and community.
4. Utilize all opportunities to relate her teaching to pupil needs. Every subject offers opportunities for guidance.
5. Build up pupil readiness for reading and all other subjects.
6. Emphasize the importance of good reading habits.
7. Be alert to identify causes of pupil maladjustment in their early stages.

Guidance personnel

In recent years a considerable number of elementary schools have established organized programs of guidance. Many schools have central guidance committees composed of counselors, special service personnel, and classroom teachers. It is the function of these committees to make a continuous study of the school's guidance program to discover ways to improve its effectiveness. While many guidance functions are performed on an individual pupil-teacher basis, some problems of pupil adjustment cut across the organizational lines of a school. Also, the solution of many of the serious problems of pupils require the cooperative efforts of the guidance staff of the school.

The classroom teacher cooperates with the counselor by providing pertinent information in regard to her pupils. She cooperates with curriculum directors in selecting and organizing learning materials in terms of pupils' abilities. She cooperates with supervisors of instruction by examining her teaching methods with a view to providing more adequately for individual pupil needs. She utilizes the information made available by other guidance personnel in assisting individual pupils and in improving her teaching of groups. She makes available to the guidance personnel anecdotal records, case histories, and sociograms she has made.

Parents

Few of the school's activities make a stronger appeal to parents than the guidance program. Parents concerned with their children's present school and future vocational success are particularly interested in any effort of the school to assist their children in making satisfactory adjustments in these respects. Some guidance activities are likely to be misinterpreted by parents. The interpretation of test scores and the methods of obtaining information in regard to home conditions have been sources of misunderstandings between parents and teachers.

Since the prevention of pupil's difficulties represents guidance at its best, teacher-parent conferences in the home and school in which a cooperative plan is worked out to assist the pupil may prevent serious difficulties. The practice in some schools of substituting or supplementing the pupil's report card by teacher-parent conferences is an excellent opportunity to obtain parental understanding and cooperation of the guidance activities of the school. In these conferences, it is important for the teacher to reveal a thorough and sympathetic understanding of the pupil. The teacher should also be aware that parents may be so involved and concerned with their own children's problems that it is difficult for them to always have an objective point of view.

Unless the teacher exercises tact and skill in applying the principles of good human relationships, the teacher-parent conference may be more harmful than helpful. The conference should not be held in the classroom during school time. A regular conference room or office, with a secretary present, should be provided. Regular appointments for the conference should be made and kept. Of course, this arrangement should not preclude the many informal contacts in the community between teachers and parents.

PRINCIPLES OF GUIDANCE

In counseling pupils the teacher should be aware of several basic principles of guidance. A few of the most important ones are these.

1. *Guidance activities should be based upon an analysis of the problems encountered by pupils of elementary school age.* While these needs vary in nature and intensity from one pupil to another, most of these problems can be broadly classified as personal, social, health, and educational. A rapidly growing concept among teachers is that, while many problems are isolated and a great many others are complex, it is often necessary to consider a number of problems which are related in some way before solving any one of them. For example, a pupil's behavior in school may be related to problems at home, problems of social acceptance, problems of health, problems of physical deficiencies, problems of unfortunate previous experiences in a related area. There is a strong tendency to gather a great deal of data about all pupils, particularly those who seem to have unusually important problems, and to interpret all data in a clinical, unified, integrated manner rather than to take hold of specific problems in an atomistic fashion.

2. *Guidance should not mean giving pupils answers to all their questions.* In some instances information is available and seems to be called for by the nature of the problem of the youngster. In many other instances there is no ready answer, and there is not under any circumstances an answer which can be definite or have any considerable degree of validity for the particular problem. Many problems have such a nature that it will take a great deal of time for their solution; for some, passage of time is the only solution. There are many problems for which there can be no definite answer or solution under the control of the teacher and the youngster. Such circumstances call for encouragement and development of faith that eventually things will work out all right. In many situations the great problem to be solved is not the specific problem that is bothering the youngster, but the problem of being able to meet the bad situation without too much worry and damage to his personality.

3. *The teacher should seek the assistance of other persons in the solution of many problems of pupils.* She may wish to confer with parents, or have the child carry certain of the problems back to his parents for discussion; it may be that one or both of the parents, the teacher, and the pupil may need to confer about the problem. There are, of course, some problems which the youngsters bring to teachers in great confidence and which the youngster would greatly prefer not to have the parents know about. The teacher must use the greatest discretion in such situations and be careful not to violate the confidence of the youngster. In addition, quite frequently the problem is of such a nature that the teacher knows of someone in the school or community who could give a better answer to the question

than she can—perhaps the principal of the school, a vocational counsellor, a school psychologist, a family physician, a minister, or a priest. In some instances, it is some other person in addition to all or any one of these.

4. *The teacher should refrain from the temptation to be the source of all information.* Teachers may give youngsters a great deal of misinformation upon many occasions. It is difficult for the teacher to take a modest position and say, "This is a question about which I am not able to advise you or counsel you," and yet that must be done in a great many situations. Perhaps a suggestion may be taken from the practice of physicians, who are very modest and very reluctant to give answers and information, particularly if they cannot be positive about the validity of their answers.

5. *The pupil should solve many of his own problems.* The role of the counsellor is that of guidance in how to approach the study of his problems. Many decisions in respect to problems that occur over and over again are either identical or in similar form. The ultimate goal of guidance is for the counsellor to make herself relatively unnecessary by reason of having helped the students in the development of attitudes, skills, methods, and sources of information for the solution of their own problems.

6. *The teacher should acquire all the data that she can about children.* She should learn by study and experience how to interpret various types of technical and personnel data and test results. (See Chapter 3 for a discussion of procedures for obtaining information concerning the pupil.)

ADAPTING INSTRUCTION TO THE INDIVIDUAL

Learning is an individual matter. Although an instructor may "teach" a class, the learning is done by the individual. Beyond the minds of the separate individuals in the group, there is no class mind capable of learning. The teacher should not make the mistake of assuming that all, or any two, individuals in the class learn alike from the same instructional materials or instructional activities. It is unfortunate that there is not a better device by means of which teachers can see in detail the variety of learnings, with respect to both nature and amount, that take place among twenty or thirty children in a class who have had practically identical stimuli.

The teacher, therefore, must focus her attention upon the learning actually taking place in the individual child rather than upon her teaching materials and activities. She must not only concentrate upon the individual, but as a means to produce the desired growth and learnings she must acquire a great deal of knowledge about each individual child, his capacities, interests, and background.

Learning activities and materials which are not organized in terms of the needs, interests, and experiences of children will frustrate and discourage some children, while other children will not work up to their capacities. A curriculum that is not flexible and that cannot be adjusted to the needs of children will cause children to be frustrated, discouraged, and uninterested in school.

Individual differences

In every age level differences within groups of children must be constantly taken into consideration in directing learning. Children differ from each other intellectually, physically, socially, and emotionally: some learn slowly, others quickly; some are of small stature, others are large for their age; some are leaders in their groups, others are lonely; some are happy and learn by failures, others are nervous and unstable whenever they face a problem. Children not only differ from each other, but they have different relative levels of aptitude and achievement. A child with a high I.Q. may be average in reading, do superior work in social studies, do poorly in art, and produce a monotone in singing; while another child with the same I.Q. may do well in reading, poorly in social studies, about average work in music and art, and be a superior basketball player.

Since each child is a unique individual, the needs of each must be met in a way which fits each individual case. Therefore, it is the teacher's responsibility to understand the needs, interests, and capacities of each child so that she may intelligently provide for these needs in the most economical and effective way. In the two preceding chapters, ways of locating, recording, and reporting needs have been discussed. By reviewing, analyzing, and evaluating the information on cumulative records, anecdotal records, sociograms, the teacher can discover the status of the child in each of the various areas of growth and development. Areas within which children vary will be presented in the following paragraphs.

Intelligence. The range in mental age among children in any single elementary class is usually four or five years in the primary grades and six or seven years in grades 7 and 8. In a second grade, the mental age will vary approximately from five years to ten years. In a typical fifth-grade class the mental age of students varies from less than the average M.A. of a typical third-grade class to more than the average M.A. of a typical seventh grade.

Children with less intelligence learn more slowly; they need a great amount of meaningful practice and more time in moving from one type of learning to another; they are not able to work with abstractions. Children with a high I.Q. usually have a good attention span, learn quickly, need less practice and less time to complete their work, can generalize and work with abstractions. A child with an I.Q. below 80 will find it difficult, probably impossible, to do much of the work that a child with an average I.Q. of 100 can do, while a child with an I.Q. of 125 would probably be bored with the same assignment.

Aptitudes. In many schools tests of special aptitude are given and the scores are available. Aptitude tests in mathematics are especially useful. Care must be exercised in interpretation of these scores. The best single basis on which to forecast what a learner will actually do in a subject is his previous school marks. In addition to capacity, they measure in a rough way the factors which generally make for achievement, such as interest, industry, promptness, and cooperation.

Children also vary significantly in their capacities or aptitudes for learning of various types. This is particularly true with respect to aptitudes for art, music, mechanical skills, and sports. Much of what is assumed to be a difference in specific aptitude is in large part the result of differences in attitude, interest, and previous preparation; for practical purposes of learning, the differences are very significant whatever their cause.

Physical fitness. Children vary in height, weight, and muscular coordination. Many physical handicaps also are very obvious, such as a need for braces and crutches in order to walk and for heavy lenses in order to see. Children with asthmatic conditions and cardiac conditions cannot play vigorously. Infections because of decayed teeth and diseased tonsils lower the child's efficiency. Some children tire easily and are not interested in activities while others are very energetic and eager to be doing something.

Social and emotional adjustments. Social and emotional adjustments are closely related. Some children are reticent, and others boisterous; some timid, others bold; some responsible, others irresponsible. Some are cooperative and others not so; some are dependent and others independent. Some are irritable and others poised; some cheerful, others depressed; some sensitive, others much less so; some suggestible, others negativistic.

Patterns of social and emotional behavior are not static but may vary within an hour or two. In one situation and with a certain

group of children a child will be happy and cooperative, whereas
with another group the same child may be annoying and boisterous.
Some children are dependent at home; these same children may be
self-sufficient at school. As environmental conditions affect children
differently at different times so will their patterns of behavior
differ.

As the result of difficulty of learning in elementary grades, junior
high school students may have developed attitudes of fear, insecurity, and dislikes for certain fields of school learning, and some have a
dislike for all fields. Others, probably because of much happier experiences, have developed feelings of interest, confidence, and belief in the value of learning.

Home background. Children differ greatly in their cultural
backgrounds and attitudes as influenced by the home. Children
come from homes which may be characterized by the following factors: poverty, with or without culture; wealth, with or without
culture; estranged parents; compatible parents; one parent at home;
both parents working; dull child in a family of bright children and
vice versa. Some homes create fears; others aid children in facing
realities of life. Because of varied home backgrounds and varied experiences in the homes, children will vary in their interests, attitudes,
appreciations, understandings of economic and social concepts,
speaking vocabulary, and in their abilities to convey their ideas to
others. They will react very differently to the same situation.
They are sensitive to different things.

Homes differ greatly in their intellectual and cultural interests and
tastes, in modes of thinking, in language and speech habits and
standards, in patterns of cooperation and regard for others, in facilities for home study and in other ways very significant for learning
and behavior at school.

Academic achievements. The chronological age of children enrolled in the first grade has a range of about one and a half years.
Every month in chronological age makes a great difference in maturity; therefore, there will be a great range in the maturity levels of
the children. In the first grade curriculum emphasis is placed upon
the development of reading skills. Those children who do not have
mental age of six years should have a curriculum especially arranged
to fit their needs; to place them with those children who are ready to
read would only mean failure.

The range of pupil status in subject-matter achievement in any
grade is usually four or five years. For example, in arithmetic the
scores in problem-solving in fifth grade may range from third-grade

level to seventh-grade level which means that some children will be doing as well with the materials as an average third-grade child would do and some as well as an average seventh-grade child would do. The rate of speed at which children work will also vary significantly; some children will work ten problems in thirty minutes while others will solve only four in the same time period. A reading assignment will be read and comprehended by one child in fifteen minutes, while another child will devote thirty minutes to the same selection and probably not understand what has been read. One child can communicate his ideas to others by means of written themes and reports very effectively, while another finds it very difficult to use that medium of expression.

Partly as the result of differences in general capacity to learn and in specific aptitudes and attitudes in a particular field, learners have widely different backgrounds in that field. Particularly in English classes in the upper grades, some children have much better than average foundation in vocabulary, grammar, and language, and much more advanced interests in literature. In ability to read, differences have become so great as to call for the establishment of special classes for those with least ability. Variability of similar importance for learning exists in all other fields, particularly mathematics.

Interests and industry. Not only will learning depend upon the degree of interest in learning and in learning activities, but as a matter of fact the degree to which the learner will participate in learning activities depends upon the degree of his interest in the particular area. Interests depend largely upon the extent, pattern, and character of previous experiences. They depend upon the nature and pattern of interests of parents, of other adults known to the learner, and of his companions. While it is among the most important services and responsibilities of the teacher to develop desired interests—that is, in good literature, in physical and mental health, and in other peoples of the world—she must also recognize the pattern of interests in the individual learner as it exists at the time and adapt instruction somewhat to it, harnessing those interests in order to insure wholehearted, effective participation in learning activities.

Individual difficulties

Schools are accepting the responsibility for fitting the school program to the many needs of children. Children who are challenged with a task that is neither too difficult nor too easy have good mental health and continue attacking problems which must be solved. Methods which have proved to be successful in providing for individual differences will be presented in the following paragraphs.

Physically handicapped. Physically handicapped children should be educated with normal children if at all possible and should be placed in play groups where they can participate without being embarrassed. They must be guided in learning to minimize their handicaps and to put forth effort to be as independent as possible. At a time when the afflicted child is not in the classroom his handicaps should be explained to his classmates; this often changes a critical attitude to sympathetic understanding. Usually children are very sympathetic and very eager to help handicapped children. Children with certain types of serious physical disabilities should be placed under the direction of a specially trained teacher and given special treatment, which in many cases involves appropriate types of physical and mental therapy.

Children who are hard of hearing must learn to live in a hearing world and those who can hear must learn something about the problems of handicapped individuals. Children who are hard of hearing should be seated so that they can hear what is being said and so that they can see the face of the person who is speaking. The teacher and children should pronounce and enunciate words clearly; if the child does not understand, the speaker should repeat in a courteous manner.

Children with poor vision should be seated where they can see what is written on the board and also all materials that are being displayed for observational purposes. Their reading materials should be printed in large type on nonglazed paper. For children with severe visual handicaps, some schools have special sight-saving classes. Children with lowered visual acuity also must be guided through socializing experiences to capitalize on their potentialities and thus make a contribution to society.

Speech difficulties. Speech is a basic tool in gaining status in a group. A child with a speech difficulty, such as stuttering, lisping, infantile speech, sound omissions and substitutions, often is silent because of the unfavorable reactions of other children. No child should ever be permitted to giggle at the handicapped child; neither should a teacher persist in asking a stutterer to keep repeating that which the teacher cannot understand. To do so only increases the child's anxiety and frustration. The child should be permitted to make his needs known without fear or embarrassment.

It is the responsibility of every teacher to understand speech difficulties of young children and to provide guidance in speech correction. In many schools a specialist in speech education is provided to whom stutterers, cleft palate cases, and others suffering from speech defects may be sent for special treatment.

Social adjustment difficulties. Social adjustment often implies gaining status in a group, which means that a child must make a contribution and must cooperate in a democratic way. It is very difficult to group children socially, as their needs of today may not be the needs of tomorrow. In organizing groups and committees, teachers should use the information secured from sociograms, observations, and interviews. For example, the child who has no friends should be placed with a group of friendly children. The child who needs recognition and has a talent in drawing could be assigned to direct a group working on a frieze. Often a teacher can help children make adjustments by discussing with them the customs of various groups and the way in which to conduct themselves on different occasions and in strange places, such as during interviews, in public buildings, etc.

The gifted child. Gifted and slow-learning children differ not only in quantity but also in quality of ability and should be taught differently. The progress of civilization depends largely upon the contributions of genius. The work of an Edison, Pasteur, Madame Curie, Franklin, or Shakespeare is of more consequence to civilization than the efforts of thousands of persons of average ability. The loss to society and to civilization because of our failure to develop fully the capacities of the ablest children is incalculable.

As the result of classroom experiences with gifted children, we are able to characterize them for the purposes of teaching. The gifted child possesses greater energy and more curiosity, is sociable, active, more capable of dealing with abstractions, perceives relationships more clearly and quickly, prefers to work under his own planning and initiative, likes to explore new and more advanced areas, becomes bored more quickly with simple routine tasks, learns mechanical processes much more quickly than an average child, dislikes tasks he does not understand, dislikes rote memorization though he is superior at it, has confidence in his own abilities, appears lazy if given uninteresting things to do, is likely to seek short cuts, and possesses a wide range of worthy interests.

The gifted learner should not only have more work to do, but it should be of a type to challenge his superior and special abilities. He should be required to locate and to organize materials, to find and state relationships and generalizations, to read more difficult material. He should be relieved of some of the easier routine tasks which may be necessary for the average or below-average child. He should be given larger units, tasks and problems with a greater number of steps. He should be freed of some of the drill of the class and permitted to work more on his own. He should be stimulated to undertake imaginative and creative tasks. For him, frequent diagnostic testing is unnecessary; he can be trained for self-diagnosis and self-planning of remedial work. The more gifted the child is, the more these suggestions should be employed and the further they should be carried. They usually apply to children with an I.Q. of more than 120 to 125. Those of definitely higher I.Q. (140 and up) should be treated as special individual cases. In many schools gifted pupils are identified not only on the basis of I.Q. but other information is taken into account such as teachers' judgments, school marks, and creative products of the pupils.

There are many individual differences within a group of gifted children. Many of them have special problems. Some of these are lack of stimulation because of slow pace and repetitions in classroom work causing boredom and resulting in poor work and study habits. Some bright children are used as "tutors" or "clerks" and thus are deprived of opportunities to explore new fields, advance in skills, or develop their own particular talents.

They are often censured by the teacher when they do not work to capacity. Some receive high marks but feel that they did not have to work very hard to master the task. Many feel that they are confronted with a too heavy work program with no time to play. Many gifted children have problems in the home. They are not always understood by parents and other members of the family. Sometimes too much is expected of them.

The slow-learning child. Until recent years the child with an I.Q. of 90 or less rarely continued in school beyond the ninth grade, and those with an I.Q. of less than 80 rarely progressed beyond the sixth grade.

The slow-learning child usually possesses to some degree most of the following characteristics which need to be held constantly in mind while teaching him. In comparison with the child of higher I.Q.—

1. He learns in shorter steps or units.
2. He needs more frequent checkups on his progress and more remedial work.
3. His vocabulary is more limited and less precise.

4. He needs to have many new words made very clear in meaning.
5. He does not see relative generalizations or meanings as readily.
6. He has less creative ability and less ability to plan for himself.
7. He is slightly slower in acquiring complicated mechanical and motor skills.
8. In proportion to his dullness he tires less quickly of mechanical routine tasks and he tires more quickly of difficult reading or abstract discussion.
9. He is quick to generalize crudely, is lacking in self-criticism, and is easily satisfied with superficial answers.
10. He is less envious.
11. He has had unhappy experiences with previous school work and is hence more likely to be irritable in class, lacking in self-confidence, and more interested in nonschool life.
12. He is more susceptible to the suggestions of other persons.
13. His difficulties are cumulative in learning.
14. He has a narrow range of interests.
15. He possesses a slow reaction time.
16. He tends to engage in overcompensating activities.
17. He is less able to see the end results of his actions. Remote, long-range goals are not impelling to him.
18. He fails to detect identical elements in different types of situations.
19. His attention span is short and must be reinforced by engaging appeal.
20. He especially needs evidence of his progress.

In planning learning activities for the slow-learning pupil, the teacher should ascertain the source of the child's difficulty. If it is due to his limited mental ability, the following suggestions are recommended:

1. Present new materials by associating them and explaining them in terms of simple familiar materials.
2. Keep the slow learner conscious of progress at all times. He must be given reason to believe he is succeeding.
3. Use real objects and other concrete and lifelike aids whenever practical.
4. Employ applications to life, not only to bridge the gap between school and life but also to promote understanding.
5. Make an effort to discover special interests on the part of individual learners and to utilize them if possible by applying learning activities to these interests.
6. Make daily assignments involving specific, meaningful tasks.
7. Be satisfied with attempting what is possible and take time to teach that little well.

8. Explore constantly to discover misunderstanding and relatively poor learning. Do remedial teaching on the spot, but do not be too critical.

9. Avoid an excessive vocabulary load. Use simple and familiar words and simple sentences. Use words in their exact and precise meanings.

10. Encourage slow learners by letting them explain but do not confuse others by too many poor explanations.

11. Help the slow learner to read better. Take more time for oral reading in order to develop comprehension and vocabulary.

12. Make a special effort to see that the child understands adequately new concepts that are essential to meaning and that will come up later. Write them on the blackboard and give concrete examples.

13. Avoid giving the slow learner, merely to keep him busy, meaningless routine tasks from which little progress in learning can be expected.

14. Avoid sarcasm or frequent criticism. Always encourage those who try.

15. Do not be irritated by symptoms of lack of interest, tension, discouragement, or mild disorder in the slow learner. These are natural symptoms of continued unsatisfying experiences resulting from being forced to attempt more than ability justifies. They diminish as children are given learning activities that are appropriate to their capacities, abilities, and interests.

16. Remember that it is very important that the slow learner like and have confidence in his teacher.

PROVIDING FOR INDIVIDUAL DIFFERENCES

Various plans have been designed to provide for individual differences, such as (1) acceleration, (2) individual instruction, (3) project and unit plans, (4) special classes for gifted pupils, (5) remedial classes for slow-learning pupils, (6) ability grouping, (7) small groups within class, (8) supervised study, (9) curriculum enrichment, (10) elective subjects, (11) differentiated assignments, (12) tutoring, (13) summer schools, (14) modifications in teaching methods within a class to provide for slow-learning and gifted pupils, and (15) individual guidance. A few of the plans which are widely used in the elementary school are described in the following paragraphs.

Accelerated and enriched programs

For many years, elementary schools followed the practice of giving gifted pupils double promotions in which these pupils were allowed to skip one or more elementary grades. Studies of the effects of this practice upon the achievement and social development of pupils have revealed that enriching the program of learning activities at each grade level is more satisfactory than skipping grades.

In an endeavor to provide for gifted pupils, the Denver schools have adopted a plan which may be summarized as follows:

1. *Identification.* In each school, the staff seeks out the individual pupils who show evidence of exceptionally great learning ability. The most common evidence is a high I.Q.—125 or above.

Gifted pupils often have excellent work habits, high marks, high scores on achievement tests, great drive.

Excellent physical development, emotional balance, and social adjustment are traits of the gifted. Early use of language and a large vocabulary mark many gifted persons.

The gifted have keen powers of observation and good memory. They have remarkable capacity for attention and concentration. They usually are attracted to books early and develop a great love of reading.

They tend to show originality in drawing, painting, music, language, and games. They like intricate things, whether toys or rules for games, and they are interested in relationships, such as cause and effect. They are attracted by number relationships, evidenced early by interest in calendar and clock.

2. *Modification of curriculum.* Each school provides the gifted pupils (if parents consent) with broader and deeper learning experiences than those of the regular curriculum, that is, enrichment

    a. individually, within the regular classroom, or

    b. in groups formed on the basis of ability, or

    c. in special classes meeting for some part of the school day, one to five days a week.

The enrichment is work added to the regular program for the purpose of developing the abilities characteristic of gifted pupils, such as the ability to learn quickly and easily, to generalize readily, to discover and use basic principles, to see relationships quickly, to deal with large concepts.

3. *Counseling and Guidance.* Each gifted child is assigned to one teacher who advises and confers with the pupil and his parents on development of his abilities.

Studies show that many successful persons, identified as gifted during childhood, attribute their success to some one or more interested adults who gave them encouragement, support, and appreciation.

4. *Articulation.* Each teacher of gifted pupils is advised of the abilities, interest, and experiences provided by previous teachers, and each school informs the next school to receive the pupils of its program.

Whenever pupils are provided a special program, close communication from grade to grade and school to school is essential to prevent unnecessary repetitions or omissions in the sequence of learning.

Elementary and junior high schools confer on programs for the gifted.

5. *Evaluation.* The success of the program is measured by the quality of pupils' learning that results.

A major goal is to enable the gifted pupil to achieve at a level commensurate with his exceptional ability. Standardized tests and other measures of achievement are used frequently.

Another major goal is to foster superior development of gifted pupils physically, emotionally, and socially. Ratings, sociograms, and teachers' observations are used to measure attainment in those respects.

In order to partially implement their general plan of enrichment, the Mathematics Committee of the Denver Public Schools [1] recently recommended that—

In Grade 2, introduction of more addition and subtraction facts to provide additional time in Grade 3 for the development of processes involved in addition and subtraction.

In Grade 3, introduction of some multiplication and division facts.

In Grade 4, fractions are introduced to remove some of the burden from Grade 5.

In Grade 5, more time is allowed for fractions which prove to be difficult to master, addition and subtraction being more difficult than multiplication and division.

In Grade 6, more time is allowed for fixing the skills involved in fractions. The introduction of percentage will be optional. It is introduced to give some realistic approach to multiplying with decimal fractions, such as .03.

Informal grouping

Some teachers have been dividing the class into groups of from two or three to seven or eight pupils. Within each of these groups, different individuals play different parts in a normal way, according to their interests and abilities. Working together in the groups in the directed study or workshop situation tends to develop interest and cause the learning activities to be more pleasant and stimulating. The pressures upon the individual to extend himself come from his peers in the group and not from the teacher—a real advantage in this day of peer culture.

The teacher acts as a consultant and moves from group to group as needed or as she is called by the leader or a member of a group. Groups are not formed on the basis of their capacities or abilities. However, sometimes a group will be working upon a set of learning activities sufficiently simple so that the teacher may suggest having certain other individuals work with them. Likewise, abler youngsters are encouraged to join a group working on complex activities. Frequently, however, the groups are not selected but are heterogeneous; individuals volunteer for groups, are chosen by the learners,

[1] *Instruction News,* XIII, 4 (Denver, Colorado: Denver Public Schools, March, 1957), p. 26.

or are assigned on the basis of class discussion. What each individual does within his group is adapted to his own interests, capacities, abilities, and needs, thus making it possible for the children to be placed at any time with the group that is working on problems which fit their particular needs and their maturity level. Advantages of grouping are:

1. The group plan provides better for very important educational outcomes, such as skill and habits of cooperation, skill in oral discussion, development of ideals from social situations, and other social attitudes, ideals, skills, and habits necessary as training for cooperation. These may be developed much better in class group teaching than where individual instruction is used.
2. Group contacts give mutual stimulus to activity which is not possible under the individual plan.
3. The group plan stimulates effort through discovery of problems and the development of interest in the group discussion.
4. The group plan is valuable because of the opportunity for the slow to learn from the discussions of others.
5. The group plan makes unnecessary duplicate explanations, as under the group organization plan one explanation or set of instructions serves for all.

Ability grouping

In the upper grades in school, in which the upper 13 or 20 per cent of a given class includes enough pupils to form a special section of bright and one of slow pupils, ability grouping can be used with definite success. While general agreement is lacking and it is impossible to draw precise conclusions from experiments in which learners are using different subject-matter materials, the consensus of scores of investigations is that results are improved when ability grouping is employed intelligently (as far as results that can be measured on tests are concerned), even though instruction was not adapted to the group as well as it could be in more than a few of these experiments. Unless great care and intelligence are used to adapt instruction to the differentiated group, it may not be very wise procedure.

Precautions must be taken to keep at a minimum the stigma attached to being in the slow group. When stigmatizing the slow group is avoided, the ill effects of grouping are probably materially less than in conventional heterogeneous classes in which the slow learner cannot hope to excel and is daily faced with competition with which he can hardly fail to contrast himself even if his teachers do not do so openly. In an increasing number of upper elementary grades, review sections are formed in the seventh grade in arithmetic and reading, reviewing if necessary fourth-grade materials.

When ability grouping is employed, there is opportunity for adaptation and differentiation of materials and methods with regard to individual students with the slow, the average, and also the bright class.

A study by the research division of the National Education Association revealed that forming separate classes for slow-learning pupils has already become a fairly widespread practice in the upper grades, especially in English, mathematics, and the social studies.

Pupils who should be placed in slow-learning classes may be best identified by means of a combination of three or all of the following criteria: (1) general intelligence test, (2) average mark in all subjects in previous year or two, (3) average mark made in previous year in subject involved, and (4) objective test covering the field concerned as taught in the previous year or two. The greatest care must always be employed to cause both bright and slow to forget that they are in special sections.

Obviously it is not practical to use the same subject matter or the same materials for all pupils, regardless of interest, capacity, ability, or background. Various plans are employed for adaptation of subject matter and learning activities, and a number of these will be considered.

Independent work

Children who are working independently must be provided with carefully planned constructive activities which vary from day to day. Workbooks, worksheets, independent reading, creative work with clay, painting, etc., are used frequently in the primary grades. In the intermediate grades children may work on individual difficulties in spelling or arithmetic, prepare special reports, or work on special committees, such as arranging the bulletin board, preparing a dramatization for literature class.

Supervised individualized period

The supervised individualized period may be a reading period in which each child is reading in a different book. Children may be doing different things in arithmetic or language, according to their individual needs. In a work period in social studies, each child (or probably groups of children in committees) may work on the same problem by attacking it in different ways, although they may be working on individual problems. In a directed individualized work period these opportunities may arise.

1. The teacher has the opportunity to gather information which will furnish a basis for diagnosis and individual treatment.
2. It is possible to adapt the problem much better to the needs of both the slower and the abler children.
3. The opportunity for personal help and conversation free from the formality of the group work period and the possibility of privacy in relationships with children may both be used to excellent advantage by a clever teacher to adapt criticism and approval, encouragement and rebuke, to the individual nature of the child without assuming before the other children the role of one who varies standards. All the special advantages that attend private talks in these connections are available to the teacher.
4. The teacher can more easily pierce the defense of sophistication and indifference assumed by many children in the presence of a group of their classmates, which weakens during personal and informal contacts.
5. An opportunity is afforded to give individual help to children on difficulties peculiar to them not only in the case of the slow but also of the average and brighter children, and also to children whose difficulties are the result of absence or the fact that they are transfers; likewise there is opportunity to give needed training in how to study.
6. The opportunity is offered to check up on the child's progress, locate weak spots, analyze difficulties, and offer individual suggestions for remedial work.
7. There is the opportunity to arouse interest by encouragement, by raising questions, and by the sheer personality and personal influence of the teacher.

Individualized instruction

Various types of *individualized* instruction have been employed. In its extreme form, each individual is given his assignments, his instructions, and his evaluation as an individual. As commonly utilized, there is at least some group work; either the class as a whole or a small group in it is given group instruction and assignments occasionally. Group tests are employed.

In some schools each pupil moves at his own rate over the same ground as the others, completing a year's work in a subject in six months, eight months, or a year and a half as the case may be. These are more important advantages claimed for individual instruction:

1. It allows the slow child to progress at his own rate, thus permitting thoroughness and avoiding discouragement.

2. It prevents the illusion of making progress when it is not really made, which misleads so many slow, uninterested, or indolent children under group discussion.
3. It tends to concentrate the attention of the children on their own individual achievements, upon which their progress through the course of study depends, instead of upon the average progress of the class.
4. It tends to focus attention upon the mastery of subject matter and upon educational growth, and away from satisfying demands imposed by the teacher.
5. It permits the more able child to make progress at his optimum rate and thereby realize the possibilities of his peculiar gifts.
6. It tends to eliminate that training undesirable for the gifted child which results from his being held down to the pace of the average and which sometimes generates habits of idleness and attitudes of satisfaction with achievement that is less than capacity.
7. It brings about personal contacts between child and teacher, for which the "child-tutor" situations are much more favorable than "teacher-class" situations.
8. It permits valuable exercise of individual initiative, especially on the part of the more capable child who now is supervised as closely as the slow or mediocre one.
9. It tends to reduce retardation and to prevent the elimination of the slower children.

Activity units and projects

The activity unit can be adapted very easily to individual differences. Reading materials such as books, magazines, bulletins, folders, and the like having a unit range from very easy to difficult are made available to the children. Children report their information to committees or to the group; by asking the slow child to report first and by requesting those who add further information not to repeat what has been said, the bright child must listen to the slow child in order to know what has been said. Provision also is made for individual instruction in the development of skills in the tool subjects. If five children are ready to learn how to interpret information represented by means of a graph, those children are given information pertaining to the graph. If all the children in a group are ready to learn how to make an outline for a report, the whole class works on the problem.

In activity programs, children also have an opportunity to develop their creative ability through the media of clay, paints, drawing, and construction. In a unit on birds, for example, one child who was interested in building bird houses learned to appreciate the fact that houses differing in construction and size were needed for different birds, with the result that number concepts took on meaning and significance.

Differentiated and flexible assignments

A great many teachers are employing differentiated and flexible assignments effectively in ungrouped classes. The major difference between these two types of assignments is that the differentiated assignment is modified in quantity and nature of work covered for gifted, average, and slow-learning children, whereas in the flexible assignment the assignment is not divided into levels, but activities or learnings varied with respect to difficulties are provided and each child is encouraged to do as much as he can in terms of his abilities and the time available beyond a designated minimum amount of work.

Differentiated and flexible assignments are used by every teacher who provides effectively for the needs and interests of children. A teacher who paces the teaching of information and the development of skills and abilities needed in learning to the needs and interests of children uses flexible or differentiated assignments. For example, a list of fifteen words is usually the spelling assignment for a week. In a heterogeneous group, some children will be working on fifteen words, other children will be assigned ten or twelve words, and a few may be given six or seven words only. In a flexible assignment a certain number of words would be required of all children and those children who have time to learn more words would work on those which they are interested in learning to spell.

The practice writing periods usually are flexible; children work on their own difficulties, found in their written work. Assignments in work-type reading periods may be differentiated and/or flexible, the determining factor being objectives for the period and needs and interests of children.

QUESTIONS, PROBLEMS, AND EXERCISES

1. Suggest how the classroom teacher can make provision for individual differences of pupils by means of guidance in the classroom.

2. How may the gap between what is *known* and what is *done* about individual differences be reduced or eliminated in the elementary school?

3. What are the chief types of exceptional children for whom special provisions should be made in the elementary school?

4. State the advantages and disadvantages of grouping pupils in the elementary school on the basis of social maturity, mental ability, chronological age.

5. List ways of providing for individual differences in reading in the primary grades and in the intermediate grades.

6. Prepare programs in mathematics for sixth-grade pupils which will fit the needs of slow-learning pupils and of gifted pupils.

7. Suggest ways in which individual pupil initiative can be fostered in the classroom.

8. Suggest how the teacher may assist a pupil in attaining social status with his age-peers.

SELECTED SUPPLEMENTARY READINGS

BAKER, HARRY J. *Exceptional Children,* rev. ed. New York: The Macmillan Co., 1953.

A practical guide for understanding the various types of exceptional children.

BLAIR, GLENN MYER. *Diagnostic and Remedial Teaching.* New York: The Macmillan Co., 1956.

Chapters on remedial work in reading and each of the other learning fields. Excellent discussion.

BUHLER, CHARLOTTE, FAITH SMITTER, SYBIL RICHARDSON, and FRANKLYN BRADSHAW. *Childhood Problems and the Teacher.* New York: Henry Holt & Co., Inc., 1952.

Chap. ix, "The Teacher's Methods of Working with Individual Children." Contains descriptions of children with different types of problems.

MCDANIEL, HENRY B. *Guidance in the Modern School.* New York: The Dryden Press, Inc., 1956.

Chap. iii, "Guidance in the Elementary School." Discussion of the responsibility of the elementary school teacher for guidance.

NATIONAL SOCIETY FOR THE STUDY OF EDUCATION. *The Education of Exceptional Children. Forty-Ninth Yearbook,* Part ii. Chicago: University of Chicago Press, 1950.

Describes procedures and services which have been found effective in meeting the needs of exceptional children within a school system.

SMITH, MARION FUNK. *Teaching the Slow Learning Child.* New York: Harper & Bros., 1954.

Describes personalities and problems of school retarded children.

WILLEY, ROY DE VERL. *Guidance in Elementary Education.* New York: Harper & Bros., 1952.

Presents various points of view concerning guidance in the elementary school.

WINGO, G. MAX, and RALEIGH SCHORLING. *Elementary-School Student Teaching.* 2d ed. New York: McGraw-Hill Book Co., Inc., 1955.

Chap. xiii, "The Guidance of Children." Specific guidance techniques are described and suggestions are given on how they might be used in functional situations.

22

PARTICIPATING IN
EXTRACLASS ACTIVITIES

The successful teacher of today does not think of extracurricular
student activities as frills or concessions to a pupil's desire to play,
but as important educational experiences that are integral parts of
the school program. How children will think, act, and feel in the
future can be influenced very materially by their experiences in
extracurricular activities. From these experiences they can acquire
important habits, skills, interests, tastes, information, understandings, and attitudes for certain of the objectives of education.

It is important for elementary schools to have a program of extracurricular activities. In graded school systems, children usually
associate most of the day with children of their own chronological
age. This is desirable in the instructional program of the more
formal subjects, but undesirable in many areas of social experience.
Many of the social experiences needed for wholesome living have
their outlets in extracurricular activities that cut across grade lines.
In order to have children of varying ages participate in activities, the
school must plan a program that will make it possible for children
not only to identify themselves with their own classmates, but also
with children in other grades.

A major problem of the school is to plan a program that will provide activities for the development of those skills which make for
effective social living. This program of extracurricular activities
supplements the part of the curriculum that deals with the work-
study skills and content subjects by providing activities that will aid
the child in becoming an integrated personality and will support the

438

development of those skills, abilities, and attitudes that will make for effective social living. Social skills desirable in a democracy include abilities to assume responsibilities, to support democratic ideals, and to use leisure time effectively. Many of the attitudes and skills needed in effective social living are learned most effectively by working and playing with others in informal groups outside the regular class periods.

Today work is generally a group organization, for very few people work absolutely alone on a job. Hence work involves interpersonality relationships. Since children do not inherit those skills, abilities, and attitudes necessary for effective cooperation in play and work, such matters must be learned. School people and laymen who are aware of this situation also recognize the value of extracurricular activities in providing experiences by which children will learn how to plan and how to manage situations that will include many children, how to budget their time and energy for both work and leisure activities, how to be an effective group member, and how to get along with others.

EXTRACURRICULAR ACTIVITIES

The philosophy of the school will determine the type of extracurricular activities that each school will support. The program should provide activities that will serve as an outlet for those interests, energies, and creative potentialities which are not provided for in the regular curriculum. It also is desirable that children engage in activities that cut across grade lines. Some of the most representative are assemblies, various kinds of clubs, safety patrols and safety councils, athletic events, music groups (rhythm bands, orchestras, bands, glee clubs), and a school newspaper. A brief review of some extracurricular activities is presented in the following paragraphs.

School assembly

The school assembly can be a great force in bringing the children from all grades together, thus making it possible for them to work together on projects, to share enjoyment of interesting experiences, and to make the entire community aware of the school program. Some schools hold frequent, short assemblies, while others hold longer but less frequent meetings. At an assembly various grades may present any phase of school work, such as culminations of units of work, musical programs, dramatizations, puppet shows. Outside speakers who understand children and have a message for them may be invited to share their experiences or talents with the school. The assembly also may serve as a clearinghouse for problems related to the whole school: observing safety measures at crossings, conduct in the lunch room, special school celebrations, and the like. Values to be derived from a school assembly are the development of leadership and poise, acquiring desirable habits of conduct in large groups, socialization through the intermingling of many children, broadening of interests and information, and securing unity in the school.

School newspaper

A school paper offers many opportunities for children in several grades to plan and work together. It also is a means of making contacts with parents. Children in upper grades can assume responsibilities for editing contributions made by the different grades and by individual children and for publication of the paper. A newspaper project is an outlet for creative literary and artistic abilities. It promotes a unified school spirit. In the various activities of publishing a school paper children learn to cooperate, to be considerate of others, to be tactful, to make decisions, and to evaluate their product.

Clubs

Every child should have an opportunity to belong to a school-sponsored club of his choice. Typical clubs related to more formal school work are book and library clubs. Hobby clubs grow out of children's interests and provide opportunities for them to explore their creative potentialities. Music clubs, such as band, orchestra, and glee clubs, provide additional opportunities for children to develop skills that would be difficult to acquire in any other way. The educational values attained through the various club activities sponsored directly by the school are development of leisure-time activities, teaching parliamentary procedures, enrichment of social experiences, and development of leadership, self-control, self-expression, and responsibility.

Similar values are found in clubs which are not sponsored directly by the school but are closely related to it, such as teacher-sponsored groups. Audubon Junior Clubs study and protect birds. Ten or more children of elementary school age may organize a club under an adult advisor. Children who are interested in science may form a science club and may affiliate, without charge, with the Science Clubs of America. Sponsors should be science teachers. These teachers should possess to a considerable degree the quality of leadership.

The Junior Red Cross is the American Red Cross in the schools. The program meets the needs of the school and should serve as a factor contributing to the regular school program. Each elementary schoolroom is entitled to receive the *American Junior Red Cross News*. The success of the program requires the combined interest and effort of school authorities and the local Red Cross chapter.

The relationship between the boy scouts and the American schools is very close. Scouts are held in high esteem by citizens in the community, by school faculties, and by students. Girl scout troops are small, democratic groups who respect the rights and beliefs of others. The ideals of the group embody a practical code of conduct and a sound basis for citizenship. Girls ten through fourteen years of age may join the troop. Girls seven through nine years of age are eligible for membership in the Brownie scout group. A boy scout prepares himself for many things, such as camp activities, rescue work, and service to his country. Scouts between the ages of nine and twelve are known as the Cub Pack. Boys living in rural areas who go long distances by bus or car may organize a Lone Scout tribe.

The objective of the camp fire girls program is to provide opportunities for girls of ten and over to work and play together, to learn to plan, to take responsibilities, and to cooperate with others in working toward a common goal. Activities include home crafts, hand craft, health, nature, business, and Indian lore. The junior group is known as Blue Birds; any girl seven to nine years may belong.

4-H Club work is designed to meet the educational needs of rural boys and girls. The age limits usually range from ten to twenty years. Local leaders may be teachers, farmers, homemakers, or men or women of other professions. Each member does a piece of work that teaches better ways in homemaking, in agriculture, in raising cattle or poultry, or the like. The general activities of the 4-H Clubs include demonstrations, club days and club picnics, nature hikes, tours to observe good practices, camps, exhibits.

Leadership and program

Much of the success of an extracurricular activity depends upon its sponsor. In many elementary schools a part of the teacher's load is to sponsor at least one extracurricular activity. When administrators select new teachers, they look for those who can and will take the responsibility for an extracurricular program as well as a person prepared to teach basic skills. The sponsor of extracurricular activity should possess the following qualities.

1. Like to associate with boys and girls of school age.
2. Enlist confidence of boys and girls.
3. Be keenly interested in the world around her.
4. Be willing to give time and thought to making the club or group activities a success.
5. Be able to plan systematically.
6. Have a contagious enthusiasm.
7. Have a democratic spirit.
8. Have a sense of humor.
9. Be able to give constructive suggestions for activities.
10. Be able to guide without dictation.
11. Be able to find chief satisfaction in child growth, rather than in expressed appreciation of her efforts.

The most desirable outcomes will not automatically result from pupil participation in haphazard extracurricular activities. If the maximum educational benefits are to result, the activities and the pupil participation must be directed toward educational objectives that are just as definite as those of the tool subjects.

When a teacher is assigned the supervisorship of a student activity, she should consider carefully its potential contributions to educational objectives and read what others have said about them. She should think of the various mental, physical, and other activities in which students participating in the activity will engage and evaluate each of these items with respect to the contributions they may make to skills, attitudes, ideals, interests, information, habits, and understandings. The results of participation should be thought of as—

1. Contributing to important objectives of a nature not provided for by the curriculum, for example, outcomes involved in cooperation, leadership, and initiative.
2. Contributing to objectives of at least moderate importance not provided for in the curriculum, such as dramatic ability.
3. Reinforcing the curriculum by contributing additional experience to important objectives not adequately provided for in the curriculum, for example, those outcomes involved in oral and written expression, understanding of community life, and social competence.
4. Contributing to relatively important objectives, for example, pride in achievement of class, feeling of oneness or unity in group endeavors, loyalty to larger groups, good sportsmanship.
5. Avoiding repetition of experiences provided in the regular curriculum, for example, practice in handwriting or music.
6. Avoiding the formation of erroneous ideas or false standards of values such as the following.

a) Wrong impressions about business and business methods.
b) Superficial or unbusinesslike methods of accounting.
c) Snobbishness and conceit among cliques.
d) Undemocratic or unsocial political practices.
e) Obsession with winning at all costs.
f) Inferior techniques in speech, writing, singing, playing an instrument.
g) Excessive participation resulting in neglect of other educational activities, overwork, loss of sleep.
7. Contributing to guidance and personality development, for example, helping socially inferior individuals to develop skills in group participation to build up self-confidence.

Good planning and supervision of extracurricular activities reduces to a minimum the waste of time and motion through repetition of activities beyond the point of diminishing returns. In the classroom, teachers usually avoid waste resulting from excessive repetition—indeed they are forced to the other extreme. In extracurricular activities, it is a rather common occurrence for children to continue a type of experience long after educational returns begin to decrease.

Good planning and supervision of activities also calls for careful consideration and analysis of the types and relative importance of outcomes. The matter cannot be dismissed by thinking of the results of participation as "training." "Training" must be thought of in more specific terms, that is, as acquisition of specific information, understanding, interests, ideals, attitudes, habits, or skills. Outcomes must be scrutinized, evaluated, and credited or charged to a particular activity.

The better-trained and more successful teacher today does not abandon educational statesmanship to cater to the whims, appetites, and prejudices of the untrained adults of the neighborhood or the untrained and immature young learners. Compromising when necessary or feasible, he steers a firm course toward a long-range educational objective.

The teachers less well trained and those lacking in character tend either to lose sight of educational objectives or to sacrifice them in the interest of expediency or personal popularity. A great many supervisors of extracurricular activities think more of putting on a public exhibition, which is pleasing to the adults and seems to reflect credit upon their achievements, than of the training received by the children who are participating.

There are other important considerations which if kept in mind and observed in the management of children's activities will contribute to greater educational returns. Among the more important are these.

1. Some individuals need the type of training provided by any given activity much more than others.
2. The importance and values of the activity should be recognized by children, teachers, and parents.
3. Activities must not be dominated and supervised too much in detail by the sponsor.

From these considerations, many suggestions for the conduct of extra-class activities may be derived. Among them may be mentioned the following:

1. Enough activities should be provided for all, for example, not merely one team, or one cast for one play.
2. Participation, particularly in the roles of leadership, should be rotated not only to provide opportunities for more individuals, but to prevent participation by a few children beyond the point where diminishing educational returns result.
3. Individuals most in need of a certain type of experience should be encouraged to participate in the activity most likely to provide that type of experience.
4. Those already well trained along certain lines should permit others more in need of particular types of training to participate.
5. Recognition of the importance of activities should be evident in the selection, promotion, and salary of teachers and in such matters as marks.
6. Teachers should recognize that the educational value of extra-curricular activities is dependent in part upon the opportunities for planning, initiative, organization, and leadership by learner-participants. An important characteristic of activities is the greatly diminished teacher domination.

The following additional suggestions apply especially to directing club activities.

1. The teacher should give careful thought to the kinds of activities the club may profitably carry on and the way in which those activities may be made most educational.
2. The teacher should meet with committees frequently, especially in the early days of the club, until sound patterns of activity are established.
3. The teacher should assist the club in determining the qualifications for its officers but should not bring pressure to bear in favor of specific individuals.
4. The teacher should guide the officers of the club in their thinking but avoid attempting to shape their conclusions too aggressively.

5. The teacher should permit the club, its committees, and its officers to use their own judgment even when their decisions seem not to be the best. The good teacher realizes that such a plan is sound educationally and should be departed from only in rare cases of fundamental principle and unusual importance.

THE PARENT-TEACHER ASSOCIATION

Teachers work directly with the local P.T.A. school unit. The local P.T.A. school units meet regularly in the respective school buildings. Even though membership is optional, it is advisable for teachers to belong to the group. By having a sympathetic understanding of the problems of the P.T.A., teachers may become very influential in helping the organization realize its goals which are stated in the *Parent-Teacher Manual* as follows:

To promote the welfare of children and youth in home, school, church, and community.

To raise the standards of home life.

To secure adequate laws for the care and protection of children and youth.

To bring into closer relation the home and the school, that parents and teachers may cooperate intelligently in the training of the child.

To develop between educators and the general public such united effort as will secure for every child the highest advantages in physical, mental, social, and spiritual education.[1]

The P.T.A. groups in practically every community are faced with at least one serious problem. Officers do succeed in getting members, but to get active participation from those who belong is another matter. Many feel that when they have paid their dues and have attended the first meeting, they have discharged their responsibilities to the organization. This situation may be due to the fact that the programs of meetings do not appeal to many of the members. Often most of the evening is devoted to business, such as the minutes, treasurer's report, and reports of special committees. Frequently an outside speaker will discuss a topic which is not directly related to local problems or issues. Often teachers will find that educational values to be derived from the meeting are negligible. A very serious weakness is that many teachers are not willing to assume a role of leadership in improving the situation. Yauch, Bartels, and Morris make the following recommendations for teachers.[2]

[1] National Council of Parents and Teachers, *Parent-Teacher Manual* (Chicago: The Congress, 1953), p. 4.

[2] Wilbur A. Yauch, Martin H. Bartels, Emmet Morris, *The Beginning Teacher* (New York: Henry Holt & Co., Inc., 1955), pp. 299-300.

1. Accept your obligations to work closely with the P.T.A. and participate as an active member.
2. Accept the present way of doing things, without negative judgments for at least the first year, or until you have become fully accepted by the parents. But don't be too much of an "eager beaver" at the start.
3. Accept offered responsibility for holding office, and don't act like a shrinking violet by assuming false modesty when asked. Volunteer only when invited and don't "horn in."
4. Win your way into the hearts of the parents by your consistent concern for their children. Be ready to discuss their problems under any and all circumstances.
5. Act like "one of the gang." Divest yourself of your academic robes on entering the meetings. This is not to suggest that you lose your dignity, but that you deliberately refuse to act according to the stereotype into which the parents may unconsciously cast you. Talk "shop" only when the parents indicate their interest in it. This will be almost exclusively restricted to a discussion of their own child.
6. After full-fledged membership has been won and recognized by the parents, you will be in a position to make suggestions about changes in the program that have a chance to be accepted.
7. Attempt to steer the concerns of parents gradually away from a narrow interest in their own child to a broader concern for the welfare of all children.
8. Try to involve a larger portion of the membership in active participation in meetings. This may call for a radical change in custom which will need to be introduced slowly.
9. Support the local organization loyally in your discussions with individual parents. You have a much better opportunity to come in contact with parents whom the P.T.A. is unable to reach.
10. Be positive about the group. Even though you may not be entirely enthusiastic about the present situation, act as though you were. This is contagious and will influence change to occur in desired directions.
11. Put the "T" back into P.T.A. You are the educational leader upon whom the parents depend for direction.

PUBLIC RELATIONS

The teacher should always be alert to possibilities of contributing to a better understanding of the work of the school. Not only should she cooperate wholeheartedly with the program of the entire school system and that of the building or school in which she is employed, but cooperatively with the principal and other teachers, she should carry on public relations activities. Among the public relations activities employed successfully by many schools and teachers are exhibits of the work of the children (handwork, musical performances, plays, playlets) before service clubs and other organizations in the community, at county fairs, or in show windows downtown; stories in local newspapers as well as in the school paper about the work of the children and developments in the school, new equipment, standard test results, honors awarded to the school or its representatives, special honors, and unusual achievements of individual teachers. In public presentation of children or of their work it is advisable to observe certain important principles:

1. School administrators should give due credit to children and teachers.
2. Teachers should give due credit to children and not monopolize the spotlight.
3. Individual children should not be praised excessively or exhibited conspicuously; keep the center of interest in the group rather than in any individual.
4. Individual teachers should be careful not to overdo publicity which seems to be boastful or center too much upon themselves.

A friendly relationship between the home and school is most desirable. Mutual understanding on the part of parents and teachers is important for all children. A child who is facing problems in making adjustments in his relationships with other children or in making progress in schoolwork benefits particularly when parents and teachers share in studying his difficulties. Often classroom problems are related to problems in the home, as home forces that have influenced the child's behavior often continue to carry over into the classroom.

Sometimes the teacher is invited into the home by the child or parent to have a meal or to see a new baby. The teacher also may make a visit of her own volition. In the latter case, she may wish to visit a child who is ill, to secure information, or to promote good home-school relationships. A friendly home call with both parents and child present gives the teacher an opportunity to clarify distorted accounts about the school by the child. An understanding among parents, children, and teacher usually clears many complex problems.

The information which a teacher receives during her home visitation should be respected. The teacher will learn much about the status of the home, the interests of parents and children, and standards of conduct in the home. The parents may give the teacher confidential information regarding family relationships and peculiarities of the child. If teachers use the information obtained in an intelligent way, parents will usually have a friendly feeling toward the school.

RESEARCH

Not only is the physician far more completely trained than the teacher, but with few exceptions he continues when in practice to read the results of medical research and findings. There are scores of journals printed in English in which medical research is published. More than 95 per cent of the physicians and surgeons in the United States receive and most of them read fairly regularly the *Journal of the American Medical Association,* in which each week there are on the average approximately ten or a dozen articles and forty or fifty large pages of reports of medical research.

Teachers are generally not well trained in reading reports of educational research, much less in doing research. They do not possess an adequate stock of concepts and terminology in statistical and experimental methods. Many journals publishing educational research insist that the writers of the articles prepare their reports in relatively nontechnical terms. There is therefore very little reason for any teacher not to keep abreast of the more important educational research.

Media of publication

Among the more useful media of publication of educational research are the following periodicals, which are here classified on the basis of the relative technicality of the reports published:

Technical
> *Journal of Educational Psychology.* Warwick & York, Inc., Baltimore.

Somewhat Technical
> *Journal of Educational Research.* All fields but more articles on elementary education. Department of Education, University of Wisconsin, Madison.
> *Review of Educational Research.* Summaries of the findings of researchers. Each issue is devoted to a single field, for example, "The Language Arts." The cycle of fields is repeated each three or four years. U.S. Office of Education, Washington, D.C.
> *Journal of Applied Psychology.* Northwestern University, Evanston, Ill.

Nontechnical
> *Understanding the Child.* A magazine for teachers. The National Committee for Mental Hygiene, New York.
> *Elementary School Journal.* Elementary education. Department of Education Publications, University of Chicago, Chicago.
> *Education Research Bulletin.* Ohio State University, Columbus.

Many of the more complete and technical reports of research are published in the form of small books or bulletins. There are several rather important series of such publications including the following:

Contributions to Education. Principally the reports of researches conducted as doctoral studies. Teachers College, Columbia University, New York.
Supplementary Educational Monographs. University of Chicago, Chicago.

Often an investigation is of such proportions that a book of several hundred pages or even a set of several books is necessary to report it. In these categories are:

Eugene R. Smith, Ralph W. Tyler, and Others, Appraising and Recording Student Progress. ("Adventure in American Education Series.") Progressive Education Association. New York: Harper & Bros., 1942. Vol. III.
Lewis Madison Terman, Mental and Physical Traits of a Thousand Gifted Children. Stanford University, 1925. Genetic Studies of Children. Vol. I.

Some volumes contain reviews or summaries of research in a given field. For example, William S. Gray's "Summary of Reading Investigations, July 1, 1954, to June 30, 1955" was reported periodically in the Journal of Educational Research (Vol. XLIX, pp. 401-36).

If teachers feel that they cannot afford to purchase personal copies of these books or subscribe to research publications they should ask the administration of their schools to buy them for the professional library which the majority of school systems now have.

Essentials for experimental study

Teachers who have not had courses in research methods, in measurement, and in statistical methods should at their first opportunity take such courses. Until they can take courses in these fields, they should read an elementary book on each of these subjects. Among the suitable books are the following.

Corey, Stephen M., Action Research to Improve School Practices. New York: Teacher's College, Columbia University, 1953.
Garrett, Henry E., Statistics in Psychology and Education. New York: Longmans, Green & Co., Inc., 1953.

From training in research methods, measurement, and statistical methods the teacher will learn to recognize the characteristics of a sound experimental study of learning and of teaching procedures, including the following essentials:

1. Employment of a control group of learners comparable to the experimental group and of the same degree and pattern of distribution of ability,

educational status, and ability to learn, and of equal status with respect to the things to be learned. Comparability is usually measured by:

    a. General intelligence test, mental age, and intelligence quotient.

    b. Tests of information, skills, understandings, habits, or other outcomes to the development of which the experimental learning experiences should make material contribution.

    c. Marks and ratings by former teachers.

2. Control of factors, other than the method or materials being investigated, likely to influence growth of the students in the areas of the more important outcomes, for example:

    a. Age

    b. Sex

    c. General home environment

    d. Relative skill of the teacher or teachers, both in general and with particular respect to the experimental and control methods and materials

    e. Opportunities to learn elsewhere, in other words, stimuli, outside the experimental group, to the development of the outcomes to be measured.

3. Selection (or development) and use of reliable and valid measures of growth outcomes during the experimental period. (These measures should grow out of the experimental method and materials and should not be more subject-matter information tests. Measures should be expressed in terms of units which are reasonably equal and comparable, so that growth as indicated by final and initial scores of 60 and 40 respectively will be equivalent to growth as indicated by scores 70 and 50, or 45 and 25.)

4. Appropriate statistical treatment, for example, determination of the statistical reliability of whatever differences are found, including the extent to which they may be the result of unreliability of the measures of growth or chance errors of sampling. (If coefficients of correlation are employed they should be appropriate, for example, not linear for nonlinear data, and they should be carefully interpreted.)

5. A painstaking and logical interpretation of the data and the findings, sufficient to pass the following tests.

    a. Were all the more important possible outcomes adequately measured?

    b. Were experimental and control groups approximately equivalent in ALL the important regards that would likely determine the amount of growth during the experimental period?

    c. Were all nonexperimental factors likely to influence growth during the experimental period eliminated or so controlled as to produce equivalent effects upon the two groups, for example, learning from outside sources or the relative lack of experience of the teacher with the experimental methods?

    d. To what extent could the differences discovered or the fact that no significant differences were discovered be attributed to chance?

    e. Were the general conclusions of the study applicable alike to bright, dull, and average learners? to boys and to girls? to younger and to older learners?

    f. To what extent could the conclusions be applied to other classes? other subjects? learners of other ages? learners in other types of communities? learners in schools employing different methods?

g. To what extent were the experimental results affected by attitudes which were not typical or permanent of the learners or of the teachers?

Cooperative research

In many of the larger cities investigations are being carried on under the leadership, planning, and direction of competent investigators. Under their direction teachers assist by cooperating in the course of their regular duties or by serving on committees or in other capacities as their training and ability qualify them. These investigations usually deal with such subjects as learning, course-of-study development, individual problem children, construction of measuring instruments, achievement, pupil adjustment, home environment, community conditions, employment opportunities, and the like. Many of the more desirable positions in larger school systems are open only to those with training, interest, and capacity to carry on or to assist in any way in carrying on investigational or creative research.

Action research

Teachers are professionally interested in the quality of their work. They have the background, experience, and ability to analyze their work and to help the school improve its program. Action research is research that is undertaken by teachers and/or supervisors so as to have a better understanding and to make more effective decisions relative to their teaching problems. In this work, participants use the scientific method of problem-solving. Steps which are used by teachers and supervisors in action research are:

1. Defining the problem.
2. Formulating tentative hypothesis.
3. Isolating crucial factors relative to the problem.
4. Collecting and analyzing data and making generalizations.
5. Using the generalizations in order to improve their instruction.

Problems that are specifically suited to action research include (1) remedial aids for retarded readers, (2) group work for children of varying abilities, (3) report cards to be sent to parents, (4) unique reading techniques, (5) improvement of science program, (6) effectiveness of various visual aids, etc.

By using a scientific approach in solving school problems, teachers are learning to identify their own problems, developing an understanding of what they are doing, and acquiring self-confidence. Often problems are of such a nature that the solution requires several teachers to work together. This is an excellent way to create a strong professional attitude on the part of teachers which results in a higher morale throughout the school system.

QUESTIONS, PROBLEMS, AND EXERCISES

1. Discuss the educational values to be derived from assembly programs; from recreation clubs.

2. Is a school council consisting of elected members from all the intermediate and upper grades desirable? Defend your answer.

3. Assume that you have been assigned (without any experience) to one of the following sponsorships—school newspaper, assembly programs, scouts. What steps would you take in preparing for the responsibility?

4. Enumerate the values of after-school recreation clubs.

5. Observe and evaluate several school assembly programs.

6. Assume responsibility for a week of activities of a Cub or Brownie group. Work out your plans beforehand. Keep notes on how your plans work out.

7. Organize a panel discussion and have the group present to the class a summary on "How the P.T.A. can function in clarifying crucial local educational problem or issues."

8. Make a list of all the more important things a teacher should endeavor to learn about the homes of children in her room.

9. What, in a sixth grade, could you exhibit or bring to the attention of the community as a means of helping the public appreciate the work of schools?

10. Find at least one issue or copy of the periodicals mentioned in connection with research and select several good research reports of interest to you. Make an abstract of one research report. Include objectives, techniques, sources and nature of data, findings, and conclusions.

11. Write four additional study topics related to this chapter.

SELECTED SUPPLEMENTARY READINGS

BUHLER, CHARLOTTE, FAITH SMITTER, SYBIL RICHARDSON, and FRANKLYN BRADSHAW. *Childhood Problems and the Teacher.* New York: Henry Holt & Co., Inc., 1952.

The book is presented effectively by using case studies as related to specific problems of children. The major issues presented are home visits, parent-teacher conferences, and group meetings.

COREY, STEPHEN M. "Action Research and Classroom Teacher," *N.E.A. Journal.* XLIII (February, 1954), 79-80.

A concise and clear presentation of what constitutes action research.

EVERETT, SAMUEL, and CHRISTIAN ARNDT. *Teaching World Affairs in American Schools.* New York: Harper & Bros., 1956.

Chapters pertinent to this topic are chap. iv, "Clubs, Forums and Youth Conferences"; chap. v, "Assemblies and Other All-School Activities." Descriptions are presented of ways in which international understanding is sought through student organizations as noted in chapter headings. More applicable to grades 6, 7, 8.

SMITH, MARY NEEL. "We Improved Instruction by Means of Action Research," *N.E.A. Journal,* XLIV (April, 1955), 229-30.

A presentation of action research used in Denver Junior High School to improve the instructional program. The results were so satisfactory that a new series of action-research investigation was put into action.

WINGO, G. MAX, and RALEIGH SCHORLING. *Elementary-School Student Teaching.* 2d ed. New York: McGraw-Hill Book Co., Inc., 1955.

Chap. xv, "The Guidance of Extraclass Activities," discusses extraclass activities from the point of view of intellectual, social, and esthetic needs of children. The qualifications and responsibilities of the sponsor and the organization of the program are presented in a concise and clear manner.

YAUCH, WILBUR A., MARTIN H. BARTELS, and EMMET MORRIS. *The Beginning Teacher.* New York: Henry Holt & Co., Inc., 1954.

Chap. xv presents clearly ways to contact parents of school children. Following techniques are analyzed: parent-teacher conferences, home visitation, open house, news sheets, and active P.T.A.

23

THE TEACHER'S GROWTH IN SERVICE

The acquisition of knowledges, attitudes, and skills essential to effective teaching is dependent upon a suitable preservice education supplemented by continual growth throughout a teaching career. For many teachers the challenge to constant growth is impelling. By the nature of her work the teacher is in an advantageous position to continue her education. Therein lies one of the main attractions of the teaching profession.

NEED FOR CONTINUING GROWTH

Teachers have not only the opportunity but the responsibility for continuing personal and professional growth. A few reasons why continuing growth is necessary are discussed briefly in the following paragraphs.

Limitations of preservice education

In an effective preservice program of education for teachers, the elements of general education and the foundations of professional orientation can be provided, but the feeling of responsibility inherent in an actual teaching situation is difficult to produce at the preservice level. In an in-service education program, discussions of principles of learning and teaching can more readily be linked to the realities of a classroom environment. The need for an in-service education program would still exist even with improved programs of teacher internship. As in other professions, it is too much to expect that one short period of training can provide teachers with the education needed for a lifelong professional career. Education provided in the preservice period must constantly be supplemented by individual and group efforts. While more realistic education programs can contribute greatly to the teacher's preparation, many of the understandings needed can only be acquired by firsthand experiences with children and adults in school and community life.

New developments in teaching

Recent studies of human relations and social progress have revealed principles which have far-reaching implications for school practice. A significant development in social processes has been the technique of democratic group discussion in which leadership is not on a *status* basis but changes from one member to another in terms of each participant's contribution to group thinking. The perfection and use of this method may easily revolutionize pupil-teacher as well as teacher-supervisor relationships.

Modern psychology has provided new insights into child development and growth. In fact, many psychologists insist that if teachers were to utilize our present knowledge of human behavior effectively our schools could produce well-adjusted individuals free from frustrations and useless fears.

Many school practices in regard to marks, examinations, and discipline lag far behind present knowledge of rational human behavior, mental health, and motivation. Many of the present plans of organizing and presenting instructional materials are based upon the generally discredited stimulus-response psychology. Methods involving drill on meaningless, isolated, and unrelated bits of subject matter are based upon the same outmoded theory of psychology. The potential value of new instructional material such as audiovisual aids has not been clearly perceived by teachers.

Developments in community-centered schools chart the path away from educational programs isolated from the realities of living. New instruments designed to measure the outcomes of teaching in terms of attitudes, interest, and ideals, rather than the mastery of subject matter, present a fruitful field of study for groups of teachers. Techniques of diagnosis have been devised which make it possible for the teacher to study the child against his background of home and community life. Sociometric techniques make it possible for the teacher to study child group structure, thereby providing an insight into the child as a member of a functioning social group.

Changing conditions in society

Much has been written in regard to the dynamic character of society and the resulting lag between education and life. Change is constantly being accelerated, especially in the areas of communication, transportation, and science. There is good reason to believe that, once momentum is established in social studies, it can be accelerated in a manner comparable to the acceleration in natural science.

The ever-increasing interdependence of peoples makes new social processes compulsory. The common man is emerging to demand respect for human personality, regardless of race, creed, or color. This is the essence of democracy. Political democracy represents only one aspect of the democratic way of life. The economic and social aspects are equally important. In order for the teacher to assist pupils to experience democracy in their school relationships, the teacher herself must experience it in her relationships with other teachers and school administrators.

In-service education programs can contribute to the teacher's orientation to the world scene. In some curriculum revision programs, the participants have spent the first year in an analysis and interpretation of the social forces which affect the thinking and behavior of people. A good point of departure is a study of conditions in the local community and participation in its affairs.

Emerging concept of education

Education has acquired different meanings from one generation to another. Today the school has undertaken the task of the all-round development of "all the children of all the people." The emphasis upon the whole child as a self-directing member of society has resulted in the introduction of new instructional materials and procedures. Both the scope and variety of teaching materials have been greatly expanded. The new emphasis upon the social aspects of education is linked with the idea that in a democratic society, civic and social education is essential for all citizens.

Despite the acceptance by many teachers of the broader concept of education, conflicting opinions exist in regard to both the responsibilities of the school and the best methods to achieve them. Group study and discussion of these matters can well be incorporated in an in-service education program for teachers.

New concepts of child development

Each child is now recognized as a unique personality, actively conditioned by his environment. He is the product of his experiences in his community, home, and school. He has been required to accept without question in the short period of his life all the taboos that civilized man has acquired through centuries of slow progress. His emancipation from complete adult domination is being consummated. His needs embrace every aspect of human existence—social, emotional, intellectual, and physical. Development in these various areas may be very uneven and slow. His efforts to maintain his personality intact are being assaulted by powerful forces from every direction. The fundamental drives to human action—desire for recognition, security, new adventure—are unrestrained. He is highly sensitive to the reactions of other children of his own age group. Frustration and emotional blocks to learning result from unsympathetic, unintelligent efforts of teachers and parents to require him to conform to adult standards of thought and behavior. Growth cannot be forced. These and other recently developed understandings of child growth and development need to be studied at length with their implication for teaching.

Clinics on child development are designed to give teachers insight into child growth. In her daily contacts in the classroom, the teacher has an excellent opportunity to observe the reactions of children to their social environment. She also is in a position to analyze the sources of children's confusions and fears. A study of the various aspects of human behavior in an in-service education program should assist the teacher in providing the basis for interpreting her classroom observations.

Growth inherent in the profession

Every social situation is novel. No two situations are composed of identical factors in the same combination or relationship. Each evolving situation makes a demand upon the individual for adjustment and orientation. The teacher carries on her work in a rapid succession of novel situations. The challenge presented by each newly developing situation requires great adaptive ability. No fixed teaching procedures or formulae will suffice. This fact makes teaching difficult but also fascinating. The alert teacher is constantly stimulated by new factors or different combinations of factors in the teaching situation. Pupils react differently in each new situation. Their behavior patterns are in process of continual modification. Teaching cannot be completely routinized. There is need for experimentation in more effective procedures, in the use of new instructional materials, and of more accurate methods of evaluation of the outcomes of instruction.

Stagnation is fatal to all forms of living organisms. When growth ceases, deterioration begins. The teacher who fails to continue her own intellectual growth soon finds it difficult to stimulate such growth in her students. Only by an extension of her own intellectual life can the teacher augment that of others.

Life soon loses its zest for the person who makes no effort to advance his own knowledge or deepen his understandings. The best insurance for mental health is the stimulus of a strong impelling interest in personal and professional improvement. In the field of intellectual achievement, the teacher should be a worthy representative of the culture she serves. The teacher's interests should be constantly deepening and widening. Her enthusiasm for life should be constantly revitalized by new ideas.

TYPES OF IN-SERVICE EDUCATION

Teachers' growth in service can be promoted by (1) participation in cooperative endeavors with other teachers and (2) individual effort. An adequate in-service education program usually includes both types of activities. While many aspects of personal and professional growth can best be provided for by sharing in group undertakings, there are many phases of the program in which it is advantageous to employ procedures which are individualistic in nature. The relative value of the two elements of the program depends upon the needs of individual teachers. Those teachers who have limited experience in working with other persons may derive greater benefit from group enterprises, whereas other teachers may need the opportunity to work at some task requiring individual thought and effort. In most instances, the individual teacher who is desirous of continuing her growth in service will find it advantageous to include both cooperative and individual projects in her program.

The elementary school teacher is afforded numerous opportunities for both types of learning experiences. Among the most effective activities are:

Cooperative Enterprises	*Individual Endeavors*
Faculty and staff meetings	Graduate work
Teacher councils	Reading—general and professional
Study groups	Travel
Workshops	Membership and participation in professional organizations
Demonstration centers	Professional writing
Study clinics	
Orientation programs	
Group excursions in community	
Observation of other teachers' work	
Teacher committees	
Action research	

Cooperative

A cooperative program of in-service education of teachers serves the purpose of vitalizing the work of the school, as well as promoting teachers' growth. The two functions are interdependent. In this chapter, however, the teacher-education aspect of the program will be emphasized. The effectiveness of cooperative programs of in-service education is closely related to democratic procedure.

As a member of a group of teachers engaged in study of a problem vital to the school, the individual teacher is presented with an excellent opportunity for personal and professional growth. As a participating member of such a group, the teacher has the responsibility for assisting in the promotion and maintenance of conditions conducive to cooperative democratic endeavor.

In a cooperative endeavor each member of the group has the responsibility of identifying and suggesting significant problems for study by the group. These problems should have their origins in the group situation and be of such a nature as can be solved by the group. The only compulsion upon members to participate is provided by the challenge of the problem. In the work and deliberations of the group, the individual teacher should exercise her influence in maintaining conditions which foster free and impartial inquiry. The individual teacher is expected to participate with the group in taking appropriate action to implement group decisions.

Teachers' meetings. The chief value of the general teachers' meeting to the individual teacher is that of providing a general orientation to the broad aspects of the education program of the school system. This purpose is achieved by familiarizing the teacher with the general objectives and policies of the system of which she is a part. Problems which are specific in nature can best be solved in meetings of smaller groups, such as the faculty of a particular school, or in conferences with administrative and supervisory officials.

In many schools teachers are expected to serve on committees which have the responsibility for planning and conducting teachers' meetings.

The following list of topics illustrates the type of problems upon which teachers have made a cooperative attack in their faculty meetings:

Dynamics of child groups
Pupil-teacher planning
Individual differences

General scope of the curriculum
Evaluation of pupil achievement
Guidance responsibilities of teachers

Orientation programs. A continuous educational program is essential to the progress of a school. This continuity is often jeopardized by the large turnover in teaching personnel. For example, many curriculum revision programs have failed of fruition because new teachers did not wholeheartedly accept responsibility for carrying it forward. This difficulty can be alleviated somewhat by the early orientation of new staff members to the ideals and objectives of the program.

New teachers may also encounter difficulty in making the necessary adjustments to the community. The older members of a school faculty can be of assistance to the new teacher in becoming oriented to the new school and community situation. A growing number of school faculties cooperate in extending various forms of hospitality to new members. Such plans have attained excellent results in maintaining cordial relationships between teachers, thus providing a sound basis for constructive, cooperative educational endeavor.

Teacher councils. Central organizations comprised of representatives of classroom teachers, administrative and supervisory staffs, and special-service personnel have been formed in several school systems. Their general purpose is to receive suggestions and opinions of other teachers in regard to different school problems, and convey constructive proposals to the superintendent and board of education. In some instances problems are referred to the council by the superintendent for study and recommendation. The council may also serve as a coordinating and unifying agency by reviewing the reports of various committees of teachers.

From the viewpoint of in-service education, obviously the greatest values accrue to the teachers who have the opportunity to serve as members of the council. However, the opportunity provided by this type of organization for all teachers in a school system to give expression to their ideas on school policies, as well as to benefit from any constructive action growing out of the council's recommendations, serves to create a favorable environment for teacher growth.

Teacher committees. One of the important objectives of a curriculum-revision program is the in-service education of teachers. The organization of a faculty for purposes of curriculum construction usually includes provision for various committees of teachers. In these committees the main work of revision is done.

The study of the multiple problems involved in curriculum revision presents excellent opportunities for teacher growth. One of the necessary and highly important phases of a curriculum development program is that of preparing courses of study for the guidance of teachers in using the suggested curricular materials. An examination of a typical course of study will reveal the great variety of problems which a curriculum committee encounters. The problems range from formulating a statement of the guiding philosophy of a course to making a list of suggestions for evaluating pupil achievement. Another significant outcome of active participation by the teacher in curriculum committee work is that it increases her efficiency in the use of curricular materials to promote more effective pupil learning.

In addition to continuing committees which study the persistent problems of the school program, many short-term committees function in connection with special problems, such as improvement of guidance, library service, and teacher welfare in times of increasing cost of living. These committees are usually terminated after the study has been completed and a report with recommendations is made to the faculty.

Numerous other school problems in addition to those described in the preceding sections of this chapter have been studied by teacher committees. Through their committees, teachers in many school systems participate in the selection of new personnel. By means of interviews, questionnaires, and visits to other schools, the committee obtains information in regard to the qualifications and viewpoints of applicants for administrative and teaching positions in their school. School-board-relations committees represent teachers at some of the meetings of the board in discussions of various instructional problems. Problems of teacher welfare, such as tenure and retirement, have been the subject of teacher group study. In fact many of the teacher tenure and retirement plans now in operation were initiated and sponsored by committees of teachers. Instructional practices likewise have come within the scope of special committee study.

Workshops. No recent development in the in-service education of teachers has attracted more widespread interest than the workshop. The distinctive aspect of the workshop is the opportunity afforded individual teachers and groups of teachers to study the problems which most directly concern them under the most favorable and democratic conditions without regard to conventional class organization and procedures.

Workshops have been conducted under the auspices of various organizations and agencies. They have been—

1. Sponsored by colleges, usually in the summer, for individual teachers from different schools, or for groups of teachers from one school. (In some instances, colleges have conducted extension classes in the form of workshops during the regular school year.)
2. Conducted by public school systems for teachers in the system. (These workshops may include teachers with a special problem or interest, or they may include all the teachers in the system. These may be conducted in the summer or during the school term.)
3. Directed under the joint sponsorship of a college and a public school system.
4. Co-sponsored by a school system and a national organization interested in the education of teachers.

A staff, consisting of a director and a group of consultants representing different fields of interests, is usually selected to direct the general activities of the workshop. The actual plans are made by a committee of teachers, staff members, and representatives of the sponsoring agencies. These plans are based upon information obtained in advance from the prospective members of the workshop. The members organize themselves into different groups on the basis of their interests or problems. Each group elects a representative to a planning committee, whose function is to plan the program from week to week.

On a typical day a workshop group engages in the following activities.

1. A general morning meeting of all members of the workshop is held. Topics of general interest are discussed by the director, consultant, visiting expert, and members of the workshop. These programs are designed to unify the workshop activities, serve as a general clearinghouse for information, and provide continuous motivation for the workshop activities.
2. At the noon hour participants have lunch together to enlarge acquaintance and to develop the spirit of good fellowship.
3. The afternoon is devoted to individual and small-group activities. Conferences with consultants are held. Suitable library materials and audio-visual aids are utilized by individuals and groups. The different groups meet two or three times each week to discuss their specific problems. Provision is made in the schedule for members to work on individual problems and exchange ideas with each other. Flexibility in the organization is provided to permit

the individual member to withdraw from one group when his purposes have been served and become a member of another group.
4. The evening meetings are largely devoted to social activities and recreation.

Evaluations of their experiences by members provide fairly convincing evidence of the importance of workshops in an in-service education program for teachers. Workshop participation, however, represents only one significant type of educative experience. It does not contain all the desirable elements in a program of teacher education. Perhaps every teacher should have some workshop experience. Equally true is the fact that every teacher needs to engage in in-service learning exercises which are not stimulated and directed by group activity.

In respect to the relative value of local school workshops in comparison with college campus workshops, it should be observed that it is easier to relate the activities of the local workshop to the actual problems of a particular school. On the other hand, it should be recognized that many local schools do not have adequate financial resources or library facilities to conduct their own workshops. In the college-directed workshop, the library and other facilities are usually more satisfactory. The exchange of ideas among teachers from different schools in a campus workshop may serve a useful purpose in broadening viewpoints in regard to many school problems.

Demonstration centers. In some city and county school systems, a school which possesses the necessary facilities and competent teachers is designated as a demonstration center. Teachers from other schools are given the opportunity to observe the use of new curricular materials and techniques of teaching. Recently many school systems have established centers to demonstrate the proper use of audio-visual materials. Socialized procedures, such as the project method and unit methods, have served as the basis of many teaching demonstrations.

The value of demonstration to the individual teacher is dependent not only upon the quality of the teaching but also upon the ability of the observer to analyze, interpret, and adapt the procedures observed to her own teaching. To assist the observing teacher in this respect, predemonstration conferences are usually held between the demonstrating teacher and the observers, in which the objectives of the lesson are discussed. The demonstration is also followed by a discussion period in which the teaching procedures and outcomes are evaluated.

Study clinics. Representative teachers from many local school systems attend study clinics conducted at some of the larger universities for the purpose of making an intensive study of some significant problem under the guidance of experts. The list of topics ranges from improved methods of pupil evaluation to methods of understanding children. Important values can be achieved by this type of professional education, especially if the teachers attending the clinic, on returning to their respective schools, share their learning with other members of their faculties.

Group excursions. A requisite for building a sound educational program is a thorough understanding of the community of which the school is a part. The attitudes and behavior of youth can be interpreted only in terms of their community background. A knowledge of community life is likewise essential to the proper utilization of community resources as curricular material.

In an endeavor to understand the economic and social conditions of their school communities, teachers have organized community-study groups. As a part of their activities in this respect, teachers make planned excursions to various places in the community for the purpose of obtaining firsthand information in regard to local housing conditions, industries, welfare, and public service agencies. In larger schools, committees interested in various phases of community life may visit different places and make reports to the entire faculty. Teachers who participate in activities of this nature are better able to assist pupils to bridge the gap between school activities and life outside the school, and to make more effective application of curricular materials to the problems and needs of children living in a particular community.

Observations. Provision is made in many schools for the teachers to observe the work of other teachers in their own and other schools. To insure the maximum benefit to the visiting teacher, the teachers and the supervisor should plan the visits carefully in the light of their purposes and possibilities. These usually are to—

1. See how some theory or method is carried out in actual practice
2. Observe the methods of other teachers and compare them with one's own
3. See how equipment is used
4. Become acquainted with students the visitor may soon have in his own classes
5. Develop an understanding of the work of other teachers

Study groups. There has been an increasing tendency of teachers within a school to form informal groups for the study of a single problem or a series of problems which appear to be pressing for solution in their school. The composition of the study group depends upon the outcomes sought. Teachers with similar professional duties may consider instructional problems within a particular area of the curriculum. For example, the teachers of the third-grade pupils may wish to study curricular materials and teaching procedures suitable for use in that grade. A problem common to persons in different types of schools may be the basis for membership and participation in a study group. For example, representatives of junior high schools, senior high schools, and elementary schools may come together to study the problem of articulation of the schools they represent.

Members of the school personnel charged with the responsibility of achieving a common objective in an educational program may form a study group to consider their common task. For example, physical education teachers, school health service representatives, science teachers, and school cafeteria managers may study means of coordinating as well as strengthening the student health program.

Study groups may be formed by teachers with similar viewpoints on a particular issue for the purpose of devising methods of arousing the interest of other teachers or persons in the matter. Or a study group may seek to promote action along the lines of the teacher's interests.

Aside from its possible value in improving school practice in a particular area, the study group may serve to demonstrate to teachers the democratic way of accomplishing a task. The stimulus of the group, the informality of the organization, and the flexibility of its procedures are conducive to understanding, initiative, and leadership on the part of the individual teacher. Participation in group activities on this basis also tends to promote feelings of comradeship among teachers, as well as a sense of belonging on the part of the individual.

Action research. Action research is a form of educational research in which a group of school personnel endeavor cooperatively to apply the scientific method to the study of a problem within their school. The persons involved in the research usually include teachers, supervisors, and administrators.

The main purpose of action research is the improvement of the local school program. An important incidental outcome of the research is the professional growth of the participating teachers who obtain valuable insights into existing school problems and gain experience in working with other school personnel.

Individual

Membership in professional organizations. The teacher who seeks to keep up in her profession and improve it should be an active member of several professional organizations. These fall into three general groups:

1. State and national general education associations
2. Organizations centering around special fields of teaching or administration
3. Organizations primarily for the improvement of working conditions, salaries, tenure

The *National Education Association,* founded as the National Teachers' Association in 1857, now enrolls more than 660,000, or 53 per cent of the teachers in the United States. It publishes the *Journal of the National Education Association,* which contains short articles on teacher growth and welfare, curriculum, and methods. Within the NEA there are departments primarily concerned with the problems of classroom teaching. In addition to these departments, the association has six deliberative groups which are known as councils or commissions.

The association and its various departments and divisions issue yearbooks and bulletins containing much useful information. While the activities of the association are designed primarily to promote growth in service, it does have a legislative program looking to better support of the schools and has been somewhat active in that field.

The goals of the National Education Association have been officially stated to be:

1. An active democratic education association in every community.
2. A stronger and more effective state education association in every state.
3. A larger and more effective National Education Association.
4. Unified dues—a single fee covering local, state, national and world services—collected by the local.
5. 100% membership enrollment in local, state, and national professional organizations.
6. Unified committees—the chairmen of local and state committees serving as consultants to central national committees.
7. A Future Teachers of America Chapter in every institution preparing teachers.
8. A professionally prepared and competent person in every school position.
9. A strong, adequately staffed state department of education in each state and a more adequate federal education agency.

10. An adequate professional salary for all members.
11. For all educational personnel—professional security guaranteed by tenure legislation, sabbatical and sick leave, and an adequate retirement income for old age.
12. Reasonable class size and equitable distribution of the teaching load.
13. Units of school administration large enough to provide efficient and adequate elementary and secondary educational opportunities.
14. Adequate educational opportunity for every child and youth.
15. Equalization and expansion of educational opportunity including needed state and national financing.
16. A safe, healthful, and wholesome community environment for every child and youth.
17. Adequately informed lay support of public education.
18. An able, public-spirited board of education in every community.
19. An effective world organization of the teaching profession.
20. A more effective United Nations Educational, Scientific and Cultural Organization.
21. More effective cooperation between adult, higher, secondary, and elementary education with increasing participation by college and university personnel in the work of the united profession.
22. A new NEA Educational Center in the nation's capital.[1]

The *National Catholic Education Association* is a voluntary organization of individuals and institutions interested in the welfare of Catholic education. In 1956 there were more than 9,000 members. The purpose of the organization is to strengthen the conviction of its members and of people generally that the proper and immediate end of Christian education is to cooperate with divine grace in forming the true and perfect Christian, and to emphasize that Christian education embraces the whole aggregate of human life—physical and spiritual, intellectual and moral, individual, domestic and social —with the goal of elevating it and perfecting it according to the example and the teaching of Christ. The Association now includes seven departments: Major Seminary, Minor Seminary, College and University, School Superintendents, Secondary School, Elementary School, and Special Education.

In 1916, the *American Federation of Teachers* was formed as an affiliate of the American Federation of Labor. Because of the opposition of the National Education Association and of superintendents and boards of education, the membership in the American Federation of Teachers did not number more than 12,000 until the

---

[1] *Handbook for Local, State, and National Associations* (Centennial edition. Washington, D.C.: National Education Association, 1956-57), pp. 13-38.

depression of the 1930's. Since then, it has grown steadily and has spread into every section of the country. It now has more than 47,000 members. The official journal of the organization, *The American Teacher,* contains many articles of educational and social significance.

The Federation has two main objectives: (1) to consolidate the teachers of the country into a strong group which will be able to protect its own interests; (2) to raise the standard of the teaching class by a direct attack on the conditions which, according to the belief of the Federation, prevent teaching from enjoying the status of a profession. These conditions are lack of academic freedom and of civil liberty and the absence of the opportunity for self-determination of policies and democratic control.

Article II of its constitution states the long-range objectives of the Federation of Teachers to be as follows:

1. To bring associations of teachers into relations of mutual assistance and cooperation
2. To obtain for teachers all the rights to which they are entitled
3. To raise the standard of the teaching profession by securing the conditions essential to the best professional service
4. To promote such a democratization of the schools as will enable them better to equip their pupils to take their places in the industrial, social and political life of the community
5. To promote the welfare of the children of the nation by providing progressively better educational opportunity for all

The rapid growth of the American Federation of Teachers in recent years may be attributed largely to the academic and timid policy of many of the state education associations in improving the welfare and working conditions of classroom teachers. Most state associations tend to be dominated and administered by school administrators, although some of the divisions, such as the classroom teachers' associations, have been free from such control and in some instances have been very effective in obtaining teacher-welfare legislation.

The *American Education Fellowship* was founded in 1924 as the Progressive Education Association. The fellowship stresses a modern philosophy of education and emphasizes the child and his growth and education for fellowship and citizenship from the community to the international level. It has had a considerable influence on educational thought and practice in recent years, despite the fact that it has never enrolled more than a few thousand members. The official journal of the organization is entitled *Progressive Education.*

A *state or territorial educational or teachers' association* exists in each state and territory. Like the national organizations, each state organization issues a journal devoted largely to professional articles, news, and state problems. Most of these journals are of rather mediocre quality as to professional content, but they contain articles of interest to the teachers of the particular state. The state associations have been more active than the national association in obtaining favorable legislation and school funds.

State education associations aim to:

1. Build an informed professional and civic intelligence among members
2. Set every teacher to work on the problems of the profession and the community
3. Improve teaching, the curriculum, and school organization
4. Improve the selection and preparation of teachers
5. Foster a unified profession—strong on local, state, and national levels
6. Support important federal legislation
7. Improve adult and higher education
8. Build public support for public schools
9. Foster world understanding and cooperation
10. Improve community life
11. Enhance teacher welfare, including:
    a) Statewide minimum salaries, with provision for progressively higher standards, and special recognition for added study or travel
    b) A modern salary schedule in each local community to meet its special needs
    c) Provision for teacher tenure and security
    d) Provision for sick leave and sabbatical leave on a cumulative basis
    e) Adequate provision for retirement on account of disability or age

Almost every locality has a number of local associations for educational purposes. The most common are the city and county associations which are formed by groups of the teachers or are branches of the national councils of teachers in the various subjects.

The teacher who wants to improve her teaching ability and keep up with the changes and advances made in educational fields should be a member of some of these organizations. The annual dues are not so high that any teacher need be kept out because of expense.

These organizations are constantly striving to improve the lot of the teacher, improve the materials of instruction, and improve the relations of the teachers with the public. They deserve the cooperation of all teachers.

General reading. As a part of her professional as well as her general cultural growth, the teacher must make definite provision for a systematic reading program. In preparing young people for the world ahead, the teacher must know that world and what goes on in it. Immediately upon beginning her teaching career, she must expand and maintain her knowledge and understanding of the world in which her students will find their lives and problems. She must continue to learn about public affairs—local, state, national, and international.

The public soon loses respect for the teacher and the school that do not prepare young people to understand the new world—the air age, the atomic age, the new era of interdependence nationally and internationally, economically, politically, and culturally.

The teacher should learn to assimilate, discount, and interpret what she reads on current problems and affairs. Few periodicals and newspapers or radio commentators can be relied upon to treat current issues impartially. Nevertheless the teacher can grow steadily in her knowledge and understanding of such matters from reading both sides of an issue.

Teachers, traditionally, are genuinely interested in world peace. World peace will come only as the result of mutual understanding among peoples of all quarters of the globe. The present generation of adults is relatively ignorant and provincial, unsuited for living in the age of atom bombs and international interdependence. Our hope lies in a new generation of better educated adults. Teachers hold the key to world peace and to the continuation of our march toward democracy and a high standard of living for all.

Many teachers take current affairs tests such as the one published by the Cooperative Test Service, attempting each year to improve their scores. It is encouraging and indicative of the trends of the times that the National Teachers' Examination—one of the means of examining prospective teachers in many cities—includes a test on contemporary affairs and culture. A well-balanced program of general reading should do more than keep the teacher informed about developments in the world: it should make provision for reading of books which entertain, new and timely books which the world outside the school is reading, books which will lead to good conversation at the dinner table, books which take one far afield to China, Mexico, or Russia, books valuable for their excellence of style.

The teacher who wishes to enrich her experiences by reading should follow a program such as the following:

1. Read regularly at least one good daily newspaper that has accurate national and international news coverage, even if it arrives a day late from a city some distance away.
2. Read a local newspaper for information about community affairs.
3. Read or scan at least two weekly periodicals:
   a) A journal with a bias in favor of the conservative view
   b) A journal with a bias in favor of progressive and liberal ideas
4. Read or reread at least one of the classics each month.
5. Read one book a month on some current problem.
6. Read one work of fiction or drama each month.

Interesting and reliable small books on current topics can be purchased at nominal cost. Such editions as the Anchor Books, Pocket Books, Penguin Books, Signet Books, and Mentor Books make good reading available to everyone. In addition, there are several series of inexpensive pamphlets written by prominent writers and dealing with domestic and foreign questions. Among these are the Headline Books, published by the Foreign Policy Association of New York and the Public Affairs pamphlets distributed by the Public Affairs Committee, Inc., of New York.

Professional reading. In planning a well-balanced program of reading the teacher should reserve some time for reading a few of the best current professional books and periodicals. No other single means of in-service education offers greater opportunities for the teacher to keep abreast of new developments and trends in the profession than those afforded by a carefully planned program of professional reading. Not only should the teacher keep informed in regard to developments in elementary school teaching but she should be familiar with the new and changing concepts, theories, and practices in education in general.

Professional reading presents the teacher with the opportunity to share in the experiences of other teachers who are seeking to make their teaching more effective. The challenge and the stimulation that come from reports of the endeavors of other teachers add zest to the efforts of the teacher who is desirous of improving her own teaching. Perhaps the greatest value which comes from reading a good professional book is that it enables a teacher to recapture waning enthusiasms and renew her faith in the power of education in human affairs.

Despite the inherent values in professional reading, there is considerable evidence to indicate that the reading materials of large numbers of teachers are very narrow both in scope and in variety. From the great mass of professional literature the teacher should carefully select materials for reading which best serve her needs. No definite prescription can be given that will meet the needs of all teachers. An adequate program of professional reading should include elements which provide information in regard to the following:

1. Significant developments and trends in public education
2. New concepts of learning and child development
3. Promising practices in curricular organization and teaching procedures
4. Newer practices and teaching materials in subjects taught

To assist teachers in selecting reading materials wisely, many educational groups and institutions periodically issue lists of selected books on education. Perhaps the best known of these is published each April in the *Journal of the National Education Association* which lists the sixty best books on education published during the year. Many teachers read the summaries of articles published in the *Education Digest* and select those in which they are particularly interested to read in their entirety in the journal in which the articles were originally published. The *Education Index* contains a rather complete list of articles on education which are published in periodicals. Some of the magazines which feature articles of particular interest to the elementary school teacher are as follows:

Elementary School Journal	*The American Teacher*
Progressive Education	*The Educational Screen*
Childhood Education	*Instructor*
The Grade Teacher	*Science Education*
The Arithmetic Teacher	

Professional writing. No other type of activity carries greater recognition than professional writing. The number and quality of published articles and books are among the most important criteria in determining teacher promotion in many schools. A consideration of the significance of professional writing reveals several good reasons why teachers engage in this type of activity.

The chief value of writing an article for publication accrues to the teacher who does the writing. The actual work of writing must be preceded by a careful study and analysis of the problem. The organization of the material requires the selection of the most relevant data and the rejection of those of minor importance. The necessity of writing the material in a manner to insure clarity, simplicity, and forcefulness of expression provides excellent training for a teacher in improving the quality of her classroom presentation.

Professional writing also enables the teacher to assist other teachers in the solution of some of their problems, thus extending her sphere of usefulness. A description or report of an effective classroom procedure may be instrumental in causing teachers in other schools to improve their own teaching. The classroom situation can be a learning laboratory for the teacher as well as for her pupils. The insights and understandings obtained as a result of firsthand experiences with the problems of pupils serve as a practical basis for significant educational writing.

Travel. Travel is an integral part of the teacher's preparation for teaching. If instructional materials are to be made meaningful to the pupil, they must first be meaningful to the teacher. The vividness and reality of verbal descriptions in books of places, persons, and events can be greatly enhanced by seeing them in their natural surroundings.

By granting salary increases for travel comparable to those allowed for summer school attendance, many school boards have recognized the importance of travel. Large numbers of teachers of modern foreign languages visit the countries where the languages are spoken. A knowledge of a people is indispensable to a genuine understanding of their language. In teaching the social studies, information and inspiration may be obtained from tours of places of current economic and social significance as well as of centers of governmental activity and historical shrines. In teaching science, there is much value in trips to different geographical regions to study at first hand the distinctive features of those areas. A vacation spent in one of the national parks should improve the teaching of teachers. Visits to great art galleries, libraries, and museums can contribute to better teaching of many subjects. By travel and wide reading the teacher can enlarge her vision and discover means of making new applications of the subjects taught.

Many organizations sponsor guided tours for teachers to different parts of this and other countries. These tours have the advantages of convenience and economy. Too frequently, however, these guided trips are organized without sufficient recognition of the interests and needs of individual teachers. Perhaps it is advisable for the teacher to plan her own trip in terms of her particular purposes, interests, financial ability, and time available.

Graduate study. The most convincing evidence that teachers as a group are desirous of improving their instruction is revealed by the fact that thousands of teachers take graduate college work after they begin their teaching careers. Large numbers of teachers attend summer schools conducted by colleges and universities. Many teachers, also, take advantage of the opportunities presented by correspondence and other extension courses to continue their college work in addition to their regular teaching duties. A considerable number of teachers spend their sabbatical leaves in graduate study.

Many school boards recognize the values of graduate study in improving the effectiveness of teaching by increases in salaries of teachers who earn additional credit either in summer school or during the school term. A few school boards require all teachers in their schools to attend summer sessions.

The chances are very great that college courses taken after a person has begun her teaching career will have more meaning and significance to her than similar courses taken before she has had any teaching experience. The content of the course can be related more directly to problems encountered in actual classroom situations. Courses can frequently be chosen in terms of the specific problems of the individual teachers. Some of the most important values of summer school attendance are derived from informal discussions of teaching with teachers from other schools.

The significance of postgraduate work in improving teaching efficiency is dependent upon several factors. Since the quality of instruction varies greatly in different summer schools, the teacher should exercise intelligent discrimination in the selection of the college in which she is to do her study. The institution, instructors, and courses can be chosen in the light of the teacher's individual teaching problems and future professional plans. If good judgment is exercised in respect to these matters, the background of teaching experience and the earnestness which characterize the study of teachers will make summer school study an invaluable experience.

In the event that college courses taken by extension during the school term are closely related to problems being encountered by the teacher in her actual teaching, they can contribute greatly to teacher improvement in service. Properly correlated, the classroom situation can serve as a laboratory for the study of topics suggested in the course. Unless the two are supplementary, it is usually feasible to postpone the course until summer school.

QUESTIONS, PROBLEMS, AND EXERCISES

1. Assume that you are a teacher in an elementary school in a town of 10,000 population. Outline in some detail a plan for your own professional growth.

2. Under what conditions are school boards justified in requiring all teachers to attend summer school once every three years?

3. What are some of the difficulties involved in a truly democratic cooperative attack by teachers on a problem existing in their school?

4. Prepare a time budget which would enable you to devote a part of each week to general and professional reading.

5. Discuss the statement: "Teacher training institutions should fully prepare teachers in order that in-service growth will not be necessary."

6. Assume that you are chairman of a faculty committee appointed to study and report the possibilities of holding a summer workshop for teachers. Outline your procedure.

7. Make an inventory of the teacher committees in your school and list the work of each.

8. List some books, magazines, and professional journals which you would recommend for teachers to read.

SELECTED SUPPLEMENTARY READINGS

ALLEN, JACK. *The Teacher of the Social Studies. Twenty-third Yearbook.* Washington, D.C.: National Council for the Social Studies, 1952.

Chaps. vi, vii, and viii. Describes ways of teacher growth in service.

ANDERSON, KENNETH E., and HERBERT A. SMITH. "Preservice and In-Service Education of Elementary and Secondary School Teachers," *Review of Educational Research,* XXXV (June, 1955), 221.

Reports the effectiveness of an in-service education program for teachers in terms of pupil achievements.

COREY, STEPHEN M. *Action Research to Improve School Practices.* New York: Bureau of Publications, Teachers College, Columbia University, 1953.

Discussion of the purpose, methods, and values of action research.

MELCHIOR, WILLIAM T. *Instructional Supervision.* Boston: D. C. Heath & Co., 1950.

Part II, "Indirect Approaches to In-Service Education Improve the Learning Experiences of Pupils and Teachers." Discussion of studying pupils using community resources, and modifying the curriculum as procedures in improving learning experiences of pupils and teachers.

MITCHELL, JAMES R. "The Workshop as an In-Service Education," *North Central Quarterly,* XXVIII (April, 1954), 421-57.

Report of a study conducted by the Subcommittee of the Association on In-Service Education of Teachers.

NATIONAL SOCIETY FOR THE STUDY OF EDUCATION. *In-Service Education, Fifty-sixth Yearbook,* Part i. Chicago: University of Chicago Press, 1957.

Entire volume devoted to a comprehensive and thorough treatment of in-service education of teachers.

REID, HALE C. *In-Service Education of the Beginning Teacher.* DeKalb Conference Report, National Commission on Teacher Education and Professional Standards. Washington, D.C.: National Educational Association, 1955. Pp. 304-9.

Report on the in-service education program for beginning teachers in Cedar Falls, Iowa.

SHARP, D. LOUISE. *Why Teach.* New York: Henry Holt & Co., Inc., 1957.

A collection of tributes from men and women in all walks of life to the members of the teaching profession. Should provide a rich source of inspiration and satisfaction for teachers.

24

THE TEACHER AS A PERSON

Numerous lists of qualities which characterize good teachers have been formulated by research workers and supervisors. It should be kept in mind that these qualities are included as separate items only for purposes of analysis and study. In reality an effective teacher can be described only by configurations of many attributes. Many of the single qualities are mutually interactive in their impact upon the child. It is pointless, for example, to ask whether the personality of the teacher has greater significance than her technical skill; these characteristics supplement and reinforce each other. It is difficult to conceive of a teacher with an effective teaching personality who is deficient in teaching skills.

Attributes of an effective teacher

Many investigations have been made in an attempt to discover the major individual factors associated with success in teaching. Among the factors which have been studied are:

Intelligence test score
Marks made in college
Age and sex
Amount of professional training
Years of experience
Amount of training in the field taught
Marks made in professional courses
Professional test scores
National Teachers' Examination test scores
Personality trait ratings
Personality adjustment scores
Marks made in courses in field taught

In most of these investigations the criterion of teaching success employed was ratings of supervisors. From these studies one is forced to conclude that none of the factors investigated seems to be closely associated with teaching success as measured by ratings of supervisors, although there is a positive correlation between teaching success and each of these factors except sex. There is very little correlation between success and age, years of experience, marks made in subject courses, and intelligence test scores. It appears that, given a reasonable minimum of intelligence and appropriate training, it cannot be shown statistically that there is very great relationship between teaching success and measures of any of the traits thought to contribute to teaching success. Of course it is more than possible that the ratings of supervisors are not reliable and valid measures of teaching success. In fact, many students of the problem have arrived at the conclusion that at least some of the coefficients of correlation, which are usually between .15 and .30, would be materially higher between the respective factors and *reliable* valid measures of teaching success.

Qualities appreciated by students

Several studies have been made of the qualities most highly appreciated by students and of the relative desirability of various characteristics for success in teaching. The characteristics ranking highest in these studies were:

Breadth of interests
Cooperation and helpfulness
Kindliness and consideration for the individual
Leadership, initiative, self-confidence
Good disposition: appreciativeness, courtesy, tact, sympathy
Patience
Interest in the students as individuals
Interest in subject matter taught
Unusual proficiency in teaching a particular subject
Magnetism: approachability, cheerfulness, optimism, sense of humor, sociability, pleasing voice
Self-control: calmness, dignity, poise, reserve
Wide interests
Enthusiasm: alertness, animation, inspiration
Attractiveness: personal appearance
Fairness and impartiality
Adaptability
Good judgment: discretion, foresight, intelligence
Honesty and impartiality
Sense of humor

Ability to explain clearly—fluency of speech
Scholarship and knowledge of subject
Use of recognition and praise
Health
Forcefulness: courage, decisiveness, firmness, purposefulness
Refinement: good taste, modesty, morality, simplicity
Promptness: dispatch, punctuality

Qualities looked for by administrators

If asked what qualities are most essential to teaching success, school administrators and supervisors almost invariably place at the top of the list what they refer to as "teaching personality." In general, personality seems to include such things as animation, personal appearance, congenial manner, effective speech, emotional stability, apparent interest in students, maturity of thought and action, a sense of humor, optimism, temperament, poise, and sociability. In analyzing teacher personality, it is necessary to consider the total impact of the entire pattern of these qualities upon the pupil. The individual qualities which make for excellence are not identical in all effective teachers. It would be as undesirable as it would be futile to attempt to fit all teachers into a common mold. Individuality and uniqueness of teacher personality is a priceless ingredient of a teaching staff. A distinctive set of personal qualities may enable a teacher to make a noteworthy contribution to the mental and social development of pupils. Moreover, personal characteristics requisite for effective teaching vary in kind and in degree at different grade levels and in different types of schools and communities.

Qualities liked by parents

It is important that parents have a favorable attitude toward teachers if possible and consistent with good teaching; it usually is.

In the Philadelphia public schools a study was made of what 160 parents expected their children's teachers to be like. Following are the conclusions as reported by Victoria Smith, who conducted the study.

Personal Attributes and Characteristics of Good Teachers

1. Well-groomed
2. Healthy
3. Full of physical vigor
4. Open-minded
5. Efficient
6. Frank
7. Patient
8. Full of imagination
9. Sense of humor
10. Tactful
11. Keen-minded
12. Sympathetic
13. Calm, collected
14. Fair, impartial
15. Kind, understanding
16. Good educational background
17. Well versed in subject matter

Teaching Techniques
1. Cooperate with parents.
2. Have ability to cope with individual differences in children. They can take the slow, uninterested child and fire him with enthusiasm, make him do difficult things and enjoy them.
3. Are progressive and keep abreast of the times.
4. Are strict—make them toe the line. They do need discipline. One "soft" teacher can ruin a child's school life. We want them modern, but yet strict and not too lax. Discipline them—yes! But know when and where to apply it.
5. Educate the whole child and train him for social life, teaching things other than the 3 R's.
6. Do not scream and "holler."
7. Teach ideals. Praise the school and surroundings and make the children realize what they have.
8. Have a hobby—so much so that the child catches it too.

Real Love and Understanding of Children
1. Love children and children love them.
2. Interested in children—not just a job.
3. Have ability to project themselves into the mind and thinking of a child.
4. Make the child feel free to come to his teacher with his problems.
5. Do not set themselves up as experts in the field of child psychology and are not too eager to say, "Take your child to a child guidance clinic."
6. Have respect for medical authorities.
7. Give an honest evaluation of the child's work.
8. Get along with children, make them comfortable and gain their confidence.
9. Friendly, warm, affectionate and breaks the barrier between, "I'm the teacher—you're the child!"
10. Make each child feel important.

Real Persons
1. Interested in other things—not just education.
2. Without prejudice.
3. Leave troubles at home.
4. Certain amount of worldliness.
5. Have hearts.
6. Courage of convictions.
7. Make mistakes and admit them.[1]

The parents and the supervisors emphasize many of the same traits as being desirable in the teachers of children. But when all is said, the fact remains that the personal characteristics of effective teachers vary greatly with the individual and are influenced by the school and the community in which the teachers work.

[1] Victoria F. Smith, "What Kind of Teachers Do Parents Like—What Kind of Parents Do Teachers Like," *Understanding the Child*, XXII (Philadelphia Public Schools, Oct., 1953), pp. 99-104.

Interpersonal relationships

From these various studies it is obvious that interpersonal relationships between the learner and teacher and consequently the personality of the teacher are tremendously important. High on the list of qualities associated with success and characteristics that students and parents like in teachers are such things as approachability, cooperation, helpfulness, a good disposition, kindness, inspiration, impartiality, pleasantness, friendliness, and ability to make others feel at ease.

Young people need affection and security. They crave obvious acceptance and status. The qualities of teachers that are rated high by pupils, particularly those of the lower elementary grades, are those which students interpret as affection or regard for their individual personalities and those which tend to give security. Among the qualifications mentioned most were leadership, initiative, confidence, self-control, calmness, dignity, poise, and reserve. These personality traits inspire confidence on the part of pupils. People in general, especially very young people, are inclined to get their cues for fears or for confidence from their elders, even older children. These cues do not necessarily have to be words; they can be mannerisms and facial expressions.

In recent years the need of American young people for affection and for a sense of security has been greatly intensified by several social and economic changes. Among them are:

(1) The increased number of working mothers. This development has resulted in less companionship between mother and child. Consequently young people are more dependent on baby-sitters and on their peers for companionship. This shift has contributed to hunger both for affection and for security. When both working parents come home from a job long after the children have come home from school, they are preoccupied with household chores and with the need for some form of recreation after the day's work. Except for sitting silently with parents in front of television sets, in an increasing number of instances the children do not participate in the recreation and social programs of their parents in the evening.

(2) Increase in time spent by adults in commercial and social recreation evenings. This change has very greatly decreased the amount of time which parents give to their children in social, educational, and recreational activities which tend to build up a feeling on the part of the children of belonging, of being accepted, and consequently of being liked and being secure.

(3) Resulting in part from the two developments just mentioned is the increased tendency for young people to find their social recreation life among those of their own age and for that reason at least partially a greater emphasis is placed upon desiring to be accepted by others. It has been observed by many students of childhood and adolescence that young people form their cliques and groups in a very selfish and heartless manner. This persists even through the rushing period for fraternities and sororities in college life.

As a result of these developments the need for personal attention, mild demonstrations of affection, and developing feelings of security have become much greater. The elementary school teacher should make it a point to see that every student feels that "the teacher likes me" and that "I belong." Care should be taken to see that no youngster experiences great or continuous feelings of inadequacy in connection with the learning activities responsibilities with which he is confronted by the teacher and the school situation.

Following is a good statement of desirable interpersonal relations between teacher and pupils:

1. Be friendly but not familiar. Your own "childishness" should be past. Children prefer you to be a sympathetic, kindly adult.
2. Know not only the children's names but also much about their personal backgrounds which affect their relationships in the classroom.
3. Recognize sensitively children's individual differences. Build constructively upon these differences rather than expect every child to fit into an identical pattern.
4. Take into account the maturation levels of the group and proceed to get better acquainted and to establish rapport in the light of these observable growth gradients.
5. Be as consistent a personality in dealing with the children as is humanly feasible. Do not be too strict one day and too lax the next.
6. Face each day's work realistically and cheerfully with the children. Even when you do not feel cheerful, you must remember the negative effect upon children if you reflect your problems and anxieties.
7. Create a permissive atmosphere in which every child is, first of all, free to be himself and free to let you see him be himself.
8. Plan with and in consideration for children in such democratic ways that your guidance is prized by the other members of the group.
9. Participate actively and naturally with children in what they enjoy doing—in their work and their play.
10. Take time to listen to the children's questions, problems, joys, and dilemmas, and treat their confidences clinically and confidentially.
11. Demonstrate to the children that you believe in them and in their potentialities.
12. Encourage every child in the cultivation of self-confidence, self-expression, independence, and social effectiveness.[2]

[2] James B. Burr, Lowry W. Harding, and Leland B. Jacobs, *Student Teaching in the Elementary School* (New York: Appleton-Century-Crofts, Inc., 1950), p. 129.

The pupil just entering the school, and indeed for some years thereafter, is confronted with the necessity of making many important social and emotional adjustments. This is especially true during the first few days and weeks that the youngster is in school, when he may become unduly disturbed over a playground incident or his inability to perform as well as others in things asked by the teacher. Children are also likely to exaggerate the degree of their unacceptability by other youngsters in the school. Many parents have found it very difficult to force youngsters to attend school in these early years; they bring them personally to school after long tearful struggles at home. These fears in the first few days, the first few months, or first few years of school very frequently result in attitudes which, if ever replaced by more wholesome attitudes, give way only after years of satisfying experiences in school.

Qualities associated with teaching effectiveness

The extent to which teachers are successful in producing desirable changes in the attitudes and behavior of pupils is the measure of teaching effectiveness. Increasing knowledge and developing skills are only the means to those ends. There are certain characteristics of teachers which appear to be closely associated with teaching effectiveness. Reference to some of the qualities of successful teachers has been made in preceding sections of this chapter. In addition to those already mentioned the teacher of children in American schools should possess an understanding of children, an understanding of the times in which she is teaching, an abiding faith in education and the usefulness of teaching, and a devotion to the ideals of democracy.

Understanding children. Understanding children involves a knowledge of human development, learning, and behavior. This information can be acquired by a study of the scientific facts which explain human growth in the terms of biology, psychology, and sociology. It is necessary, however, to supplement these facts with knowledge obtained by observation of, and association with, all types and conditions of men. Familiarity with the isolated factors in human development has little significance unless one is able to recognize their interdependence.

The prevailing idea that teachers, by the nature of their work, are necessarily isolated from life is erroneous. Every classroom is a psychological and sociological laboratory in the truest sense of the term. The teacher who is interested in people has unparalleled opportunities not only to observe at first hand the development of human beings but also to promote that growth. To the alert, intelligent teacher, the local community serves as a social laboratory to increase her understanding of human behavior. Careful study of children in school and out has given her significant insights into social living. Among the most important of these are:

1. The uniqueness of each individual child in regard to mental abilities, interests, social adaptability, and emotional drives
2. The potential contribution each individual can make to the general welfare
3. The need for a series of "common developmental tasks" in the education af all children
4. The advisability of withholding judgment of a child until all relevant facts are available
5. The necessity of recognizing that there is a *cause* underlying all forms of child behavior. (An analysis of behavior usually reveals that an individual's "actions are based upon his past experiences, shaped by his present situation, and influenced by his desires and hopes for the future.")

Understanding the times. Teachers who seek to assist children in making adjustments to the world in which they live must know that world. They must be aware of the economic and social forces which shape it and influence the thoughts and actions of men. They should be well informed in regard to the economic interdependence of the various peoples of the earth. They should be cognizant of the degree to which political democracy in some sections, and economic democracy in all sections, of our country have failed of attainment. Basic to service in democracy's schools is a realization that the cornerstone of democracy is respect for human personality, regardless of race, color, or creed.

A knowledge of America, her past struggles, her present strengths and weaknesses, and her aspirations for the future, should be part of the equipment of every American teacher. Above all, she should recognize the dynamic character of our democracy and be tolerant of social and economic change. Finally, the teacher should be a student of international affairs with a full knowledge of the need for political and economic cooperation among all peoples.

Faith in education. Our system of universal education is based upon a faith in the improvability of the individual through a process of formal education. This belief in the inherent value of the individual is linked with the idea that the existence of a democratic society is dependent upon the ability and willingness of society to provide the means of guaranteeing a constant flow of intelligent, well-informed citizens into its life stream.

It is essential that the teacher be convinced of the soundness of these assumptions. Unless she firmly believes that education is a potentially great force in the lives of men, the greatness of teaching will evade her. A blind acceptance of the significance of education is equally tragic. The teacher must recognize that education is not a formula which can lift men by magic out of their ignorance and selfishness. Human progress is painfully slow. Agencies other than the school influence the actions of mankind for good or ill. At times it may appear that the efforts of the school are fruitless, thwarted as they are by other forces. Only a vital, realistic program of public education can hope to counteract these influences. Herein lies the constant challenge to the teacher to vitalize her teaching.

In spite of the disappointing outcomes of many of the efforts of teachers, there is ample evidence to demonstrate the power of education. Unless a person senses the social significance of teaching, and unless she is desirous of rendering a service which will ennoble mankind, she should not engage in teaching.

Devotion to democratic procedures. Democracy is not achieved by a people in a single supreme effort and enjoyed forever afterwards. To be retained, it has to be rewon daily. Eternal democratic effort is the price of democracy. The school has the responsibility of rekindling the spirit and replenishing the substance of the democratic way of life.

The individual counts for much in terms of the general welfare in a democracy. It is of the greatest importance, therefore, that he be educated in schools dedicated to the principles of human rights, individual opportunities, and social responsibilities. Dictatorial practices in the classroom subdue and frustrate the child rather than assist him in becoming a self-directing, effective member of a democratic society.

A teacher who is intelligently devoted to the democratic process will in her relationships with pupils advance the general welfare by being concerned with the welfare of each child, regardless of his intelligence, race, social status, or economic conditions. She guides the child to a recognition of the fact that in a democracy the individual has responsibilities as well as rights and privileges. She assists the child in translating democratic ideals into action in her daily association with other children in the classroom, on the playground, and at school dances, as well as in out-of-school activities. She arranges situations in which all the children will have meaningful experiences in sharing responsibility in planning, managing, and evaluating their own activities.

MENTAL HEALTH OF THE TEACHER

Many of the causes of personality maladjustments have their origins in childhood experiences. In many instances the feelings of inadequacy and insecurity among teachers can be traced to the overemphasis by parents and teachers on such matters as school achievement or slight deviations from the norm in personal appearance and behavior. The inner conflicts which arise as a result of the individual's inability to attain social acceptability and other desired goals represent a prolific source of personality maladjustment.

It is doubtful that a direct attack, in which each undesirable personality trait is made the object of an intensive effort for improvement, results in personality development. Since the traits function in combination, no one of them can be isolated for emphasis. Likewise, resolutions by teachers not to be impatient, irritable, depressed, or dull do not always result in any material improvement.

In some teachers favorable qualities of personality seem almost to be inherited; they develop early with little conscious effort. In most teachers, at least a few of the traits have to be cultivated systematically over a considerable period of time. Consequently, teachers vary a great deal with respect to the quality of teaching personality. Some persons of good minds and adequate or superior training are failures or at most very limited successes at teaching.

In a realistic program designed by the teacher to overcome her personality deficiencies, cognizance should be taken of the difficulty of eliminating maladjustments of long standing, especially if certain elements in the teaching situation aggravate the problems. A knowledge of some of the basic concepts of mental health should assist the teacher in meeting her own problems of personality adjustment as well as those encountered by her pupils.

Concepts of mental health

Mental health is an emotional and mental condition characterized by thought and behavior patterns that are satisfying to the individual and in reasonable harmony with the group of which he is a member. Life is a series of adjustments between the living organism and its social and physical environment. A well-adjusted individual is one who utilizes the resources available in his environment to meet his personal and social needs. Thus conceived, adjustment is the individual responsibility of each person.

Failure on the part of the individual to make adequate adjustments to physical environments results in physical disharmony and ineffectiveness. The inability of the individual to adjust to the social environment results in the impairment of personality. There are many degrees of mental illness, varying from the milder forms characterized by irritability and nervousness to the more serious types which are indicated by emotional instability, delusions, feelings of inferiority, moodiness, isolationism, imaginary persecution, and extreme melancholy. To the extent that human behavior patterns are specific, a person may be well adjusted to one situation and poorly adjusted to another. He may be well adjusted at one time in life and not at another.

The really crucial issue involved in the mental maladjustment of teachers is its unwholesome effect upon pupils. Numerous investigations have revealed that the number of maladjusted pupils is much greater in classes taught by poorly adjusted teachers than in the classes of well-adjusted teachers.

While the maintenance of mental health is largely an individual responsibility, there are present in many teaching situations certain factors which serve to intensify personal difficulties of long standing in the life of the teacher. In their extreme form, some of the unsatisfactory conditions under which teachers work may cause mental illness. In most instances, however, the conditions merely aggravate existing difficulties.

The factors which help and handicap a teacher in maintaining good mental health vary markedly from one teaching situation to another. In most instances the unwholesome influences can be modified or minimized and the wholesome features can be capitalized by an intelligent teacher. In the event the teacher's tendencies toward maladjustment and the undesirable factors in a teaching situation combine to produce a serious form of mental illness, the teacher should seek medical advice. Unless the difficulty can be eliminated, the teacher owes it to herself and her pupils to withdraw from teaching.

Suggestions for maintaining mental health

Many less serious forms of mental disturbance can be removed by a prompt, practical, common-sense program, instituted and carried out by the teacher herself. The teacher who is desirous of maintaining good mental health may find some of the following suggestions helpful.

1. *Recognize the significance of teaching.* A clear vision of the social significance of teaching may be gained by a consideration of

the opportunities the teacher has to make desirable changes in the thinking and behavior of children under her jurisdiction. Protecting the personality of the child from the forces that constantly tend to disintegrate it presents a challenge to the highest humanitarian instincts of the teacher.

Unless the teacher can establish a strong faith in the improvability of the individual through the process of education, she should seek employment in a vocation more suited to her interests. Only a firm conviction that teaching is important can serve as a bulwark against the petty annoyances, irritations, and stresses of professional life.

The teacher who likes people and is genuinely interested in their welfare experiences little difficulty in developing a keen interest in teaching. Nothing short of a strong desire to help children meet their numerous complex problems can give purpose and dignity to the work of the teacher. Endeavors of teachers who seek more tangible rewards in the form of financial returns and social status are both disappointing and futile.

2. *Formulate a sound philosophy of life.* Reference has been made in the preceding paragraphs to the teacher's need to accept a satisfactory philosophy of education which incorporates among other things a strong conviction in regard to the value of teaching as a form of human endeavor. This educational philosophy should be an aspect of a larger all-embracing philosophy of life. One's philosophy of life is a highly personal matter; however, sound social values should be given due recognition. A proper sense of values tends to give perspective and direction to one's life at all times, particularly in periods of extreme stress and strain.

A teacher's mental health is highly dependent upon a guiding philosophy of life which is satisfying and gives purpose and direction to all her personal and professional activities. The details of an individual's philosophy of life are subject to constant modifications within the limits of its broader framework. A sound philosophy is ever evolving, always in the process of being acquired. It should however, have sufficient stability to enable an individual always to relate his ideas and experiences to it; otherwise, it fails to be a guide to thought and action.

3. *Keep physically fit.* There is considerable evidence to indicate that a close relationship exists between physical and mental health. They are mutually dependent. An unsatisfactory condition of one contributes to the failure of the other. Adherence by the teacher to a sensible physical fitness program is therefore essential to the maintenance of mental health. In planning a physical health

program consideration should be given to the simple rules of health, such as exercise, sufficient sleep, and a well-balanced diet. The indoor work of the teacher should be counterbalanced by outdoor recreational activities. Adequate provision should be made for relaxation from the work of the classroom. An excellent means of achieving this is to engage in leisure-time activities which take one's mind away from one's work.

Chronic fatigue and irritability may be symptoms of ailments which can be revealed by diagnosis and alleviated by competent medical treatment. The periodic physical examination, which is recognized as essential for pupils, is likewise important for teachers. Undue worry over minor ailments is both a cause and a symptom of emotional instability. Those who seem to be depressed or discouraged a considerable amount of time or who seem to have spells of general depression should consult a physician and raise the question of whether or not there is need for supplementing the diet or other therapeutic measures. Teachers who are inclined to eat small meals should probably supplement their diet with vitamins and minerals, or better still be certain to include in their diet foods containing high quantities of essential proteins, vitamins, and minerals, for example, liver and derivatives of soy beans.

4. *Cultivate a sense of humor.* It has been said facetiously that everyone needs a sense of humor to console him for what he *is* and a vivid imagination to compensate for what he *is not.* While the work of the teacher should be taken seriously, there is an ever-present danger that the teacher will take herself too seriously. An individual should be able to laugh at other people, with other people, and especially at himself. The position of the teacher tends to encourage pupils to accept her word as final authority. This automatic acceptance often causes her to overestimate the wisdom of her own words. Such an attitude may result in maladjustment of the teacher to out-of-school situations in which other persons may take issue with her.

In the classroom a sense of humor will often serve to "calm the troubled waters." The possessor of a sense of humor tends to avoid overemphasis upon minor difficulties and other trivial matters. To acquire a sense of humor, the teacher must learn to see matters in their true perspective and not to engage in a major struggle over a minor issue.

5. *Develop strong avocational interests.* No one can prescribe leisure-time activities for another person. Each individual is free to "write his own ticket," to choose his activity or hobby. Aside from the practical limitations of money and time, the teacher because of

her training should be able to make a wise choice of leisure-time activities. Certainly the teacher should have some strong intellectual interests beyond the requirements of her teaching. Hobbies in art, music, and books present opportunities to satisfy the creative and intellectual urge. If the need for achievement is not met by one's professional activities, gardening and use of materials may give a feeling of mastery that is conducive to mental health. Perhaps every person should engage in some activity "just for fun." The teacher who knows how to play seldom becomes blue, discouraged, or bored with life.

Beyond special interest in a hobby, a satisfactory leisure-time program should include a variety of activities which bring one into contact with people, music, poetry, and the beauty of nature. The sources of interests in activities are numerous. A slight interest in a particular activity may grow, if properly cultivated, into an all-consuming enthusiasm which enhances and adds zest to professional activities.

6. *Know yourself, accept yourself, and be yourself.* Objective self-analysis in which one assesses one's own strength and weaknesses is difficult, but it is essential in overcoming deficiencies in personality development. Equally important is the discovery of the causes of one's maladjustment. An individual tends to overrate himself on those traits which appear to be important and underrate himself on those of little importance; for example, a person may underrate his handwriting ability, hence the common expression, "I cannot read my own handwriting," yet he seldom admits he is dishonest or untruthful.

If limitations cannot be removed they should be accepted. Attempts "to do the impossible" in terms of one's ability lead to discouragement and frustration. On the other hand, failure to utilize one's abilities fully and a shirking of responsibility tend to destroy the keen enjoyment of living.

Likewise necessary to mental health is the ability to discard all forms of pretense and be oneself. Efforts of teachers to identify themselves with persons in the self-styled socially elite class are tragic to both teacher and pupils. A well-known writer recently portrayed a teacher who was desirous of lifting herself out of her own social class by catering to all the "nice little boys and girls" from the wealthy families and ignoring and humiliating the children from the poorer homes. Teachers should recognize the dignity of a profession that serves "all the children of all the people." Indulgence in self-pity and expressions like "I am just a teacher" reveal a distressing type of vocational maladjustment with its concomitant lack of personal and social adjustment.

7. *Develop associations with other adults.* For most teachers it is a definite hazard to spend almost all of their time alone or with children and books. These types of experiences need to be supplemented by at least a few hours each day or a considerable number of hours each week in association with adults. Otherwise the teacher is likely to become disoriented to the adult world and to exaggerate the importance of the little problems, worries, and frustrations growing out of association with pupils. While it is desirable to have satisfying recreation with adults, such recreation need not be either hilarious or formal. It does, however, need to be sufficiently satisfying that nerves become relaxed and minds taken away from the petty irritations and worries of working with young people.

Teachers whose time is monopolized rather exclusively by association with children and schoolbooks have a tendency not to develop the mature, detached attitudes of adults toward young people but to sink to the level of immaturity of the children. They fail to make adequate allowances for the fact that little folks are little folks and that they are immature in their social and emotional growth.

8. *Develop a well balanced emotional life.* Teachers or others engaged in occupations that are specialized or somewhat detached from normal activities of life tend to lack sufficient rich emotional experiences and to develop as a result a typical personality.

The teacher should avoid developing too high a sensitive, emotional attitude toward children. Being deprived of children of their own, many unmarried teachers tend to shower their pent-up affections upon their pupils, particularly upon certain selected ones who are more satisfying in behavior and in intellectual achievements. This trend or tendency must not be permitted to become an obsession or too strong an emotional experience. Teachers must develop friendships with adults and an interest in community problems and activities of local, state, national, and indeed worldwide nature.

Mental health precepts. A study of the foregoing list of suggestions, along with others which might be added, reveals that the teacher's task of maintaining good mental health is similar to that of any other person. The following useful summary of mental health precepts has been formulated by McKinney.[3]

[3] Reprinted by permission from *Psychology of Personal Adjustment* (2d ed., by F. McKinney, published by John Wiley & Sons, Inc., 1949), pp. 548-49.

1. Keep yourself physically fit through hygienic habits of rest, exercise, diet, and cleanliness.
2. Face your troubles, worries, and fears; do what you can about them, then turn your attention to more pleasant things.
3. Have several absorbing hobbies, interests, social games, or sports in which you like to participate.
4. Guide your impulses and emotions in desirable channels rather than suppress them.
5. Strive to become a balanced personality instead of an extremist.
6. Develop a sense of humor; be willing to admit your own mistakes and laugh at yourself.
7. Have several major goals in the line of your abilities and enjoy working toward them.
8. Acquire real friends and companions who will share your fortunes and troubles.
9. Avoid strain; develop serenity; relax all muscles that are not necessary for the task at hand.
10. Build the habit of enjoying the present by drinking in the beauties of the world around you.
11. Be courageous in crises; don't run from them.
12. Grow daily by creating things yourself rather than being merely a spectator, dreamer, and nonproducing consumer. There is fun in striving.
13. Don't be overconscious of your uniqueness. Realize that most of us are ordinary people.
14. Realize time heals many wounds; be patient and hopeful.
15. Seek love, adventure, safety, and success—but be sure they are the kind that you can fully enjoy.
16. Develop your philosophy; know where you stand and adjust to the conditions you must meet.

While these precepts have universal significance, the teacher has special need to reduce tensions. Stevenson and Milt have given the following useful suggestions for teachers.[4]

1. Share your troubles.
2. Work off your anger.
3. Stop thinking about yourself and do something for somebody else.
4. Pitch in and take your tasks one at a time.
5. Put your major efforts on things you can do well and do not fret about the things in which it is impossible for you to excel.
6. Accept the fact that things cannot go well all the time.
7. When things go wrong do not feel it is a mistake to escape for a little while.
8. Show people you like them rather than constantly expecting them to show you that they like you.
9. Control the urge to edge out the other fellow.
10. Take time out regularly for recreation.

[4] G. S. Stevenson and Harry Milt, "Ten Tips to Reduce Teacher Tension," *The National Educational Association Journal*, XLV, 9 (December, 1956), pp. 545-47.

PARTICIPATION IN COMMUNITY LIFE

The superior teacher today recognizes that the school is one of the more important community agencies. It is of and for the community. As a responsible leader in such an organization, she cannot escape her responsibility of active participation in community life. Whether the people of the community expect it or not, the teacher should participate in activities of the community which have for their objectives the improvement of social and economic conditions. Her participation may not only serve to make those agencies more effective but also be of service to the school. Frequently the adverse criticism directed toward teachers is a result of a lack of acquaintance with and understanding of the teacher. If the person who hears derogatory statements relative to the teacher's activities knows the teacher personally, he may properly discount the remarks. A teacher gains status in a community by assuming appropriate responsibilities in its affairs. Effective community participation is based upon an understanding of the resources, needs, and customs of the community.

As an adult individual, the teacher benefits immeasurably by association with mature adults. Perhaps nothing is more conducive to the impairment of the teacher's mental health than her exclusion from the normal social activities of adults. The teacher has been characterized as a "creature set apart" in the typical American community. Too often this is a self-imposed role. In most instances the apparent social ostracism can be overcome by the teacher's taking a genuine interest in the affairs of the community. The fact that the customs of the community may be different from those in other communities in which the teacher has lived should serve to stimulate, rather than discourage, her participation in community life.

It is a truism to state that the teacher's primary responsibility is to teach the pupils enrolled in the school. This suggests that the teacher should exercise discrimination with respect to the type and number of community activities in which she participates. There is the ever-present danger that the teacher may dissipate her energies by becoming a "professional joiner" of organizations which have little significance to her own or the community welfare. In making decisions in regard to which activities should be given priority, the teacher should give preference to those which are most closely related to the educational and social welfare of the youth of the community and to those which will give her opportunity for social relaxation. This decision is not so simple as it may appear, since the child's development is influenced by practically every aspect of his community environment. This suggests another important reason for the teacher to participate in community activities. Only as the growing youngster is considered against the background of community life is it possible to understand his attitudes, aspirations, and behavior.

Also the leadership of the teacher is needed in most communities in matters which tend to promote better racial relationships and more intelligent understanding by all the people of vital economic, political, and social issues. Effective community participation is dependent upon an understanding of the resources, needs, and customs of the community. Failure to recognize the peculiar social cleavages which exist in a community may result in the teacher's becoming identified with, if not actually embroiled in, factional rivalries, thus detracting from her usefulness as a potential leader. While the teacher has the right as a person and as a citizen to participate in those activities from which she derives the greatest satisfaction, the basic criterion is the probable effects of such participation upon her position as a responsible leader.

In a previous chapter it was suggested that prior to beginning her work in a new school the teacher should acquire considerable information about the community—its industries and civic institutions, its religious attitudes, and attitudes about social practices. The gathering of information of this sort should continue throughout the teacher's experience in the community. She should always be in search of opportunities to relate her instruction to the community, using the community as a basis for making verbal instruction more concrete and more meaningful.

Establishing good public relations

The teacher should proceed cautiously but definitely and systematically to become a part of the local community. Because of the fact that the teacher's personal contacts are largely with the children instead of with adults, it is an easy matter to live aloof from the community life. This, together with the fact that teachers new to the community are usually young unmarried people, who already have other home community connections, makes for the unsatisfactory and somewhat dangerous situation of the teacher living in a community, being a community servant paid with tax money, yet not being a part of the community. No other type of public official would risk such an untoward condition.

The teacher in the small community should attend some local church from the outset even if not a church member. She should learn the names of adults in the community and form the practice of calling them by name, greeting them and "passing the time of day" with them upon every occasion. The teacher should accept all reasonable invitations to participate in the social life in the community. She should not associate exclusively with other teachers but mingle freely with other persons. Above all, the teacher should attend all meetings of the P.T.A. and should at the meeting greet those whom she has met, meet others, and learn as quickly as possible the names of as many parents of her students as possible. The importance of establishing, maintaining, and extending good public relations is far greater than many teachers realize.

Conforming to local standards

The teacher, like many others in her community, particularly the other professional people, is dependent for success upon the good will and respect of the people of the community. Every community has its standards of social conduct which it expects to be met. Because of her close association with young people and the fact that high school students and the community youth in general pattern themselves after the younger teachers, the teacher is in a particularly public position. Young people in the community who oppose the wishes and restrictions of their parents by saying, "Why shouldn't I do that or go there? Mr. (or Miss) Teacher does!" are making trouble for the teacher.

The teacher, therefore, must learn what the community standards are. If they are intolerable to her, she should move to another community at the end of the year. The teacher should always be sure to observe the local standards as long as she is in the community.

The first year in the community is the most critical one. After a teacher has lived there for several years, particularly if she has made many friends and has a wide acquaintance, she may do and say things which would have been most unwise before she gained acceptance as a member of the community group.

Particularly in small communities the teacher, especially the teacher relatively new in the community, should observe the following cautions:

1. Be careful not to criticize publicly individuals in the community. It is amazing how quickly and surely such remarks get to the individual criticized or to his friends.
2. Conversely, do not praise individuals in public except in the manner of seconding praise of others. Enemies of the praised individuals are prone to assume that you belong to "the other crowd."

3. Never speak disparagingly of the community or its institutions, no matter how pitiful they are or how much you hear others criticize. Criticism from the "outsider" is rarely acceptable.

4. Be cautious in speaking your views on controversial matters—particularly if they do not concern your students and the welfare of young people. Do not attempt, particularly at first, to indoctrinate your community.

5. Discuss with your principal and superintendent school and community questions that trouble you.

6. Never criticize and rarely discuss other teachers, your administration and administrative school officials, or the board of education with others than your very close confidants—and then most cautiously.

7. Be careful at all times to avoid being thought of as belonging to a "faction."

8. Remember at all times that you may be the "provincial" person who needs to learn to be tolerant and understanding.

9. Patronize local stores for the very great part of your expenditures.

Increasing contact with parents

In recent years, growing out of the increased need for better public relations and attacks upon and criticisms of the public schools, there has been a very noticeable stepping up of the efforts and activities of teachers to increase their contacts with parents. Teachers in general are planning more opportunities for getting parents to visit the schools to get acquainted with the teachers and with the work of the school. Particularly in the elementary school, teachers are visiting the home of their pupils. In many schools teachers have office hours after school, inviting all parents in general and especially those parents with whom a conference seems desirable.

The teacher should be reluctant to use a conference for complaints about students; whenever used these should grow out of an attempt to make an analysis of the youngster's progress in school and the development of a program for the pupil's greater growth.

One of the major purposes of parent-teacher conferences is to avoid and to alleviate misunderstandings. With this in mind it seems wise that the conference be held before misunderstandings develop or at least before they have become long standing. Particularly in the lower grades report cards may well be supplanted by or supplemented by parent-teacher conferences.

One of the most important purposes of the parent-teacher conference is to understand and to develop confidence on the part of the parent in the work of the school in general and in particular in the group of youngsters in which the pupil is a member.

A. PROFESSIONAL RELATIONS	No Improvement Needed	Little Improvement Needed	Some Improvement Needed	Considerable Improvement Needed	Much Improvement Needed
1. Do I read professional literature in an attempt to increase my competence?					
2. Am I a participating, contributing member of the faculty organization?					
3. Do I assume my share of group responsibility?					
4. Do I have a genuine interest in professional organizations and utilize the opportunities afforded by them?					
5. Do I contribute to group thinking on problems of a general nature as well as those of particular interest to me?					
6. Am I genuinely tolerant of the opinions of others and open-minded on all matters under consideration?					
7. Having had an opportunity to voice my opinions, do I give wholehearted support to the decisions and accepted policies of the school without derogatory private comment?					
8. Do I inspire the confidence of the children by an understanding and friendly manner?					
9. Do I inspire the confidence of parents so that they feel free to talk frankly with me?					
10. Do I have the poise to withstand petty annoyance and maintain an emotional stability?					
11. Do I welcome opportunities to learn from and share with my fellow teachers and those in near-by schools?					
12. Have I sincere regard for and interest in the adjustment and development of beginning teachers and student teachers?					
13. Do I utilize opportunities for improving my professional competence through university study, travel, membership in study groups?					
14. Do I seek opportunities of broadening my experience and understanding through summer work of widely varied kinds quite apart from work with children?					
15. Am I as courteous to and thoughtful of children and colleagues as I expect them to be?					

496

B. Nonprofessional Relations	No Improvement Needed	Little Improvement Needed	Some Improvement Needed	Considerable Improvement Needed	Much Improvement Needed
1. Do I keep myself currently informed on social and political affairs?					
2. Do I read widely for my personal enrichment?					
3. Have I some intensive interest or hobbies that I follow?					
4. Have I a wide variety of other interests?					
5. Do I make it a point to be outdoors enough?					
6. Is there some form of exercise that I enjoy regularly in each season?					
7. Do I take time for rest and relaxation even when busy?					
8. Do I set aside some time for things of the spirit: church worship or quiet thought, etc.?					
9. Do I maintain active social contacts with people outside the profession as well as in it?					
10. Am I able at times to "shed my profession" completely?					
11. Do I assume some responsibilities in the larger social sense, contributing time or services or money to needy causes or people?					
C. Community Relations					
1. Am I thoroughly informed on the setup and functioning of the village government?					
2. Am I familiar with organizations in the community and do I participate in or make use of their services? Woman's Library Club / Junior Auxiliary / Rotary Club / Chamber of Commerce / Threshold Players / D. A. R. / Garden Club / Historical Society / Community Council / Scouts / Local churches / American Legion / Others					
3. Do I make use of the facilities offered by the Park Board?					
4. Do I use and encourage the use of the local library?					
5. Am I aware of civic needs within the community? If so, do I seek opportunity to offer suggestions and support measures undertaken?					
6. Do I contribute within my means to charitable and religious activities in the community?					
7. Am I familiar with and do I utilize in my work with children the many facilities which the community has to offer?					
8. Do I make use of resource studies such as Community File, Excursion Files, etc.?					

D. TEACHER-PUPIL RELATIONSHIPS	No Improvement Needed	Little Improvement Needed	Some Improvement Needed	Considerable Improvement Needed	Much Improvement Needed
1. Do I recognize the value in group planning and provide for it?					
2. Do I guide children in their plans rather than dominate them?					
3. Do I encourage my children to do their own thinking?					
4. Do I realize the value of thinking in the learning process?					
5. Do I establish certain routine procedures and responsibilities?					
6. Are the arrangement and order of my room and materials conducive to individual and group control?					
7. Is my relationship with children one of sincerity and rapport?					
8. Do I recognize the needs of each of my children and provide for their individual difficulties?					
9. Do I take time for the problems and interests of the individuals of my group?					
10. Do the children of my group have a feeling of status and "belonging"?					
11. Do I recognize my mistakes and admit my inadequacies to children?					
12. Do my children respect me because of my contributions to the group and not because of my status as a teacher?					
13. Whenever possible, do I regard undesirable behavior as an educational opportunity and use it as such?					
14. Do I recognize and care for the fatigue element in the individual and group control?					
15. Do I encourage thoughtful evaluation and discussion on the part of my children rather than do most of the talking myself?					
16. Does my group give evidence that I strive for self-control rather than imposed control?					
17. Does our planning make provision for a definite quiet period?					
18. Do I use supervisory services effectively?					
19. Do I avoid overstimulation by careful guidance and selection when opportunities such as assemblies, movies, etc., are offered?					

MEASUREMENT OF TEACHING COMPETENCES

In their efforts to improve the quality of their teaching, teachers in schools have cooperated in preparing self-rating scales. In other school systems the self-rating sheets have been devised by supervisory officers to encourage teachers to think through their teaching competencies as a basis for a program of self-improvement. The faculty of the Glencoe, Illinois, elementary school developed the teacher self-evaluation scale shown on pages 496–98.

QUESTIONS, PROBLEMS, AND EXERCISES

1. Outline a program designed for the acquisition of a desirable personal trait.

2. Suggest how an individual might change or eliminate an undesirable personal trait.

3. What are some of the symptoms of an inferiority complex in a teacher?

4. What are some of the factors which may influence social maladjustment among teachers?

5. Plan a schedule of your daily activities which provides time for recreational activities in addition to provision for those of a personal and professional character.

6. Prepare a paper in which you list your recreational interests, indicating the sources of these interests, and describe in some detail your favorite hobby.

7. What factors should a person take into account in considering teaching as a career?

8. Indicate ways in which a teacher may acquire an effective teaching personality.

9. Recall the teachers you had in high school. How many of them exercised a lasting influence upon your thinking or behavior? Describe the most outstanding characteristic of those teachers who had a lasting influence on your thinking.

10. What are the chief values of self-rating devices for teachers?

SELECTED SUPPLEMENTARY READINGS

CANTOR, NATHANIEL. *The Teaching Learning Process.* New York: The Dryden Press, Inc., 1953.

"Toward a New Teacher," pp. 226-62. "The Professional Self in Teaching," pp. 264-84. Presents seven characteristics of a good teacher with a unique section on how the teacher might improve herself.

DANIEL, J. McT. *Excellent Teachers: Their Qualities and Qualifications.* Columbia, S.C.: The Steering Committee of the Investigation of Educational Qualifications of Teachers in South Carolina, 1944.

Chap. iii, "Excellent Teacher Qualities, the Point of View of Teachers and Patrons." The reasons why administrators and supervisors pick certain teachers as the most excellent are described in this chapter.

GOTHAM, R. E. "Personality and Teaching Efficiency," *Journal of Experimental Education,* XIV (December, 1945), 157-65.

A research study of the relationship between personal qualities essential to teaching success and four criteria of teaching success. The four criteria are (1) teacher rating scales, (2) measures of qualities commonly associated with teaching success, (3) changes produced in pupils, and (4) a composite of all three.

HILDRETH, GERTRUDE. *Child Growth Through Education.* New York: The Ronald Press Co., 1948.

Chap. 23, "The Teacher's Part in the Guidance of Learning." The understanding teacher is one that possesses certain skills in guiding children. Those skills are described and evaluated in the chapter.

LARUE, DANIEL W. *Educational Psychology.* New York: Thomas Nelson & Sons, 1939.

Chap. xx, "The Personality of the Teacher." Four basic aspects of teaching personality are presented and evaluated.

McDANIEL, INGA CARTER. "Establishing Effective Home School Relationships," *California Journal of Elementary Education,* XVI, No. 3 (February, 1948), 160-75.

A good discussion on how to improve home-school relations. Some excellent specific suggestions are given.

OLIVA, PETER F. "Personality of the Teacher," *The Bulletin of the NASSP,* XL, 216 (January, 1956), pp. 39-43.

An excellent summary of the important aspects of the teacher's attitude and the resulting reflection on her personality.

OTTO, HENRY J., HAZEL FLOYD, and MARGARET ROUSE. *Principles of Elementary Education.* New York: Rinehart & Co., Inc., 1955.

Chap. 15, "The Teacher as Person, Citizen, and Professional Worker." A good description of what is needed to become an outstanding teacher.

RICHEY, ROBERT W. *Planning for Teaching.* New York: McGraw-Hill Book Co., Inc., 1952.

Chap. 9, "What Teachers Are Like." A very concise presentation of the misconceptions held by lay people about teachers and a discussion of what their life is really like. Chap. 10, "The Teacher's Work." The teacher's work day is described as well as the responsibilities of the profession.

WILES, KIMBALL. *Teaching for Better Schools.* Englewood Cliffs, N.J.: Prentice-Hall, Inc., 1952.

Chap. 14, "How Do We Improve Our Teaching?" A very practical discussion of how to improve one's teaching day by day in the classroom. Many questions are raised and answers suggested.

WITTY, PAUL (chairman). *Mental Health in the Classroom.* Washington, D.C.: Department of Supervisors and Directors of Instruction, National Education Association, 1940.

NAME INDEX

SUBJECT INDEX

Ability, Mental
  individual differences in, 421-22, 426-29
  and pupil behavior, 140
  pupil grouping according to, 432-33
Academic achievement
  as factor in marking systems, 393
  individual differences in, 423-24
  measurement of; see Evaluation
Acceptance, need for, 46
Achievement tests, 23, 38-39, 342, 386-87
  Stanford, 395-98
Action research, 451-52, 465
Activities
  creative; see Creative activities
  developmental, 30-31
  extraclass; see Extraclass activities
  of interest, 110
  learning
    effects of, 96-97
    objectives of, 286-87
    teacher's responsibility for, 9-10, 295-96
  problem-solving; see Problem-solving activities
  routine, 290-93
    time allotment for, 294
  show-and-tell, 313; see also Oral communication
Activity, principle of, 95
Activity units, 181-84, 435-36; see also Units of instruction
Adjustment, pupil, 135-52; see also Behavior; Discipline
Adjustment
  emotional

    evaluation of, 46-47
    individual differences in, 422
  social
    evaluation of, 44-46
    individual differences in, 422-23, 26
  Symonds Inventory for, 48
Advancement, opportunities for, 15
Affection, need for, 46, 138
Allotments, time, 203-5, 206, 294
American Education Fellowship, 468
American Federation of Teachers, 467-68
American Junior Red Cross News, 441
American Library Association, 217
American Teacher, The, 468
Anecdotal records, 41-42, 376-77, 399-403
Annoyance, effect of, on learning, 96
Apperception, principle of, 101
Appreciation
  development of, 130-32
  music
    phonograph records for, 239-41
    radio for, 234
    tape recordings for, 241
Aptitudes, individual differences in, 422
Arithmetic instruction, 319-21, 339-42
  computational phase of, chart for, 83-85
  drill and practice, 341
  in early curriculum, 5
  evaluation in, 280, 341-42
  fraction concepts, 340-41
  guided, 339-40
  informal, 319-20

Date Due

NOV 5 '58	APR 2 9 1969	
NOV 1 7 58	NOV 1 9 1970	
DEC 1 5 '58	DEC 3 '70	
MAR 1 '60	NOV 1 2 196	
FEB 1 6 1961		
MAR 2 1961		
APR 1 1 1961		
APR 2 5 1961		
DEC 1 1 1961		
JAN 3 1962		
MAR 8 1962		
FEB 2 7 1963		
MAR 1 3 1963		
MAR 9 1964		
Mar 14'67		
Mar 29'67		
Apr 4'67		
May 16'67		
Feb 27 68		
Mar 5 68		
May 20 68		